# Powering Office 2003 with XML

# Powering Office 2003 with XML

Peter G. Aitken

Wiley Publishing, Inc.

Powering Office 2003 with XML

Published by
**Wiley Publishing, Inc.**
10475 Crosspoint Boulevard
Indianapolis, IN 46256



Published simultaneously in Canada

LOC: 2003105847

ISBN: 0-7645-4122-6

Manufactured in the United States of America

10 9 8 7 6 5 4 3 2 1

1B/RV/RQ/QT/IN

# Credits

ACQUISITIONS EDITOR
Jim Minatel

TECHNICAL EDITOR
Sundar Rajan

DEVELOPMENT EDITOR
Maryann Steinhart

PROJECT EDITOR
Pamela M. Hanley

COPY EDITOR
Foxxe Editorial Services

EDITORIAL MANAGER
Mary Beth Wakefield

VICE PRESIDENT & EXECUTIVE GROUP PUBLISHER
Richard Swadley

VICE PRESIDENT AND EXECUTIVE PUBLISHER
Bob Ipsen

VICE PRESIDENT AND PUBLISHER
Joseph B. Wikert

EXECUTIVE EDITORIAL DIRECTOR
Mary Bednarek

PROJECT COORDINATOR
Courtney MacIntyre

GRAPHICS AND PRODUCTION SPECIALISTS
Beth Brooks, Carrie Foster,
Joyce Haughey, LeAndra Hosier,
Michael Kruzil, Ron Terry,
Scott Tullis

QUALITY CONTROL TECHNICIANS
Brian H. Walls, Angel Perez,
Carl Pierce, Dwight Ramsey

PROOFREADING AND INDEXING
Sharon Hilgenberg,
TECHBOOKS Production Services

# About the Author

**Peter G. Aitken** has been writing about computer applications and programming for almost 20 years, with more than 35 books and hundreds of technical articles to his credit. His specialties include Office applications, graphics, XML, and Visual Basic programming. Peter is proprietor of PGA Consulting, providing application development and technical writing services to clients in business and academia. He lives in Chapel Hill, North Carolina, with his wife, Maxine.

# Preface

Microsoft Office has for years been the preferred suite of office productivity applications. This popularity was well deserved – the Office applications provided powerful and flexible tools for performing word processing, spreadsheet analysis, and other tasks. In particular, Office stood out in the ways that the different applications could share information with each other. An Excel chart could easily be embedded in a Word document, or an Excel worksheet could be automatically updated with information from an Access database, to give only two examples.

Over the past few years, however, the world of computing has undergone a sea change. We have moved away from application programs that exist in isolation on a single computer or, at most, a local area network (LAN). The trend is toward meeting the needs of businesses and other organizations with integrated solutions comprising multiple components existing on different computers and linked by the Internet or an intranet. In order to provide maximum flexibility, an individual application program must provide *interoperability* – the ability to exchange data with other programs regardless of the platform on which they are running. For reasons that are detailed in Chapter 2, Extensible Markup Language, or XML, has emerged as the de facto standard for data exchange.

Microsoft was well aware of the need for interoperability, and it has addressed it in a big way in the new version of Office. First, it's created a new Office application called InfoPath designed for creating forms for entering and editing XML data. Second, it's added powerful XML support to several of the existing Office applications. Yes, I know that the previous version also had some XML support, but that pales in comparison with what's available now.

# Structure of the Book

This book contains four parts plus appendices. The material is organized as follows:

- Part 1 provides an introduction to the XML capabilities of the Office applications and gives an overview of XML technology.
- Part 2 deals with the new InfoPath application. You'll learn how to use InfoPath forms, how to design your own forms, and how to use scripting to enhance the functionality of forms.
- Part 3 explores the XML functionality of the other Office applications: Word, Excel, Access, and FrontPage. Each application gets its own chapter that explains its XML tools in detail.

- Part 4 presents a series of case studies showing how to use XML to integrate Office applications with each other to tackle real-world tasks.
- Appendix A details what's on the book's CD-ROM. The remaining appendices provide a concise overview of XML and the important related technologies XSD schemas and XSLT stylesheets.

I recommend that everyone start by reading Chapters 1 and 2. After that you can skip around as your needs and interests dictate.

# Web Updates

I am maintaining a Web page for this book at `http://www.pgacon.com/PoweringOfficeWithXML.htm`. Any corrections or clarifications to the book will be posted here. You can also contact me with comments, suggestions, and suspected errors – I always enjoy hearing from readers. Please note that I can respond only to book-related messages; I simply do not have the time to deal with general XML or Office queries.

– Peter Aitken

# Acknowledgments

This book has only one author listed but is in many ways a team effort. There's no way this book could have come into being without the help of many talented people at Wiley, including: Maryann Steinhart, Development Editor; Jim Minatel, Acquisitions Editor; Sundar Rajan, Technical Editor; Pamela Hanley for her overall coordination and editorial input; and Foxxe Editorial Services/Jeri Friedman, Copy Editor. Thanks, everyone!

# Contents at a Glance

# Contents

## Part III XML and Other Office Applications

# Part I

## Enhancing Office with XML

## IN THIS PART:

Part I describes the XML technology that is part of Microsoft Office 2003, with an emphasis on features that are new in this version of Office, and explores how this XML capability puts Office in the forefront of compatibility solutions. This part also explains the fundamentals of XML, how it developed, and why it is so well suited for certain tasks.

Chapter 1

# Office and XML Technology

IN THIS CHAPTER

- Exploring what's new in Office
- Previewing XML's role in Word
- Previewing XML's role in Excel
- Previewing XML's role in Access
- Previewing XML's role in InfoPath

THE LATEST VERSION of Microsoft Office, called Office 2003, brings many changes and improvements to the desktop. The most important of these changes have to do with the way Office can interact and exchange data with other programs. These new capabilities are implemented by means of a technology called Extensible Markup Language, or XML. This chapter explains why interoperability is so important for today's computing needs, and provides an overview of the related features in Office. Chapter 2 provides you with a basic look at XML and how it works.

## Why XML?

Office applications have always had the ability to exchange data with other Office applications. These capabilities were very useful, and at the time quite impressive. Aside from the obvious and trivial use of the Windows clipboard for "cut-and-paste" operations, you could always do things such as inserting a slide from a PowerPoint presentation into a Word document or embedding a Word document in an Excel worksheet. There was even some data exchange possible with programs outside of the Office suite, although these capabilities were rather limited.

As computing has evolved from a single program operating in isolation on a single computer, to various software components running on a corporate LAN, to applications that use components in different cities or different countries via the Internet, the need for smooth interoperability has increased. Components need to communicate with each other. This was much easier, of course, when the entire program ran on one computer, or even ran on different components on a single network under the control of one Information Systems (IS) department that could enforce the required compatibility. But now, a worker using an application in the San Francisco office might be interacting with components located on systems in New York and Paris, where different applications and even different operating systems might be in use. At the same time that it became more important to maintain compatibility, it became far more difficult to do so.

Simultaneously, the very concept of an "application" was becoming less meaningful. Developers and systems integrators tend to think more in terms of business processes – capabilities or actions that a business or other organization needs. For example, think of a hospital, the information it needs to keep track of, and the various uses that information is put to. On the "input" side of things, the following is needed (this is surely a simplification, but still serves well as an example):

- Personal information about a patient
- Insurance and/or Medicare information
- Details of procedures that were performed: X-rays, lab tests, surgery, physical therapy, and so forth
- Accounting of supplies used: prescription drugs, dressings, intravenous solutions, and so on
- Records of visits from consulting physicians and other specialists

Then think of the multiple uses to which this information may be put:

- The Billing department uses the information to submit insurance claims and prepare patient bills.
- The Ordering department uses the information to keep track of inventory of supplies and to place orders as needed.
- The Records department keeps track of all information as part of each patient's medical record.
- The physicians and nurses need access to the information to keep track of each patient's progress.

When designing a computerized solution to fill needs such as this, the focus is on the tasks that need to be done rather than on individual application programs. The fact is, however, that in order to be potentially useful in a business solution, an individual program should have as much flexibility as possible when it comes to exchanging data with other parts of the solution.

The answer to this problem clearly lay in the widespread adoption of a common standard for data transfer. Any proprietary technology, under the control of a single organization was unacceptable. As a public and freely available technology, XML was, as they say, "just the ticket."

# XML in Office 2003

Previous versions of Office, such as Office 2000 and Office XP, integrated XML to some degree into the various applications. For example, Excel XP could open and save XML files, and Access XP could import and export XML data. But those features are kitten's play in comparison to the extent to which XML is integrated with Office 2003.

The deeper integration of XML technology into Office 2003 brings a host of important enhancements to the suite. These enhancements are not the type that are obvious to the user right away. XML does not provide a snazzy new user interface, new formatting commands in Word, better charts in Excel, or automated data entry in Access. For the most part the XML-related improvements in Office 2003 have to do with how the Office applications can exchange data with other programs. This includes data exchange between Office programs, but much of the emphasis is on exchange with non-Office programs. What other programs? It doesn't matter—that's the beauty of XML. By supporting the XML standard, Office can interact with any other program that also supports XML.

XML support is not spread throughout all of the Office applications. When speaking about XML and Office, the only traditional Office applications that are included are Word, Excel, and Access, plus the new application InfoPath. FrontPage, the Web site development application, has some new XML features, as well.

XML support permits Office applications to communicate with any other software that also supports XML, regardless of the system it is running on. Some of the consequences of this are:

- Office apps can exchange data with complex back-end data stores.
- Data can be retrieved from and sent to disparate and otherwise incompatible systems.
- Information can be reused and repurposed without the need to re-key or recode.

- Information of various kinds can be structured in a way that makes it easier to search and organize.
- Because the structure of XML data is independent of its display, the same information can be presented in different formats and on different devices as needs dictate.

A central aspect of XML in Office is support for schemas, which are also called data models. A *schema* is like a database template in that it describes the types and relationships of data. You can work with your own business-specific XML schema, using Office applications to access and reuse important information that may have been hidden away in documents sitting on file servers or on hard-to-access back-end systems.

Some schemas will be specially designed for use within an organization. In other cases, it makes more sense to use one of the many published schemas that are designed for various tasks. One example is the Extensible Business Reporting Language (XBRL), an open specification that uses an XML schema to describe financial information. Another example is H7, which was designed for the healthcare industry. By utilizing such standard schemas, different organizations can easily share information even if they are using technologies from different vendors on different platforms.

Office provides several of its own schemas. The XML Spreadsheet Schema is designed for saving spreadsheet data in XML format. Word has its own XML schema, called WordML, that lets you save a document along with its formatting and other information as an XML document. The choice of your own custom schema, an industry standard schema, or Office's schemas provides great flexibility.

## XML and Word

Word 2003 has its own XML schema called WordML. When you save a document as an XML file using this schema, all of the formatting and layout information is preserved along with the document text. WordML does not provide semantic markup, so it gives no information about the meaning of the document contents. Such meaning can be provided by another schema. This gives you a great deal of flexibility because the WordML schema preserves layout and formatting information, while a custom schema can simultaneously provide semantic structure to the document.

The support for XML in Word 2003 creates a new way of looking at documents. In previous versions of Word, a Word document was really nothing more than a combination of raw text data with formatting. Searching the document or attempting to retrieve information from it was limited to a regular text search. There were at best very limited ways for the document to denote what its contents meant. With XML, a Word document can take on a dual identity, as both document (text with formatting and layout) and a data store (structured information). For example, Figure 1-1 shows an XML file open in Word with the XML tags visible. You could hide the tags and apply formatting to the data, but the tags would still be present and providing structure to the data.

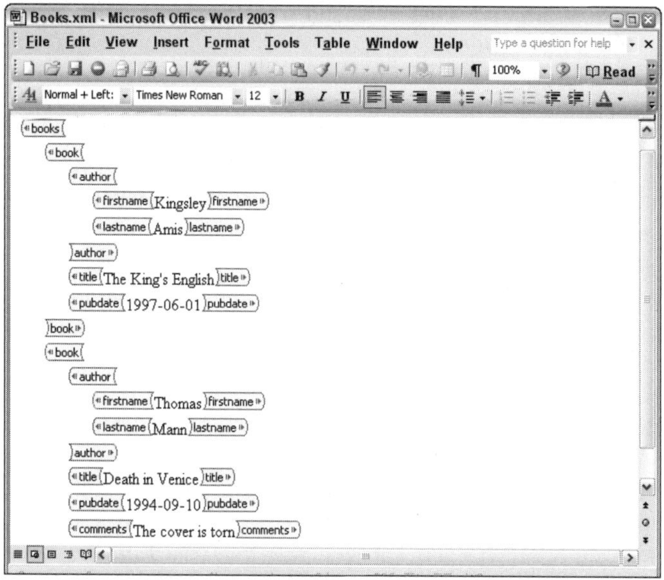


**Figure 1-1: Word can display XML data and retain the structure provided by the tags.**

Here's an illustration: Suppose that your company requires prospective employees to submit a resume as a Word document. This is fine for printing and viewing on-screen, but suppose you are asked to see if any of the several hundred applicants have a degree in economics and speaks French? In the past, the only way to do this would be for someone to examine each resume looking for the relevant information. With XML, however, the resume documents could be structured in such a way that locating the relevant information would be a simple automated process.

Word also supports XSLT (XML Stylesheet Language for Transformations), a language for defining transformations to XML data. When a Word document uses a custom schema, you can create an XSLT transform, which takes the original document as input and creates a new document based on applying the transform rules to the original document contents. There are few limitations to what you can accomplish using XSLT. Here are some examples of what you could do:

- Extract parts of the document and output them as an HTML (Hypertext Markup Language) document for publishing on the Web
- Perform calculations and create summaries based on data contained in tables within the document
- Embed commands for outputting the document to a typesetter, text-to-speech converter, or other specialized presentation device
- Create a table of contents or an index

You can learn more about Word and XML in Chapter 7, "Word and XML," and Chapter 11, "Connecting Word and InfoPath."

## XML and Excel

Excel has its own XML schema, XML Spreadsheet Schema (XMLSS), and can read and save data using this schema. In addition, Excel can read XML data based on any other schema without any need for reformatting. This means that the powerful presentation and analysis features of Excel can be brought to bear on essentially any data as long as the original source of that data has the ability to save in XML format. Manipulation of external XML data is simplified by Excel's *Field Chooser*, which lets the user select data elements from an external schema and simply drag them to the worksheet for inclusion. The link between an Excel worksheet and external XML data is dynamic. Tables and charts in Excel will be updated in real time when the underlying XML data changes.

The Field Chooser acts like a visual mapping tool. When you open an XML file, it presents a visual representation of the data elements. This can be based on the file's schema or, if there is no schema, Excel can generate one based on the file's internal structure. Figure 1-2 shows an example; the hierarchical tree under "sampleData" shows the structure of the XML data. Any of these elements can be dragged to the desired location in the worksheet.

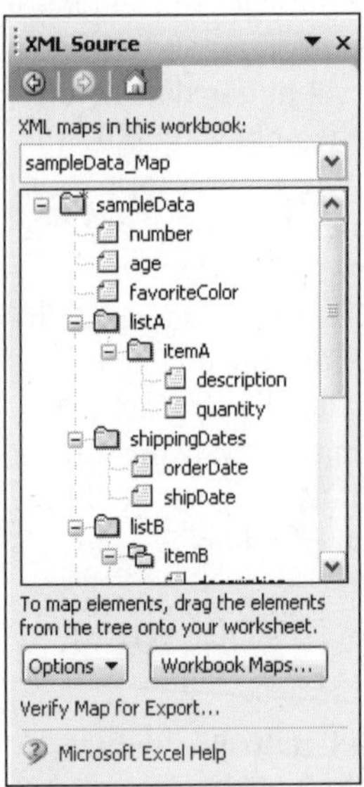


**Figure 1-2:** The Field Chooser lets you map elements of an XML file to your worksheet.

- The Field Chooser greatly simplifies many tasks that in the past have required programming. For example: Map XML data to existing worksheet structure for data import.
- Design dynamic workbooks load XML data, display it, and write it out in any format.
- Create information repositories are based on existing Excel workbooks.

You can learn more about Excel and XML in Chapter 8, “Excel and XML,” and Chapter 12, “Connecting Excel and InfoPath.”

## XML and Access

Access is a database management program designed for organizing, structuring, and manipulating data. As such it has a natural relationship with XML. In fact, in earlier versions of Office it was Access that first received the capability to work with XML data.

Access can work with XML data, importing data into any one of the various types of databases that Access supports. When you import XML data, you can select which parts of the XML file to import, as is shown in Figure 1-3.

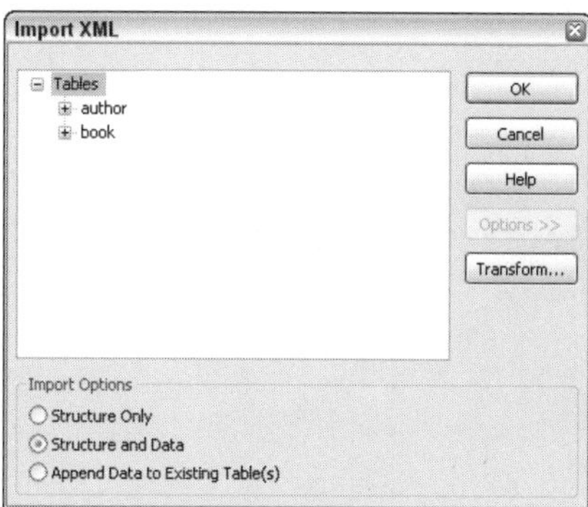


**Figure 1-3: Access can import data from XML data files.**

Access can also export data from an existing database into an XML document. You have the option of applying an XSLT transform during the import process to convert the XML data into a format that the database can accept.

Access can also work with XML schemas. During the importing of data, a schema can be used to ensure that the data being imported adheres to a certain structure. You can also choose to export the structure of an Access database as an

XSD (XML Schema Definition) schema. The same is true when exporting Access data to XML. XSLT transforms can be applied during the data exporting process.

ReportML is a custom XML schema that is supported by Access. It permits exporting to go beyond just the data so that you can export the details of an Access datasheet, report, form, query, or table. The resulting XML file contains the associated presentation and connection information.

You can learn more about Access and XML in Chapter 9, "Access and XML," and Chapter 13, "Connecting Access and InfoPath."

## XML and InfoPath

InfoPath is a new application in the Office suite. On the surface, InfoPath is a forms designer that lets you create forms for data entry and editing. Beneath the surface, InfoPath provides much more. Its forms are dynamic and can be associated with a schema to ensure that the form and the data that is entered meet the schema's data model. InfoPath forms are based on XML technology and can be integrated with back-end databases and other applications that also support XML. For example, a form can be designed so its data is saved as an XML file, submitted to a Web service, or submitted to a database. The ability to integrate script into forms provides additional power and flexibility. Figure 1-4 shows an example of an InfoPath form.

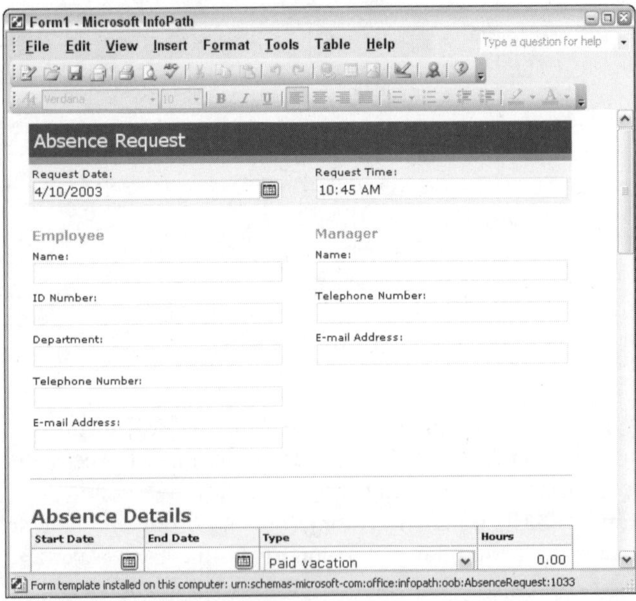


Figure 1-4: An InfoPath form.

InfoPath provides for both the design of forms and the use of forms. Forms can be used offline as needed.

You start exploring this exciting new application in Chapter 3, "Introduction to InfoPath," and learn to design InfoPath forms in Chapter 4, "Designing InfoPath Forms, Part 1" and Chapter 5, "Designing InfoPath Forms, Part 2." Chapter 6, "Scripting with InfoPath," shows you how to add scripts to your forms for additional functionality. Then, you see how InfoPath works with other Office applications and with Web publishing in Part IV.

Chapter 2

# What Is XML?

IN THIS CHAPTER

- Understanding XML
- Exploring XML technology
- Looking at related technologies

THE NEW INTEROPERABILITY features in Office are all based on XML technology. For most of these features, XML works behind the scenes and you will not have to work with it directly. Even so, you should have a good understanding of what XML is and how it works. In this chapter, you will learn the fundamentals of XML, how it developed, and why it is so well suited for certain tasks. The rest of the chapters provide you with the details of using XML and some important related technologies in Office applications.

# XML Overview

XML stands for eXtensible Markup Language. XML is designed to provide structure to data. This means that with XML data can be organized in a way that each individual piece of information is clearly identified as to what it is and how it is related to other data. This may sound like pretty basic stuff – after all, isn't the data in an Excel spreadsheet or an Access database well organized? Yes, that's true, but there are several factors that have resulted in wide acceptance of XML as a standard for structured data.

## XML Is a Markup Language

What does *markup* mean? Let me use an example to explain. Look at the following information:

```
1999 BMW 540i, dark blue, 49000 miles, $34500
```

You and I know perfectly well what this information represents – it's a for sale listing for a car with details about the make, model, color, and so on. A computer, on the other hand, is not nearly as smart. There's no way that a computer can reliably and accurately interpret this information. What the computer needs is some additional information about what the individual pieces of data mean. That's exactly what markup does. Here is the same data in XML format:

```
<car>
  <year>1999</year>
  <make>BMW</make>
  <model>540i</model>
  <color>dark blue</color>
  <miles>49000</miles>
  <price>34500</price>
</car>
```

The data is the same, but it is now marked up – given structure – by identifying labels. From this example, you can already see some of the fundamentals of XML syntax:

- Markup information, called *tags*, is enclosed in brackets.
- Data is located between tags.
- The beginning of each unit of data, or *element*, is marked by a tag. The name of the tag identifies the data.
- The end of each element is also marked by a tag. This end tag is identical to the start tag with the addition of a leading slash (/).

You can see, for example, that the `<year>` tag identifies the start of the "year" data. The text "1999" is the data itself, and the `</year>` tag marks the end of the "year" data. You can also see that some elements such as `<year>` and `<make>` contain data, while some elements – `<car>` in this example – contain other elements.

This may seem very simple to you, and in fact XML is quite straightforward – you'll learn more details throughout this book. Even so, how can such an uncomplicated idea provide all the power and flexibility that XML is supposed to have? Read on to find out.

## XML Is Plain Text

XML data is always stored as plain text files. You can open, read, and edit any XML file using the simplest of tools, such as Microsoft's Notepad text editor. In truth, you will rarely, if ever, work with XML in this manner, but use of the text format has important implications. By using an open and universally accepted format, XML breaks down the barriers that are created when data is stored in a format that is proprietary to a particular application, operating system, or hardware platform. XML data can be transferred between Windows PCs, Macintoshes, Unix machines, and even mainframes without problems. No one is going to object to XML because they cannot easily use it on their platform.

XML being plain text does not mean it cannot be used with binary data, such as images, that cannot be represented as text. Binary data is stored separately, and then referenced from within an XML file.

## XML Is Extensible

As its name implies, XML is extensible, meaning that it can be extended as needed to meet any data structuring needs that may arise. When you decide to use XML for your data needs, you can be confident that this decision places essentially no limitations on future expansion and change.

XML's extensibility derives from the fact that it is, technically speaking, a *metalanguage*, or a language that is used to define other languages. The languages that can be defined with XML, called *schemas*, are each tailored for a specific purpose. One developer might use XML to define a language for storing medical records data, for example, while another person might define an XML language for keeping track of an auto-parts inventory. From its inception, XML was designed to provide this flexibility.

## XML Supports Data Modeling

A *data model*, or schema, describes the permitted data structure of an XML file. It will specify the elements and attributes the XML file can contain, which ones are required and which are optional, what the relationship between them is, and what kind of data each can contain. The data model for an XML file that contains inventory data for a clothing retailer will be totally different from the data model of an XML file that holds data for an oil-drilling exploration company. Schemas are an essential element of using XML in Office.

## XML Separates Storage from Display

Data is not much use unless it can be displayed in some way. Display can mean many things. It might be a standard desktop computer monitor or the small screen of a Palm or other personal digital assistant. There are many other types of "display" that most people do not think about, such as data

- Converted to speech for audio output
- Presented as a Web page
- Sent to a typesetter for publication as a magazine or book

The XML language places absolutely no constraints on how data is displayed. In fact it was designed this way intentionally. The display of the data (when it is required) is totally separate from the storage and structure of the data.

## XML Is a Public Standard

The "rules" of XML, technically called the XML Recommendation, were developed by the World Wide Web Consortium (commonly knows as the W3C). The W3C is a public organization that receives input and assistance from industry, government, academia, and individuals. In addition to XML, the W3C is responsible for a lot of other well-known standards, such as Hypertext Markup Language (HTML), Portable Network Graphics (PNG), and Hypertext Transfer Protocol (HTTP). Because W3C is a public organization, standards that it develops are available to all. There are no commercial interests with control over the standards, and thus no way anyone can be charged royalties or licensing fees to use a standard. Because the standards-making process is open and public, the standards that emerge tend to be well thought out and complete. This also means that the standards-making process is unavoidably slow. For example, the W3C worked on the XML Recommendation for two years before finally releasing it in 1998.

It's important to note that the W3C has no authority to impose its standards on anyone. This is why they are properly called Recommendations rather than standards. You are perfectly free to create a variation of XML, but what's the point? It's the wide use and acceptance of "official" XML that makes it so useful.

You can learn more about the W3C and its activities at `www.w3.org`.

# Background and Development of XML

The origins of XML stretch back some 40 years, to the era of mainframe computers, when IBM was looking for a method for structuring documents. IBM's goal was to facilitate the exchange and manipulation of data. The result of these efforts was Generalized Markup Language (GML). While GML was used internally by IBM, it never achieved acceptance elsewhere. Other organizations developed similar document-structuring languages, but at that stage everything was proprietary and each markup language was incompatible with the others.

The first successful effort at creating a standardized markup language was Standard Generalized Markup Language (SGML), which also originated at IBM. SGML started as a markup language for structuring and organizing legal documents, but was soon expanded to function in other settings as well. The International Organization for Standardization (ISO) released SGML as an official standard in 1986. SGML is extremely powerful and flexible, with all the corresponding complexity and processing overhead. For many if not most uses, SGML is overkill.

The development of the Internet prompted the next major step in the evolution of markup languages. Huge numbers of documents were becoming available on the Internet, and early methods for accessing these documents were proving unsatisfactory. People in the industry knew that accessibility would be facilitated if the documents could be linked to one another in a meaningful way so that users could easily find and move between related documents. The solution, HTML, was developed by Tim Berners-Lee, who was a software engineer at the European Laboratory for Particle Physics in Switzerland. HTML not only allows documents to be linked to one another but also provides markup tags for controlling document display. With HTML was born the World Wide Web, consisting of the entire web of linked HTML documents.

Despite its enormous success, HTML has some significant limitations. During the early days of the Web it was more than adequate, but as the Web expanded developers started to "push the envelope," trying to be more and more creative with their Web pages. Tasks for which HTML was never intended, such as animation, database access, and user interactivity pushed Web designers to the limit. With the assistance of nonstandard enhancements to HTML as well as ancillary technologies, Web developers have created the exciting Web pages that we see today.

Eventually, however, it became painfully clear that HTML was being pushed beyond its limits. One major limitation is that HTML has a fixed set of markup tags, and you cannot create new tags to meet new needs. In other words, HTML is not extensible. The other limitation is that HTML combines tags for structure with tags for display. Thus, structure and display are inextricably linked. The new markup language had to overcome these limitations. Specific goals that the W3C set for the new markup language included the following:

- **Extensibility.** The language provides for defining new elements as needed.
- **Validation.** A document should be able to be validated against a data model.
- **Structure.** The language syntax must follow a well-defined set of rules.

XML is the result of this effort by the W3C.

# XML and Related Technologies

The XML Recommendation as issued by the W3C consists of two parts:

- A set of rules for structuring data with tags and attributes.
- A set of rules for creating a data model for XML data called Document Type Definitions (DTD).

The rules for creating tags and attributes are in a sense the real core of XML. The ability to define a data model is equally important. A data model specifies how an XML file is structured and what data it can contain. An XML document that stores an auto-parts inventory will have a very different data model from one that stores medical records. DTDs were the original technology for defining a data model and are still widely used. They are not supported by Office, however, so are not covered in this book. Office uses a more recent and powerful method for defining a data model, called XML Schema Definition Language (see the next section).

As mentioned earlier, the base XML Recommendation includes only XML itself and DTDs. Several related technologies have been developed. These are not, technically speaking, part of XML itself, but they are important for maximizing the benefits of Office's XML features. The following sections do not by any means constitute a complete list of XML-related technologies, but are limited to those that are relevant for Office 2003.

## XML Schema Definition Language

The original method for defining an XML data model, also called a schema, was Document Type Definitions, or DTDs. While still widely used, DTDs have some limitations that make them less than ideal for certain uses. The W3C developed a new and more flexible data-modeling tool called XML Schema Definition Language, or XSD. Office uses XSD schemas for data modeling.

## Cascading Style Sheets

I've already mentioned that one of XML's advantages is that it keeps data structure totally separated from data display. This does not mean, however, that XML data never needs to be displayed! Cascading Style Sheets (CSS) is a language that lets you associate display attributes (such as font, color, and line spacing) with the elements of an XML file. A display program such as a browser uses the information in the style sheet to control the display of XML data. A style sheet is separate from the XML file. This provides the following two advantages:

- You can display the same XML data in different ways by simply using a different style sheet.
- If the same style sheet is used for multiple XML documents, you can change the display of all of them by changing only the one style sheet.

## Extensible Stylesheet Language for Transformations

Extensible Stylesheet Language for Transformations (XSLT) is a language for defining transformations that can be applied to XML data. A transform can change the structure of an XML document as required by the current situation. The order and organization of the data can be modified, and new elements such as an index or table of contacts can be created. One common use of XSLT is to transform XML data into HTML for display in a Web browser.

# Part II

## Getting Going with XML and InfoPath

## IN THIS PART:

Part II introduces InfoPath, a new application in the Office suite that lets you design and distribute sophisticated forms for entry, editing, and sharing of data. An InfoPath form's data is maintained as XML, permitting forms to interact dynamically with back-end databases, Web services, and other applications that support XML. You learn to design InfoPath forms, with their many options, and then look at the capability to integrate script into forms to provide additional power and flexibility.

Chapter 3

# Introduction to InfoPath

IN THIS CHAPTER

- Exploring InfoPath
- Using InfoPath forms
- Formatting and correcting InfoPath forms
- Merging InfoPath forms
- Saving and sharing InfoPath forms
- Examining InfoPath form security

INFOPATH IS THE NEW member of the Office family. It provides a forms-based interface that lets users enter and share data. This chapter covers the basics of InfoPath and shows you how to fill out InfoPath forms.

## What InfoPath Does

To quote from the Microsoft documentation, InfoPath "streamlines the process of gathering, sharing, and using information." The way that InfoPath does this is through the use of forms. I'm sure that you have worked with on-screen forms before, when placing an order with a Web merchant, for example, or when registering at an online job site. The notion of forms is clearly not new. What's new is the way InfoPath lets you work with forms, and the way that the data entered into a form is stored. Specifically, data from InfoPath forms is maintained as XML, which means that InfoPath can exchange data with any other program or system that supports XML. This in fact is what sets InfoPath apart – the ease with which it can integrate with other applications. For the most part the XML is hidden away behind the scenes – you, as an InfoPath user, will not need to work directly with XML.

### InfoPath's Two Modes

When you use InfoPath you are always working in one of two modes. In one mode you are filling out forms – adding, viewing, and editing data on InfoPath forms. Many users will only use this mode. I refer to this as Data mode, even though that is not a term used by Microsoft. The other mode is called Design mode and is used to create and modify the underlying design of forms. In Design mode you can view and set a form's schema, define data validation rules, and specify other aspects of a form that determine its appearance and behavior. Generally speaking, InfoPath's Design mode is used by systems administrators, programmers, and advanced users. Chapter 4, "Designing InfoPath Forms, Part 1," and Chapter 5, "Designing InfoPath Forms, Part 2," cover Design mode extensively. This chapter deals primarily with InfoPath's Data mode.

## Forms and Form Templates

InfoPath works with forms and with form templates. It's important to understand the distinction between them. A *form template* defines the structure and functionality of a form, including:

- The XML schema that defines the structure of the form data
- The controls on the form
- The data validation rules for the form
- The form's default data (if any)
- Rules about what the user can and cannot modify on the form
- The views associated with the form (data layout)

A form template consists of a single file with the XSN extension that is stored locally on your computer or at a remote network server or Microsoft SharePoint Server. When you design a form in InfoPath, you are creating a form template. The InfoPath installation also includes a selection of form templates.

A *form* is based on a form template. When you are working with data in InfoPath you are using a form. A good analogy with paper forms is a blank master form that is used for photocopying – this is the form template. The photocopies that the users actually fill out are the forms.

## The InfoPath Screen

The InfoPath screen, sometimes referred to as the *workspace*, has two main sections, the form area on the left and the task pane on the right, as Figure 3-1 shows. The form area is where you work with forms, either in Design mode or Data mode (as shown in the figure). The task pane can contain a variety of elements. Most often it displays commands for InfoPath actions, such as opening a form, performing a spell check, or adding a control to a form in Design mode. The task pane can also display online help, clip art galleries, and other such information. Depending on what you are doing, InfoPath may display special task panes that contain commands and other elements related to the task at hand. To work with the task pane:

- Click the left and right arrows at the top of the task pane to move backward and forward through the task panes that have been displayed.
- Click the Home button at the top of the task pane to return to the initial task pane.
- Click the down arrow at the top of the task pane to view a menu of commonly needed commands.
- Point at the vertical dotted line at the top-left corner of the task pane to drag the pane to another screen location. Drag to the left or right edge of the screen to dock the task pane.
- Click the Close button at the top of the task pane, or press Ctrl-F1, to hide the task pane.
- Press Ctrl-F1 or select View → Task Pane from the InfoPath menu to display the task pane.

When you design a form you can also design one or more custom task panes that will be available to users when filling out the form.

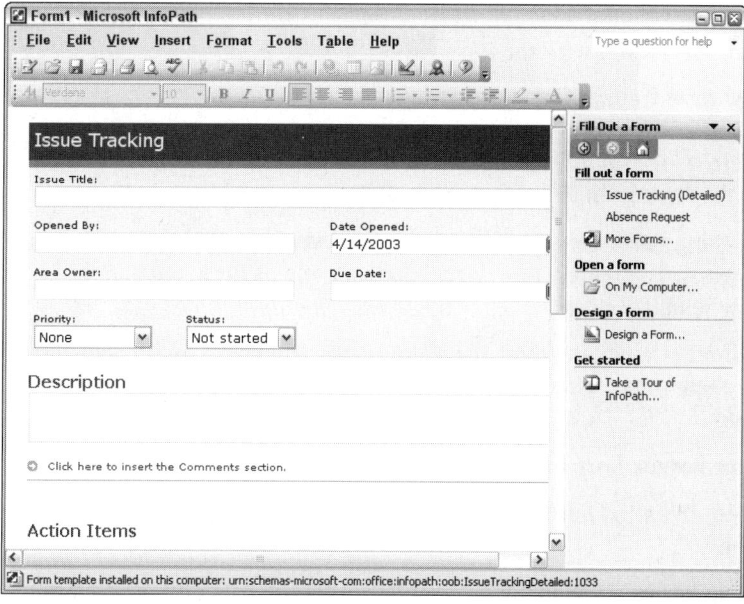


Figure 3-1: The InfoPath screen.

## Sample Forms

The InfoPath installation includes a selection of sample forms that are designed for commonly used data entry tasks, such as expense report, resumes, and performance reviews. You can use the forms as they are provided, and you can also use them as the starting point for designing your own custom forms. You will learn how to access these sample forms in the next section.

# Opening Forms

Naturally, before you can fill out a form, you must open it. You can either open an existing form that you or someone else has already started to fill out, or you can open a new form based on a form template. To open an existing form:

1. Select File→Open to display the Open dialog box.
2. If necessary, navigate to the folder or shared network location where the form is located.
3. Select the form.
4. Click Open.

To start a new form from a form template:

1. Select File→Fill Out a Form. This step is not required if the task pane is already displaying the Fill Out a Form page.
2. The Fill Out a Form section of the task pane lists form templates you have used recently. To create a new form based on one of these templates, select the template name.
3. To use another template, click the More Forms command on the task pane to open the Forms dialog box (see Figure 3-2). This dialog box has three tabs:

   **Recent Forms.** Lists form templates you have used recently.

   **Custom Installed Forms.** Lists custom form templates that are available to you.

   **Sample Forms.** Lists the form templates that are part of the InfoPath installation.
4. Select the desired form template, then click OK.

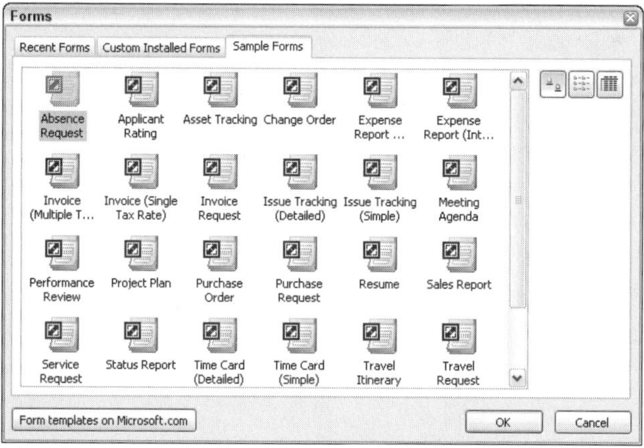


Figure 3-2: The Forms dialog box lets you select a form template.

Once you have opened a form you can proceed to fill it out as described in the next section.

# Filling Out Forms

An InfoPath form is composed of controls. Each control is designed for a certain kind of information, although there is some overlap. For example, both the Text Box and the Rich Text Box controls are designed for display and/or entry of text, but the latter control offers significantly more formatting options.

## Navigating a Form

Only one item, or control, on the form is active at a time and will respond to input from the user. You can activate a control by clicking it. As you move the mouse pointer over a form (without clicking), InfoPath indicates the controls with a special outline so that you can easily identify the control you want. You can also press Tab or Shift-Tab to move forward or backward from control to control (in the order determined when the form template was designed). The arrow keys also move between controls in most situations. The exception is when you are editing text, in which case the arrow keys move the insertion point in the text. If the insertion point has reached the end of the text, however, an arrow key moves to the next control.

An InfoPath form also can display buttons and other elements for carrying out actions such as sending the form or inserting an optional section. Several of these elements are shown in Figure 3-3. You need only to click one of these buttons or other elements to initiate the action.

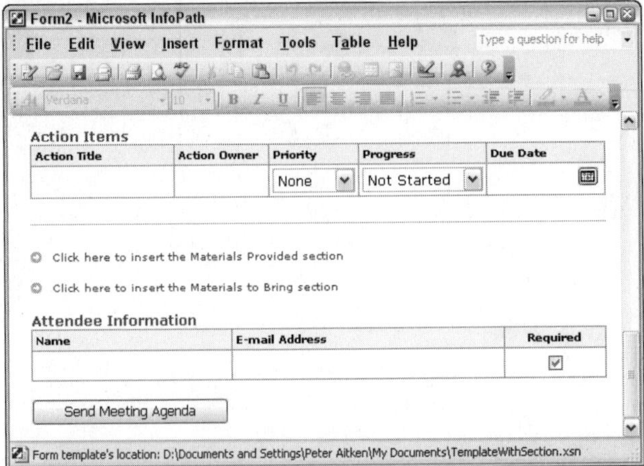


Figure 3-3: An InfoPath may contain elements that you click to carry out an action.

# The Date Picker Control

The Date Picker control is usually used for fields on a form that require entry of a date. This control displays as a Text Box with an adjacent calendar icon. You can type a date directly into the field, or you can click the calendar icon to select a date from a graphical calendar (shown in Figure 3-4).

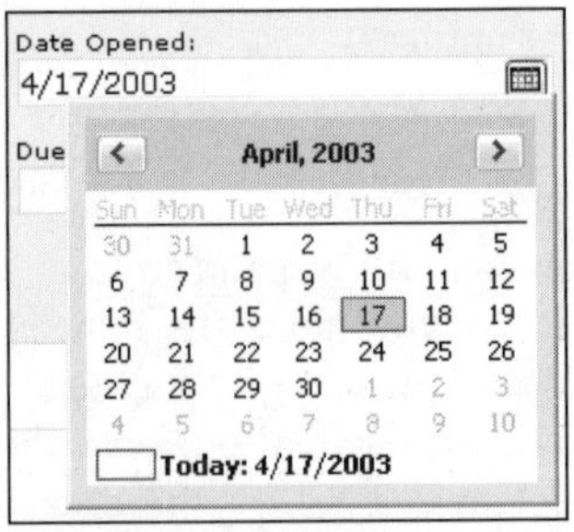

Figure 3-4: Selecting a date with the Date Picker control.

When the Date Picker calendar is displayed, select a date by clicking it. Use the left and right arrows at the top of the calendar to display different months. Today's date is marked with a red outline. If the control already has a date entered, that calendar day is shaded in gray.

## Inserting Hyperlinks

In some form locations you can insert a hyperlink to a document or graphic on the Internet. Hyperlinks are displayed as blue underlined text; anyone viewing the form in InfoPath can right-click a hyperlink and select Open Hyperlink to view to link target in his browser. If you type a URL such as `www.microsoft.com` in a form location that supports hyperlinks, it automatically becomes a hyperlink. To create a hyperlink from other text:

1. Select the text that you want to turn into a link, or place the insertion point at the link location.
2. Press Ctrl-K or select Insert → Hyperlink. The Insert Hyperlink dialog box is displayed (see Figure 3-5).
3. Enter the hyperlink target's URL in the Link To field.
4. If you selected text in Step 1, it is displayed in the Display This Text field. Otherwise, enter the text that you want displayed as a link in the form.
5. Click OK.

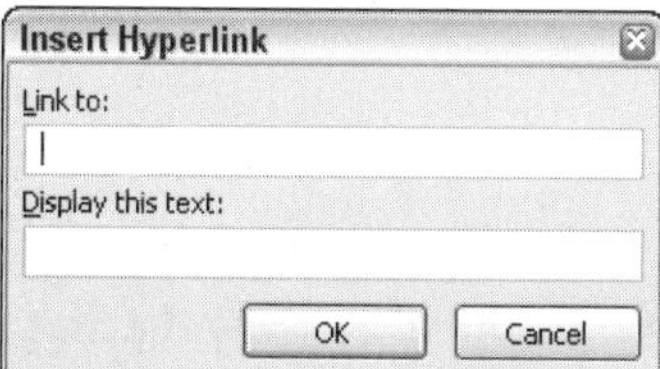


**Figure 3-5: Defining a hyperlink on a form.**

To modify an existing hyperlink, right-click the hyperlink and select Edit Hyperlink from the pop-up menu. In the Edit Hyperlink dialog box, make the necessary changes to the link target and/or the link text.

To delete a hyperlink, right-click the hyperlink and select Remove Hyperlink from the pop-up menu. The text remains in the form but is no longer a hyperlink.

## The Picture Control

The Picture control is used to insert image data in a form. This can be useful in many situations, such as a resumé form that includes a picture of the individual. When you open a form, a Picture control may already contain an image or it may be empty, depending on how the form was designed. In the latter case, it is displayed as shown in Figure 3-6. In filling out a form, you can click the control (whether it is empty or already contains an image) and then follow the prompts to specify the image for the control. When a form template is designed, a Picture control can be marked as read-only, which means that the user won't be able to change the image in the control. In this case, clicking the control has no effect.

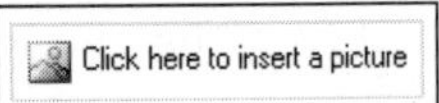


Figure 3-6: An empty Picture control.

A Picture control can hold an image in two ways: as actual binary image data, or as a link to an image file that exists elsewhere, on a network server or Web site. The form designer decides how the control holds its data.

A Rich Text control also can be used to insert images on a form. This control is discussed later in the chapter.

It's important to distinguish between two types of images that can be on a form. An image that is in a Picture control or a Rich Text control is part of the form's data, and is saved or submitted along with the form's other data. An image can also be part of the form's visual interface, purely part of the form's design and not part of its data. The latter kind of image is static and cannot be manipulated by the user. Designing a form's visual interfact is covered in Chapters 4 and 5.

## Working with Views

When a form template is created, the designer has the option of defining multiple views for a form. A resumé form, for example, could have a detail view that displays all of the information in the resumé and a summary view that displays only the most important sections. Some views allow for the entry and editing of information, while others are for display and printing only. The designer can also create a special print view that can be used when the form is printed. Every form has a default view that is used when the form is first opened and is also used for printing if no print view is defined.

To switch between views use the View menu, which lists all the views that are defined for the form in use. The default view for a form has the same name as the form template.

## Working with Repeating Tables

Repeating tables are designed for data that repeats, when you don't know ahead of time how many individual entries there will be, and are often used in InfoPath forms. A meeting agenda form, for example, may include a section for attendees, with fields for name, phone number, and e-mail address for each. Because the number of attendees can't be known ahead of time, this part of the form would be created as a repeating table. This kind of table is initially displayed as a single row containing one or more controls for data entry. The user fills out the original table row for the first attendee, and then adds additional rows for other attendees as needed. Each new row contains the same controls as the original.

When the focus is in a repeating table, InfoPath displays a blue down-arrow icon at the left end of the table row that has the focus. Figure 3-7 shows the icon in a single-row table.

Action Items

| Action Title | Action Owner | Priority | Progress | Due Date |
|---|---|---|---|---|
| | | None | Not Started | 6/6/2003 |

Figure 3-7: You can insert new rows into a repeating table.

Click a repeating table's icon to view a menu with the following commands:

- **Insert Above.** Inserts a new table row above the current row.
- **Insert Below.** Inserts a new table row below the current row.
- **Remove.** Deletes the current row (and its data, if any).
- **Cut, Copy.** Cuts or copies the current row, with its data, to the clipboard. These commands are available only if you have selected the entire row by dragging over it with the mouse.
- **Paste.** Pastes a previously cut or copied row into the table.

# Inserting Sections

A form template can be designed with optional sections. As you work on a form, you can insert these sections as needed. For example, a loan application form could have an optional section titled "Spouse's Income." If the loan applicant is married, this section can be inserted and filled out. If the applicant is not married, the section is not needed. Some optional sections can be inserted multiple times. In a resumé form, for instance, the "Personal Reference" section can be inserted zero, one, or more times, depending on how many personal references are being included.

Some forms include links that you can click to insert an optional section; Figure 3-8 shows an example. Near the bottom of the screen you can see an arrow icon next to the text "Click here to insert the Comments section." This technique lets the form designer specify where in the form a section can be inserted.

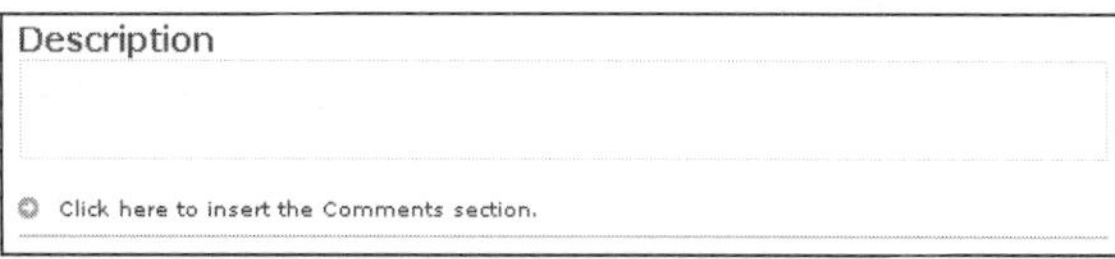


Figure 3-8: Some forms display links to click to insert an optional form section.

Other optional sections provide more flexibility as to where they can be inserted. For these sections there is no link in the document. Rather, you move the insertion point to the form location where you want the section inserted, then choose Insert → Section followed by the section name. InfoPath simplifies things for you by enabling only those section names that can be inserted at the current form location. If a section name is grayed out in the Insert → Section menu, you know it cannot be inserted at that location.

To remove a section, you must first select it. To do so, point at the section until a dashed border appears around the section, and then click. A selected section is displayed with a gray background and a dashed border. For example, the Comments section is selected in the form shown in Figure 3-9. Press Del to delete a selected section. Some sections of a form are not optional and cannot be selected.

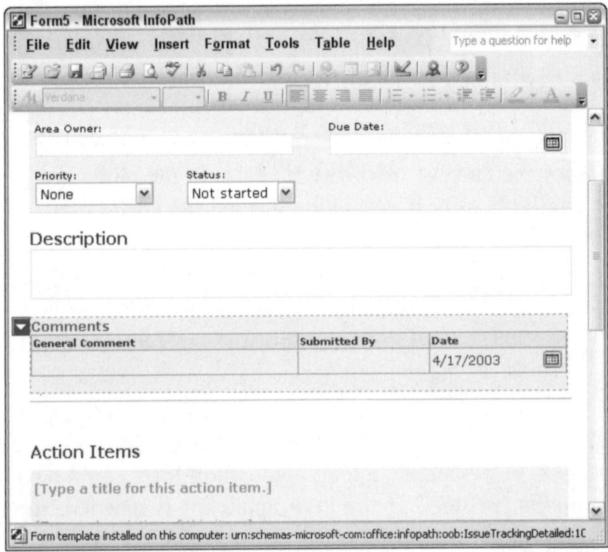


**Figure 3-9: A selected section displays with a gray background and a dashed border.**

Sections can also be cut or copied and pasted at a new location using the Windows clipboard. If, after cutting or copying a section to the clipboard, the Edit → Paste command is not available, it means that the section cannot be pasted into the form at the current location.

# Formatting with Rich Text Controls

InfoPath provides two controls for entering text data: the Text Box control and the Rich Text control. A Text Box control provides no formatting options; its font is specified when the form is designed, and the user (the person filling out the form) can make no changes to the format of the text.

The Rich Text control, however, provides the user with extensive control over formatting so that he or she can do such things as change the font, insert lists and tables, and display graphics. The Rich Text control is used on forms for entry and display of longer sections of text.

Text formatting works pretty much the same as text formatting in other Office applications such as Word. If you are familiar with applying text formatting in those applications, you probably already know the material in this section.

When you design forms, you can place some limitations on which formatting options are available for a specific Rich Text control. For example, you can have a Rich Text control that permits the user to change the font but not to insert tables and images. One way users can tell when text formatting is permitted is by looking at the Formatting toolbar. In a given situation, if the buttons on the toolbar are grayed out (unavailable), the corresponding formatting cannot be changed.

In some cases, text must be selected before applying formatting. Selected text is displayed in reverse video, white text on a black background. You select text by dragging over it with the mouse or by double- or triple-clicking to select a word or paragraph, respectively. You can also use the keyboard, holding down the Shift key while using the cursor movement keys to expand or contract the selection.

When working with formatting you should have InfoPath's Formatting toolbar displayed, as shown in Figure 3-10. To display this toolbar (or to hide it when you are done using it), choose View → Toolbars → Formatting.

Figure 3-10: The Formatting toolbar provides access to InfoPath's text formatting commands.

## Font Formatting

The term *font formatting* refers to the appearance of text characters. This includes the font itself (the style of the text) as well as its color, size, and additional attributes such as underlining. You can apply font formatting in two ways:

- To format existing text, select the text then apply the formatting.
- To format text you are about to type, move the insertion point to the desired location, apply the formatting commands, and then start typing.

Most aspects of font formatting, such as bold and underlining, are well known and need no further explanation. Some users may not be familiar with the following:

- **Size.** Font size (height) is expressed in points; one point is 1/72 inch. The default for most InfoPath controls is 10 points.
- **Strikethrough.** Text is displayed with a line through it, `like this`.
- **Superscript.** Text is displayed at a smaller size, higher than surrounding text.
- **Subscript.** Text is displayed at a smaller size, lower than surrounding text.

You can change any aspect of font formatting using the Font task pane, shown in Figure 3-11. To display this task pane, select Format → Font or press Ctrl-D. You can also change most aspects of font formatting — all except strikethrough, superscript, and subscript — using the Formatting toolbar.

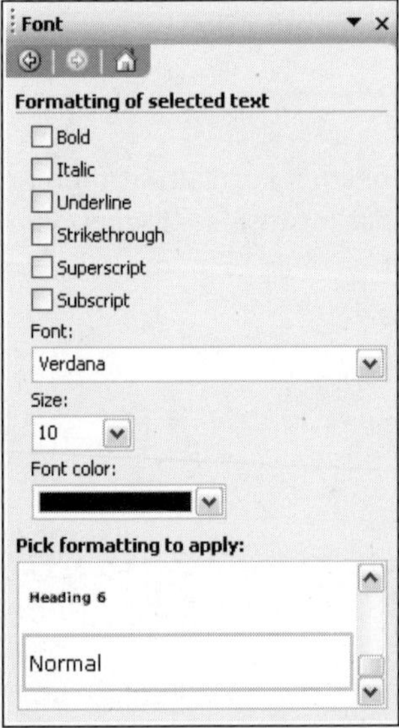


Figure 3-11: The Font task pane displays commands for font formatting.

To remove formatting from text, you can remove the individual formatting attributes, such as italics or bold, one at a time. It's usually quicker, however, to select the text and, in the Pick Formatting to Apply list in the Font task pane, select Clear Formatting.

## Inserting Images

If the InfoPath form designer chooses, users may be permitted to insert images into Rich Text controls. The image becomes part of the form's data.

To insert an image, place the insertion point at the location in the Rich Text control where you want the image. Choose Insert→Picture, and then choose either From File or Clip Art. If you select From File, InfoPath displays the Insert Picture dialog box. Use this dialog box to browse for the desired image file, then click Insert. If you select ClipArt, InfoPath displays the Clip Art task pane, shown in Figure 3-12. Use the commands on this task pane to locate and select the desired clip art image.

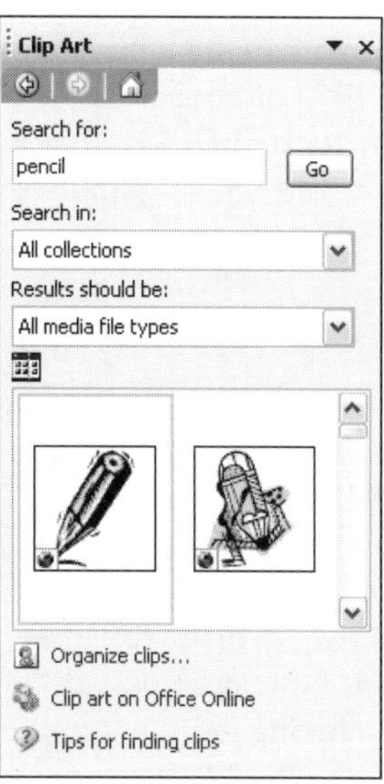


Figure 3-12: The Clip Art task pane.

When you or another user insert an image in a document, either from clip art or a file, the binary image data is embedded in the form and is included when the form is saved or submitted.

You can select an image in a Rich Text Control by clicking it. A selected image displays small white squares called *handles* at its corners and the midpoints of its edges. When an image is selected you can perform the following actions:

- Press Del to delete the image.
- Point at a handle and drag to change the image's shape and/or size.
- Right-click the image and select Format Picture to display the Format Picture dialog box in which you can specify how text should wrap around the image.
- Right-click the image and select Borders and Shading to display the Borders and Shading dialog box, from which you can add a border to the image.

What's the difference between an image in a Rich Text control and an image in a Picture control (discussed earlier in this chapter)? An image in a Picture control is independent and can be treated separately from any other form data, while an image in a Rich Text control is just part of the control's data, which may also include text and formatting.

## Highlighting

Highlighting changes the background color of text. It can be used to call attention to sections of text, for example. To apply highlighting to text (either text you have selected or text you are about to type), click the Highlight button on the Formatting toolbar. The current highlight color is displayed on the Highlight button. To apply a different highlight color, and also change the current color, click the arrow that is adjacent to the Highlight button and select the desired color. To remove highlighting from text, apply a white highlight.

## Lists

InfoPath has the ability to automatically create numbered and bulleted lists in Rich Text controls. In a numbered list, items are numbered automatically, with the numbering being adjusted as needed if items are added to or removed from the list. Each list is available in different styles. For example, a numbered list can be 1, 2, 3 or i, ii, iii, and so forth. A bulleted list can use different symbols for bullets.

To create a list, select the paragraphs that will be in the list, or place the insertion point at the location where you will type the list. Each individual paragraph will be a list item. Then, click either the Bullets or Numbering button on the Formatting toolbar. To select a list style other than the default, click the arrow next to the Bullets or Numbering button and select the desired style.

Another way to create a list is to right-click in the document and select Bullets and Numbering from the pop-up menu. This displays the Bullets and Numbering task pane, shown in Figure 3-13 Click the desired list style, or click None to change text from a list back to a regular paragraph.

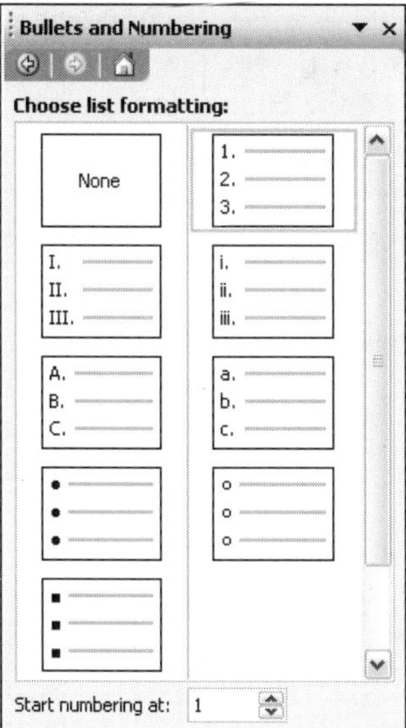


Figure 3-13. The Bullets and Numbering task pane.

By default, a numbered list starts with "1" and continues in sequence. If you want to start a list at another number, right-click the list element and select Bullets and Numbering to display the Bullets and Numbering task pane (see Figure 3-9). Change the value in the Start Numbering At box to specify the new list number.

## Text Alignment and Indentation

Text alignment, sometimes called *justification*, determines how text aligns with the left and right margins. Alignment applies to entire paragraphs of text. There are four types of alignment:

- **Align Left.** Text is aligned at the left margin and ragged on the right. This is the default.
- **Center.** Text is centered between the margins.
- **Align Right.** Text is aligned at the right margin and ragged on the left.
- **Justify.** Text is aligned at both margins, being stretched to fit.

To change the alignment of text place the insertion point anywhere in the paragraph, then click the Formatting toolbar button for the desired alignment.

Indentation controls how far the left edge of a paragraph is offset from the margin. To change indentation, place the insertion point anywhere in the paragraph and click the Increase Indent or Decrease Indent button on the Formatting toolbar.

To indent only the first line of a paragraph, place your cursor at the beginning of the paragraph and press Tab.

## Heading Styles

InfoPath provides six levels of predefined headings styles that you can use in text on a form (in places that permit formatting). A style applies to an entire paragraph. To apply a heading style to text:

1. Put the insertion point in the paragraph.
2. If necessary, press Ctrl-F1 to display the Font task pane.
3. In the Pick Formatting to Apply list (see Figure 3-14), scroll to bring the desired style name into view.
4. Click the style name.

To remove a style from a paragraph, follow the preceding steps, selecting Normal from the Pick Formatting to Apply list.

## Tables

You can insert a table in a Rich Text control to present data in a row and column format. Here are the steps required:

1. Place the insertion point at the location for the table.
2. Choose Insert→Table to display the Insert Table dialog box (see Figure 3-15).
3. Enter the desired number of rows and columns.
4. Click OK.

A newly inserted table displays as a grid of lines as shown near the bottom of Figure 3-16. To enter data, click the desired cell and type the data. You can also move between table cells by pressing Tab to move to the next cell and Shift-Tab to move to the previous cell. If you are in the last cell of the table, pressing Tab inserts a new row at the bottom of the table. The arrow keys either move the insertion point within a cell's text or move to the next cell, depending on the position of the insertion point.

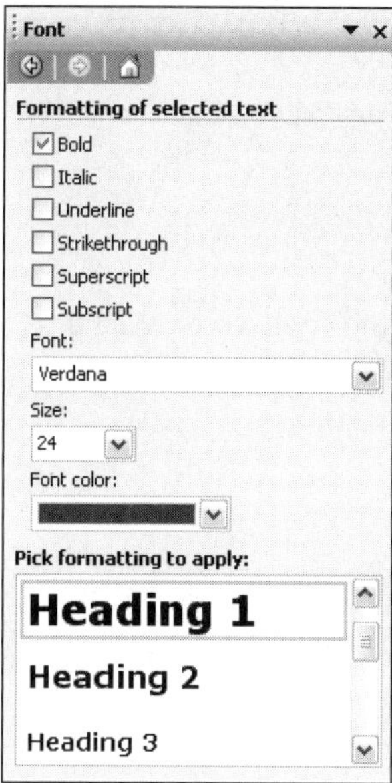


Figure 3-14: Selecting a heading style for text.

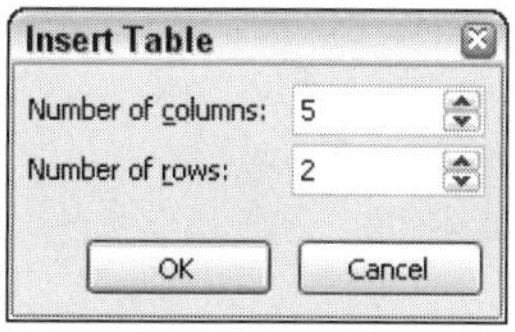

Insert Table

Number of columns: 5

Number of rows: 2

OK Cancel

Figure 3-15: Inserting a table in a Rich Text control.

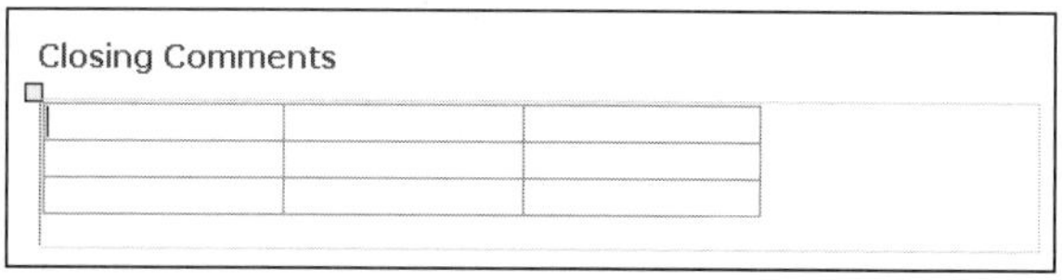

Closing Comments

Figure 3-16: A new, blank table.

Text within a table can be formatted just like any other text using the procedures outlined in this chapter. Thus, you could display a table's headings in a larger font or a different color, or use highlighting to set certain rows or columns off from other ones. You can also format the table itself using the following techniques.

To change the cell borders and background:

1. Select the cells you want to change by dragging over them. Selected cells are displayed with a gray background.
2. Choose Format → Borders and Shading to display the Borders and Shading dialog box.
3. In the dialog box, use the Borders tab to specify the style, color, thickness, and placement of cell borders.
4. Use the Shading tab to select the cell background color.
5. Click OK.

To insert or delete rows and columns, place the insertion point at the desired location in the table, and then:

- Choose Table → Insert followed by the appropriate command to insert a row or column.
- Choose Table → Delete → Rows or Table → Delete → Columns to delete the row or column containing the insertion point.
- Choose Table → Delete → Table to delete the entire table.

To set properties of the entire table, right-click anywhere in the table and select Table Properties from the pop-up menu. In the Table Properties dialog box (see Figure 3-17), you can:

- Use the Table tab to specify how the table aligns with surrounding text.
- Use the Row tab to control row height. The default is for rows to automatically adjust their height to fit the text they contain.
- Use the Column tab to set column width.
- Use the Cell tab to control the vertical alignment of text in a cell and also to set the amount of padding (space between a cell's text and its borders).

You can adjust a table's row and column size manually by pointing at a cell border and dragging to the desired size.

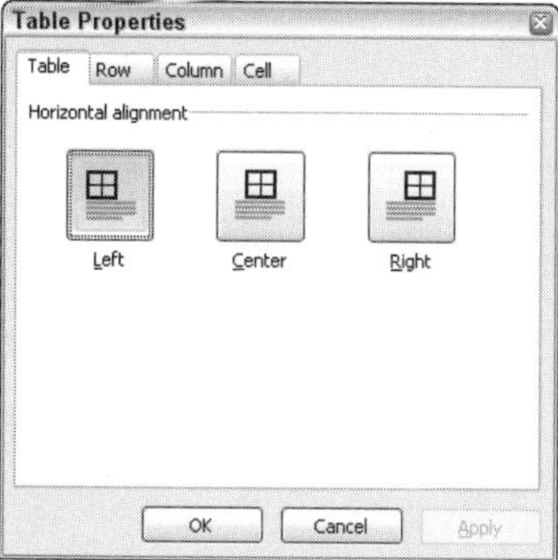


Figure 3-17: The Table Properties dialog box.

# AutoComplete

InfoPath has an AutoComplete feature that keeps track of data that's been entered into fields on a form. It's much like the Word AutoComplete feature – when the user starts typing in a field, AutoComplete compares the first few characters with previous entries the user has made and displays a list of possible matching data. The user can select from this list or continue typing. AutoComplete is available only for Text Box controls and may be disabled for specific controls by the form designer.

When filling out a form in InfoPath, the user can control AutoComplete as follows.

1. Choose Tools → Options to display the Options dialog box, and click the General Tab.
2. Under System Options, click the Internet Options button, and then click the Content tab. (Note: InfoPath uses the same AutoComplete feature as the Internet Explorer browser. That's why the options are under Internet Options.)
3. Click AutoComplete in the Personal Information section. InfoPath displays the AutoComplete Settings dialog box (see Figure 3-18).
4. In the Use AutoComplete For section, select the items for which to use AutoComplete. The Forms option refers to general data entry in Text Box controls on forms. Deselect all items to turn AutoComplete off.
5. In the Clear AutoComplete History section, click the Clear Forms button to erase all stored AutoComplete data.
6. Click OK until all dialog boxes are closed.

Initially, it is the form designer who decides whether AutoComplete is enabled or disabled for a Text Box. If it's enabled, the user can turn it off, as explained in Step 4.

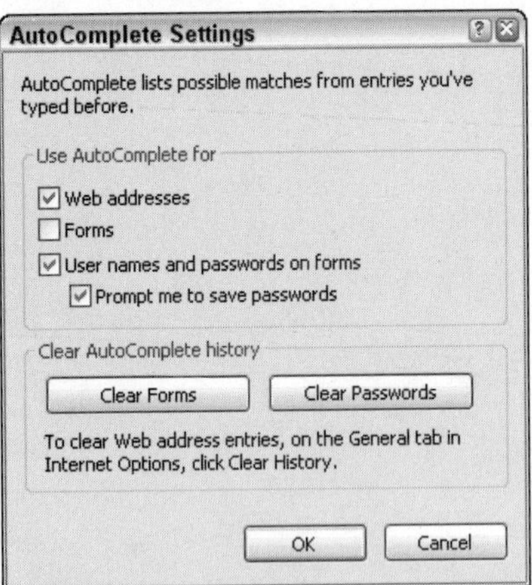


Figure 3-18: Setting AutoComplete options.

# Correcting Forms

InfoPath can check for and detect two types of error on forms: spelling errors and data errors.

## Check Spelling

InfoPath's default setting is to check spelling as you type. Words that are not found in the dictionary are marked with a wavy red underline. If you right-click such a word, a pop-up menu offers you one or more suggested corrections as well as command to ignore the word throughout the form or to add the word to the dictionary. You can also left-click a misspelled word to display the Spelling task pane, shown in Figure 3-19. This task pane offers the same commands as the pop-up menu, plus the Find Next command, which ignores the current misspelled word and looks for the next one.

If you do not want InfoPath to check spelling as you work, choose Tools→Options to open the Options dialog box, and click the Spelling tab (see Figure 3-20). (You can also display the spelling options dialog box by clicking the Spelling Options link at the bottom of the Spelling task pane.) Turn off the Check Spelling as you Type option, and then close the Options dialog box. You can set several other spelling options here, too. If InfoPath is not checking spelling as you work, you can check the entire form's spelling at one time by clicking the Spelling button on the toolbar.

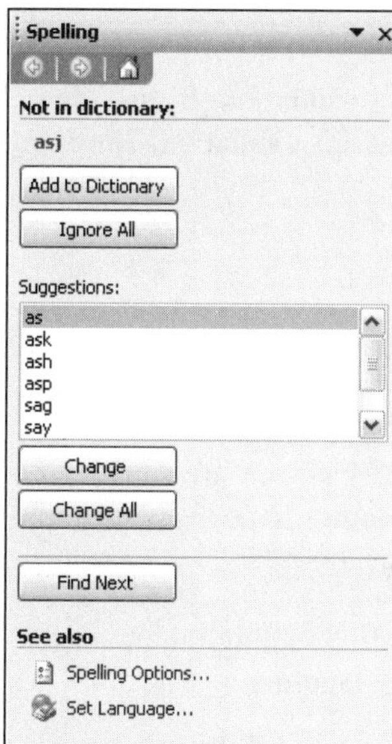


Figure 3-19: The Spelling task pane.

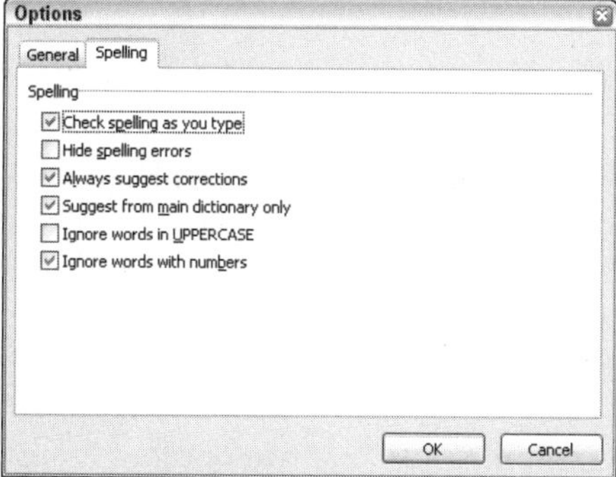


Figure 3-20: Setting spelling options.

Spell checking does not cover words that are part of the form itself. When a form is designed, certain fields can be designated as excluded from spell checking. A user who is filling out a form has no way to override these settings.

## Data Validation

Most InfoPath forms are designed with some sort of data validation. If the form is based on an XML schema, then the schema rules are used for validation. The form designer can add other data validation rules, such as:

- A field may not be left blank.
- A numeric value must be within a certain range.
- A date must be a weekday.

InfoPath checks data against the form's validation rules as you are working on the form. When a validation error is found, one of two things happens (depending on the control where the error occurred and the nature of the error):

- A dialog box is displayed describing the error. After reading the message, close the dialog box and edit the data to fix the violation.
- An inline alert is displayed as a dashed red border around the control. Right-click the control to view a short description of the error; select Full Error Description from the pop-up menu to view a more detailed description.

When working with data validation errors, use the Tools→Go to Next Error command (or press Ctrl-Shift-E) to move to the next error on the form.

You can save a form that contains data validation errors, but you cannot submit it to a Web service or database.

# Merging Forms

Some InfoPath forms are designed to be merged, meaning that two or more forms, and their data, can be combined into one form. For example, you might design a Meeting Overview form to be filled out by the meeting coordinator, and a Session Report form to be completed by each of the meeting attendees. After the forms are filled out, they can be merged so that all the individual session reports are part of the meeting summary. The ability of a form to be merged is part of its design and cannot be changed by the user when filling out a form. The form template also determines the appearance of the final merged form.

To merge the form you are currently working on with another form, choose File→Merge Forms. (If this command is not available, it means the open form does not permit merging.) In the Merge Forms dialog box, select the form to merge, and then click Merge. When forms are merged, the resulting XML data contains the data from all of the individual forms, and the screen display shows the visual elements of all forms.

# Saving and Sharing Forms

Once you have filled out a form, what then? There are several possibilities, which is part of InfoPath's flexibility. Some of these choices are always available, while others may or may not be available, depending on the design of the form template.

## Save the Form

When you save a form, InfoPath saves the data as an XML file. This file contains the form data as well as information that identifies the file as an InfoPath form and that identifies the InfoPath form template that the form is based on. The elements in an InfoPath XML file are all associated with a namespace that identifies the form template. Because the form's schema is part of the template definition, the namespace serves to "connect" the XML file with its Data model.

To save a form, choose File → Save or click the Save button on the toolbar. When you save a form for the first time after starting it, you're asked to specify a location (path) and name for the form. The name is up to you; InfoPath automatically adds the XML extension. The save location depends on the situation. You can save the file locally and work on it even if you do not have a network connection. You may want to save it to a shared folder, for example on a Windows SharePoint Services site, to make it available to others.

If you have opened an existing InfoPath form, whether created by you or someone else, or if you have already saved a new form at least once, then the File → Save command saves the form with its current name and location. To change the name and/or location use File → Save As.

## Save the Form as a Web Page

InfoPath can save a form as a Web page, permitting the form data to be viewed in a browser. When saved in this manner, the data and form are read-only and cannot be modified in any way. To save a form as a Web page:

1. Choose File → Export To → Web.
2. In the Export To dialog box specify a name and location for the file. InfoPath automatically adds the HTM extension to the filename.
3. Click Export.

Note that the Web page created by exporting a form is not dynamic. In other words, subsequent changes to the form are not reflected in the Web page.

### Working Offline

Forms that you will work with are often saved to a network location to make them available to others. What if you want to work on the form when a network connection isn't available – when using your laptop on an airplane, for example? First, when you have a connection to the network, open the form from its original location. Then, use the Save As command to save it locally on your laptop's hard disk. You can then work on the form as needed regardless of whether you have network access. The next time you are connected to the network, use Save As to save the form back to the network server.

## Submit a Form

When a form template is created, it can be designed to permit the form data to be submitted directly to a database or a Web service. If that's the case, the Submit command on the File menu is available. Simply select this command to submit the form data. The details of the submission are part of the form template so there's no need for further input on your part.

## E-Mail a Form

A form can be e-mailed to someone either in the body of the e-mail message or as an attachment to the message. To send a form in the body of a message you must be using Microsoft Outlook 2003. Then:

1. Choose File → Send To Mail Recipient. InfoPath opens the mail form, as shown in Figure 3-21.
2. Enter the recipient's address in the To box, or click the adjacent book icon to select a recipient from your address list.
3. Enter a subject and, if desired, an introduction in the corresponding boxes. The introduction will be included in the message along with the form.
4. Click Send.

If you do not have Outlook 2003, you are limited to sending a form as an attachment to an e-mail message (you can do this with Outlook 2003 as well, of course). This is done outside of InfoPath. You must save the form as an XML file, as described earlier in this chapter, then use your e-mail program to locate the file and attach it to a message.

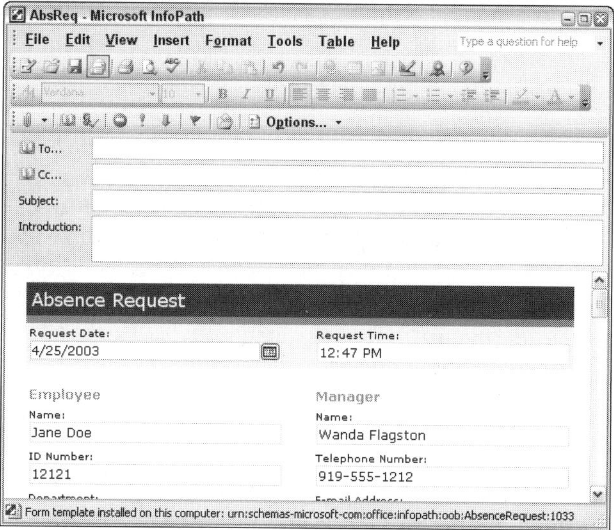


Figure 3-21: Sending a form to an e-mail recipient.

# InfoPath Form Security

An InfoPath form can gain access to files, settings, and resources on your computer. You may want to restrict the extent to which forms have this access.

## Basic Security

Part of the security for InfoPath forms is related to what the form is and is not allowed to do on the user's system. This is particularly relevant when a form contains script code (covered in Chapter 6, "Scripting with InfoPath") that can access a system's files and settings and therefore has the potential to cause mischief. In this regard, a form falls into one of two categories – trusted or sandboxed – depending on the origin of the form. Basic security for InfoPath forms, then, is organized around the source of the form, as follows:

- Sample forms, those that are installed as part of the InfoPath installation, are trusted.
- Custom installed forms, those that are installed with a custom setup program, are trusted.
- Other forms, those that are opened from a location on the network, are sandboxed.

Trusted forms are by default given access to files and settings on your computer. You can restrict the access of trusted forms if you think it wise, as follows:

1. Choose Tools→Options to display the Options dialog box.
2. On the General tab, remove the check mark from the option "Allow forms that I install . . . ."
3. Click OK.

Security for sandboxed forms is based on the same security model used by the Internet Explorer Web browser. This works by assigning network locations to zones. Each zone has security settings defined for it. When you open a form based on a network template, its security settings are determined by the zone that the template source is in. You can refer to your Internet Explorer documentation for more details.

Chapter 6 presents more information about creating trusted forms.

## Digital Signatures

A digital signature is a technique by which the author of a form can "sign" the form with digitally encoded identification. Digital signatures are encrypted and are essentially impossible to forge, permitting the recipient of a signed InfoPath form to be confident that the form did, in fact, come from the owner of the digital signature. A Web service, for example, could be set up to accept submissions of forms only if they are signed with a known signature, preventing the acceptance of spurious or malicious data. Once a form has been digitally signed, it cannot be modified, ensuring the integrity of the data.

To sign a form, you must have a digital certificate installed on your system. You obtain such a certificate from a commercial certification authority such as VeriSign Inc. In most organizations, you should ask your network administrator or IT contact for a certificate. InfoPath can use only those certificates created for client authentication and that have a digital signature value for the key usage attribute.

To add a digital signature to a form, be sure that the form data is complete. Then:

1. Choose Tools→Digital Signatures to display the Digital Signatures dialog box.
2. Click the Add button to display the Add Signature dialog box.
3. Click the Select Certificate button and select the certificate to use.
4. Optionally, enter a comment to be associated with your signature.
5. Click OK to return to the Digital Signatures dialog box. You signature is listed.
6. Click Close.

You can use the Digital Signatures dialog box to view the digital signatures that have been applied to the form, and also to remove signatures.

Chapter 4

# Designing InfoPath Forms, Part 1

IN THIS CHAPTER

- Exploring form design
- Beginning a new form
- Working with a data source
- Examining form layout
- Understanding views

INFOPATH PROVIDES a sophisticated design capability for creating forms for display and entry of data. You can create custom interactive forms to meet essentially any data requirements. This chapter and the next teach you the fundamentals of InfoPath form design.

## Form Design Overview

Every InfoPath form has two components: the data source that provides the structure and storage for the form's data, and the visual interface that provides for display and entry of the form's data. It's important to understand these two components and how they relate to each other before getting to the details of form design.

### The Data Source

Every InfoPath form has a data source. It is the data source that stores the data that is displayed and entered on the form. A data source is composed of fields and groups:

- Fields contain data, such as text, a number, or a date.
- Groups organize fields. A group can contain fields as well as other groups.

For example, take a look at Figure 4-1, which shows the structure of a data source for an InfoPath form.

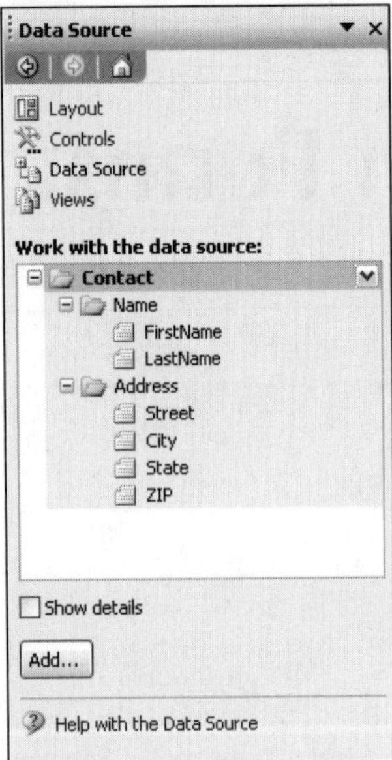


Figure 4-1: An InfoPath data source.

When displaying a data source, InfoPath uses a folder icon to represent groups and a page icon to represent fields. You can see from this figure that the data source is organized as follows:

- Contact is the top-level group. It contains two other groups, Name and Address.
- Name is a group; it contains two fields, FirstName and LastName.
- Address is a group; it contains four fields, Street, City, State, and ZIP.

This a very simple data source, but it serves perfectly well as an illustration. It is clear that the way data sources are structured has direct parallels to the way XML is structured. The data source structure shown in Figure 4-1 would be represented in XML as follows (with data added):

```
<contact>
  <name>
    <firstname>John</firstname>
    <lastname>Doe</lastname>
  </name>
  <address>
    <street>12 Oak Street></street>
    <city>Anytown</city>
```

```
    <state>CA</state>
    <zip>98765</zip>
  </address>
</contact>
```

In fact, this is exactly how InfoPath works – data from an InfoPath form is stored as XML, with the groups and fields in the data structure corresponding to elements, and in some cases attributes, in the XML.

When you are filling out a form, you need not be concerned with its data source – that's handled behind the scenes. The data source is, however, an integral aspect of form design. As you'll see later in this chapter, you can base a form's data source on an existing defined data structure. You can also start from scratch and define the data source yourself.

## The Visual Interface

The second main component of an InfoPath form (the first being the data source) is its visual interface. This, after all, is what the user sees when using the form, and the design of a form's interface can make the difference between a form that is clear and easy to use and one that is confusing and error-prone. A form's interface comprises controls and a layout.

The controls are individual screen elements that are used for the display, entry, and editing of data. InfoPath supports a variety of controls specialized for different types of data – Text Box for text data, Date Picker for dates, Check Box for yes/no options, and so on. The controls you can use on a form are very much like the controls that you are accustomed to seeing in various Windows applications. On an InfoPath form, each control is linked, or bound, to a field in the data source.

The form layout determines how controls are arranged on the form. You can think of the layout as a table of rows and columns, much like a table you would create in a word-processing document. Each cell in the table can hold a control, and because you have complete freedom to split and merge cells, you have a great deal of flexibility in arranging controls on the form. The use of layout tables instead of freehand form design makes it easy to create neat, orderly forms.

# Starting a New Form

You can start a new form based on an existing data structure, such as an XML schema or a database. The data source of the form will have the same structure. You can also start a new form from scratch and define its data source as part of the form-design process.

## With an Existing Data Structure

You can define a new form's data source based on an XML schema, and XML data file, a database table, or a Web service. In each case, the data source has the same structure as the item on which it's based.

### FROM AN XML DATA FILE OR XML SCHEMA

To base a new form on an XML schema or data file, choose File→Design a Form to display the Design a Form task pane. Then:

1. Click the New From Data Source link to open the Data Source Setup Wizard.
2. Select the XML Schema or XML Data File option, and then click Next.
3. Enter the path and name of the XML schema or data file you want to use, or click the Browse button to locate the file.
4. Click Finish.
5. If you selected an XML data file (rather than a schema), InfoPath asks you if you want to use the data in the file as default values for the fields in your form. Select Yes or No. You can always specify default data values later.

InfoPath creates the data source based on the information in the schema or data file and displays it in the Data Source task pane. You are now ready to start working with the data source and designing the form's visual interface, which is discussed later in this chapter.

### FROM A WEB SERVICE

A Web service is a program that resides on a Web server and interacts with clients by exchanging XML data. A Web service can make public information about the structure of the data it works with. InfoPath can retrieve this information and create a form's data source based on it. An InfoPath form can be set up to receive data from a Web service, send data to a Web service, or both.

When a form uses a Web service for its data source, it is essential that the final form accurately match the data structure that the service uses. This means that when you create a form's data source from a Web service, the following limitations apply:

- You cannot modify existing groups or fields in the data source.
- You cannot automatically create the data source when adding controls.
- You can add new fields and groups only to the data source's root group.

In order to base a form's data source on a Web service, you must first have some information about the service. You must be able to locate the service, which requires that you know the location of the service's WSDL (Web Services Description Language) file. Alternately, if you are going to search for the service on a UDDI (Universal Description, Discovery, and Integration) server, you must know the address of the UDDI server. You must also know the Web service operation that is used to send data to or receive data from your form. In addition, some Web services require that you provide some sample data values during the process of setting up the data source, and you need to know the details of the samples you should provide. Once you have all of this information, you can proceed as follows:

1. Choose File→Design a Form to display the Design a Form task pane.
2. Click the New From Data Source Link to open the Data Source Setup Wizard.
3. Select the Web Service option, and then click Next.
4. On the next screen, choose whether the InfoPath form will receive data, submit data, or both.

The details of the remaining steps depend on the specific service you are connecting to, and also on whether your form will be submitting data, receiving data, or both. Note that forms that both receive and submit data may use different services for receiving and submitting.

If your form will receive data from the Web service, InfoPath creates two views for the form. One is a query view that users will use to submit queries to the Web service. The other is the data entry view, which is used to display the results of queries and also to enter data. You are asked which one you want to design first. The design process is covered later in this chapter.

### FROM A DATABASE

InfoPath can create a form's data source from an existing database. At present, only SQL Server and Microsoft Access databases are supported. When you use this technique, the data source is created based on the tables and fields in the database. These are the steps to follow:

1. Choose File→Design a Form to display the Design a Form task pane.
2. Click the New From Data Source Link to open the Data Source Setup Wizard.
3. Select the Database option, and then click Next.
4. Click the Select Database button and select the database you want to use.
5. If the database contains more than one table, InfoPath displays a list of tables from which you must select one to be the primary parent table in your form's data source.
6. InfoPath displays the selected table in the Data Source Setup Wizard dialog box, as shown in Figure 4-2. If the Show Table Columns option

is selected (as in the figure), InfoPath displays the names of the columns, or fields, in the table. Otherwise, only the table name is displayed.

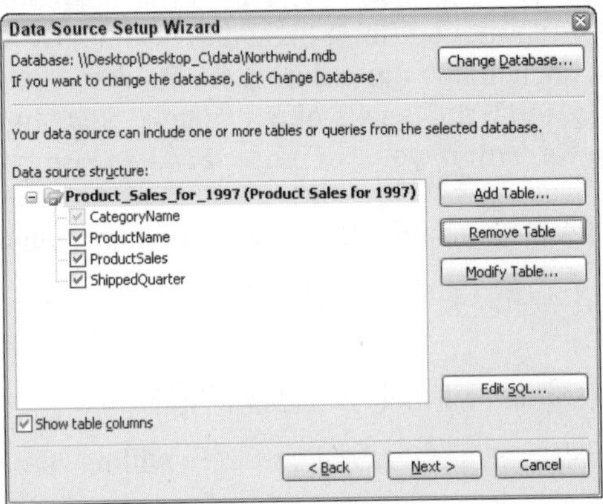


Figure 4-2: The Data Source Setup Wizard dialog box.

7. To add another table, click the Add Table button and select the table. You are asked to edit the relationship between the parent table and the table being added, as shown in Figure 4-3. This relationship identifies the fields that link the two tables. InfoPath tries to identify the proper relationship by the use of field names. Otherwise, you must click the Add Relationship button and select the two linked fields. When the relationship is defined, click Finish to close the Edit Relationship dialog box and return to the Data Source Setup Wizard, which now lists the new table along with other tables.

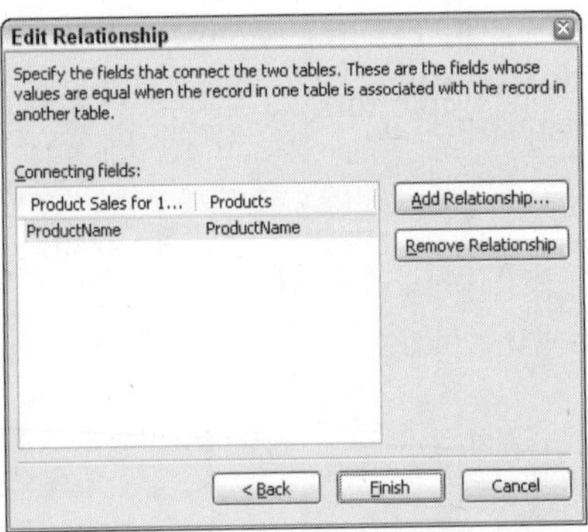


Figure 4-3: Editing a relationship between tables.

8. Use the Add Table button to add more tables, if needed. You can also use the Modify Table button to change the sort order for a table. When you are finished, click Next.

9. Check the Data Source Setup Wizard summary information to make sure that it is correct. Use the Back button to make any corrections, if needed.

As the last step in creating a data source from a database, InfoPath creates two views for you: a query view for querying the database, and a data entry view for viewing and entering data. The query view has some controls placed on it – you can always modify it later. The data entry view is blank. You'll learn more about views and form design later in the chapter.

When a form uses a database for its data source, it is essential that the final form accurately match the data structure of the database tables. When you create a form's data source from a database, you face the same limitations you have when you create a form from a Web service:

- You cannot modify existing groups or fields in the data source.
- You cannot automatically create the data source when adding controls.
- You can add new fields and groups only to the data source's root group.

### FROM A SAMPLE FORM

You can design a form that is based on one of the sample forms that are installed with InfoPath. You are, in effect, customizing that form to meet your specific needs. Your new form inherits the data source of the sample form, and there are limitations as to what you can do:

- You cannot modify existing groups and fields in the data source.
- You cannot automatically create the data source by inserting controls.
- Depending on the sample form, you may not be able to add fields or groups to certain parts of the data source.

Using this technique is suitable when a sample form and its data source come pretty close to what you want in your own form. You can add groups and fields to the data source (with some limitations), and you can change the form's layout and appearance. If your desired finished form is significantly different from a sample form, then you are better off using another technique.

To design a form based on a sample form:

1. Choose File → Design a Form to display the Design a Form task pane.
2. On the task pane, click Customize a Sample.
3. In the next dialog box, locate the same form and double-click it.

You can now proceed to modify the sample form as described later in this chapter.

## Creating a Data Source from Scratch

If your form does not need to conform to an existing data structure, you will create it from scratch. There are two ways to do this:

- You can define the groups and fields of the data structure first and then proceed to designing the form's interface, which is discussed later in this chapter.
- You can define the data source as you add controls to the form. This technique is covered in the "Controls" section of Chapter 5, "Designing InfoPath Forms, Part 2."

To create a new form with a blank data source, choose File → Design a Form to display the Design a Form task pane. Then, click the New Blank Form link. InfoPath displays the Design Tasks task pane, as shown in Figure 4-4. Click the Data Source link to open the Data Source task pane. You can now proceed with designing your data source, as described in the "Working with the Data Source" section later in the chapter.

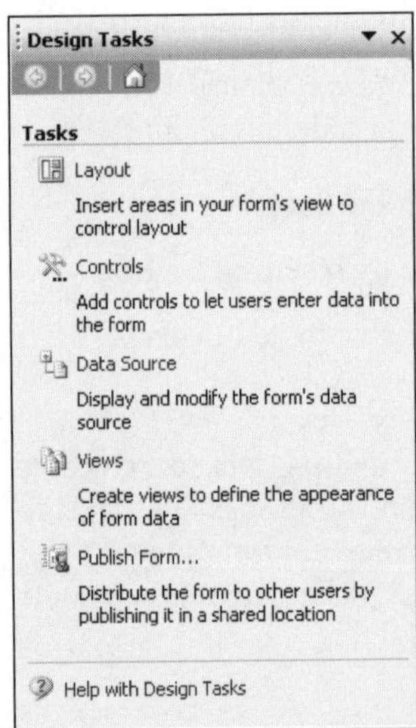


Figure 4-4: The Design Tasks task pane.

# Saving and Opening Forms

When you are designing a form, you can save a local copy as you work to guard against data loss from power outages and also to let you work at your own pace. To save a form you are designing, choose File→Save. If you are asked to choose between saving and publishing the form, select Save. Then, select a location and enter a name for the form. Saving a form in this way is different from publishing a form. Publishing makes the form available for others to use and is covered in Chapter 5.

To open a form template that you saved previously so you can continue designing it, choose File→Design a Form to display the Design a Form task pane. In the Open a Form in Design Node section of the task pane, select the form you want from the list of forms that were open in design mode recently, or click the On My Computer command to locate other forms.

# Working with the Data Source

You use the Data Source task pane (see Figure 4-5) to work with a data source. Its elements include the following:

- The links at the top enable you to open other task panes for working with layout, controls, or views.
- The list in the center displays the current structure of the data source.
- The Show Details option controls whether the list displays just the names of the data source groups and fields, or also displays details about fields such as the data type.

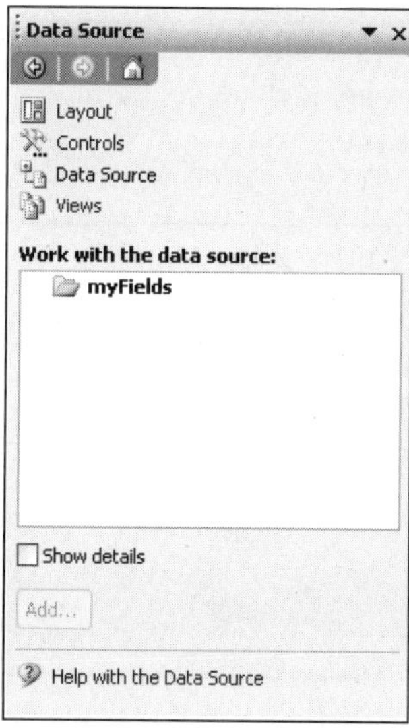


Figure 4-5: The Data Source task pane.

If you are starting to design a data source from scratch, the Data Source task pane shows a data source that contains only one group, named myFields (as shown in the figure). If you are working with an existing data source or one that was created from a database, an XML schema, or a Web service (as described earlier in this chapter), the structure of the data source is displayed as a hierarchical tree, with groups represented by folder icons and fields by page icons. Click the plus and minus signs in the tree to expand or collapse nodes of the tree to see the details as required.

In the data source view, groups and fields that cannot be modified are indicated by a small padlock on the folder or page icon. You can view but not change the properties of locked items. An item is locked if it originated in an XML file, schema, Web service, or database on which the data view was based.

An item in a data source can be one of three things:

- A group
- A field that is an XML element
- A field that is an XML attribute

## Adding to a Data Source

When adding an item to a data source, the new item is always the child of an existing item. Table 4-1 shows which parent-child relationships are and are not permitted in a data source. Also, you cannot add new children to locked items.

TABLE 4-1 PARENT-CHILD RELATIONSHIPS IN A DATA SOURCE

| Item | Can Be Child of Group | Can Be Child of Element Field | Can Be Child of Attribute Field |
|---|---|---|---|
| Group | Yes | No | No |
| Element field | Yes | Yes | No |
| Attribute field | No | Yes | No |

To add an item to a data source:

1. Select the item in the data source that will be the parent.
2. Click the Add button on the Data Source task pane to display the Add Field or Group dialog box (see Figure 4-6).

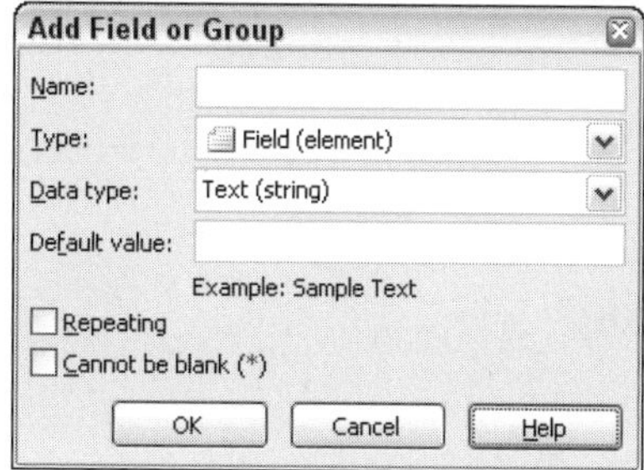


Figure 4-6: The Add Field or Group dialog box.

3. Make entries in this dialog box as follows:

   **Name.** The name of the field or group being added. Remember that XML is case-sensitive.

   **Type.** The type of item being added. This list offers only those types that are permitted for the parent you selected.

   **Data type.** Select the data type of the item (see the following section on data types). Not relevant for groups.

   **Default value.** Optional. This is the data that displays in the field when the form is first opened, before the user has made any entries. If omitted, the field will initially be blank. Not relevant for groups.

   **Repeating.** Select this option to create a repeating field or group. A repeating field is a field in the data source that can occur more than once. You use repeating fields with controls such as List and Repeating Section.

   **Cannot be blank.** Select this option to create a data validation rule that requires entry of some data into the field. Not relevant for groups.

4. Click OK.

Field names must begin with a letter or the underscore character. They can contain letters, numbers, and the characters period (.), underscore (_), and hyphen (-). Other characters, including spaces, are not permitted.

# Data Types

The data types that are available for InfoPath fields are a subset of the data types that are supported by XML. It is important that you select a data type that is appropriate for the data that the field will hold. Table 4-2 lists InfoPath's data types and describes the data they are designed for. You can change a field's data type later if you need to.

**TABLE 4-2 INFOPATH'S DATA TYPES**

| Data Type | Use for |
| --- | --- |
| Text | Plain, unformatted text |
| Rich Text | Formatted text |
| Whole number | Numbers without a decimal part |
| Decimal | Numbers that may have a decimal part |
| True/False | Yes/No, on/off values |
| Hyperlink | URLs |
| Date | Dates with no time information |
| Time | Times with no date information |
| Date and time | Combined date and time information |
| Picture | Images |

# Viewing Data Source Details

Each item in the data source has a set of properties that specify its name, data type (for fields), and so on. You can view these properties on the Data tab of the Field or Group Properties dialog box, as shown in Figure 4-7. This tab shows the item's properties from InfoPath's perspective.

If you need to see the item's properties from an XML schema perspective, click the Details tab in this dialog box (see Figure 4-8). This tab shows the item's namespace, data type, and other information.

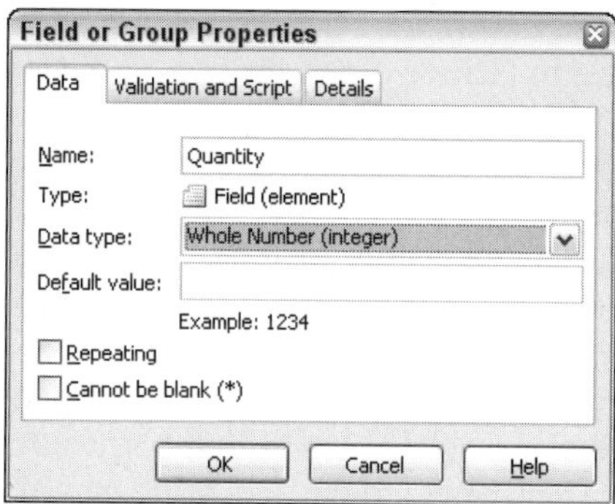


Figure 4-7: The Data tab of the Field or Group Properties dialog box.

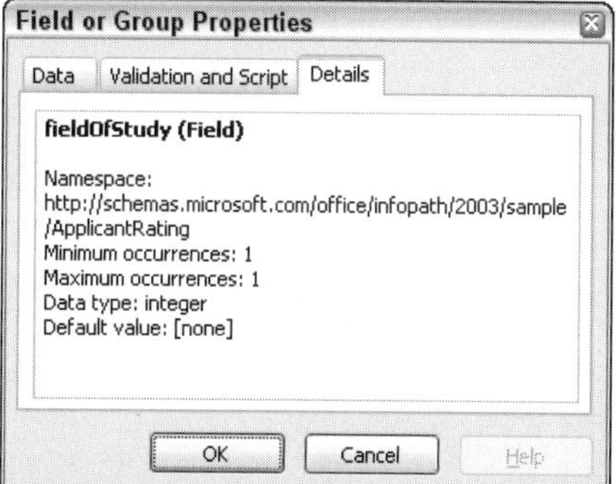


Figure 4-8: The Details tab in the Field of Group Properties dialog box shows a data source item's schema description.

# Modifying a Data Source

The extent to which you can modify a data source depends on where it came from. If the data source originated with an XML file or schema, a Web service, or a database, you are permitted to modify only those parts of the data source that you added. Other elements are locked and cannot be changed.

If a form template has already been put into use, and users have already filled out forms based on that template, be very careful about making changes to the data source. Depending on how the form data is used, changes to the data source can lead to loss of data.

To modify a field or group in the data source, display the Data Source task pane then right-click on the field or group you want to change. From the pop-up menu select Properties to display the Field or Group Properties dialog box. The Data tab, which was shown earlier in Figure 4-7, provides the current details of the field or group. You can change only the name of a group. You can change any aspect of a field, including its data type and name, but you cannot change its type. That is, you cannot change an element field to an attribute field, or vice versa. Click OK when you have made the desired changes.

To move an item to a new location within the data source, right-click the item and select Move from the pop-up menu. InfoPath displays a dialog box with the structure of the data source. Click the item that will be the new parent of the item being moved, then click OK. When you move an item, any children that it has move along with it.

To delete an item from the data source, right-click the item and select Delete from the pop-up menu.

# Form Layout

A form's layout determines the general structure of a form – how the controls are arranged, how many columns are on the form, and other similar aspects of the form's visual appearance. This section shows you how to create and modify a form's layout.

## Layout Tables

A *layout table* determines the basic structure of a form's visual interface. A layout table is similar in many ways to the tables you may use to organize data in a word-processing document. It contains rows and columns, and each cell (where a row and column intersect) can contain controls and other elements that make up an InfoPath form. The flexibility of designing forms based on layout tables derives from several factors:

- A form can contain more than one table, permitting you to create sophisticated designs.
- A table can be inserted in a cell of another table, further enhancing design flexibility.
- A table cell can be split into two cells either vertically or horizontally.
- Multiple adjacent cells can be merged into a single cell.

Figure 4-9, for example, shows a new form that has two layout tables on it (with controls or other content added yet). The upper table has three columns and two rows, and two of the cells have been split. The lower table has two rows and five columns.

It is possible to design a form without using a layout table, or to use a table but place some form elements outside the table. Because of the way InfoPath forms work, however, this makes it difficult to design attractive forms and makes the design process more time-consuming. I strongly recommend that you use layout tables for all form design. You can experiment with tableless design on your own, but it isn't covered in this book.

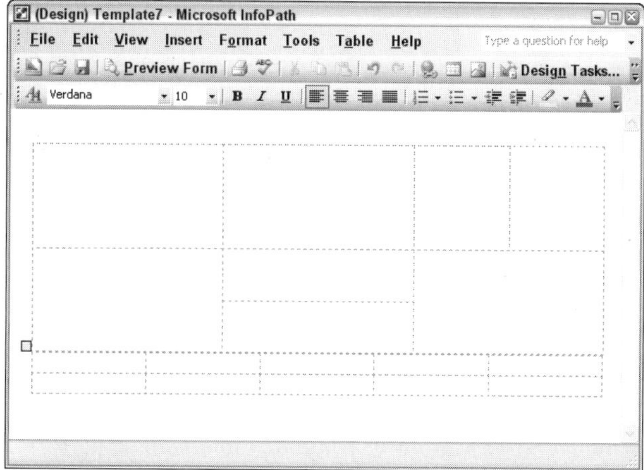


Figure 4-9: Examples of layout tables.

## Add a Layout Table

To add a layout table to a form, click at the form location where you want the table placed. This can be at the top left of a new, blank form, inside a cell of an existing table, or on the form outside of an existing table. The insertion point, a blinking vertical line, shows the location where the new table will be added.

In addition to using the mouse, you can move the insertion point on a form with the standard movement keys (the arrow keys, Home, End, PgUp, PgDn). You can also move the insertion point to a new line by pressing Enter.

When the insertion point is at the desired location, use the Layout task pane (see Figure 4-10) to insert a table.

The Insert Layout Tables list contains several predefined tables that you can insert simply by clicking the one you want. If you select the Custom Table item, InfoPath prompts you for the number of rows and columns in the table before inserting it.

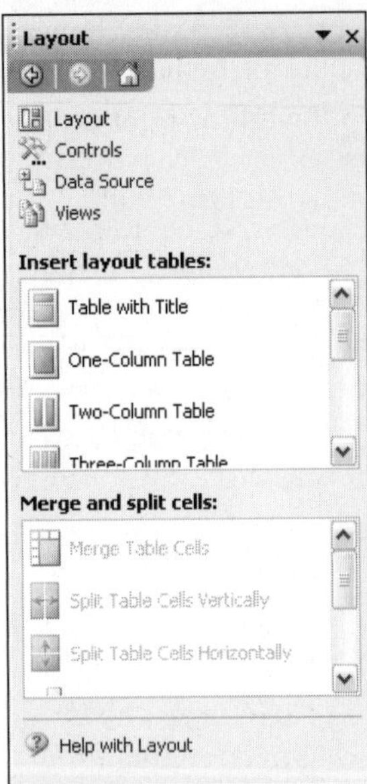


Figure 4-10: The Layout task pane.

## Modifying a Layout Table

There are several ways in which you can modify a layout table into your form. Most importantly, you can split and merge cells, and you can add and delete rows and columns.

When you split a cell, a single cell is divided to create two cells in the same space. A cell can be split either vertically or horizontally. Merging cells creates a single table cell from two or more existing cells. By merging and splitting cells, you can get away from a strict row-and-column arrangement to create essentially any layout that your form requires. To work with cells, the Layout task pane must be displayed. Then:

- To split a cell, place the insertion point in the cell, and select Split Table Cells Vertically or Split Table Cells Horizontally from the Merge and Split Cells list on the task pane.
- To merge cells, first select two or more adjacent cells by dragging over them with the mouse (selected cells display a gray background). Then, select Merge Table Cells from the Merge and Split Cells list on the task pane.

You can also add and delete rows and columns in a layout table:

- To add a row at the bottom or a column at the right edge of the table, be sure that the insertion point is in the table, and select Add Table Row or Add Table Column from the Merge and Split Cells list on the task pane.

- To add a row or column at a specified location in the table, right-click at the desired location. From the pop-up menu select Insert followed by the appropriate command. You can insert a column to the left or right of, or a row above or below, the clicked location.
- To delete a row or column, right-click the row or column to be deleted, then choose Delete→Columns or Delete→Rows from the pop-up menu.

## Formatting a Layout Table

You may be content with the default appearance of a layout table. If not, there are several ways in which you can change its appearance. You can select the portion of the table to be affected with either of the following methods (selected cells display with a gray background):

- Drag over one or more cells to select them.
- Put the insertion point at the desired location in the table, then choose Table→Select followed by Table, Column, Row, or Cell, depending on what you want to select.

You can click anywhere in the table to cancel the selection.

Some formatting commands don't require that you make a selection first, although you can. For example, a column formatting command affects the entire column that the insertion point is in even if the column is not selected. As you work with layout tables, you'll soon become familiar with which formatting commands require you to make a selection first, and which don't.

### TABLE PROPERTIES

Some properties of a layout table affect the entire table, while others affect individual rows, columns, or cells. To work with these properties, select the cell(s) to be affected (if necessary), then choose Table→Table Properties. InfoPath displays the Table Properties dialog box, which has four tabs:

- **Table.** Specify table alignment, which controls how the entire table aligns with respect to other content on the form: left, center, or right. This property is relevant only when the layout table is narrower than the form.
- **Row.** Set row height. You can specify that the row height change automatically to fit its contents (the default), or that the row have a certain minimum height. Use the Previous Row and Next Row buttons to set the height for other table rows without having to close and reopen the dialog box.
- **Column.** Set column width. Use the Previous Column and Next Column buttons to set the height for other table columns.
- **Cell.** Set the vertical alignment of cell contents and also set the cell padding (the space between the cell's contents and its edges).

You can also set column width and row height visually by dragging the table's grid lines with your mouse.

Horizontal alignment of cell contents is not a table property, but is controlled by the alignment buttons on the Formatting toolbar.

### BORDERS AND SHADING

Borders control the appearance of the lines around table cells, and shading determines the background color in tables. Do not confuse table shading with a form's background color (which is set with the Format→Background Color command and controls the background of the entire form or, to be more precise, the current view). If you do not specify shading for a table, the form's background color is visible under the table.

To work with a table's borders and shading, start by selecting the part of the table you want to format. This can be anything from a single cell to the entire table. Then, choose Format→Borders and Shading to display the dialog box, which has two tabs: Borders and Shading.

The Borders tab (see Figure 4-11) lets you specify the borders for the selected region of the table, with the following options:

- **Style.** Select the style of the border – solid line, dotted, dashed, and so on.
- **Color.** Select the border color.
- **Width.** Select the border width.
- **Presets.** Select commonly used border arrangements: none, outside edges of the selection, or inside boundaries of the selection.
- Border. Click the buttons or on the diagram to place and remove borders at the specified locations.

You use the Borders tab to specify all the details of the selection's borders at once. For example, suppose that you want the entire table to have a thick black border around its outside edges and a thin red border between all of the cells. After selecting the entire table and displaying the Borders and Shading dialog box, here's what you would do:

1. Select black from the Color list.
2. Select a thick line from the Width list.

3. Click the Outline preset to define the table's outer border.
4. Select red from the Color list.
5. Select a thin line from the Width list.
6. Click the Inside preset to define the table's inner borders.
7. Click OK.

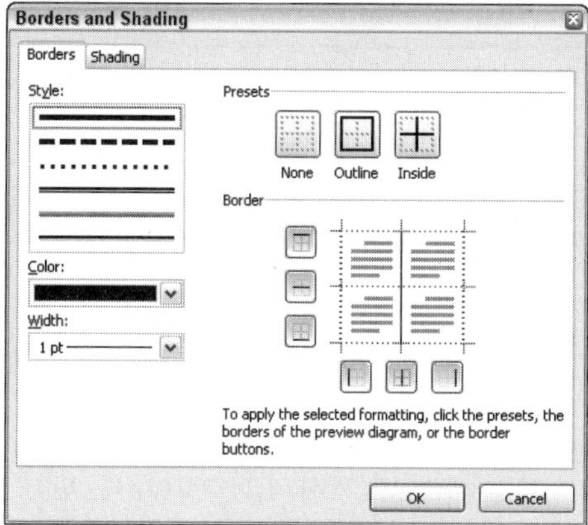


Figure 4-11: Setting borders for a layout table.

You use the Shading tab in the Borders and Shading dialog box to specify the table's background color. Just select a color from the Color list. If you select the No Color option, the form's background color shows through.

## Adding Content to a Layout Table

Placing controls in a table is an essential part of form design, and is covered in Chapter 5. There are other design elements that you can place in a table. Anything that you insert in a table is placed at the location of the insertion point.

- To insert text, just type the text.
- To insert a horizontal line, choose Insert → Horizontal Line.
- To insert clip art, choose Insert → Picture → Clip Art, and use the Clip Art task pane to locate the desired image.
- To insert an image from a file, choose Insert → Picture → From File, and use the Insert Picture dialog box to locate the file.

## Form Elements versus Form Data

It's important to understand the distinction between form *elements*, which are items such as text and pictures that are part of the form's design, and form *data*, which is linked to the form's data source. Data is always displayed in controls, while elements, such as text placed directly on the form, are not. A picture that is placed on the form, and is part of the design, may *look* exactly like a picture that is displayed in a control and is part of the form's data.

### FORMATTING TEXT

Text that is part of the form's design can be formatted with different fonts, sizes, colors, and attributes such as underlining and bold. The techniques are the same as for formatting text that is entered when a form is being filled out, which was discussed in Chapter 3.

### WORKING WITH PICTURES

You have a variety of options for formatting a picture, either clip art or from a file, that has been inserted as part of a form's design. To work with a picture, you must first select it by clicking. A selected picture has small handles displayed around the edges. Then, you can take the following actions:

- Press Del to delete the picture.
- Drag a handle to change the picture's size.
- Right-click the picture and select Borders and Shading from the pop-up menu to define borders for the picture.
- Right-click the picture and select Format Picture from the pop-up menu to display the Format Picture dialog box to change formatting.

The Format Picture dialog box, shown in Figure 4-12, has three tabs that let you control certain aspects of the picture's appearance, as follows:

- **Text Wrapping.** Controls how the picture is displayed with respect to surrounding text (if there is any)
- **Size.** Enables you to specify a precise pixel size for the picture
- **Text.** Allows you to specify alternate text to be displayed by a browser if the image is not available

Figure 4-12: The Format Picture dialog box.

# Sections

When designing an InfoPath form, you can use *sections* to organize the form and to group controls. A section can contain layout tables and controls that are related in some way. The controls in a section are bound to a group in the data source. There are three types of sections:

- **Optional.** The user can insert or delete this type of section in the document as needed. You use optional sections for information that may or may not be needed. For example, a resume form might have an optional "Professional Certifications" section for data about the user's credentials. If a given user has such credentials, she would insert the Professional Certifications section and fill out its controls with her information. A user who does not need to list professional certifications would leave the section out.
- **Repeating.** This section can be inserted in a form as many times as needed. As its name implies, it's used for information that may be repeated. On a resume form, for instance, you could design a repeating section called "Previous Position" that holds information about one job the applicant held in the past. When an applicant is filling out the form, he inserts as many Previous Position sections as are needed to list the jobs he has held.
- **Regular.** A regular section, called simply a section in InfoPath, has no special capabilities. It is used as an aid in form design and organization.

A section is always bound to a group in your data source. Although it is possible to insert a section in a form before there is any data source to bind it to, you eventually have to bind it to a section. InfoPath provides techniques for adding a section and defining its binding in one step, provided that the data source has been defined.

## Sections and Schemas

When working with optional and repeating sections, InfoPath requires that the characteristics of the group in the data source, as defined in the schema, be suitable for the type of section. Specifically, an optional section can be bound only to a group that is also optional – in other words, not marked as "required" in the schema. Likewise, a repeating section can be bound only to groups that are allowed to occur more than once (a repeating group).

Although it is possible to bind a section to a single field in the data source, this is rarely done. One of the main benefits of sections is the capability to quickly and easily bind them to groups. This not only simplifies the form designer's task, but helps to organize the form in a way that parallels the data source. Binding a section to a single field has none of these advantages.

### INSERTING AND BINDING SECTIONS

There are two ways to insert and bind a section. These techniques require that the data source be defined and that the insertion point be at the location where you want the section.

The first method requires that the Controls task pane be displayed. Then:

1. Scroll the Insert Controls list until the desired item is visible: Section, Optional Section, or Repeating Section.
2. Click the type of section you want to insert. InfoPath displays the Section Binding dialog box, shown in Figure 4-13, which displays the form's data source. The title of this dialog box reflects whether you are inserting a section, an optional section, or a repeating section, but its function is the same in all three cases.
3. Select the group that you want the section bound to. If necessary, expand the data source to display the desired group. Click the group, and then click OK.

If you selected a group that is not appropriate for the type of section – that is, a nonrepeating group for a repeating section or a nonoptional group for an optional section – InfoPath displays a message and requires you to select another group. When the process is complete, InfoPath inserts the section into the form. The section is blank at this point (contains no controls); adding controls is discussed in Chapter 5.

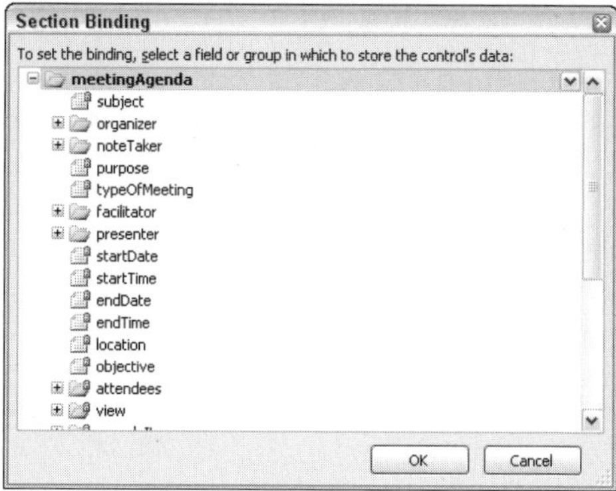


Figure 4-13: Binding a form section to a group.

The second method of inserting a section requires that the Data Source task pane be displayed. It inserts a regular or repeating section into the form, depending on whether the bound group is repeating. In the case of a regular section, you can change it to an optional section later (if permitted by the data source). For this method:

1. On the Data Source task pane, right-click the group that the section will be bound to.
2. From the pop-up menu, select either Section or Section with Controls (the commands are Repeating Section or Repeating Section with Controls if the group is a repeating group).

   **[Repeating] Section.** InfoPath inserts a blank section that is bound to the group. You will need to add controls to the section later.

   **[Repeating] Section with Controls.** InfoPath inserts a section that is populated with controls that are bound to the fields in the group. For each field, InfoPath selects the type of control that is best suited to the field's data type.

### SECTION PROPERTIES

To work with the properties of a section, right-click the section and select Section Properties (or Repeating Section Properties) from the pop-up menu. InfoPath displays the Section Properties dialog box, shown in Figure 4-14.

The tabs in the dialog box control various aspects of the section's properties:

- **Data.** Properties related to the type of section (regular, repeating, or optional). These properties are explained further in the text.
- **Display.** Properties related to conditional formatted (covered later in this chapter).

- **Size.** Properties that control the size of the section and its margins.
- **Advanced.** Properties that control the section's screen tip (text that is displayed when the mouse hovers over the section) and its position in the tab order.

The Data tab contains the properties that are most important in terms of the section's type and behavior. At the top in the Binding section, it displays the name of the group that the section is bound to. You cannot change this; it is for informational purposes only.

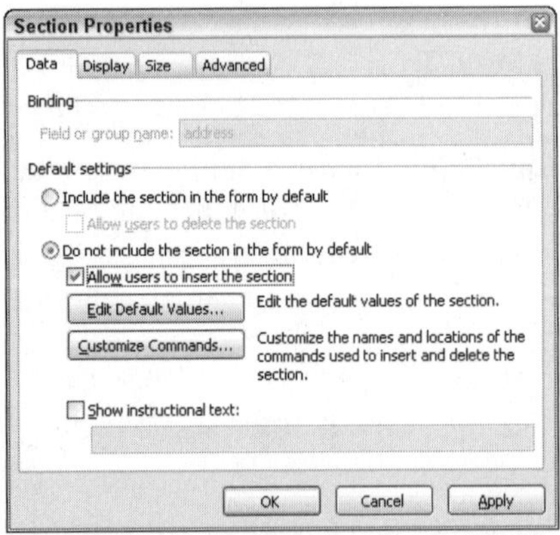


Figure 4-14: The Section Properties dialog box.

You cannot change the binding of a section. You must delete the original section and then insert a new section with the new binding.

The remainder of the Data tab is different depending on the type of the section. For a regular section, there are no options available on the Data tab. The options for repeating and optional sections are described in the following sections.

## OPTIONAL SECTION PROPERTIES

The main choice on the Data tab for a nonrepeating section (which was shown in Figure 4-14) is whether the section is to be included in the form by default, that is, be present when the form is first opened by the user. If you select that option, the only other choice you have is whether the user is permitted to delete the section.

If you decide not to include the section in the form by default, then you must also choose whether users can insert the section. If you select the Allow Users to Insert the Section option, you also have these settings to make:

- **Edit Default Values.** Click this button to edit the default data values that will be placed in the section when it is inserted.
- **Customize Commands.** Click this button to specify where the command to insert the section will be available in InfoPath.
- **Show Instructional Text.** Select this option and enter the desired text if you want users to be able to insert the section by clicking text that is displayed on the form.

By default, the command that lets the user insert or delete an optional section will be available on the Insert Section menu and also on the section's shortcut menu. You may want to customize the form so that the command is available in other locations when the user is filling out the form. To do so, click the Customize Commands button in the Optional Section Properties dialog box. InfoPath displays the Section Commands dialog box, shown in Figure 4-15.

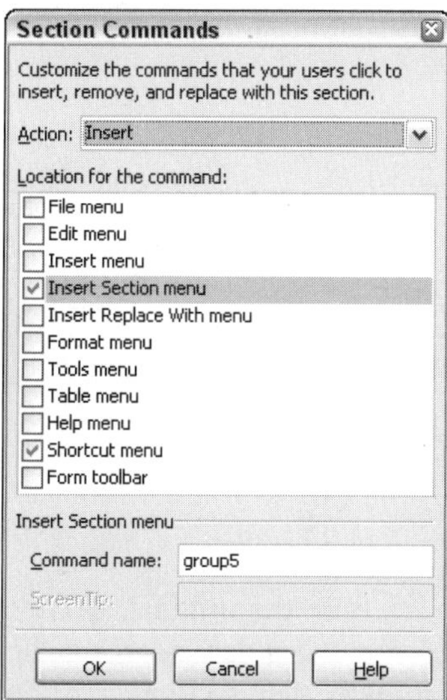


Figure 4-15: Customizing the commands for an optional section.

Make settings in this dialog box as follows:

- **Action.** Select the action. For an optional section, the available actions are Insert and Delete.
- **Location for the Command.** Lists the locations where the command can be displayed. Checked items indicate where the command are actually displayed.

- **Command name.** Specifies the name that will be displayed for the command. By default, this is the name of the data source item to which the section is bound.
- **Screen Tip.** For some command locations, you can specify a screen tip that displays when the mouse hovers over the command.

I recommend that you be consistent when customizing commands. If a form has more than one optional section, the commands should be located in the same locations for all of them.

### REPEATING SECTION PROPERTIES

The Data tab of the Repeating Section Properties dialog box is shown in Figure 4-16. If you want users to be able to add and delete the section, make sure the Allow Users to Insert and Delete the Sections option is checked. Otherwise, the section can be added and deleted only by script code (which is beyond the scope of this book).

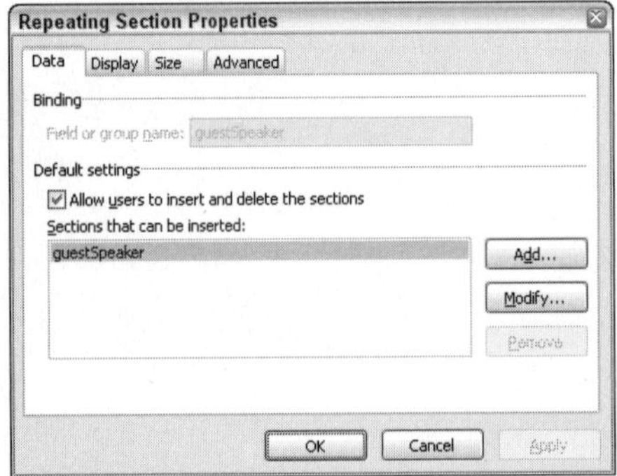


Figure 4-16: The Data tab for a repeating section.

The Sections That Can Be Inserted box initially lists only the original, default repeating section. You can define additional sections that users can insert on the form. It is important to understand that these are not really new sections, but are variations on the original repeating section that have been customized with a different name and/or default values.

# Color Schemes

Rather than specifying a form's visual appearance yourself, you may want to use one of the predefined color schemes offered by InfoPath. A color scheme assigns complementary colors to various elements of a form, including body and heading styles, tables cells, and borders. You can always modify a form's appearance after applying a color scheme, but color schemes are professionally designed and provide you with an easy way to create attractive forms.

To apply a color scheme to a form, choose Format→Color Schemes to display the Color Schemes task pane, shown in Figure 4-17. Then, select the desired scheme. Select None to remove a previously assigned scheme.

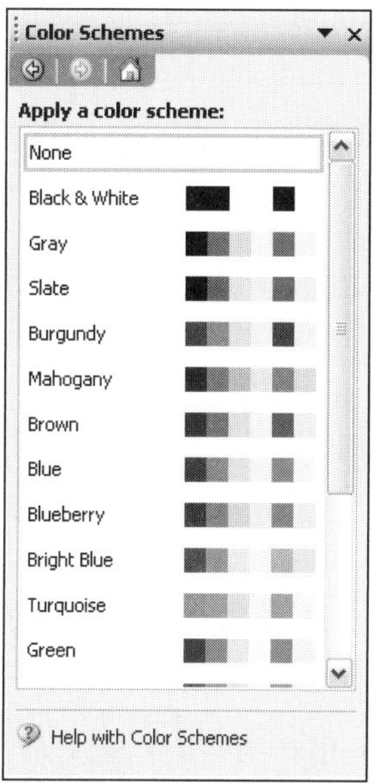


Figure 4-17: The Color Scheme task pane.

# Form Views

Every form has a default view that is displayed when a user first opens the form. When you design a form, you can give it additional views that make it easier to work with. No matter how many views a form has, the underlying form data is always the same. Views differ only in the way they organize and display the data. A detail view, for example, might display all of the form's data, while a summary view would hide most of the data and display only the summary fields. In either case, the same data is present in the form. When a user is filling out a form, the available views are listed on the View menu, enabling the user to switch between views as needed.

## Creating a New View

To work with views, display the Views task pane (see Figure 4-18), which shows the form's current views (two in the figure) and some view-related commands. Click a view's name to display it for design and modification. To add a new view, click the

Add a New View command. InfoPath prompts you for the new view's name, and then displays the new view, initially blank, for you to design.

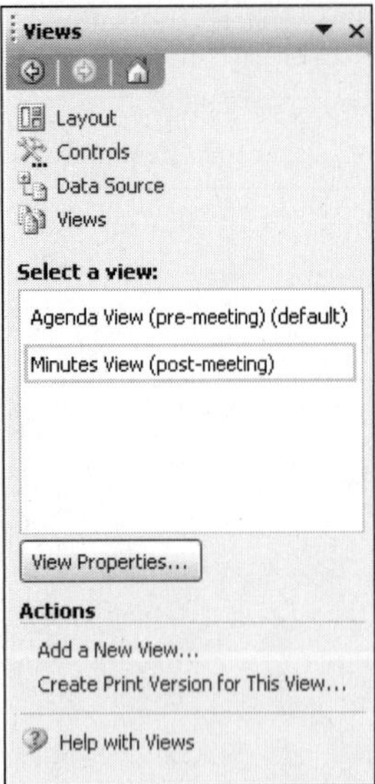


Figure 4-18: The Views task pane.

There's nothing special about designing or modifying a view. You use the same form design techniques that you have learned in other parts of this chapter, such as creating sections and using layout tables.

## View Properties

Each view has a set of properties associated with it that control certain aspects of the view's appearance and how it is printed. To access these properties, select the view on the Views task pane, and click the View Properties button to display the View Properties dialog box, which has three tabs: General, Text Settings, and Print Settings.

On the General tab you can view and set the following properties:

- **View name.** The name of the view.
- **Set as Default View.** Select this option to make this view the default view (the one that is displayed when a user opens the form). A form can have only one default view.
- **Show on the View Menu.** If this option is selected, the user will be able to select the view from InfoPath's View menu when filling out the form.

- **Background Color.** The view's background color.
- **Layout Width.** The width of the form in this view.

On the Text Settings tab you can specify the font to be used for certain controls. Select a control type and then enter the details of the font; that font becomes the default for all controls of the specified type on the form. You could, for example, specify that all Text Box controls use Verdana 18-point italic. You can still change the font of individual controls, if desired.

On the Print Settings tab you set these properties:

- **Designate Print View.** Select the view to be used when the current view is printed. By default each view is its own print view.
- **Orientation.** Choose whether the view will print with portrait or landscape orientation.
- **Headers and footers.** Text that will be printed at the top and/or bottom of each page.

There's much more for you to learn about designing InfoPath forms, including how to work with controls, validate data, and use formulas on forms, all of which is covered in the next chapter.

## Print Views

By default, each view is its own print view. This means that when the user selects the Print command in InfoPath while filling out a form, the same form that is on-screen is printed. The form designer has the option to associate a print view with any view. For example, suppose that the designer has specified that View A is the print view for View B. Then, when the user is working with View B and selects the Print command, InfoPath will print View A. There's nothing special about a view that is designated as a print view except it is designed specifically for printing — using less color, for example, or including headers and footers. Views that have been designed as print views are typically not included in the View menu because they are not intended for on-screen use.

Chapter 5

# Designing InfoPath Forms, Part 2

IN THIS CHAPTER

- Exploring controls and how to use them
- Understanding data validation on forms
- Using formulas on forms
- Setting user options
- Testing and publishing forms

CONTROLS ARE KEY components of InfoPath forms and are an important part of the form design process. This chapter explains all about controls, and then discusses other fundamental design issues, including data validation, the use of formulas in forms, and setting user options.

# Controls

On any InfoPath form, controls provide the link between the user and the data source. Placing controls on a form and binding them to the data source is a central part of form design. This section describes the controls that are available and shows you how to use them on a form.

## Control Overview

InfoPath provides almost 20 different controls. Some of them are directly related to data, such as the Text Box control, which is used for short sections of text data. Others are used to organize a form, such as the Section, Repeating Section, and Optional Section controls (which I discussed sections in Chapter 4, "Designing InfoPath Forms, Part 1"). While I can't cover all of InfoPath's controls in this book, I describe the most often used ones, which are described in Table 5-1.

**Table 5-1 FREQUENTLY USED INFOPATH CONTROLS**

| Control | Description |
|---|---|
| Button | Displays a button that the user can click to carry out an action. |
| Check Box | Presents an on/off, yes/no option. The control has two data values associated with it: one for the "checked" state and one for the "unchecked" state. A single Check Box is bound to a single field in the data source. The value of the field is the same as the checked or unchecked data associated with the control. |
| Date Picker | Designed for date data. The control displays a date next to a small calendar button. When the user clicks the button, a graphical calendar is displayed, permitting the user to select a date. The user also can simply type a date into the control. The control is bound to a single field in the data source; the value of the field is equal to the date that is currently displayed in the control. |
| Expression Box | Performs calculations based on form data. |
| List | Provides for entry and display of lists of items. There are three List controls: Bulleted List, Numbered List, and Plain List. The List controls are explained in more detail later. |
| List Box | Displays a list of values from which the user can select. It can obtain its list of values from various sources, including XML files and databases. The control is bound to a single field in the data source; the value of the field is equal to the item that is currently selected in the list. |
| Option Button | Used to select mutually exclusive options. That is, in a group of option buttons, one and only one can be selected at a time. A group of option buttons is bound to a single field in the data source. The field's value is equal to the value of the option button that is selected. |
| Picture | Used to display images. It can be bound only to a field of type base64Binary. The picture data is stored as a binary representation in the data source. A Picture control also can be bound to a field of type string, which permits it to hold a link to the picture but not the picture data itself. |
| Repeating Table | Displays data in a tabular structure. This control is not directly bound to the data source, but rather contains other controls that are bound. Each row in a Repeating Table is identical, containing the same controls as all the other rows. When filling out the form, the user can add and delete rows as needed. The Repeating Table control is more involved than most other controls, and is discussed further later in this chapter. |

| Control | Description |
|---|---|
| Rich Text Box | Stores formatted text. The text in this control can be formatted with different fonts, bulleted lists, paragraphs, images, and more. The control is bound to a single field in the data source; the value of the field is equal to the text and formatting codes in the control. |
| Text Box | Stores unformatted text. While the form designer can specify different fonts for the display of data in a Text Box, the stored data consists of plain text with no formatting. |

# Placing Controls on a Form

InfoPath provides the form designer with several techniques for placing controls on a form. You can, for example, place controls on a form before the data source exists, then create the data source later and bind the controls to it. You can also have InfoPath automatically create the data source during the process of placing controls on a form. To cover all control placement techniques is beyond the scope of this chapter, so coverage is limited to what I believe are the easiest and fastest methods for placing controls on a form.

## Choices for Repeating Data

InfoPath offers the form designer three choices for data that repeats: repeating sections, repeating tables, and List controls. It's important to understand the differences among these controls and when you would select each for use in a form you are designing.

- A repeating section is used when the repeating data contains multiple individual data items, such as an address book entry that contains name, address, city, state, and so on. A repeating section gives you maximum flexibility in laying out the controls that are bound to the individual data fields.
- A repeating table is also used when the repeating data contains multiple individual data items. In this sense it provides the same functionality as a repeating section. You have less flexibility in laying out the individual controls in a repeating table because they all must fit in a single table row.
- A List control is used when the repeating elements are individual data items.

Both repeating sections and repeating tables are bound to repeating groups or fields in the data source. A List control must be bound to a repeating field with a text (string) or rich text (XHTML) data type.

When you are using sections on your form, it is often easiest to have InfoPath automatically insert the controls in the section as was described in Chapter 4.

## PLACING CONTROLS WHEN THE DATA SOURCE EXISTS

To use this method, the data source must already be defined (as described earlier in this chapter). If you are inserting controls in a section, you must place the section on the form first. Remember that sections are bound to groups in the data source, and you should not place a control in a section that is bound to a field outside this group. Then, to insert a control:

1. Place the insertion point at the location where you want the control.
2. Display the Data Source task pane.
3. Right-click the field that you want the control bound to.
4. On the pop-up menu, click the name of the type of control you want to insert. If the name is not visible, click the More command. If the name is still not visible, it means that the control is not suitable for the data type of the selected field.

If you are inserting an Option Button control, in the last step you are asked how many to insert in the form. This corresponds to the number of options the user will have for the field data. After the control has been inserted, you usually set its properties, as described later in the "Control Properties" section.

## PLACING CONTROLS WHEN THE DATA SOURCE DOES NOT EXIST

If you are not basing your form on a Web service or database, and are defining your own data source, you have the option of creating the data source automatically while you place controls on the form. The way this works is that when you place a control on the form, InfoPath creates an element in the data source to which the control is bound. The nature of the element (field or group) and its data type depend on the type of control that is inserted.

I do not find this technique to be particularly useful for two reasons:

- The fields and groups created by InfoPath are assigned default names in the form *field1, group1.* It is necessary to edit the data source later to assign meaningful names to the data source elements.
- The organization of the data source is not always easy to predict as you place controls on the form.

Even so, some form designers find this technique useful, particularly for relatively simple forms. Here are the steps to follow:

1. Choose File → Design a Form to display the Design a Form task pane.
2. Click the New Blank Form command. InfoPath displays a blank form in the design area, and also displays the Design Tasks task pane.
3. On the task pane, click the Controls command to display the Controls task pane.
4. Make sure that the Automatically Create Data Source option at the bottom of the task pane is checked.
5. Begin inserting controls on the form.

As you insert controls, InfoPath creates elements in the data source bound to the controls. For example, if you add a Section to the form, a group is added to the data source. If you then place a Text Box control in the section, InfoPath adds a field as a child of the group. As you work, you can switch between the Controls task pane and the Data Source task pane to see the structure of the data source that is being created. When you are finished designing the form's interface, you almost always need to edit the data source to change field names and modify the structure. The "Modifying a Data Source" section in Chapter 4 explains how to do this.

## Using the Repeating Table Control

There are several ways you can place a Repeating Table control on a form. You can right-click a repeating group in the Data Source task pane and select Repeating Table from the pop-up menu. (If Repeating Table is not available on the pop-up menu, then the group is not appropriate for a Repeating Table controls, that is, it is not a repeating group.)

InfoPath inserts a table in the form with the number of columns equal to the number of fields in the group. The top row of the table contains the field names as column headers; you can edit these as needed. The second row contains controls bound to the fields in the group; it is this row that users will be able to insert and delete when filling out a form. InfoPath chooses controls for the table based on the data type of the fields – Text Box for type string, Check Box for type Boolean, and so on. You can always change the control types later, within the limitations imposed by the field's data type.

Another way to insert a repeating table is to click Repeating Table in the Insert Controls list on the Controls task pane. What happens next depends on whether the Automatically Create Data Source option on the Controls task pane is selected. If it is, InfoPath prompts you to specify how many columns you want in the table, then creates the table with controls and a group in the data source bound to these controls. All controls are text boxes and all fields default to type string, but you can change these later as needed.

If the Automatically Create Data Source option is not selected, InfoPath opens the Repeating Table Binding dialog box in which you select the group to which the table will be bound.

After inserting a Repeating Table, right-click it and select Repeating Table Properties to view the properties for the table. The Properties dialog box, shown in Figure 5-1, lets you change the data binding and enter default values for the table's controls. The Customize Commands button is used to specify the commands that will be available to the user to add and delete table rows when filling out the form. This is essentially identical to the way you customize commands for working with optional sections. Please refer to the Optional Section Properties section earlier in this chapter for details.

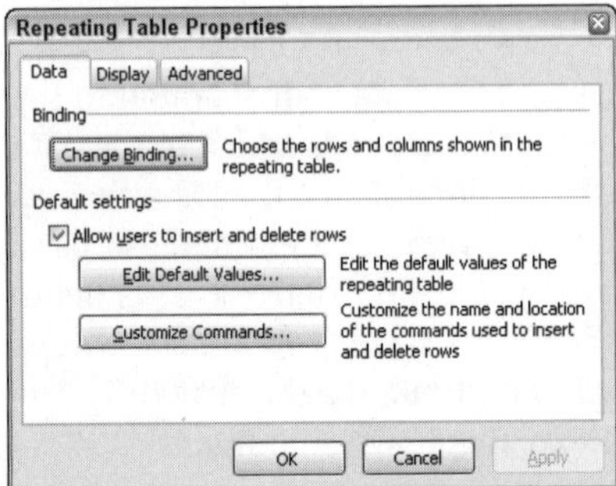


Figure 5-1: The Repeating Table Properties dialog box.

# Using the List Controls

The three types of List controls (bulleted, numbered, and plain) are identical except for the way they display on the form. Each of these controls can be bound only to a repeating field that is of the text or rich text data type. The methods for inserting List controls on a form you are designing are the same as for a Repeating Table, as described in the previous section.

When the user is filling out the form, the List and the data source remain synchronized. If the user adds items to or removes items from the list, InfoPath automatically increases or decreases the number of fields in the data source so there is only one for each list item.

# Changing Control Type

Once a control has been placed on a form, you can change it to a different control. This capability is useful if you change your mind about form design, or when dealing with the default controls that InfoPath chooses when you insert a repeating section or a repeating table. When changing a control to another type, InfoPath permits only types that are appropriate for the data type of the field to which the control is bound. Suppose that your form includes a Text Box control that is bound to a nonrepeating string field. You could change it to a Check Box control because a Check Box is compatible with that data type. You could not, however, change it to a Numbered List control because a Numbered List cannot be bound to a nonrepeating field.

To change a control, right-click it and select Change To from the pop-up menu. The next menu lists the control types that are allowed for the bound field.

## Changing Data Binding

To change the binding of a control, right-click it and select Change Binding from the pop-up menu. InfoPath displays the Binding dialog box for the control, as shown in Figure 5-2.

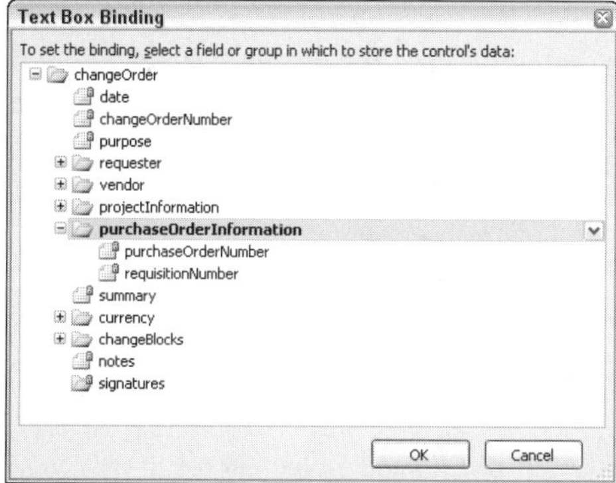


Figure 5-2: Changing the data binding of a control.

This dialog box displays the form's data source, with the current control binding highlighted. Then:

- To bind to an existing group or field in the data source, select the item, then click OK.
- To create a new item to bind to, right-click the existing group that will be the parent of the new item and select Add. Then, follow the prompts to define the new item.

## Data Binding Status

When a control is selected (by clicking), or when you point at it with the mouse, InfoPath displays a small pop-up window with the name of the field that the control is bound to along with an icon indicating the status of the data binding. The icons are

The binding is correct.

Warning – the binding may not function correctly.

Error – the binding will not function correctly.

When a control is displaying a warning or error icon, you can right-click the control and select More Details from the pop-up menu to view additional information on the nature of the problem.

# Control Properties

Each control has a set of properties that reflect its binding and other aspects of its behavior and appearance. To view and change a control's properties, right-click the control and select *XXXX* Properties (where *XXXX* is the control type) from the pop-up menu. InfoPath displays the Properties dialog box for the control. The following sections describe the properties on the Data tab. The properties on the other tabs are largely self-explanatory.

## CHECK BOX PROPERTIES

The properties of a Check Box control are

- **Default State.** Whether the control is checked or unchecked when the form is first displayed.
- **Value When Cleared.** The data value of the bound field when the control is not checked.
- **Value When Checked.** The data value of the bound field when the control is checked.

The permitted settings for the last two properties are constrained by the data type of the field the control is bound to. If, for example, the control is bound to a type Boolean field, the permitted values are 0, 1, True, and False. In contrast, if the control is bound to a type String field, you can specify any text you like for the data values.

## DATE PICKER PROPERTIES

The Date Picker control has two properties. The Default Value is the value displayed in the control when the form is first opened. Format determines how the date is displayed. You select the desired date format from the Date Format dialog box, shown in Figure 5-3.

> ## Data Validation
>
> Most controls include a Validation section in their Properties dialog box. You use these settings to define validation rules for the control, to prevent users from entering invalid data. You could, for example, specify that a Text Box control cannot be left empty, or that a Date value be within a certain range. The fundamentals of data validation are covered later in this chapter.

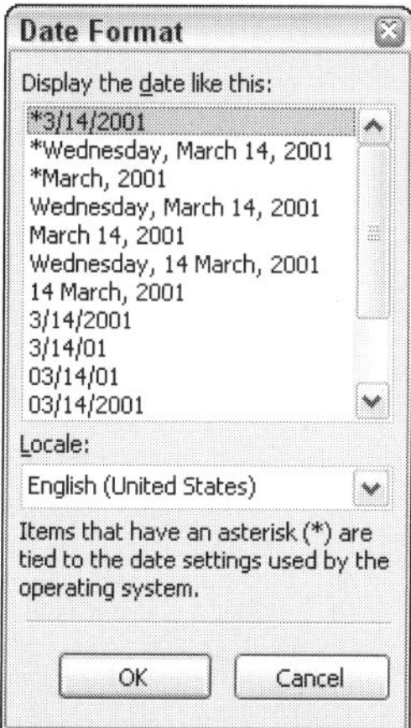


Figure 5-3: Selecting a date format.

### LIST BOX PROPERTIES

One property of the List Box control is essential – specifying the items that will be displayed in the list. You specify this information on the Data tab in the Properties dialog box. There are two options: You can enter the list items manually or you can specify that they be retrieved from a file, database, or Web service.

If you select the manual entry option, the Data tab displays a list with buttons you use to add, modify, and delete list items. Note that each list item has two parts: a display name that is displayed in the List Box, and a value that is stored in the linked field when the list item is selected. Often these two items are the same – for example, if the user selects New York in the list, the text New York is stored in the linked field. You could, however, set the property so that selecting New York in the list would cause NY to be stored in the linked field.

One item in the list is designated as the default, which is selected when the form first displays.

If you select the file, database, or Web service option for populating the control, the Data tab in the properties dialog box displays the settings shown in Figure 5-4. Click the Secondary Data Source button and follow the prompts to select the source for the list entries. The process is similar in many respects to creating a data source from an external source, as was described earlier in this chapter.

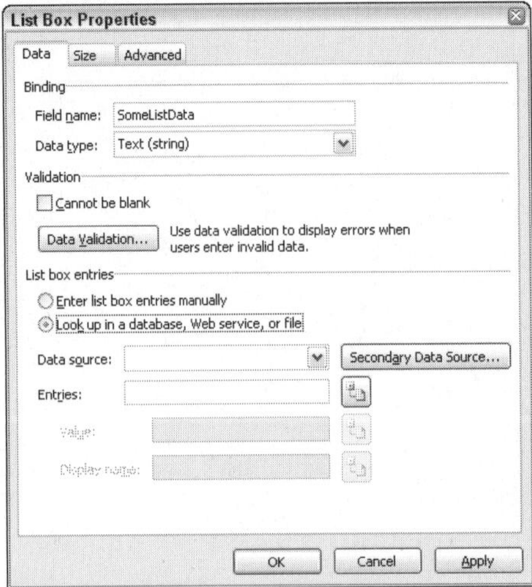


Figure 5-4: Getting List Box entries from a Web service, database, or file.

## OPTION BUTTON PROPERTIES

You never insert just one Option Button control on a form, but insert two or more, depending on the number of options the user will have for the bound field's data. Although these Option Button controls work as a unit in that they are all bound to the same field in the data source, you must still set each individual button's properties separately (unless, of course, the default properties are suitable).

## PICTURE PROPERTIES

The Picture control has the following properties on the Data tab in the Properties dialog box:

- **Show Picture Placeholder.** The control displays a placeholder.
- **Specify Default Picture.** The control displays a default image, which you select by clicking the Browse button.
- **Allow the User to Browse for New Pictures.** If this option is selected, the user will be able to click the control and browse for a picture when filling out the form.

## Picture Controls versus Pictures

It's important to distinguish between Picture controls and other images that are part of the form's design. A Picture control holds the binary pixel data that makes up the picture, and this data is included when the form is saved or submitted by the user. An image on the form, in contrast, is simply part of the form's design and has no connection to the form's data. You learned how to insert images in the "Form Layout" section of Chapter 4.

### RICH TEXT BOX PROPERTIES

In the Properties dialog box, the Rich Text control has only one property on the Data tab, namely its default value. Other properties of this control are found on the Display tab, shown in Figure 5-5.

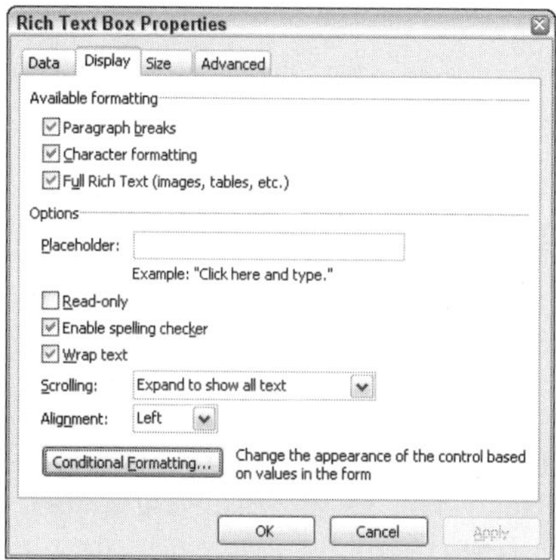


Figure 5-5: Display properties of the Rich Text control.

These properties control the formatting that the user is allowed to apply to text in the control, as well as other aspects of the control's appearance and behavior. They're described in Table 5-2.

**TABLE 5-2 PROPERTIES OF THE RICH TEXT CONTROL**

| Property | Description |
|---|---|
| Paragraph breaks | If selected, the user is allowed to insert paragraph breaks in the control. |
| Character formatting | If selected, the user is allowed to change character formatting (font, underlining, and so on) in the control. |
| Full Rich Text | If selected, additional rich text formatting, such as images and tables, is available to users. |
| Placeholder | Text that is initially displayed in the control and is erased as soon as the user starts entering data. |
| Read-only | If selected, the user cannot modify the text in the control. |
| Enable Spelling Checker | If selected, the text in the control is included when a spell check is run. |
| Wrap text | If selected, lines of text that extend past the right edge of the control are automatically wrapped to a new line. |
| Scrolling | Select the desired text scrolling option from the list. |
| Alignment | Specifies how text is aligned in the control. |

## TEXT BOX PROPERTIES

In the Properties dialog box, the Text Box control has only one property, its default value. Other properties are located on the Display tab, as shown in Figure 5-6. They are a subset of the properties for the Rich Text control, and were described in Table 5-2.

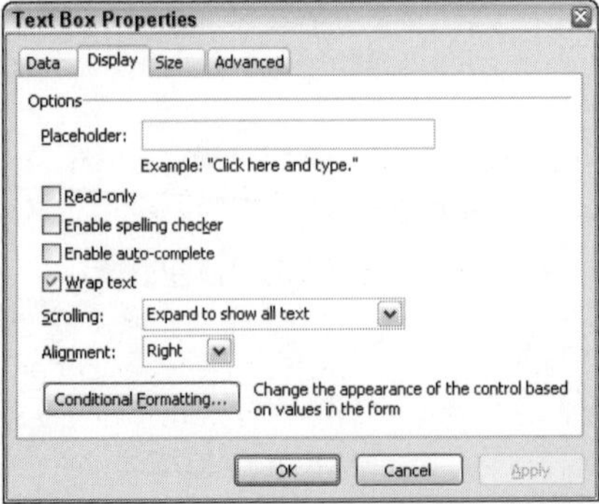


Figure 5-6: Display properties for the Text Box control.

If the Text Box control is bound to a field with a numeric data type, the Format button on the Data tab is enabled. Click this button to display the Decimal Format dialog box, shown in Figure 5-7. You use the settings in this dialog box to control the way numbers are displayed in the control.

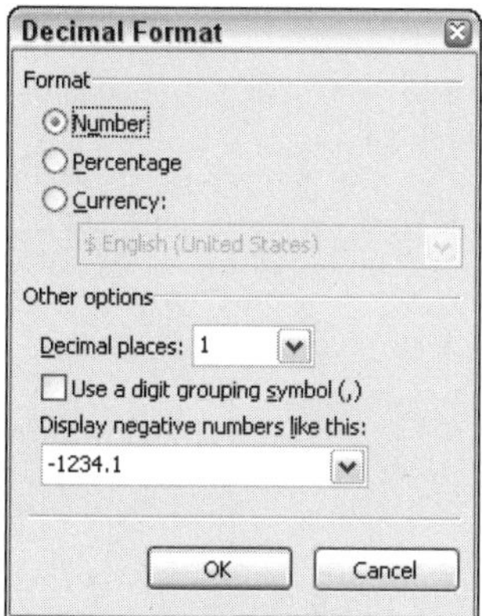


Figure 5-7: Setting number display format for a Text Box control.

# The Button Control

The Button control can be placed on a form to make it easier for the user to take some action. Most of the things you can do with this control could also be accomplished with the menus, but having the Button visible on the form makes how to carry out the action more obvious to the user. Unlike many other controls, a Button is not bound to the data source. The actions that can be associated with a button are:

- **Submit.** Submits the form to a database or Web service or using HTTP.
- **Run Query.** Queries the database or Web service that the form is connected to.
- **New Record.** Switches to data entry view and clears the values for entry of a new record.
- **Delete & Submit.** If the form is connected to a database or Web service, deletes records that have been returned by a query from the database.
- **Script.** Runs a custom script (see Chapter 6, "Scripting with InfoPath").

When you add a Button control to a form, the actions available to you will depend on the design of the form. Submit and Script are always available; the other actions are available only when the form is connected to the Web service or database.

To add a Button control, place the cursor at the desired location on the form, and click Button on the Controls task pane. The next step is to set the control properties by right-clicking the button and selecting Properties from the pop-up menu. The Button Properties dialog box (see Figure 5-8) is displayed.

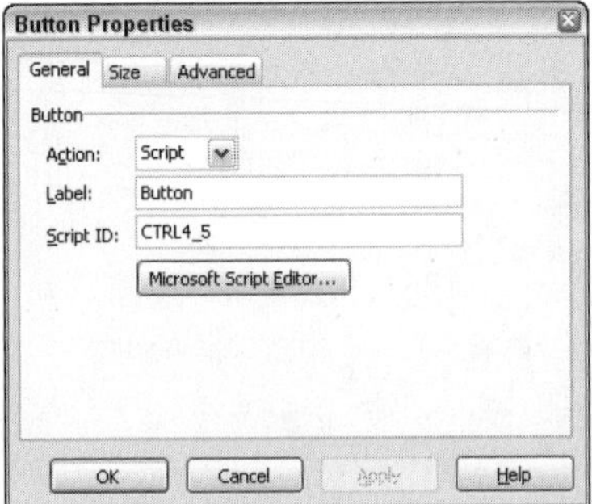


Figure 5-8: Setting Button control properties.

The properties on the General tab are as follows:

- **Action.** Select the action to be carried out when the button is clicked.
- **Label.** The text displayed on the button.
- **Script ID.** The name used to refer to the control in script. You rarely need to change this.
- **Microsoft Script Editor.** If you select Script for Action, click this button to open the Microsoft Script Editor and edit the script. This is explained in detail in Chapter 6.

The Size tab in the Button Properties dialog box lets you specify the size, padding, and margins for the button. The Advanced tab lets you specify a screen tip and shortcut key.

# Conditional Formatting

InfoPath's conditional formatting capability lets you define rules so that a control's appearance changes depending on the data in the control. Among the aspects of appearance that you can change are the font and the color, and whether the control is visible at all. The appearance of a control can be based on its own data or on data in other controls on the form. Some examples of things you can do are:

- Display negative monetary values in red
- Display a Text Box control only if a specific Check Box control is selected

- Change the color of rows in a Repeating Table control based on data in the row
- Display fields that require data to be entered in red if they are blank

Conditional formatting can be applied to the following controls: Text Box, Rich Text Box, Section, Optional Section, Repeating Section, Repeating Table, and Expression Box. To define conditional formatting for a control, or to modify existing conditional formatting:

1. Click the control to select it.
2. Choose Conditional Formatting from the Format menu. InfoPath displays the Conditional Formatting dialog box, which lists existing conditional formatting for the control, if there is any.
3. To add a new condition, click Add. To modify an existing condition, select it in the list and click Modify. InfoPath displays the Conditional Format dialog box, as shown in Figure 5-9.

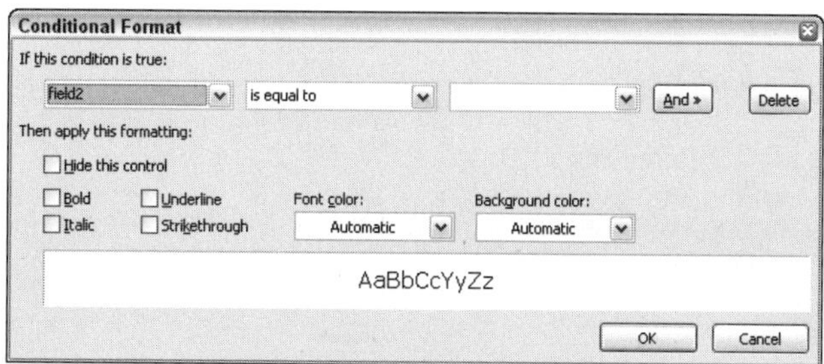


**Figure 5-9: The Conditional Format dialog box.**

4. The three fields across the top of the dialog box define the condition that must be true for the formatting to be applied. The left field displays the name of the data source field bound to the control you are formatting. If you want the condition based on the value of another field, pull down this list and select it.
5. The middle field defines the type of condition, such as *is equal to*, *contains*, and *is not blank*. Select the desired type of comparison from the list.
6. The third field is not required for some types of conditions, such as *is not blank*. For other types of conditions you must enter the comparison value here. Pull down the list and select the type of item you are entering, such as *type text* or *enter a date*, and then type in the comparison value. You can also select another field to have the comparison be performed against its value.

7. To add additional conditions to the rule, click the Add button. InfoPath inserts another row into the dialog box. Repeat Steps 4–6 to define the new rule condition. When there are two or more conditions defined, you must use the list at the right end of each row (except the last one) to select (both conditions must be true) or (only one condition, or both, must be true).
8. Use the remainder of the dialog box options to define the formatting to be applied if the condition is true. The formatting choices that are available will depend on the type of control being formatted.
9. Click OK to return to the Conditional Formatting dialog box. The condition you defined is now listed here.
10. Click OK to close the dialog box and return to form design.

Figure 5-10 shows an example of a conditional formatting rule that is based on the value of two fields. If the field Total is less than 0 and the field MarkNegatives is true, the control text is displayed in boldface and red color.

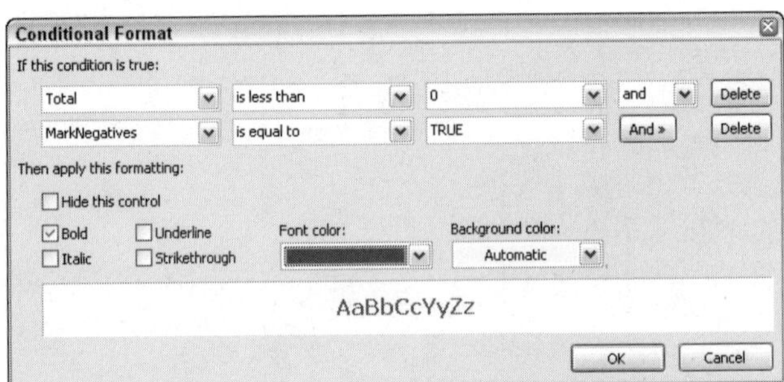


**Figure 5-10: A rule that formats a Text Box depending on the data in two fields.**

It is possible to define multiple rules for a control and have more than one rule be true at the same time. In this case, rules are evaluated in the order they are listed in the Conditional Formatting dialog box, and only the first one that is true is applied. You can use the Move Up and Move Down buttons in this dialog box to change the rule order.

# Data Validation

InfoPath's data validation capability lets you define rules for the data in any field of the data source. A rule might be as simple as requiring that a text field not be left blank, or as complex as requiring that the value in one field be less than the value in another field. When the user is filling out a form, InfoPath applies data validation rules as she works and displays alerts when a rule is violated. There are two types of data validation alerts:

- An inline alert marks the offending control with a dashed red border. The user can right-click the control to view information on why the alert is displayed.
- A dialog box alert displays a small dialog box with an explanatory message.

For some types of data validation you can choose the type of alert to be displayed. For others, an inline alert is always used. The types of data validation that InfoPath supports are described in the following sections.

Data validation rules are associated with the data source and not with the form's controls. This is relevant when you change the binding of a control. It will lose its existing validation (if any) and gain the validation rules of the newly bound field.

## Required Data Validation

This kind of validation requires that a field not be left blank – the user must enter some data into the bound control. You specify required data validation in the Properties dialog box for a field, as shown in Figure 5-11 (reminder: right-click the field name in the Data Source task pane and select Properties). Check the Cannot be Blank option to enable this kind of validation for the field. In the Data Source task pane, fields that cannot be blank are displayed with a red asterisk next to their name.

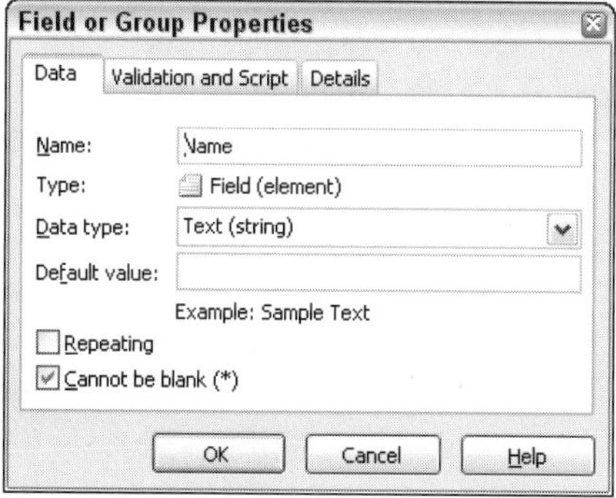


Figure 5-11: Specifying that a field cannot be blank.

## Data Type Validation

Data type validation checks to see if the proper type of data was entered into a control. What is proper for a control is defined by the data type of the bound field. For example, entering text into a control that is bound to a type Integer field results in a violation. So does entering a nondate into a type Date field. Data type validation is automatic—you do not have to take any special actions when designing your form to enable it.

## Data Value Validation

Data value validation defines rules for the value of a data item. You could require, for example, that a numeric value be within a certain range, or that a text entry contain a specific word. Data validation is an important part of form design because it prevents the entry of incorrect data before it can cause any problems, such as when it is submitted to a database.

When you base a form's data source on an XML schema (as described in Chapter 4), the data constraints that are defined in the schema are automatically imported into the form as validation rules. You can't change these validation rules, but you can add to them if needed.

To define a value verification rule, display the Properties dialog box for the field and then click the Validation and Script tab. Depending on whether the field already has a validation rule defined, this tab displays two of the following three buttons:

- **Add.** Create a validation rule for the field.
- **Change.** Change the existing validation rule.
- **Delete.** Delete the existing validation rule.

It's important to remember that a validation rule does not define what data is acceptable, but defines data that is *not* acceptable. Acceptable data is, by definition, anything that is not excluded by the validation rule.

If you click Add or Change, the Data Validation dialog box (see Figure 5-12) displays. If you're adding a rule, the dialog box is blank (contains no rule) as in the figure. If you are changing an existing rule, the dialog box displays the details of the rule.

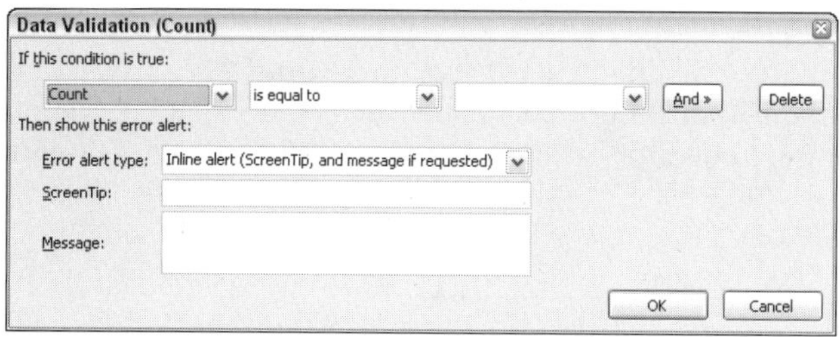


**Figure 5-12: Defining a data validation rule.**

Then, define a rule as follows:

1. The first field displays the name of the data source field that the rule will be applied to (`Count` in the figure). You can pull down this list and select another field (see the following section on multifield rules).
2. The second field is a list of the supported comparisons, such as "is equal to" and "contains." Select the desired comparison from this list.
3. The third field is a list of comparison values you might enter, such as *type a number*, *type text*, and *type a date*. Select an item from this list, then type in the comparison value. For some types of comparison (as specified in the previous step), such as *is blank*, you don't need to enter a value in this field.
4. To add another rule, click the And button. InfoPath inserts another row into the dialog box, which you complete as described in Steps 1–3.
5. In the Error Alert Type list, select either Inline Alert or Dialog Box alert, depending on the type of alert you want displayed when the validation rule is violated.
6. In the Screen Tip and Message fields, enter the details to be displayed to the user in the alert.
7. Click OK to return to the Field or Group properties dialog box, and click OK again to close this dialog box.

If you click the And button (Step 4 above) to add another rule, the button is replaced by a list that offers you the choice of And and Or. You must choose which of these logical operators to use when evaluating the two rules:

- And requires that the conditions specified by both of the rules be met for a violation to occur.
- Or requires that the condition specified by either one of the rules, or both rules, be met for a violation to occur.

For example, look at Figure 5-13. This shows a validation rule for the field Count that requires the value to be between 10 and 20, inclusive. The rule is expressed by saying that if Count is less than 10 or if Count is greater then 20 a violation occurs. It's important to use the correct operator, And or Or, when defining multiple-part validation rules.

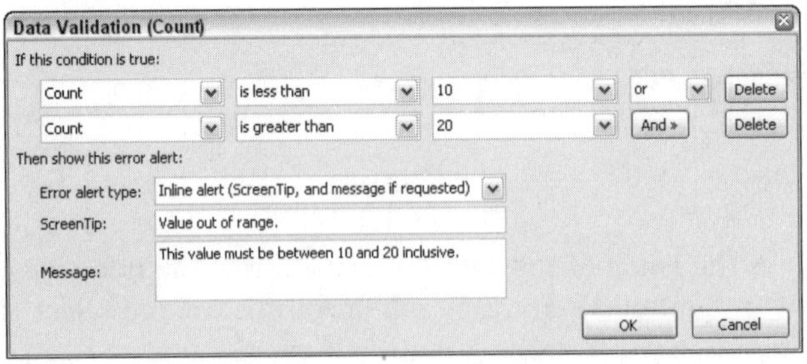

Figure 5-13: A validation rule with two parts.

## MULTIFIELD RULES

Although most validation rules involve only a single field, you also have the ability to define rules that involve two or more fields. For instance, suppose that your company's policy is to provide free shipping on orders over $500. You could define a validation rule requiring that if the Total field is 500 or greater, the ShippingCost field must be 0.

To define a rule that involves multiple fields, follow the same steps described in the previous section. The difference is that in Step 1 you also select the other field to be used by the rule. Figure 5-14 shows a validation rule defined for the conditions described in the previous paragraph. Note that the And operator is used to connect the two parts of the rule because they both must be met for a violation to occur.

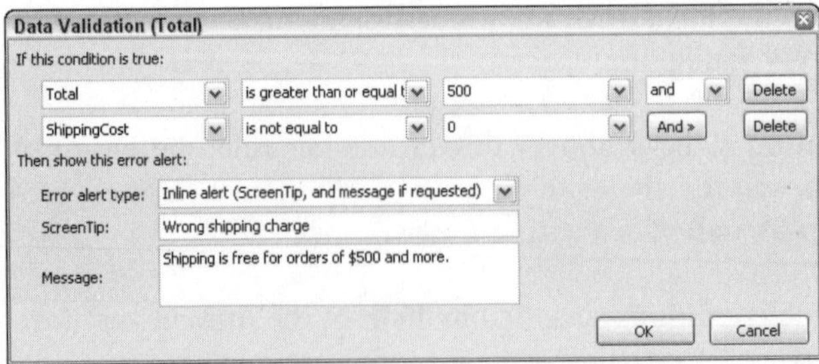


Figure 5-14: A validation rule that uses two fields.

### DYNAMIC COMPARISON VALIDATION

This type of validation compares a field value against another field value rather than against a fixed value. They work the same as the value validations described earlier in this section. The one difference is that in Step 3, in the third field of the Data Validation dialog box, you choose the Select a Field or Group option, and then select the field whose value is to be used for the comparison.

# Using Formulas on Forms

InfoPath lets you put formulas on a form using the Expression Box control. A formula performs calculations using data on the form and displays the result. An Expression Box is not bound to the data source, and the result of its calculation is not considered to be part of the form's data. Formulas are for the convenience of the form user.

To create a formula, the fields that are to be used in the calculation should already be defined in the data source. Calculations are based on fields, not controls. For the regular arithmetic calculations, you use the operators + for addition, - for subtraction, * for multiplication, and div for division. When creating a formula for an Expression Box control, InfoPath helps you by providing identifiers for the elements in the form's data source. You must provide the other parts of the formula yourself, as follows:

1. Place the insertion point at the location on the form where you want the formula.
2. On the Controls taskbar, click Expression Box in the Insert Controls list. InfoPath displays the Insert Expression Box dialog box, as shown in Figure 5-15.

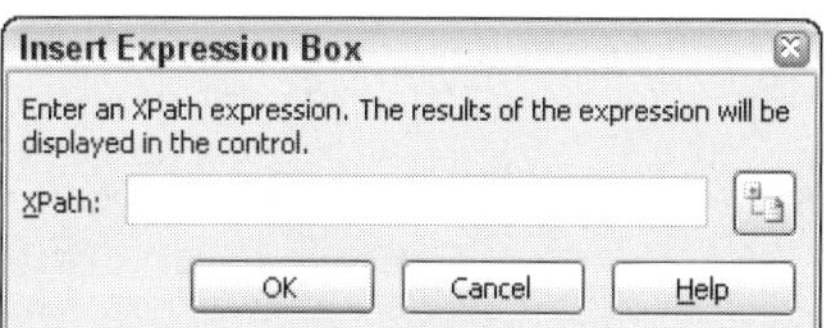


Figure 5-15: Entering a formula in an Expression Box control.

3. Click the XPath button at the right side of the dialog box. InfoPath displays the Select a Field or Group dialog box with the form's data source from which you select the first field for the formula. When you return to the Insert Expression Box dialog, the identifier for the selected field is displayed in the XPath field.

4. Repeat Step 3 as needed to add other data source element identifiers to the XPath field.
5. Add additional parts of the formula as needed, such as operators and functions.
6. Click OK to close the dialog box and insert the Expression Box into the form.

To test the formula, preview the form by clicking the Preview Form button on the toolbar. Enter values into the input fields and verify that the Expression Box displays the correct result. If any of the fields used in a calculation are empty, the result displays a NaN, meaning Not a Number, instead of an erroneous result.

Here's an example: Suppose you wanted to display the sum of a repeating field. The field, of course, must contain numeric data. Then:

1. Place an Expression Box control on the form. The Insert Expression Box dialog is displayed.
2. Click the XPath button to display the form's data source.
3. Select the desired field and close the Select a Field or Group dialog box. The field identifier will not be displayed in the XPath box.
4. Move the cursor to the start of the field identifier and enter sum(.
5. Move the cursor to the end of the field identifier and enter ).
6. Click OK to close the Insert Expression Box dialog box and add the formula to the form.

After an Expression Box is inserted on the form, right-click it and select Expression Box Properties to display its properties dialog box. On the General tab, shown in Figure 5-16, you can modify the formula in the control and also specify the format used to display the result.

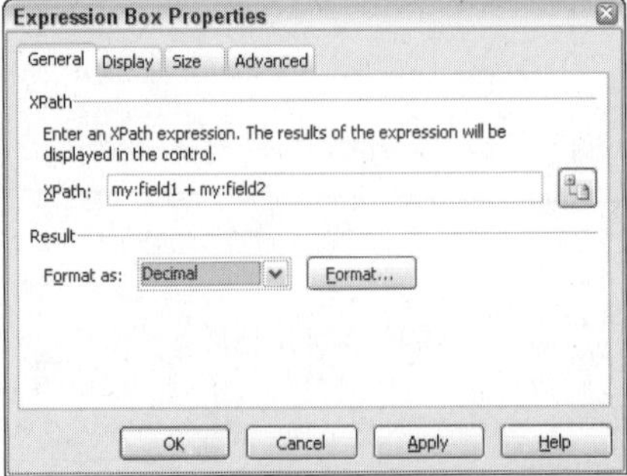


Figure 5-16: Setting properties of an Expression Box control.

You can enter field identifiers directly into the XPath expression box, but using the XPath button to select the field always ensures that the field identifier is correct, including any namespace prefixes and group identifiers.

InfoPath provides some functions that assist with certain types of calculations in Expression Box controls. They are described, with examples, in Table 5-3.

TABLE 5-3 FUNCTIONS FOR USE IN EXPRESSION BOX FORMULAS

| Function | Description | Example and Notes |
|---|---|---|
| concat(field1, field2,...) | Combines data from two or more fields into a single string | concat(my:firstname, " ", my:lastname) displays the data in the firstname and lastname fields separated by a space. |
| count(field) | Counts the number of occurrences of a repeating field | count(my:item) displays the number of times the my:item element occurs in the data source. |
| position() | Displays the row number in a repeating table | The Expression Box must be a part of the repeating table whose rows are being numbered. |
| sum(field) | Sums the values in all occurrences of a repeating field | (sum(my:price) div count(my:price)) displays the average of all values in the my:price field. |

# Setting User Options

InfoPath provides a number of user options that you can set while designing the form. These options are discussed here.

## Form Submission

When a user has completed filling out a form, one of the things that can be done with the form is to *submit* it. Submitting and saving forms were covered in Chapter 3, "Introduction to InfoPath." There are three types of form submission available: submit to a Web service, submit to a database, and submit via Hypertext Transfer Protocol (HTTP). In the first two cases, the InfoPath form is designed based on the

Web service or database from the very start (this was explained in Chapter 4). This means that the form is automatically set up to submit to the Web service or database that it was designed for, and there are no further actions required on the part of the form designer.

HTTP submission is different. There's no method by which InfoPath can learn about the requirements of the server application that will receive the submission, so the form must be designed specifically to meet these requirements (or, the server application can be created to suit the structure of a form). In either case, you must enable HTTP submission on the form and specify the URL to which it will be submitted. You can also set other submit options at this time:

1. When designing a form, choose Tools → Submitting Forms to display the Submitting Forms dialog box.
2. Select the Enable Submit option, and select Submit through HTTP from the Submit list (see Figure 5-17).

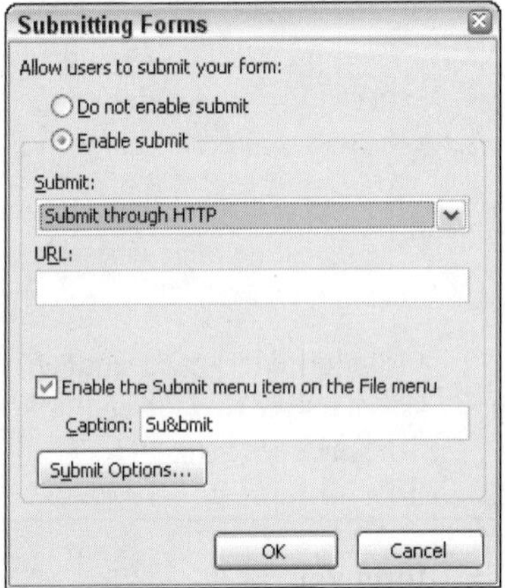


Figure 5-17: Enabling HTTP submission for a form.

3. Enter the submission URL in the URL field.
4. If you want the Submit command available on the File menu when the form is being filled out, check the Enable the Submit Menu Item option.
5. To set additional submission options, click the Submit Options button to display the Submit Options dialog box.

6. In the Submit Options dialog box, specify what happens to the form when it is submitted (close, create new blank form, or leave open), and also the messages displayed when submission succeeds or fails.
7. Click OK twice to close both dialog boxes and return to the form.

## Form Merging

Sometimes it is useful to allow users to merge forms so that the data from two or more forms can be combined and saved or submitted as a unit. Almost always, merged form data is bound to repeating fields. The methods of merging forms were explained in Chapter 3. For a user to be able to merge forms, merging must be enabled when the form is designed. To set merging permission for a form you are designing:

1. Choose Tools → Form Options to display the Form Options dialog box.
2. Click the General tab.
3. Select or clear the Enable Form Merging option.
4. Click OK.

## Form Protection and Security

Form protection prevents users from opening or modifying the form template. Unless you have a specific reason not to, I recommend that you enable protection on all InfoPath forms that you design. Form security is provided by digital signatures and applied to a form by the user when he fills out the form. The details of digital signatures were covered in Chapter 3. Digital signatures must be enabled when the form is designed.

To set protection and security options for a form you are designing:

1. Choose Tools → Form Options to display the Form Options dialog box.
2. Click the General tab.
3. Set the Enable protection option to enable or disable protection.
4. Click the Security tab (see Figure 5-18).

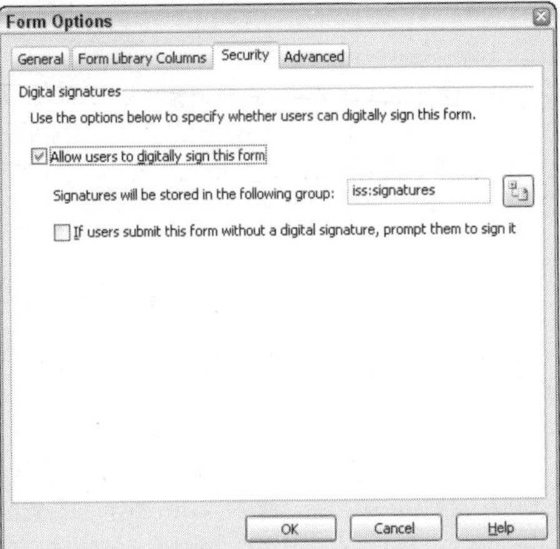


Figure 5-18: Setting form security options.

5. Set the Allow Users to Digitally Sign this Form option to enable or disable digital signing.
6. If digital signing is enabled, the second line of the dialog box displays the name of the data source group where digital signatures will be stored. If a group has not been selected yet, this line displays New Signatures Group.
7. Select the If Users Submit option if you want InfoPath to prompt users if they try to submit the form without applying a digital signature.
8. Click OK.

Form submission must be enabled first in order to enable digital signatures. You cannot enable digital signatures on a form whose data source is derived from a Web service, a database, or an XML schema unless a digital signature namespace is present.

# Testing Your Form

It is very important that you test your InfoPath form before distributing it to users. Form errors can cause serious problems if they are not caught before people start using the form with real data.

To test a form, click the Preview Form button on the toolbar. InfoPath will open the form in a new window as it would appear to a user who is filling out the form. You can test the form from the user's perspective, entering data, checking formatting, and verifying other aspects of the form's appearance and behavior. While a form is in Preview mode, the text *Preview* appears in the InfoPath title bar to indicate you are in Preview mode and not Design mode. You cannot make any changes to the form design in this mode. To exit Preview mode and return to Design mode, click the Close Preview button on the toolbar.

Another way to test a form is to display sample data in all the controls. This feature is available in Design mode by selecting View → Sample Data. By displaying sample data, you can check how real data will display in your form, and make any necessary changes to formatting and control properties. To remove the sample data from the form, select View → Sample Data again.

# Publishing Your Form

You must publish a form template in order to make it available for others to use. You publish a form to a shared location so that others can access it. This might be a shared location on the company network, a SharePoint 2003 site, or a Web site.

Before publishing your form, gather any necessary information, such as the details of the location to which it will be published. Then, select File → Publish and follow the Publishing Wizard prompts to complete the process.

You may want to make your form available as a trusted form, so it can have access to the user's system settings and files. I cover this in Chapter 6.

Chapter 6

# Scripting with InfoPath

IN THIS CHAPTER

Understanding scripting

Exploring the Script Editor

Examining InfoPath events

Checking out security and debugging

Using script examples

SCRIPTING IS a technology that enables you to include program code in an InfoPath form. Not all forms require scripting, but for certain more complex and sophisticated InfoPath applications, you can use script to obtain functionality that is not otherwise available. This chapter provides an overview and some examples of scripting in InfoPath.

## Scripting Overview

Script is computer code that is associated with a form. The code is executed when certain events occur, such as a button on the form being clicked, data in a field being changed, or the user switching to a different view. Script code has access to many of the inner workings of an InfoPath form, including its data. Some of the simpler things you can do with script include:

- Inserting today's date in a form field when the form is opened
- Performing complex calculations using form data
- Preventing the user from closing a view if a certain field is blank
- Performing certain kinds of data validation that are difficult or not possible using other validation methods
- Displaying one view or another based on data in the form when the form is loaded
- Adding an element to the data source if it is not already present

Scripts can perform much more sophisticated actions as well. Script code can use COM (Component Object Model) components such as ActiveX objects, and because the Windows operating system itself and most applications are also based on COM, this provides the potential for a lot of power.

Scripting opens a lot of possibilities for the InfoPath form developer. It is not a simple topic, however. To write scripts you need some background knowledge in several technologies, which are detailed in the next section. It is well beyond the scope of this book to cover these related technologies or, in fact, to cover scripting in its entirety. Instead, this chapter provides an overview of scripting and some examples of how you could use it in your forms.

# Background Information

Because InfoPath scripting is based on several technologies, the InfoPath script programmer needs to have a good grounding in several areas, including:

- **The scripting language.** InfoPath supports two scripting languages, VBScript and JScript. You need to know the syntax and elements of at least one of these languages.
- **The Document Object Model (DOM).** The DOM provides an interface between the script and the data source (XML document). In a script you use DOM objects, methods, and properties to access the form's data.
- **XPath.** This is a vocabulary designed for identifying specific elements in an XML document. When you use the DOM to manipulate the data source, you will often use an XPath expression to identify the part of the data source to be acted upon.
- **The InfoPath object model.** InfoPath exposes its own object model that script code uses to access InfoPath components, such as task panes, controls, and views.

The Microsoft Script Editor online help provides a great deal of useful information, including both VBScript and JScript language references, an InfoPath Developer's Reference, and debugging information. This should be the first place that you turn for assistance when working with scripts in InfoPath.

# Setting the Scripting Language

InfoPath supports two script languages, VBScript and JScript. A specific InfoPath form can use only one of these languages, and you must set this option before editing or viewing the form's script. To do so:

1. With the form open in design mode, choose Tools→Form Options to display the Form Options dialog box.
2. Click the Advanced tab.
3. In the Script Language section of the dialog box, select the desired language from the drop-down list.
4. Click OK to close the dialog box.

If you forget to set the script language, it defaults to JScript. Be aware that many of the sample forms that are provided with InfoPath already contain script, and if you are designing a new form based on one of these samples, you're stuck with the sample form's script language (usually JScript). Some of the examples in this chapter use VBScript and others use JScript. If you know one language, it shouldn't be too difficult to translate code from the other.

Please note that the Script Editor is not automatically included in all InfoPath installations. If it isn't installed on your system, then the first time you try to use it you'll be prompted to install it. Simply follow the prompts to complete the installation and then continue.

# The Script Editor

You use the Microsoft Script Editor (see Figure 6-1) to create and edit scripts for InfoPath forms. While you're designing a form, you can open the Script Editor by choosing Tools→Script→Script Editor or by pressing Alt-Shift-F11. The Script Editor also opens automatically at other times when it is needed, as you'll see later.

There are three areas of the screen with which you will be most concerned:

- The Document Outline on the left side of the screen, which lists all of the procedures and functions in the current form (only a single one in this case). Double-click a procedure or function name in this window to display it for editing.
- The editing window in the middle of the screen, which displays the form's script code. If more than one form is open for design (as in the figure), each one's code is on its own tabbed page in this part of the screen.
- The Project Explorer at the top right of the screen, which lists the open forms. In the figure there are two, Template1 and Template2.

Each form in the Project Explorer has a script file associated with it, named Script.js or Script.vbs, depending on whether JScript or VBScript is the selected script language for the form. You won't find this file on your disk, however, because all of the files that comprise the definition of a form are combined into a single XSN file.

## InfoPath XSN Files

An InfoPath template is stored as a single file with the XSN extension. In reality, this file is a CAB (cabinet) file that contains, in compressed format, the various individual files that comprise a form template, including but not limited to the following:

- A schema file (XSD) for the form's data model
- A stylesheet (XSL) that defines the form's views and transformations
- A script file (JS or VBS) that holds the form's script (if any)
- Bitmap and other image files for images that are part of the form's user interface

You can extract the individual files for a form template by choosing File → Extract Form Files while designing a form.

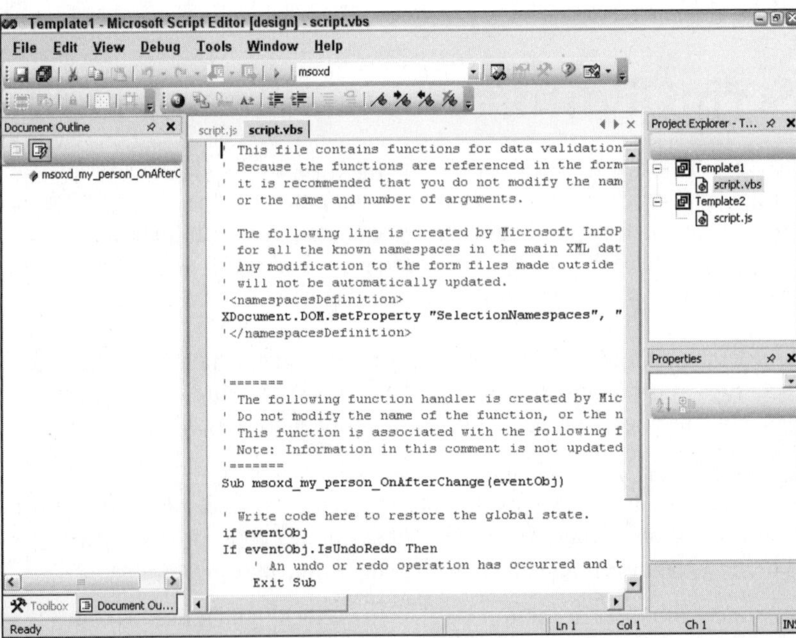


Figure 6-1: The Microsoft Script Editor.

The Script Editor is used for a variety of purposes by Microsoft and is not designed specifically for use with InfoPath. As a result it has many features and commands that aren't relevant for InfoPath form scripts, and those items won't be available to you (for example, a menu command might be grayed out).

When you are editing a script, you can save it by choosing File → Save in the Script Editor. Saving the form template from InfoPath has the same effect of saving changes to the script.

# InfoPath Events

An *event* is something that the user triggers while filling out an InfoPath form, such as clicking a button on the form, changing the data in a field, or merging a form. If you want script to be executed when an event occurs, you must create an *event handler* (also called an *event procedure*) for the event and put the script there. If there is no event handler for an event, it is ignored (as far as script processing is concerned).

InfoPath events are divided into three categories: form-level, data validation, and `OnClick`. These are discussed in the following sections, which also explain the techniques you use to create a handler for each type of event. Examples for selected events are presented later in the chapter.

## Form-Level Events

*Form-level* events are so named because they occur when something happens to the form as a whole rather than to a component of the form. These events are:

- `OnLoad`. Occurs when the form is opened, either when creating a new form from a template or when opening an existing form that has been saved
- `OnSwitchViews`. Occurs when the user switches views
- `OnVersionUpgrade`. Occurs when the version number of the form being opened does not match the version number of the template in use
- `OnSubmitRequest`. Occurs when a form is submitted

You must create an event handler to respond to any of these events. Although in theory you can type the outline of an event handler into the Script Editor, it's better to let InfoPath do it for you, eliminating the possibility of typos and other errors. It's easier and faster, too! Table 6-1 shows how. While you are designing a form in InfoPath, you can perform any action listed in the table and InfoPath will open the Script Editor and insert the outline of the designated event handler. You can then proceed to add the script to be executed when the event occurs.

TABLE 6-1 CREATING HANDLERS FOR FORM-LEVEL EVENTS

| Event | To Create the Handler |
|---|---|
| OnLoad | Choose Tools → Script → On Load Event. |
| OnSwitchViews | Choose Tools → Script → On Switch Views Event. |
| OnVersionUpgrade | Choose Tools → Form Options to display the Form Options dialog box. On the Advanced tab select Use Script Event in the On Version Upgrade list, and then click the Edit button. |
| OnSubmitRequest | Choose Tools → Submitting forms. In the dialog box, select Submit Using a Custom Script in the Submit list, and then click OK. |

## Data Validation Events

*Data validation* events are, as their name implies, typically used to validate data. They are associated with elements in the data source. There are three of these events – `OnBeforeChange`, `OnValidate`, and `OnAfterChange` – and they occur, in the order given, when the data in the underlying XML document (the data source) changes. From the user's perspective, this means when the data in a form control is changed. It's important to remember, however, that the events are associated with the data source and not with the controls on the form.

Here's how the data validation events are used:

- `OnBeforeChange` occurs when the change has been made but not yet accepted or finalized. Code in this event procedure can examine the new data value and, if it doesn't meet the form's requirements, reject it and keep the old data value.
- `OnValidate` occurs after `OnBeforeChange`, when the change has still not been finalized. It is like `OnBeforeChange` in that code examines the data value to see if it is acceptable. It differs from `OnBeforeChange` in that it does not offer the ability to automatically roll back the data to the previous value. Rather, it lets you display a *validation error* message to users to prompt them to fix the data.
- `OnAfterChange` occurs when the change has been accepted and finalized. It is typically used to perform calculations or other updates to the form based on the new data. Strictly speaking, this event really isn't used for data validation but rather to initiate some action after the data has been accepted.

The way that the InfoPath event model works results in these events being called twice in some situations. For example, suppose the user tabs to a field, deletes the data that is already there, and then enters new data. The `OnBeforeChange`, `OnValidate`, and `OnAfterChange` events are triggered twice, once in response to the delete and once in response to the new data being entered. Code in the event procedures must take this possibility into account. The code must also take into account the possibility that the change is the result of an undo or redo operation. I'll show you how this is done in the examples later in the chapter.

When an `OnBeforeChange` or `OnValidate` event procedure is executing, the data source is locked so that no changes can be made to it. This prevents the endless sequence of events that could occur if code in one `OnBeforeChange` or `OnValidate` event procedure makes changes to the data, which in turn triggers another `OnBeforeChange/OnValidate` event sequence. The data source is not locked, however, during the `OnAfterChange` event procedure.

To create a data validation event handler, follow these steps:

1. Display the Data Source task pane.
2. Right-click the element that you want the event associated with and select Properties from the pop-up menu to display the Field or Group Properties dialog box.
3. Click the Validation and Script tab (see Figure 6-2).
4. In the Script section, pull down the Events list and select the desired event: `OnBeforeChange`, `OnValidate`, or `OnAfterChange`.
5. Click the Edit button.

Figure 6-2: Creating a data validation event procedure.

An element in the data source can have handlers for one, two, or all three of the data validation events.

## The OnClick event

The `OnClick` event is in a category by itself. It is relevant for the Button control, and is triggered when the user clicks a button. To create the `OnClick` event procedure for a button, the button must already be on the form. Then:

1. Right-click the button and select Button properties from the pop-up menu to display the Button properties dialog box.
2. Click the General tab (see Figure 6-3).
3. Select Script in the Action list.
4. Enter the button's caption (the text displayed on the button) in the Label field.
5. Click the Microsoft Script Editor button.

**Figure 6-3: Creating an OnClick event handler for a button.**

Notice the Script ID field just below the Label field in the figure. This is the name that will be used to refer to the button in script. You can accept the default name that InfoPath suggests, or you can enter a more descriptive name. When you assign descriptive names, the resulting script code is easier to read because it is clear which button each procedure is attached to.

# Event Procedure Arguments

Every event procedure is passed a single argument named `eventObj`, which makes relevant information available to the code in the event procedure. The type of object passed in the argument depends on the specific event procedure. Table 6-2 lists these objects and provides a brief description of each.

**Table 6-2 OBJECTS PASSED TO EVENT PROCEDURES**

| Object | Passed to | Description |
|---|---|---|
| `DocEvent` | `OnSwitchView` | Provides a reference to the underlying XML document. |
| `DocReturnEvent` | `OnLoad`, `OnSubmitRequest` | Provides a reference to the underlying XML document and to the load or submit status. |
| `VersionUpgradeEvent` | `OnVersionUpgrade` | Provides a reference to the underlying XML document, the return status, and the template version numbers. |
| `DataDOMEvent` | `OnBeforeChange`, `OnValidate`, `OnAfterValidate` | Provides a reference to the underlying XML document, the return status, and other properties that contain information about the XML node. Also includes a method for raising an error. |
| `DocActionEvent` | `OnClick` | Provides a reference to the underlying XML document, the return status, and the source XML node. |

You'll see some of these objects used the example scripts presented later in this chapter. You can find more information about them in the Object Browser (discussed in the chapter) and in the Script Editor online help.

# The InfoPath Object Model

Like all other Office applications, InfoPath has an *object model* that describes the objects the program exposes. These objects are the components that make up the InfoPath application itself. When an object is *exposed*, its methods and properties are made available to other programs – in this case, the script code that can be part of an InfoPath form. Two of the more important elements in the InfoPath object model are the `Window` object, which provides access to the InfoPath user interface, and the `XDocument` object, which provides access to the underlying XML document (the data source). Table 6-3 summarizes the InfoPath object model.

**TABLE 6-3 OVERVIEW OF INFOPATH'S OBJECT MODEL**

| Object | Description |
|---|---|
| `Application` | The top-level object in the InfoPath object model. Provides properties and methods for accessing lower-level objects in the object model to perform various general-purpose tasks. |
| `Window` | Provides properties and methods for programmatically interacting with InfoPath windows, such as activating or closing a window, and also for interacting with task panes. Also has a property for accessing the underlying XML document that is associated with the window. |
| `XDocument` | Provides properties, methods, and events for programmatically interacting with the form's underlying XML. |
| `MailEnvelope` | Provides properties for programmatically creating an e-mail message in Outlook 2003 and for attaching an InfoPath form to the message. |
| TaskPane | Provides properties for working with built-in and custom task panes. |
| `DataObject` | Provides properties and methods for programmatically interacting with data adapter objects and accessing the data to which they are connected. |
| `Error` | Provides properties for working with InfoPath-generated errors. |
| `Solution` | Provides properties for getting information about a form template, such as its version number, the URL of its form files, and the URL from which it was loaded. |
| `UI` | Provides methods for displaying custom and built-in dialog boxes. (UI stands for user interface.) |
| `View` | Provides properties and methods for programmatically interacting with an InfoPath view, including selecting data contained in the view, switching between views, and synchronizing the view with the underlying XML document. |
| `ViewInfo` | Provides properties that can be used to get a view's name and to determine whether a view is the form's default view. |
| `ExternalApplication` | Implements a small set of methods that can be used to automate InfoPath by a COM-based programming language. |

Detailed coverage of the entire InfoPath object model is well beyond the scope of this book. You'll see some of the objects used in the examples presented later in this chapter. You can find information about the InfoPath objects and their properties and methods in the InfoPath online help, and you can also use the Object Browser, described in the next section, for assistance.

# Using the Object Browser

You can use the Object Browser to obtain information about the contents of the InfoPath object model. To display the Object Browser from the Script Editor, choose View → Other Windows → Object Browser. The object model displays in the browser as shown in Figure 6-4.

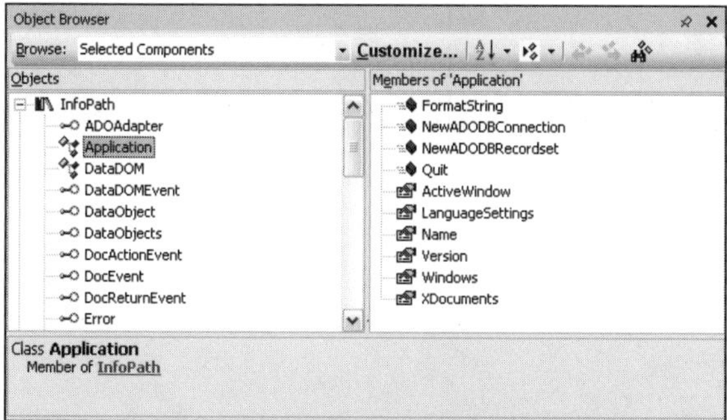


**Figure 6-4: The InfoPath object model displayed in the Object Browser.**

If the object model doesn't display, follow these steps to load it:

1. Be sure that Selected Components is selected in the Browse list.
2. Click the Customize button to display the Selected Components dialog box.
3. Open the Other Packages and Libraries node. If Microsoft Office InfoPath 1.0 Type Library is displayed in the list, select its check box, and click OK. If it isn't, continue to the next step.
4. Click the Add button to display the Component Selector dialog box. Depending on your system, this dialog box may take a moment or two to load.
5. On the COM tab, scroll down and click the Microsoft Office InfoPath 1.0 Type Library entry.
6. Click the Select button to move the library to the Selected Components list.

7. Click OK to return to the Selected Components dialog box. Microsoft Office InfoPath 1.0 Type Library is now listed.

8. Click OK to close the dialog box and return to the Object Browser.

The left pane in the Object Browser lists the library's objects. The three categories of objects – classes, interfaces, and enumerations – are identified by the icon next to the object name. When you click an item in the object list, the pane on the right lists the object's members. The object's properties, methods, and events are distinguished by icons in the Members list.

When you select an item in the Members list, the panel at the bottom of the Object Browser window displays details about the selected member. For example, Figure 6-5 shows the details about the `GetDataVariable` method of the `XDocument` object. This information includes the method's argument and return value.

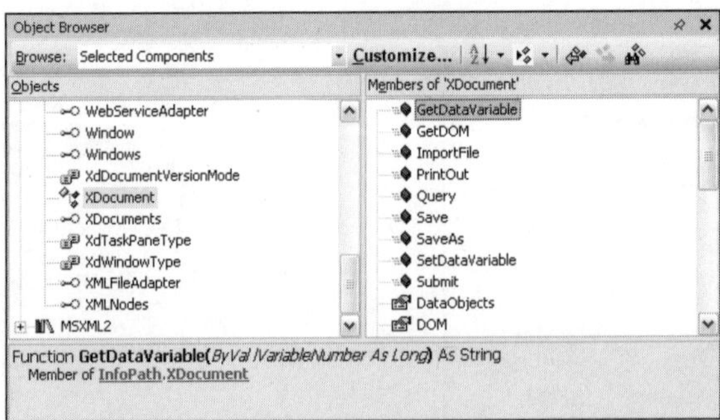


**Figure 6-5: Displaying information about a specific member.**

# Scripts and Security

A script has the potential to cause a lot of mischief on a user's system. For example, a script can use the `FileSystemObject` to read, write, and delete files. Clearly you do not want to allow just any script to run – you need some way to differentiate forms whose scripts should be allowed access to the system's files and settings from other forms. The InfoPath security model is similar to that used by Internet Explorer browser; it uses the concept of trusted versus standard forms.

To use an InfoPath form, InfoPath must have access to the template on which the form is based. By default, the form definition file contains the URL of the template. A form that's URL-based this way is said to be *sandboxed*. When it is filled out, the form is placed in the local cache and its permissions are based on the domain in which it is opened. Thus, script in a sandboxed or standard form typically cannot access system files or resources. Any attempt to do so will result in a *permission denied* error.

A form can be created so that is it based on a URN (Uniform Resource Name) rather than a URL. This, combined with a custom installation program for the form template, makes a form fully trusted. As such, the script in the form has access to the system's settings and files. Trusted forms are listed on the Custom Installed Forms tab in the Forms dialog box (displayed when the user selects More Forms on the Fill Out a Form task pane).

InfoPath provides a command-line utility called RegForm that you use to convert a standard form into a trusted form. This utility makes the necessary changes to the form and creates the installation program. Please refer to InfoPath help for more information on trusted forms and using this utility.

# Debugging Scripts

Scripts, particularly more complex ones, almost never work right the first time. You can use the Script Editor to debug your script. The debugging tools that are available greatly simplify the task of locating and fixing problems in your script code.

To use script debugging, you must make sure that it is not disabled in Internet Explorer. To do so:

1. Start Internet Explorer.
2. Choose Tools→Internet Options to display the Internet Options dialog box.
3. Click the Advanced tab.
4. If present, clear the check next to the Disable Script Debugging option.
5. Click OK.

Debugging is based on the concept of suspending the execution of the script. While execution is paused you can examine the value of variables and execute subsequent code a line at a time (called *single stepping*) to find the source of the problem. A script pauses on two conditions: when an actual error occurs, and when a break statement is encountered. The break statement is `debugger` in JScript and `Stop` in VBScript. For example, here are `Load` event procedures in both languages with a break statement:

```
function XDocument::OnLoad(eventObj)
{
    debugger;
}

Sub XDocument_OnLoad(eventObj)
    Stop
End Sub
```

You would not, of course, use a break statement by itself in a `Load` event procedure (or elsewhere). You would place it with other code that you suspect might be the location of the problem you are trying to fix. You can have multiple break statements in a form's script.

When an executing script encounters an error or a break statement, the Just-In-Time Debugging dialog box (see Figure 6-6) is displayed.

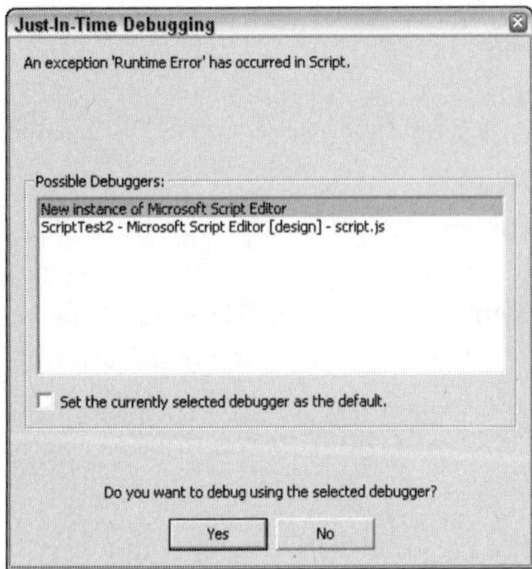


**Figure 6-6: The Just-in-Time Debugging dialog box.**

Select New Instance of Microsoft Script Editor and click Yes. The next dialog box asks you the program type that you want to debug. Put a check mark next to Script, and click OK.

At this point the Script Editor opens and displays the script code where the error occurred or where the break statement is located. A yellow arrow in the left margin indicates the line of code at which execution is paused. You can now use the Script Editor's debugging commands to examine program variables and control execution to try to locate the problem. When you are finished debugging, choose Debug→ Stop Debugging.

# Script Examples

Now that you understand the basics, I want to provide some scripting examples using many of the events available in InfoPath. The scripts perform a variety of functions that could be useful in a real-world InfoPath form. Most of the examples are in JScript, and the rest in VBScript. These examples are as simple as possible while still adequately demonstrating each technique.

An example of using script in the `OnClick` event can be found in Chapter 16, "Connecting Web Publishing and InfoPath."

# Inserting the Date

It could be useful to have today's date automatically inserted into a form field when the form is opened. This example shows you how to write a script that does this, and also shows you how to write a function, which is a separate section of code that performs a specific action. To work this example, start a new, blank form in design mode. Then:

1. In the data source, add an element named date as a child of myFields. Leave the element's data type as text, the default setting.
2. Place a Text Box control on the form that is bound to the date element you just created.
3. Choose Tools → Script → On Load Event to open the Script Editor and insert the handler for the OnLoad event procedure.
4. Add the code shown in Listing 6-1.

**Listing 6-1: The Form's Load Event Procedure**

```
function XDocument::OnLoad(eventObj)
{
  var dateField = XDocument.DOM.selectSingleNode("//my:date");
  dateField.text = todaysDate();
}
```

This function's code has only two lines. The first creates a variable named `dateField` that refers to the date element in the data source. (Note the use of an XPath expression to identify the element.) The second line sets the value of this element to today's date, obtained from the `todaysDate` function (which we'll write next).

A function is a separate named section of script code. It is not connected to any event but is executed only when called by other code. In this example, the second line in the `OnLoad` event procedure calls the `todaysDate` function. To write this function, move the cursor to a line in the Script Editor that is outside of any other function or event procedure. Then, simply type in the code shown in Listing 6-2.

Remember that JScript is case-sensitive so you must use extra care when entering and editing code.

**Listing 6-2: The todaysDate Function**

```
function todaysDate()
{
  var d = new Date();
  var s = (d.getMonth() + 1) + "/";
  s += d.getDate() + "/";
  s += d.getFullYear;
  return(s);
}
```

The code in the function starts by creating a `Date` object (this is one of JScript's built-in objects), which refers to the current date. Then, it uses the members of the object to retrieve the month, the day, and the year to create a date in the form 9/22/2003. The resulting string is returned by the function. Note that the `getMonth` method returns the month as a number 0–11 for January-December. By adding 1 to this value you get a month number in the commonly used range 1–12.

Two additional considerations bear mentioning. First, in a case such as this where a data value is automatically entered into an element, you may not want the user to be able to change it. This is most easily accomplished by not including a control that is bound to the field on the form. The data still exists in the data source and will be included when the form is saved or submitted, but it won't be available for the user to change.

The second consideration relates to the form being saved and opened again. You may want the date to reflect the date on which the form was first created. As written, the script executes each time the form is opened, so if the form is saved and opened again on a later date, then that date is entered into the date field. You can retain the original date by modifying the code to check if the date element already contains data. If not, then it means the form is being opened for the first time and today's date should be entered. If it does, then the form was previously created and today's date should not be entered. This is accomplished by changing the second line of code in the `OnLoad` procedure to the following:

```
if (dateField.text == "") dateField.text = todaysDate();
```

# Performing Calculations

Forms often need to perform calculations of one sort or another. A common example is an order form where the total needs to be calculated as the sum of the prices of the individual items. This example shows you how to do this, and also demonstrates some of the useful script code that is provided with the sample forms that come with InfoPath.

The invoice form that this example uses is a lot simpler than any real-world form would be, but it serves to illustrate the technique under discussion. The data source consists of a repeating item group that contains name and amount child elements, plus a nonrepeating total element. The name element is type string while the two other elements are type double. The total element is required and has a default value of 0. Figure 6-7 shows the form's data source.

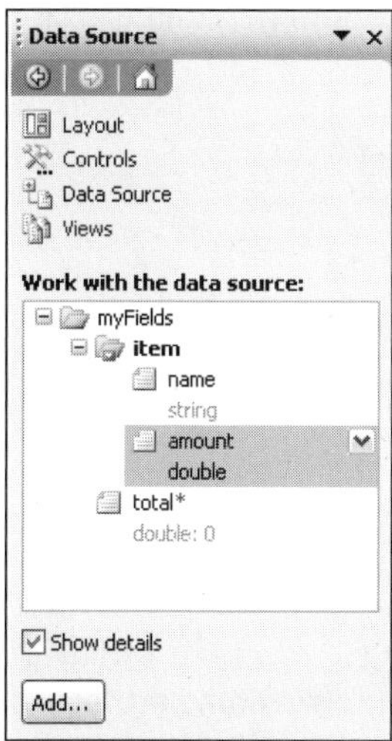


Figure 6-7: The data source for the invoice form.

Follow these steps to create the form's visual interface:

1. Place a single column layout table on the form.
2. Drag the item field from the data source and drop it on the table. From the options offered in the pop-up menu that appears, select Repeating Table. InfoPath inserts a table with two columns and controls for the name and amount elements.
3. Drag the total field from the data source and drop it on the form, inside the layout table but not in the repeating table. InfoPath adds a control and label for this element.
4. Format the Amount and Total fields as currency.

That completes the form's visual interface. Next, I'll show you how to write the event handler that will respond to changes and calculate the total. The field to connect the code to is amount because that's the field being totaled. The event to use is

`OnAfterChange` because it is after the value in an amount field has been changed that the total needs to be recalculated. Here's what to do:

1. Right-click the amount element in the data source and select Properties from the pop-up menu. InfoPath displays the Field or Group Properties dialog box.
2. On the Validation and Script tab, select `OnAfterChange` from the Events list.
3. Click the Edit button to open the Script Editor.
4. Add the code shown in Listing 6-3 to the event procedure that you just created.

**Listing 6-3: The OnAfterChange Event Procedure for the Amount Field**

```
function msoxd_my_amount::OnAfterChange(eventObj)
{
  if (eventObj.IsUndoRedo)
  {
  // An undo or redo operation has occurred and the
  // DOM is read-only.
    return;
    }

  var items =
      XDocument.DOM.selectNodes("/my:myFields/my:item/my:amount");
  var subtotal =
      XDocument.DOM.selectSingleNode("/my:myFields/my:total");
  var total = 0;
  for (var i=0;i<items.length;i++)
  {
    var value = parseInt(items(i).text);
    if (!isNaN(value))
      total += value;
  }
  subtotal.text = total;
}
```

The Script Editor automatically places the first section of code in this event procedure. It uses the `eventObj` object passed to the procedure to check if an undo or redo operation has occurred. If the amount field has changed because of such an operation, there's no need to recalculate, so execution exits the procedure.

The remaining code is what you will add. Here's what it does:

1. Creates a variable named items and uses the `selectNodes` method of the DOM to make this variable refer to all instances of the amount element in the XML document.
2. Creates a variable named `subtotal` and uses the `selectSingleNode` method of the DOM to make this variable reference the total node in the document.
3. Creates a variable named `total` that will be used to accumulate the total.
4. Loops through items (this loop executes once for each amount field), checking each amount field to see if the value is a number and, if so, adds it to the total.
5. Displays the total in the element referenced by the subtotal variable.

The form template is ready to try out. Save the form template, and then start filling out a form based on this template. Add a few rows to the table, as shown in Figure 6-8. As you add new items to the table, change prices, or delete items, the total field is automatically updated to reflect the sum of all the amounts.

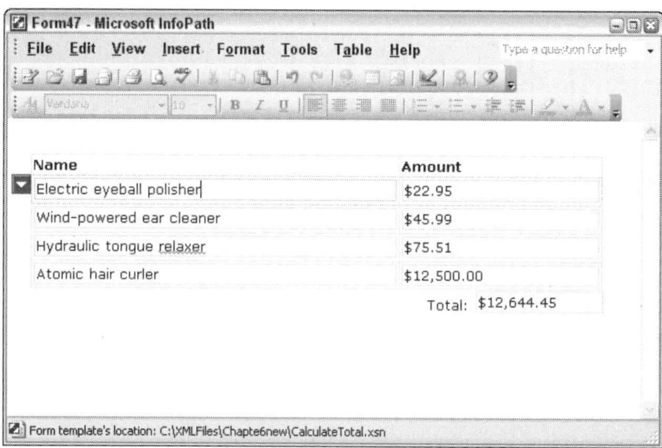


**Figure 6-8:** A form that displays a running total.

## The Sample Form Code

The sample forms that are installed with InfoPath include some interesting and useful script code. Several of them include code to calculate a sum using a different technique than was used in this example. You can and should examine the sample form code in the Script Editor. It provides quite a few functions that you may find useful in your own forms. In addition, the code in the sample forms can be very instructive in terms of accomplishing various tasks with InfoPath script.

## Validating Data

Now, let's look at two methods of validating data using script. The first one uses the `OnBeforeChange` event. If the user enters invalid data, the control reverts to its previous data and a message is displayed. The second one uses the `OnValidate` event. If the data is invalid, the field is marked with a red line and an error message is displayed when the mouse cursor hovers over the control (just like a schema validation error). These examples are in VBScript. Here are the steps to follow:

1. In InfoPath, choose File→Design a form to display the Design a Form task pane.
2. Click the New Blank Form command.
3. Choose Tools→Form Options to display the Form Options dialog box.
4. On the Advanced tab, select VBScript in the Form Script Language list.
5. Click OK to close the dialog box.
6. Display the Data Source task pane.
7. Right-click the myFields element to display the Add Field or Group dialog box.
8. Enter "theFirstPresident" in the name field.
9. Click OK to close the dialog box.
10. Drag the new theFirstPresident element and drop it on the form. InfoPath adds a Text Box control with a label The First President.
11. Right-click the theFirstPresident element in the data source and select Properties from the pop-up menu. InfoPath displays the Field or Group Properties dialog box.
12. Select the Validation and Script tab.
13. In the Events list, select `OnBeforeChange`.
14. Click the Edit button to open the Script Editor.
15. Enter the code from Listing 6-4 into the event procedure.
16. Switch back from the Script Editor to InfoPath and click OK to close the dialog box.
17. Save the form template under a descriptive name such as ValidateData.

**Listing 6-4: The OnBeforeChange Event Procedure**

```
Sub msoxd_my_theFirstPresident_OnBeforeChange(eventObj)

Dim answerField
Set answerField = eventObj.Site

' Assume data is OK.
eventObj.ReturnStatus = true

' Do not invalidate field if blank.
if answerField.Text = "" then exit sub

' Check the entered value.
' If not correct reject it and display an alert.
if UCase(answerField.Text) <> "GEORGE WASHINGTON" then
  eventObj.ReturnMessage = "That's not right!"
  eventObj.ReturnStatus = false
end if

End Sub
```

The first two lines of code within the procedure create a variable and set it to refer to the XML element to which the event procedure is attached. This is one example of using the object that is passed as an argument to the event procedure – it lets you easily identify the element that received the event.

Then, `eventObj.ReturnStatus` is set to true. If the event procedure ends with this property set to true, InfoPath assumes that the data value is acceptable and takes no action. If this property is set to false, InfoPath deletes the new value and reverts the element and its bound control to the previous value.

The code then checks to see if the element is blank, which is acceptable. If so, the procedure terminates.

The remaining code checks the data in the element against the correct answer. Note the use of the `UCase` function to convert the data to all uppercase, which is then compared to GEORGE WASHINGTON. This ensures that the answer will be counted as correct even if capitalized oddly. If the data does not match the correct answer, the `eventObj.ReturnMessage` is set to the message that will be displayed to the user, and the `eventObj.ReturnStatus` property is set to false.

Try out the form by entering your answer and pressing Tab. If you enter the correct answer, nothing happens. If you enter an incorrect answer, a dialog box appears with the programmed message, as shown in Figure 6-9. When you close the dialog box, the data in the text box is deleted.

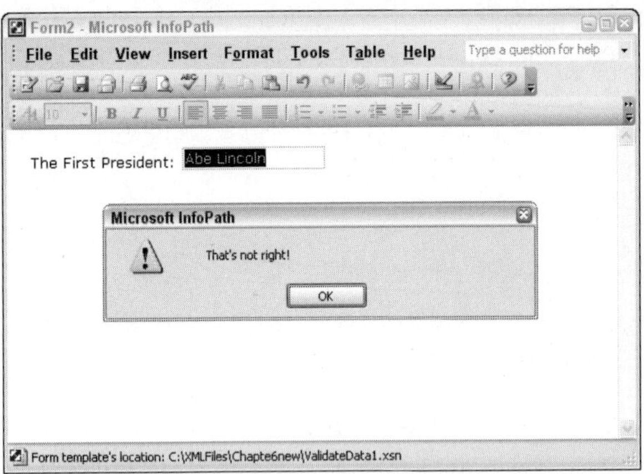


**Figure 6-9: Validating data with the OnBeforeChange event.**

To try the example that uses the `OnValidate` event, follow the preceding steps with the following exceptions:

- Step 13: Select the `OnValidate` event (instead of `OnBeforeChange`).
- Step 15: Enter the code from Listing 6-5 into the event procedure.

**Listing 6-5: The OnValidate Event Procedure**

```
Sub msoxd_my_theFirstPresident_OnValidate(eventObj)

Dim answerField
Set answerField = eventObj.Site

' Remove a previous error.
XDocument.Errors.Delete answerField, "ValidationError"

' If the answer in not correct, add an error condition.
If UCase(answerField.Text) <> "GEORGE WASHINGTON" then
  XDocument.Errors.Add answerField, "ValidationError", _
    "This answer is wrong", _
    "The correct answer is 'George Washington'"
end if

End Sub
```

The first two lines of code in the procedure are the same as in the previous event procedure and serve to get a reference to the element that has changed.

The next line makes sure that there is no earlier validation error still associated with the element.

The final code checks the data and, if it is not correct, generates a validation error by calling the `XDocument.Errors.Add` method. This method takes four arguments:

- The first argument identifies the element to which the error applies.
- The second argument describes the type of error.
- The third argument specifies the short error message that is displayed when the mouse pointer hovers over the bound control.
- The fourth argument specifies the detailed error message that is displayed when the user requests more information.

Figure 6-10 shows the form with incorrect data in the field and the mouse pointer hovering over the control. Perhaps not visible in the figure is the red border around the control. If the user right-clicks the control and selects Full Error Description from the pop-up menu, the more detailed error message is displayed.

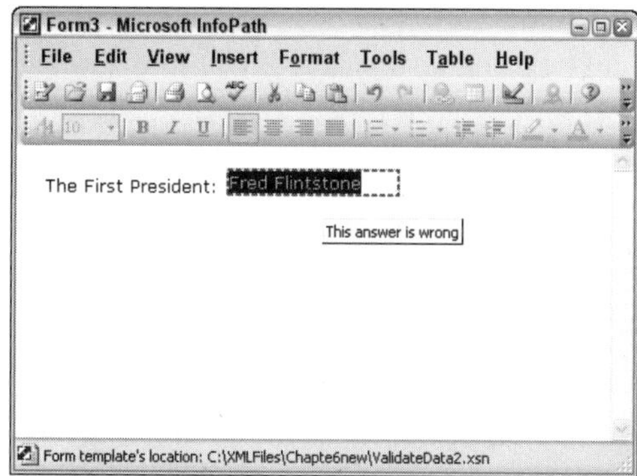


**Figure 6-10: Validating data with the OnValidate event.**

# Selecting a View Based on Data

An InfoPath form can have multiple views. One of these views is designated the default view when the form template is designed, and it is the first view displayed when the form is opened. This example shows how you can display a different view when a form is opened, based on the value of an element in the data source. This applies primarily to forms that have already had some data entered, been saved, and then are opened again. The `OnLoad` event is used to read the element value and set the view accordingly. Here's what to do:

1. Create a new form template based on a new, blank form.
2. Type the text "This is the default view" on the form.

3. Add an element named “select” to the data source. Its type should be true/false.
4. Drag the select element from the data source and drop it on the form beneath the text that you added. InfoPath adds a check box to the form.
5. Display the Views task pane.
6. Click the Add a New View command on the task pane. InfoPath displays the Add View dialog box.
7. Enter “Edit” as the view name then click OK. The new view is displayed for design.
8. Enter the text “This is the edit view” on the form.
9. Choose Tools → Script → On Load Event to open the Script Editor and display the `OnLoad` event procedure.
10. Enter the code shown in Listing 6-6 into the procedure.
11. Switch back from the Script Editor to InfoPath. The form template, with the default view and the Data Source task pane displayed, will look like Figure 6-11.

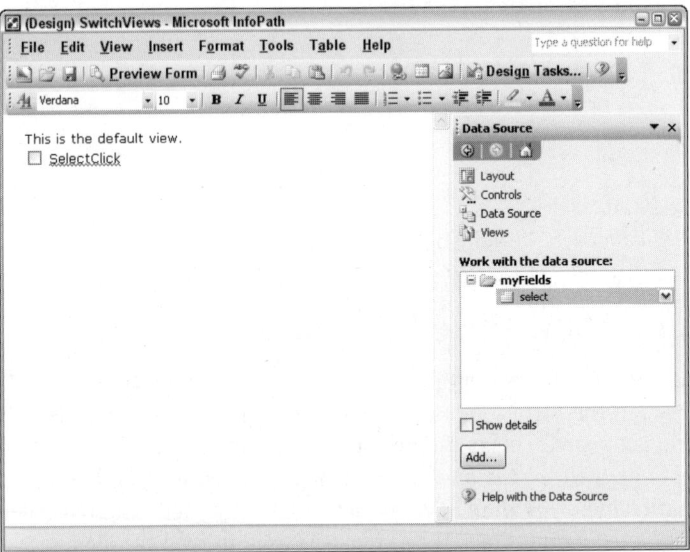


Figure 6-11: The completed form with default view displayed.

**Listing 6-6: Code in the OnLoad Event Procedure**

```
function XDocument::OnLoad(eventObj)
{
  var oSelectNode =
    XDocument.DOM.selectSingleNode("/my:myFields/my:select");
  if (oSelectNode.text == "true")
    XDocument.ViewInfos("Edit").IsDefault = true;
}
```

The code for this example is quite simple. It creates a reference to the select element in the data source. It then checks the value of the element and, if it is true, makes the Edit view the default, which is then displayed. If the value is false, no action is taken and the regular default view displays.

You can test this form in two ways. One is to change the default value of the select element from false to true. When you start filling out a new form based on the template, the Edit view is displayed first. You can also create a form based on the template and then save it. When you again open the form, the view displayed will depend on the value of the selected element when the form was saved.

Scripting is an extremely powerful tool that can bring a lot of flexibility and ease of use to your InfoPath forms. This chapter has provided an introduction to InfoPath scripting and given you a taste of the kinds of things that you can do with scripts.

# Part III

## XML and Other Office Applications

## IN THIS PART:

Part III explores how XML is integrated in four of Microsoft Office 2003's applications: Word, Excel, Access, and FrontPage.

## Chapter 7

# Word and XML

IN THIS CHAPTER

Understanding the WordML schema

Converting Word documents to XML

Editing XML documents

Validating documents

Exploring transforms

Examining XML options

WORD PROVIDES a wide range of tools for editing and formatting text. The data in a Word document, however, is difficult to access in an efficient manner. Word's ability to work with XML data helps to overcome this limitation by permitting the data structuring capability of XML tags to be combined with the text formatting capabilities of Word. This chapter shows you how to use Word's XML capabilities.

# Using the WordML Schema

Microsoft Word has its own XML schema called WordML. This schema is designed specifically to represent Word documents as XML data, with all aspects of document content, formatting, and layout encoded as XML elements. Given the sophistication of Word's formatting tools, you might expect that WordML is extremely complex, and you would be right. To see how WordML is structured, save a simple document as XML (you'll see how in just a minute) and then open the resulting XML document in Notepad.

WordML is not intended to be manipulated directly, but is a means for data to be exchanged between Word and other applications. For example:

- When saved as WordML, Word documents become available for searching and data mining by other applications. This is possible because WordML separates the content, or data, of the document from its formatting and layout.
- WordML documents can be generated by back-end processes that gather information from various sources. These documents are then available for editing and printing as needed.

> **Word, WordML, and Other Schemas**
>
> It's important to understand how Word can work with WordML and other schemas. XML is designed to be able to use multiple schemas for a single XML file, using namespaces to identify XML elements that are to be validated against each schema. Thus, a Word document can use WordML and/or one or more additional schemas. When WordML is used along with another schema, it is WordML that marks up the document in terms of formatting and layout, and the other schema marks up the document in terms of structuring the data.

To save a Word document as XML, choose File→Save As and then select XML Document in the Save As Type list. Enter the filename – Word adds the XML extension automatically. When saving a document as XML, you are offered the options to apply a transform and to save the data only. These options are covered later in this chapter. At this point you should leave them both unchecked.

Opening a WordML file is no different from opening a standard Word document. Word's Open dialog box lists files with the XML extension along with standard Word documents (DOC extension) and other file types that Word can open, such as rich text documents (RTF extension). When you open a WordML document, Word recognizes it as a WordML document and treats it accordingly. From the user's perspective, editing and formatting a WordML document is no different from editing and formatting a regular Word document. When you save such a document, it is automatically saved as WordML. If you open a WordML document and want to save it as a Word Document (`*.doc`), you must use the File→Save As command and select Word Document from the Save as Type list.

If you open an XML document that isn't a WordML document in Word, it is treated very differently, as you'll see next.

# Opening Other XML Files

Word can open any XML file, not just those that follow the WordML schema. When you open an XML file that has another namespace (that is, non-WordML), the process depends on the contents of the file:

- If the XML file's namespace matches a schema that is in the Schema Library, Word attaches the schema to the XML file.
- If the XML file's namespace does not match a schema in the Schema Library, but the file contains a pointer to a schema file (in an `xsi:schemaLocation` element), Word gives you the option of opening that schema as an XML expansion pack.

◆ If the XML file's namespace doesn't match a schema that is in the Schema Library, and the file doesn't contain a pointer to a schema file, Word opens the XML file without an attached schema.

In any of these scenarios, the end result is that you have an XML document opened in Word either with or without a schema attached. The practical differences, from the perspective of editing XML data, are that without an attached schema you cannot validate the document, and that the information available in the XML Structure task pane is not as complete. Once the document is open, you can begin editing it, as described in the next section.

# Creating a New XML Document

When starting a new XML document in Word, you may want to attach one or more schemas to it so that the schema elements are available to you on the XML Structure task pane while you are creating and editing the document.

1. Choose File→New, then click the XML Document command on the New Document task pane.
2. Word creates the new document and displays the XML Structure task pane. Click the Templates and Add-Ins command on the task pane to display the XML Schema tab of the Templates and Add-Ins dialog box (see Figure 7-1).
3. The Available XML Schemas list displays the names of the available schemas. Place a check next to each schema that you want attached to the document.
4. Click OK.

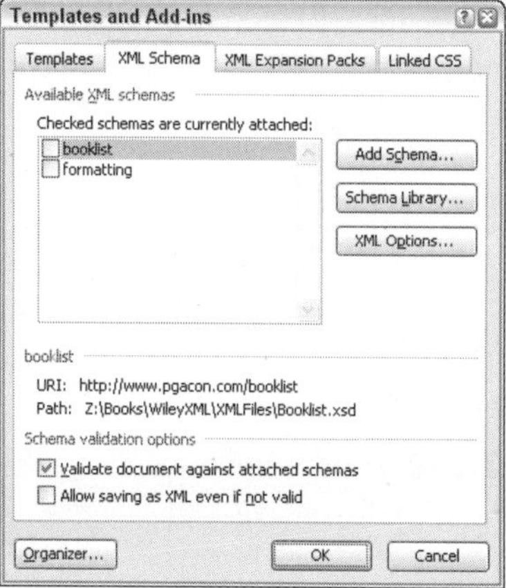


Figure 7-1: Selecting schemas to attach to a document.

Once you have created the new document, you are ready to start editing it, as described later in this chapter.

If the schema that you need is not listed in the Available XML Schemas list, you must add the schema to the Schema Library. I discuss how to do this in "The Schema Library" section later in this chapter.

# Converting a Word Document to XML

You can also attach a schema to an existing Word document, apply the schema elements to the document content, and save the document as an XML document. The parts of the document that you mark up with XML are then available to other XML applications. First, you should ensure that the schema you want to use is part of Word's Schema Library ("The Schema Library" section later in this chapter discusses this). Attaching the schema then is pretty much the same as attaching a schema to a new XML document in Word:

1. Open the Word document in the usual manner.
2. Choose Tools → Templates and Add-Ins to open the Templates and Add-Ins dialog box, and click the XML Schema tab (shown earlier in Figure 7-1).
3. In the Available XML Schemas list, put a check mark next to the schema(s) that you want attached to the document.
4. Click OK.

At this point you can start editing the document, applying tags to document contents as required. The procedures for editing an XML document are presented later in this chapter.

When it's time to save the document, do *not* simply click the Save button or choose File → Save because this saves the document in its original DOC format and not as an XML document. Here's how you save it as an XML document:

1. Choose File → Save As to display the Save As dialog box.
2. Select XML Document in the Save as Type list.
3. Make sure that neither the Apply Transform nor the Save Data Only options are selected.

4. Enter a new name for the file if desired, or accept the name that Word suggests (the original document name). Word automatically adds the XML extension.

5. Click Save.

When you have attached a schema to a Word document, you may want to select the Ignore Mixed Content option under XML Options, which are discussed later in this chapter. With this option selected, validation ignores mixed content text.

# Editing Other XML Documents

As mentioned earlier in this chapter, Word treats a WordML document like any other Word document – there are no elements or attributes for the user to be concerned with. So, let's take a look at editing XML documents that use a schema other than WordML.

The sample XML data file in Listing 7-1 contains data about a book collection, containing only two books at present. Note that this file is associated with a schema named `Booklist.xsd`, which is shown in Listing 7-2. This XML data file and schema are used for the following examples. It is assumed that the schema has been attached to the XML file as described earlier in the section "Opening Other XML Files."

Later in this chapter you'll learn how to use a transform, or solution, to modify the way an XML document is displayed in Word. For now, assume that there is no transform in use, so the document is displayed on-screen using the Data-Only view.

**Listing 7-1: The Sample XML Data File MyBooks.xml**

```
<?xml version="1.0" encoding="UTF-8"?>
<books xmlns="http://www.pgacon.com/booklist"
   xmlns:xsi="http://www.w3.org/2001/XMLSchema-instance"
   xsi:schemaLocation="http://www.pgacon.com/booklist
   c:\xmlfiles\Booklist.xsd">
  <book binding="hardcover">
    <title>The King's English</title>
    <pubyear>1997</pubyear>
    <author>
      <firstname>Kingsley</firstname>
      <lastname>Amis</lastname>
    </author>
  </book>
  <book binding="softcover">
    <title>Death in Venice</title>
    <pubyear>1994</pubyear>
```

*Continued*

**Listing 7-1** *(Continued)*

```
    <author>
      <firstname>Thomas</firstname>
      <lastname>Mann</lastname>
    </author>
    <comments>There is a small tear in the cover.</comments>
  </book>
</books>
```

**Listing 7-2: Booklist.xsd Schema for MyBooks.xml.**

```
<?xml version="1.0" encoding="UTF-8"?>
<xs:schema targetNamespace="http://www.pgacon.com/booklist"
   xmlns:xs="http://www.w3.org/2001/XMLSchema"
   xmlns="http://www.pgacon.com/booklist"
   elementFormDefault="qualified"
   attributeFormDefault="unqualified">
  <xs:element name="books">
    <xs:complexType>
      <xs:sequence>
        <xs:element name="book" maxOccurs="unbounded">
          <xs:complexType>
            <xs:sequence>
              <xs:element name="title" type="xs:string"/>
              <xs:element name="pubyear">
                <xs:simpleType>
                  <xs:restriction base="xs:int">
                    <xs:minInclusive value="1800"/>
                    <xs:maxInclusive value="2020"/>
                  </xs:restriction>
                </xs:simpleType>
              </xs:element>
              <xs:element name="author" maxOccurs="unbounded">
                <xs:complexType>
                  <xs:sequence>
                    <xs:element name="firstname" type="xs:string"/>
                    <xs:element name="lastname" type="xs:string"/>
                  </xs:sequence>
                </xs:complexType>
              </xs:element>
              <xs:element name="comments" type="xs:string"
                    minOccurs="0"/>
            </xs:sequence>
            <xs:attribute name="binding" use="required">
              <xs:simpleType>
                <xs:restriction base="xs:string">
```

```
                <xs:enumeration value="hardcover"/>
                <xs:enumeration value="softcover"/>
              </xs:restriction>
            </xs:simpleType>
          </xs:attribute>
        </xs:complexType>
      </xs:element>
    </xs:sequence>
  </xs:complexType>
</xs:element>
</xs:schema>
```

When you open an XML document in Word, both its data and its tags are displayed on-screen, and the XML Structure task pane is displayed as well. Figure 7-2 shows `MyBooks.xml` open in Word.

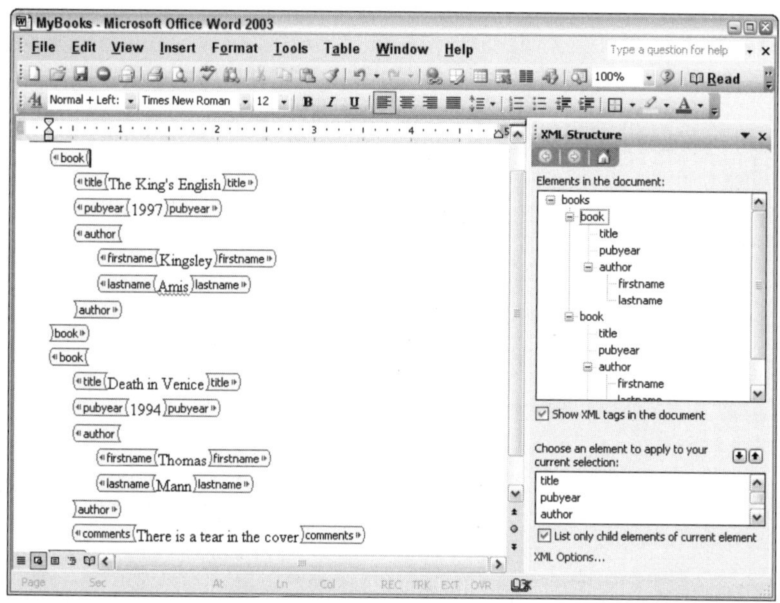

Figure 7-2: In Word, an XML document displays its data and tags by default.

The XML Structure task pane is very useful when editing XML. Its elements include the following:

- **Elements in the document.** This list displays the document structure using the names of the XML elements in the document. The current element (the one containing the insertion point) is indicated by an outline. In Figure 7-2 this is the first <book> element. Click an element in this list to select it in the document.

- **Show XML tags in the document.** Controls whether the document displays tags and data, or just data.
- **Choose an Element to apply to your current selection.** Lists the XML elements that can be applied at the current location in the document.
- **List Only Child Elements of current element.** Controls what is displayed in the Choose an Element... list.
- **XML Options.** Displays the XML Options dialog box, which is explained later in this chapter.

To include XML tags when the document is printed, choose Tools → Options and click the Print tab. Under Include With Document, select the XML Tags option.

If you want to work with the XML data without the tags getting in the way, turn off the Show XML Tags in the Document option in the XML Structure task pane. Figure 7-3 shows how the same XML file looks with the tags hidden. You can see that the data is organized on screen according to the structure of the document. It is not particularly convenient to work with data that is displayed like this. As you'll see later in the chapter, you can use Word's formatting tools to give the document a more pleasant and functional appearance.

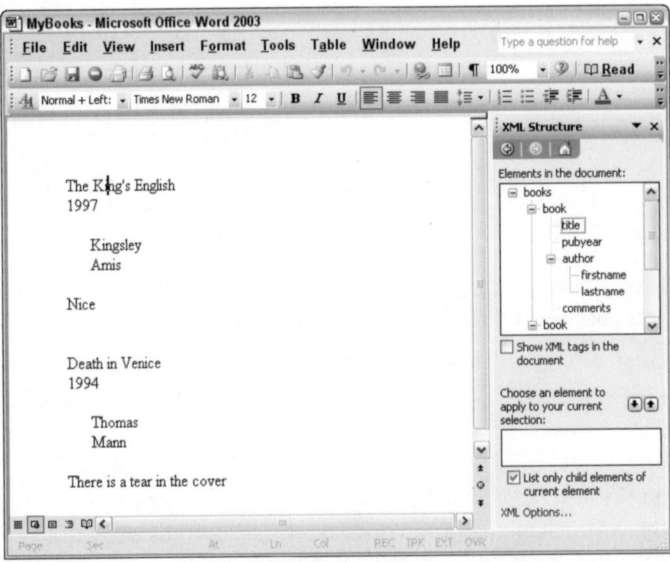


Figure 7-3: An XML document displayed without its tags.

It's important to understand how the List Only Child Elements option works. If it is selected, the Choose an Element list displays only those elements that are children of the current element (the one containing the insertion point). Put another way, the list shows only those elements that would be valid (according to the schema) at the current location. If the List Only Child Elements option isn't selected, the list displays all of the document's XML elements regardless of whether they would be valid at the current location. You can still distinguish valid from invalid elements because the latter are displayed with a red "no" symbol (a circle with a line through it).

If the XML Structure task pane is not displayed, open the task pane menu by clicking the down arrow in the task pane's title bar, then select XML Structure.

## Adding Elements

There are two ways to insert an element in an XML document. One is to insert the tags first and then the data:

1. Place the insertion point at the location where you want the element.
2. Click the element name in the Choose an Element to Apply... list on the XML Structure task pane. Word inserts the start and end tags for the element.
3. Type the data between the tags.

The second method is used when the element data is already present in the document:

1. Select the data to be in the element.
2. Click the element name in the Choose an Element to Apply... list on the XML Structure task pane. Word inserts start and end tags around the selected data.

## Deleting Elements

To delete an element, select it by double-clicking its start tag. Then, press Del. This method deletes the entire element – tags and content.

If you want to delete an element's content while leaving the tags in the document, click the element in the Elements in this Document list in the XML Structure task pane. This selects all of the element's content but not its tags. Then, press Del.

If the element contained child elements, these are completely deleted (tags and content), but the parent element's tags are left in place.

You can also remove an element's start and end tags while leaving the content intact. Right-click the tag (either the start or end tag) and select Remove *XXXX* Tag (where *XXXX* is the tag name) from the pop-up menu.

# Working with Attributes

XML attributes are not displayed in the Word document but can be accessed separately for each element by right-clicking the element's start tag and selecting Attributes from the pop-up menu. Word displays the Attributes dialog box, as shown in Figure 7-4.

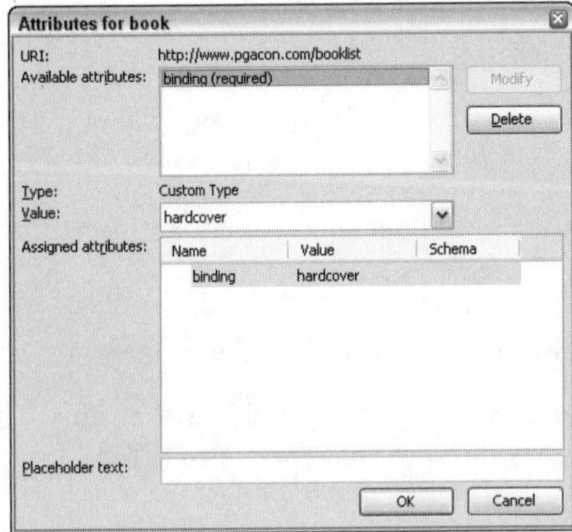


**Figure 7-4: The Attributes dialog box.**

The items in this dialog box include the following:

- **URI.** The namespace of the element.
- **Available Attributes.** Attributes that are available for this element (as defined in the schema). Required attributes are marked with (required) after their name, like the binding attribute in the figure. Optional attributes are listed with no special marking.
- **Type.** The data type of the attribute selected in the Available Attributes list.
- **Value.** The value of the attribute selected in the Available Attributes list, or blank if no value is assigned for this element.
- **Assigned Attributes.** Lists the names and values of attributes that have been assigned values for this element.

To add an attribute to the element:

1. Click the attribute name in the Available Attributes list.
2. Enter the value for the attribute in the Value field.
3. Click the Add button.

To modify the value of an existing attribute, select the attribute in the Assigned Attributes list, and then edit the value in the Value field.

To delete an attribute from the element, select it in the Assigned Attributes list, and then click Delete. You are allowed to delete required attributes even though it results in a violation when and if the file is validated.

# Formatting and Layout

When editing an XML document, you can apply any of Word's formatting to get the visual appearance that you desire. You can organize document content in tables, change fonts, use borders and shading, and so on. Note that some of Word's formatting commands, such as inserting a table, are available only when the Show XML Tags in Document option on the XML Structure task pane is turned off.

When formatting an XML document, particularly when working with tables, you must pay close attention to the element tags. As you cut and paste document content, it is essential that the tags be moved, too, so that the structure of the document is maintained. Mistakes here can lead to document validation errors. For this reason, it is better to work with tags displayed in the document.

For example, Figure 7-5 shows the MyBooks.xml file formatted with the data in a table and the book titles in boldface.

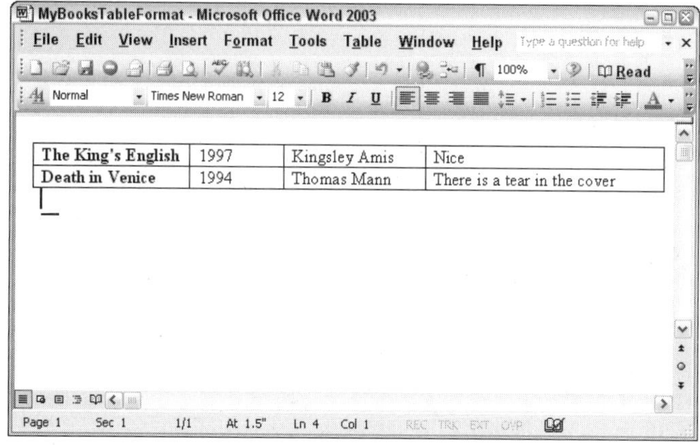


Figure 7-5: An XML document formatted as a table.

The document is still valid because the tags were carefully moved with the content into the table so that the logical structure of the document was maintained. You can see this in Figure 7-6, which shows the same document with the tags displayed.

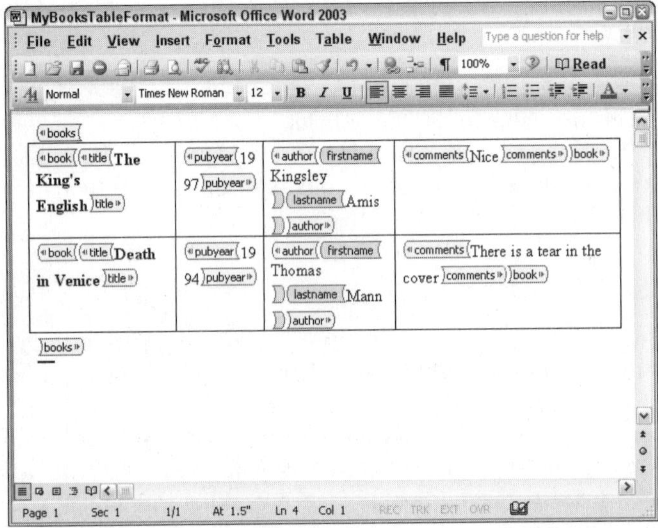


Figure 7-6: Within the table format, the XML tags are positioned so as to preserve a valid document structure.

Word simplifies the task of working with XML data in tables. If you add a row to a table that contains XML data, empty tags are automatically inserted in the new row to duplicate the structure of other rows. You can then simply type the data for the new row within these tags.

What about adding additional text to a document? For example, in the document shown in Figure 7-6, you might want to add headings to the table to identify the data in the columns. You can add text to the document, but always under the restrictions of XML validation. In other words, the content that you add must be legal within the constraints of the document's schema. You have several options:

- You can modify the document's schema to define one or more elements for extra text that is not part of the document's core data.
- You can use Word's Text Box control to display text. Because the text in a Text Box control is not regular document text, it is subsumed under the WordML schema and is not validated against other schemas used in the document.

- You can select the Ignore Mixed Content option under XML Options. *Mixed content* refers to an XML element that contains both text and other elements. With this option selected, the text part of mixed content in the document is ignored by validation. (See the section "XML Options" later in this chapter for details.)
- You can define another schema that provides for these additional text elements, and then associate that schema with the document along with its other schema(s).

You can turn validation off for an XML document in Word, but I strongly recommend against this. If a document has a schema attached, there is a reason. Allowing a document to be saved without validation can result in all kinds of problems down the road when other applications try to use the document.

## Saving Documents

When you are working with a document that has one or more schemas attached to it, the process of saving the document is pretty much the same as it is for any other Word document, with one major difference: the Save Data Only option. This option appears in the Save As dialog box only when the document type is XML Document. If this option is off (the default), the document is saved using its attached schemas as well as the WordML schema. The end result is that all formatting and extra elements are saved along with the document data. If you select this option, the document data is saved without any formatting. The setting you select depends on what the saved document will be used for. Be careful using the Save Data Only option, particularly if you have applied a lot of formatting to the document, because the formatting will be lost permanently. It may be wise to keep a backup copy of the document with the formatting, just in case.

When saving a document using the Save As dialog box, you also have the option of applying a transform to the document when it is saved. See the "Transforms for Saving Documents" section later in this chapter for more information.

# Document Validation

Validation means to check an XML document's structure and data against its attached schema. If the document meets all of the requirements and restrictions in the schema, it is said to be *valid.* Word can validate any XML document as you work on it and flag violations in the document. Document validation is affected by several option settings, which we'll discuss later in the "XML Options" section.

When Word finds a validation violation, it marks the violation two ways: with a wavy purple line in the left margin of the document, and with a red violation icon next to the offending element's name in the XML Structure task pane. This is shown in Figure 7-7, where there is a violation for the first `pubyear` element. The problem in this case is that the element value is `197` while the schema (Listing 7-2) specifies that the value must be in the range `1800-2020`.

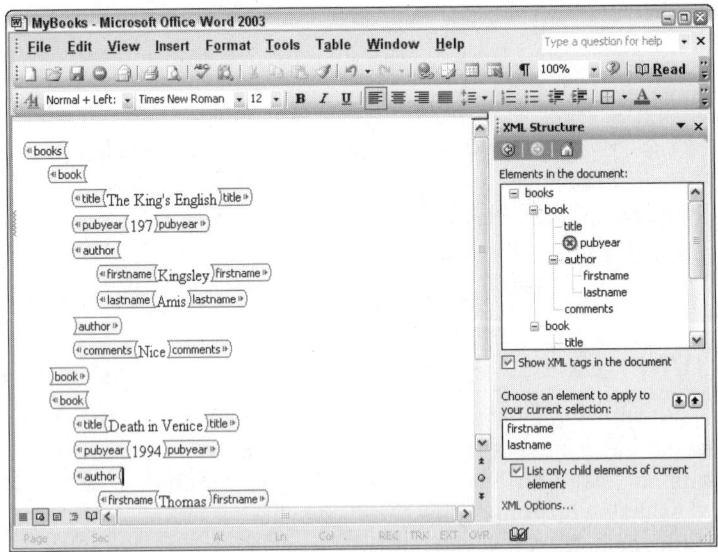


Figure 7-7: Word marks schema violations in the XML document and the XML Structure task pane.

You can find out the details of any schema violation by right-clicking the element's name in the XML Structure task pane. The first item on the pop-up menu is a description of the violation, as shown in Figure 7-8. You can use this information to edit the document's content or structure to resolve the violation.

You can have Word display more detailed messages about schema violations by selecting the Show Advanced XML Error Messages option in the XML Options dialog box. (See the "XML Options" section later in this chapter for details.)

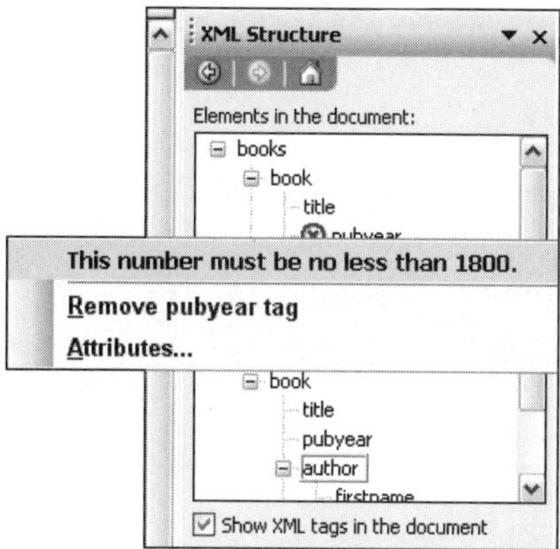


Figure 7-8: Word displays an explanation of why a document element is in violation of the schema.

# Using Transforms

A *transform*, or more specifically an Extensible Stylesheet Language Transformation (XSLT), is a file that contains rules for modifying an XML file. Word supports the use of transforms when working with XML.

Word can use transforms two ways: for display and for output. You can, for example, assign a transform to be applied when an XML document is opened so that Word displays the output of the transform rather than the raw XML data. You can also use a transform when saving an XML document to convert an XML file into an HTML document for Web display, or to convert an XML file into another XML file with a different organization and structure.

## Transforms for Displaying Documents

A transform that is used for displaying documents is called a *solution* in Word. When a solution is applied to an XML document, the output of the transform is displayed on-screen. A document can have multiple transforms associated with it, providing you with multiple ways of viewing the document by switching from one solution to another. You can also view the document without a transform applied (data only). You can write your own solutions using the XSL Transformation language, and software vendors or your IT department also can provide solutions.

To use a solution, it must be loaded into the Schema Library. Each solution is associated with a schema in the library. When you load an XML document, Word uses its namespace to associate it with a schema and with any solutions that are linked to that schema. Then these solutions are available for use with the document. Here's how to add a transform to the library:

1. Choose Tools→Templates and Add-Ins to display the Templates and Add-Ins dialog box.
2. Click the XML Schemas tab.
3. Click the Schema Library button to display the Schema Library dialog box, shown in Figure 7-9.

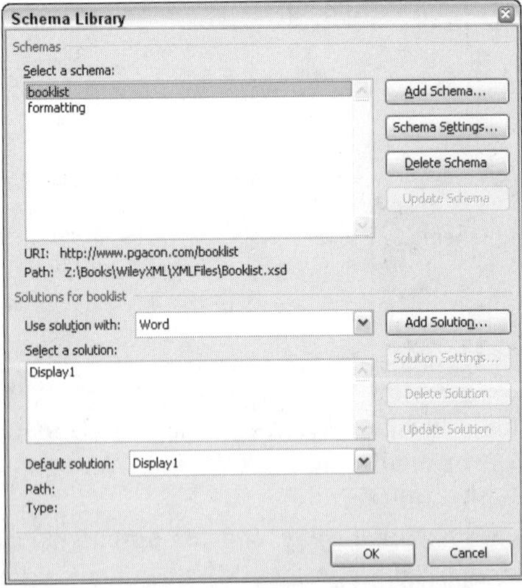


**Figure 7-9: Adding a solution to the schema library.**

4. In the Select a Schema list, select the schema that you want the transform associated with. If the schema is not listed here, you must add it using the techniques described in the section "The Schema Library."
5. The Select a Solution list displays the names of the transforms, if any, that are currently associated with the selected schema. To add a transform, click the Add Solution button and browse to locate the XSL file.
6. After selecting the file, enter an alias, or name, for the transform.
7. The alias of the new transform is listed in the Select a Solution box of the Schema Library. Make sure that Word is selected in the Use Solution With field.
8. If there is more than one transform for the selected schema, select one to be the default for the document in the Default Solution list. The default solution is applied automatically when a document is opened.
9. Click OK twice to return to the document.

When you open an XML document in Word, here's what happens:

1. Word checks the document's namespace against the schemas that are in the schema library. If it finds a match that schema is associated with the document.
2. If the matching schema has one or more solutions associated with it, those solutions are also associated with the document.
3. The document is displayed with the default solution applied. The XML Document task pane (see Figure 7-10) lists the following in the Data Views list:
   - **The name(s) of the solutions associated with the document.** Click a solution to apply it.
   - **A Data Only command.** Click this command to view the raw XML data with no solution applied.
   - **A Browse command.** Click this command to browse for another transform to apply to the document.

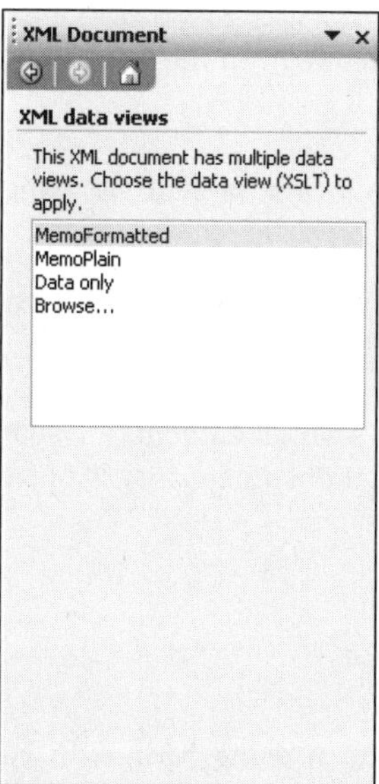


Figure 7-10: When an XML document is opened, its associated solutions, if any, are listed in the XML Document task pane.

When a document uses the WordML schema, a solution is never applied even if one is associated with the document.

When you save a document that has a solution applied, the output of the solution and not the original XML document is saved. The same goes for printing. Chapter 11, "Connecting Word and InfoPath," presents an example of using solutions in Word.

## Transforms for Saving Documents

You can also apply a transform to an XML document in Word when you save the document. There are two ways to do this, both of which have the same result:

- In the XML Options dialog box you can specify a transform to be applied automatically every time the document is saved. See the section "XML Options" later in this chapter for details.
- Specify a transform at the time you save the document.

These steps show you how to use the second method:

1. Choose File → Save As.
2. In the Save As dialog box, select XML Document in the Save as Type list.
3. Select the Apply Transform option.
4. Click the Transform button and browse to locate the XSL file containing the desired transform.
5. Back in the Save As dialog box, enter a name for the saved file, and then click Save.

When you apply a transform when saving an XML document, any data that is not used by the transform is discarded. The original document that is open in Word is not affected.

# The Schema Library

The Schema Library provides tools that assist you in using XML with your Word documents. Specifically, the Schema Library lets you organize XML schemas and XSLT transforms (also called *solutions*) in a way that makes them easier to use. The Schema Library also assists in working with namespaces. The use of solutions in the Schema library was covered earlier in the section "Transforms for Displaying Documents." Working with schemas in the library is covered here. To attach a schema to a Word document, the schema must be present in the Schema Library. To work with schemas in the Schema Library:

1. Choose Tools → Templates and Add-Ins to display the Templates and Add-ins dialog box, and click the XML Schema tab.

2. The list displays the names (aliases) of the schemas that are already in the library. To add a schema to the library, click the Add Schema button and browse to locate the schema (XSD) file.

3. After you have selected a schema file, Word displays the Edit Schema Properties dialog box, shown in Figure 7-11. Enter a descriptive name for the schema in the Alias field. This is used to identify the schema in Word.

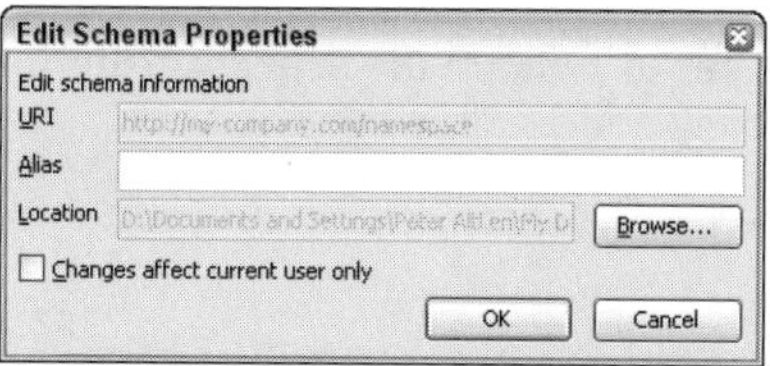


Figure 7-11: Assigning an alias to a schema.

4. Click OK to return to the Templates and Add-In dialog box. The alias of the schema you just added is listed and is also checked, indicating that it is attached to the document. You can leave this checked or unchecked, depending on your needs. (See the section "Creating a New XML Document" earlier in this chapter for more information.)

5. If you are finished, click OK to close the dialog box. Or, if you need to take more actions with the Schema Library, click the Schema Library button to display the Schema Library dialog box, shown in Figure 7-12.

Figure 7-12: You use the Schema Library dialog box to organize schemas and transforms (solutions).

6. The top part of this dialog box lists the aliases of the schemas that are currently in the library. You can take the following actions:

   Click Add Schema to add a schema to the library using the same method that was described earlier in Steps 2 and 3.

   Select a schema and click Schema Settings to view the settings, including the namespace URI and schema file location. You can also edit the schema's alias if desired.

   Select a schema and click Delete to remove the schema from the library.

7. Click OK twice to return to your document.

When you add a schema to the Schema Library, Word automatically uses the namespace URI defined in the schema file. If, however, there is no namespace defined in the schema file, Word prompts you to enter a namespace URI at the same time you are prompted to enter an alias for the schema. This namespace is used within Word.

# XML Options

You can access the XML options in several ways, including clicking the XML Options command on the XML Structure task pane or clicking the XML Options button on the XML Schema tab of the Templates and Add-Ins dialog box. The XML Options dialog box is shown in Figure 7-13.

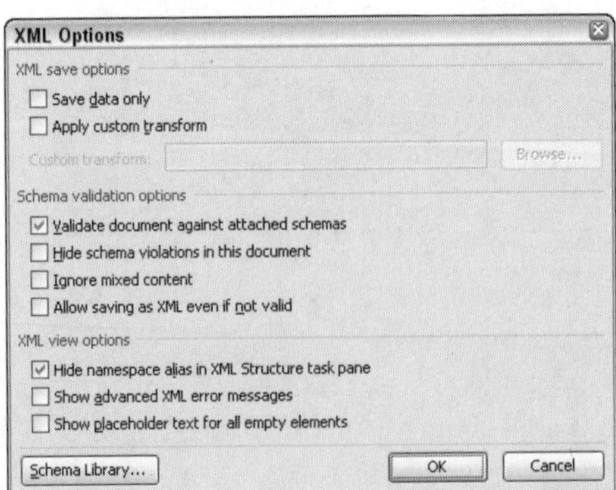


Figure 7-13: Setting XML options.

Table 7-1 explains the options available for XML.

**TABLE 7-1 XML OPTIONS**

| Option | Effect If Option Is Selected |
|---|---|
| Save data only | When the document is saved, only data (content in XML tags) is saved. All formatting and other document elements are lost. |
| Apply custom transform | This applies an XSLT transform to the file each time it is saved. The saved file is the output of the transform. Use the Browse button to select the transform to apply. (See the section "Transforms for Saving Documents" earlier in the chapter for details.) |
| Validate document against attached schemas | Word checks the document data against the attached schemas and flags violations on-screen. See the earlier section "Document Validation" for more details. |
| Hide schema violations in this document | The document is validated against the attached schemas but violations are not flagged in the document on-screen. |
| Ignore mixed content | The validation process ignores mixed content. |
| Allow saving as XML even if not valid | This permits saving an XML document that has validation violations. |
| Hide namespace alias in XML Structure task pane | Element names are displayed alone in the task pane, without the namespace alias. |
| Show advanced XML error messages | Error messages, including validation violation descriptions, provide greater detail than the default messages. |
| Show placeholder text for all empty elements | When XML tags are not displayed in the document, empty elements are indicated by placeholder text consisting of the element name in brackets. |

Now, let's take a look at some details of these options.

The Apply Custom Transform option is used when you want to apply a transform to the document each time it is saved. To apply a transform on a one-time basis, use the Apply Transform option in the Save As dialog box.

The Allow Saving as XML Even If Not Valid option should be used with care. When this option is not selected, Word does not let you save an XML document that has validation violations (you can save it as a Word DOC document but not as an XML document). There's a good reason for this: an invalid XML document can cause all sorts of problems if another application tries to process it. Use this option only if you are sure it won't cause problems.

The Ignore Mixed Content option is useful under several circumstances. Here's an example:

```
<name>
This is some text.
<firstname>John</firstname>
<lastname>Doe</lastname>
</name>
```

The <name> element has mixed content because it contains the text This is some text. as well as the <firstname> and <lastname> elements. Although mixed content is legal in XML, most schemas avoid it because it is easier to work with document structures in which an element can contain data *or* other elements but not both. When working with XML in Word, however, there are times when permitting mixed content can be helpful, such as:

- When adding text to an XML document for formatting purposes – adding column headings to a table that contains XML data, for example
- When marking up a document in which only part of the document content is to be in XML tags

By selecting the Ignore Mixed Content option, you permit the document to contain mixed content while remaining valid.

# Protecting XML Tags and Data

There may be times when you want to let other users edit the data in an XML document but prevent them from editing or deleting the XML tags. You may also want to lock some of the data, while letting other data be edited. Word lets you do this by protecting parts of the document. Here are the steps to follow:

1. Make sure that XML tags are displayed in the document by selecting the Show XML Tags in the Document option on the XML Structure task pane.
2. Choose Tools → Protect Document. Word displays the Protect Document task pane (see Figure 7-14).

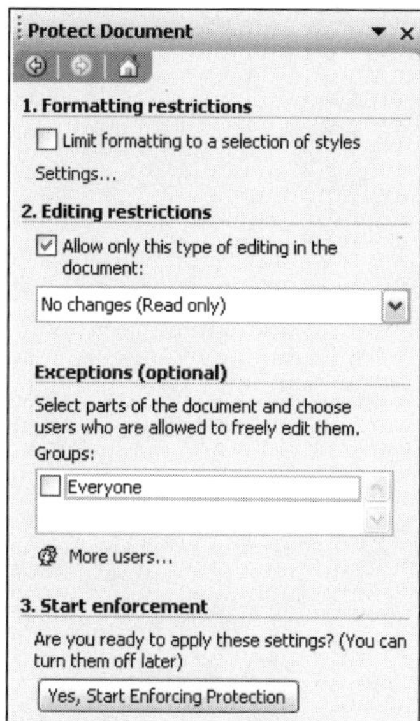


Figure 7-14: Assigning protection to a document.

3. In the Editing Restrictions section of the task pane, check the Allow Only This Type of Editing option, and select No Changes (Read-only) from the drop-down list.
4. In the document, select the contents of an element that you want users to be able to edit.
5. In the task pane, put a check mark next to Everyone in the Groups list.
6. Repeat Steps 4 and 5 for each XML element that you want users to be able to edit.
7. Click the Yes, Start Enforcing Protection button at the bottom of the task pane. Word displays the Start Enforcing Protection dialog box.
8. Select the Prevent Accidental Changes option and enter a protection password.
9. Click OK.

When a user is editing a protected document, the Protect Document task pane is displayed, as shown in Figure 7-15.

The user can use the commands on the task pane to locate regions of the document that can be edited. To remove protection, click the Stop Protection button and enter the password.

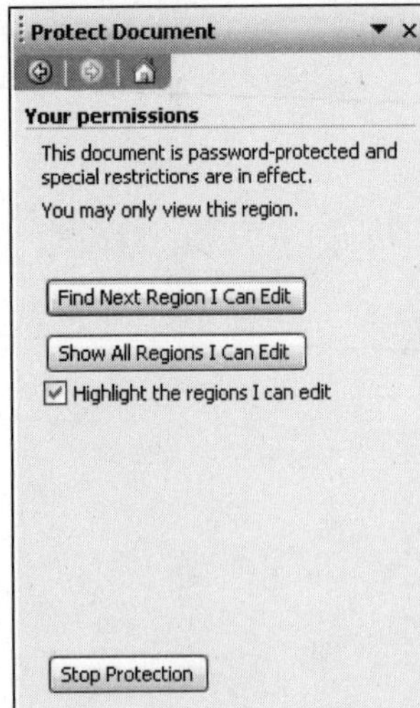


Figure 7-15: Working with a protected document.

Chapter 8

# Excel and XML

IN THIS CHAPTER

- ◆ Understanding lists (tables)
- ◆ Using the XML Source task pane
- ◆ Opening XML files
- ◆ Importing XML data
- ◆ Examining XML data validation

EXCEL IS A SPREADSHEET program designed for the manipulation and analysis of data. It provides numerous tools, such as functions and charts, that give you great flexibility in working with your data and extracting the required information. Regardless of what you are doing with the data, there is always the need to get the data into the workbook in the first place. Other than typing the data in manually, Excel offers several ways to link a worksheet to an external source of data. One of these techniques lets you use data from XML files in a workbook, and that's the topic of this chapter.

## XML and Lists

Excel has powerful capabilities for working with data in lists (sometimes called *tables*). A *list* organizes data with descriptive headings at the top of the columns and the data in the cells below. With an address list, for example, the data headings might be Name, Street, City, State, and so on. Then, below the headings, each person's data would be contained in a single row. Excel's tools for working with a list include the capability to sort the list and to filter it so that only data that meets certain criteria is displayed.

When you import XML data into a workbook, it's placed in a list. Excel offers other ways to import data to a list, such as linking to a database. The important thing to remember is that once the data is in the list, its source ceases to matter for the most part. A list is a list, whether the data is typed in, comes from a database, or is imported from an XML file. In any case, Excel's data analysis and manipulation tools are the same. Because these tools are not directly related to XML, we won't cover them in this book.

A list that contains data imported from an XML is file is sometimes referred to as an XML mapping.

# The Sample Data and Schema

Most of the examples in this chapter are based on an XML data file that is used to hold information about an organization's employees. This file, with sample data, is shown in Listing 8-1, and the associated schema is shown in Listing 8-2. The structure of the file is quite simple, consisting of an `<employee>` element for each employee. This element contains:

- A `<name>` element, type string.
- An `<ID>` element, type positiveInteger, that must be between 50000 and 99999.
- A `<dateOfHire>` element, type date.
- A `<department>` element, type string.
- A `<salary>` element, type positiveInteger.
- A gender attribute, type string, with permitted values "male" and "female."

All of the elements and attributes are required by the schema – that is, none is optional in the data file.

If you decide to use these files to explore Excel's XML capabilities, you may want to change the namespace from one that uses my URL to your own. You *must* change the location in the `xsi:schemaLocation` attribute to accurately reflect the path where you have placed the schema file. I saved these files as `Employees.xml` (Listing 8-1) and `EmployeeList.xsd` (Listing 8-2). If you use a different name for the XSD file you must change the filename in the `xsi:schemaLocation` attribute in the XML data file to reflect this name.

**Listing 8-1: The Employees XML Data File**

```
<?xml version="1.0" encoding="UTF-8"?>
<employeeList xmlns="http://www.pgacon.com/employeelist"
  xmlns:xsi="http://www.w3.org/2001/XMLSchema-instance"
  xsi:schemaLocation="http://www.pgacon.com/employeelist
  C:\XMLFiles\EmployeeList.xsd">
    <employee gender="female">
```

```
        <Name>Wendy Smith</Name>
        <ID>78234</ID>
        <dateOfHire>1998-05-01</dateOfHire>
        <department>Sales</department>
        <salary>34500</salary>
    </employee>
    <employee gender="male">
        <Name>Arthur Jackson</Name>
        <ID>61439</ID>
        <dateOfHire>1995-06-01</dateOfHire>
        <department>Marketing</department>
        <salary>54900</salary>
    </employee>
    <employee gender="female">
        <Name>Carlotta Gomez</Name>
        <ID>73219</ID>
        <dateOfHire>1996-09-15</dateOfHire>
        <department>Sales</department>
        <salary>48000</salary>
    </employee>
    <employee gender="male">
        <Name>Wilson Anderson</Name>
        <ID>51432</ID>
        <dateOfHire>2000-10-01</dateOfHire>
        <department>IT</department>
        <salary>31200</salary>
    </employee>
    <employee gender="female">
        <Name>Elizabeth Poe </Name>
        <ID>77812</ID>
        <dateOfHire>1997-12-01</dateOfHire>
        <department>Marketing</department>
        <salary>43600</salary>
    </employee>
</employeeList>
```

**Listing 8-2: The EmployeeList .xsd Schema File**

```
<?xml version="1.0" encoding="UTF-8"?>
<xs:schema targetNamespace="http://www.pgacon.com/employeelist"
    xmlns="http://www.pgacon.com/employeelist"
    xmlns:xs="http://www.w3.org/2001/XMLSchema"
    elementFormDefault="qualified"
    attributeFormDefault="unqualified">
```

*Continued*

Listing 8-2 *(Continued)*

```
  <xs:element name="employeeList">
    <xs:complexType>
      <xs:sequence>
        <xs:element name="employee" minOccurs="0"
                maxOccurs="unbounded">
          <xs:complexType>
            <xs:complexContent>
              <xs:extension base="employeeType">
                <xs:attribute name="gender" use="required">
                  <xs:simpleType>
                    <xs:restriction base="xs:string">
                      <xs:enumeration value="male"/>
                      <xs:enumeration value="female"/>
                    </xs:restriction>
                  </xs:simpleType>
                </xs:attribute>
              </xs:extension>
            </xs:complexContent>
          </xs:complexType>
        </xs:element>
      </xs:sequence>
    </xs:complexType>
  </xs:element>
  <xs:complexType name="employeeType">
    <xs:sequence>
      <xs:element name="Name" type="xs:string"/>
      <xs:element name="ID">
        <xs:simpleType>
          <xs:restriction base="xs:positiveInteger">
            <xs:minInclusive value="50000"/>
            <xs:maxInclusive value="99999"/>
          </xs:restriction>
        </xs:simpleType>
      </xs:element>
      <xs:element name="dateOfHire" type="xs:date"/>
      <xs:element name="department" type="xs:string"/>
      <xs:element name="salary" type="xs:positiveInteger"/>
    </xs:sequence>
  </xs:complexType>
</xs:schema>
```

### Excel and XML Limitations

Excel supports a wide range of XML schema constructs and can be used with most XML data. There are a few constructs that Excel does not support:

- Abstract elements that are declared in the schema but never actually used, being replaced by other elements.
- `<anyAttribute>` elements, which permit an XML file to contain attributes that are not defined in the schema.
- `<any>` elements, which permit an XML file to contain elements that are not defined in the schema.
- Recursive structures that are more than one level deep.

# The XML Source Task Pane

Much of what you will do with XML in Excel involves the XML Source task pane. This task pane displays one or more *maps* that you use to link data in the worksheet with elements in an XML file. A map is simply Excel's term for a schema – it contains the elements and attributes in the schema and the permitted relationships between them.

To display the XML Source task pane, choose Data → XML → XML Source. When first displayed, the task pane is blank unless the current workbook already has one or more maps associated with it.

## Adding Maps

In order to use the XML Source task pane, you must add one or more maps to it. You can add a map as part of the process of opening an XML file, as described later in the chapter in the section "Opening XML Files." A map can be based on an XML data file or an XSD schema file. Here's how you add a map:

1. Click the Workbook Maps button on the XML Source task pane. Excel displays the XML Maps dialog box, shown in Figure 8-1.
2. Click the Add button.
3. Browse to locate the XML file or XSD schema file on which the map will be based, and then click Open. You return to the XML Maps dialog box with the newly added map listed as follows:

**Name.** The name of the map that will be displayed on the XML Source task pane. The default name consists of the schema's root element name followed by an underscore and "Map." To change the name, click the Rename button and enter the new name.

**Root.** The name of the root element in the schema.

**Namespace.** The schema's namespace.

4. Repeat Steps 2–4 if necessary to add more maps.
5. Click OK to close the XML Maps dialog box and return to Excel. The map(s) that you added are listed in the XML Source task pane.

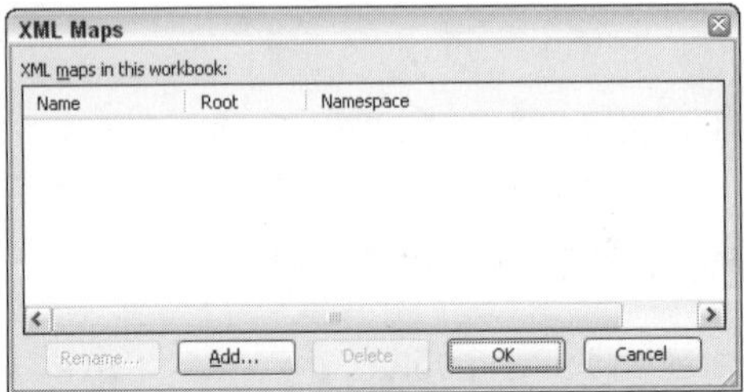


Figure 8-1: You use the XML Maps dialog box to add XML maps to a workbook.

When one or more maps are available in a workbook, the XML Source task pane displays the structure of the map that is selected in the list at the top of the task pane. The display is in the form of a hierarchical tree, and can be expanded or collapsed by clicking the plus and minus symbols that are adjacent to elements in the tree. Figure 8-2 shows the map corresponding to the employee list schema (see Listing 8-2).

Some specific items are used in the map display:

- The root element is displayed as a large folder (employeeList in the figure).
- An element that contains child elements is displayed as a pair of folders (employee).
- An attribute is displayed as a tilted piece of paper (gender).
- An element that contains data is displayed as a piece of paper with a corner folded down (name, ID, and so forth).
- An element or attribute that is required is displayed with a red asterisk (gender, name, and so on).

When you import a map based on an XML data file, Excel gets the map information from the schema that the XML file references. If the XML file does not reference a schema, or if the referenced schema is not available, Excel infers the schema structure from the content of the XML data file.

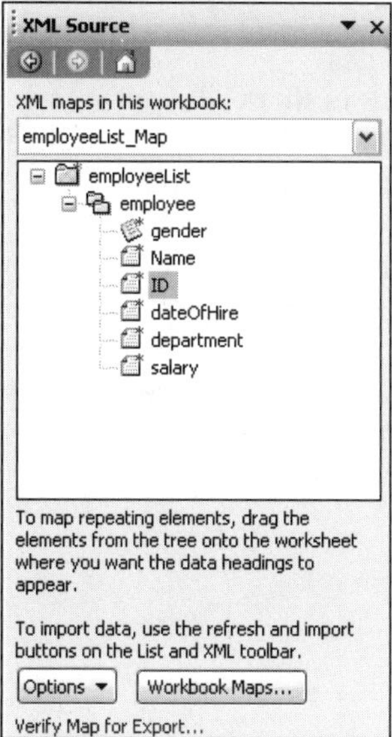


Figure 8-2: The XML Source task pane displays the structure of an XML map.

# Using Maps

An XML map is used to map XML elements to your worksheet. In other words, you use the map to specify where in the worksheet the XML data is to be placed. For example, you could specify that the `<name>` element is to be mapped to column B in Sheet1. When you open or import the XML data, the data from the `<name>` element is placed in column B.

The term *map* is used in two ways in Excel. It is used to refer to an XML schema as displayed in the XML Source task pane, as was shown in Figure 8-2. It is also used to refer to the way that XML elements are assigned, or mapped, to worksheet ranges, as described in this section.

A workbook can have multiple maps in it. Multiple maps can come from the same or from different schemas. Once created, each map is used to import XML data into the worksheet. As you might expect, a map can only be used to import data from an XML file that uses the same schema that the map is based on.

Once you have a map in the XML Source task pane, you are ready to start mapping the XML elements to worksheet ranges. Here's how:

- To map a single element, drag it from the XML Source task pane and drop it at the desired location in the worksheet.
- To map multiple elements, select the first element in the XML Source task pane, and then hold down Ctrl while selecting the others. When all desired elements are selected, drag them to the desired worksheet location.

If you map a repeating element, such as `<employee>` in the map shown in Figure 8-2, all of its child elements are automatically mapped in the worksheet. For example, Figure 8-3 shows the result of mapping the `<employee>` element to cell B4. You can see that the children of `<employee>` are mapped in the order they are present in the XML Source task pane so that the element names are in cells B4:G4 and the data, when imported, will be placed in the rows below.

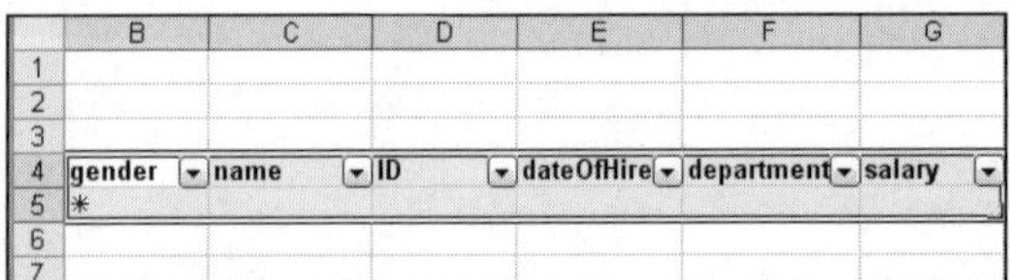


Figure 8-3: After mapping the <employee> element to cell B4.

# The List and XML Toolbar

The List and XML toolbar, shown in Figure 8-4, provides access to several commands that are frequently used when working with XML. Excel automatically displays this toolbar when you perform certain XML-related actions such as opening an XML data file. You can display or hide it as needed, as with other toolbars, by using the View→Toolbars command.

Figure 8-4: The List and XML toolbar.

Some of the commands on this toolbar aren't relevant to XML lists, so we won't discuss those here. Others are available or not, depending on the context. For example, the `Print List` command is available only when the cell pointer is in a table. The use of these commands is covered throughout the chapter, but knowing that they are available on the toolbar can make your work easier and faster:

- **List.** Displays a menu of commands for the list, including inserting and deleting rows and columns, sorting, and resizing the list
- **Toggle Total Row.** Toggles the display of formulas that sum the data in each column containing numbers
- **Refresh From XML.** Refreshes the table from the linked XML data file
- **Import.** Imports XML data into the workbook
- **Export.** Exports the table data as an XML file
- **XML Map Properties.** Displays a dialog box for setting properties of the XML map
- **Chart Wizard.** Opens the Excel Chart Wizard
- **Print List.** Displays the list in the Microsoft Document Imaging application for annotation and printing

If you can't tell from the icons which button is which, use the ScreenTip that appears when the mouse pointer hovers over a button.

# Opening XML Files

Excel can open XML data files so that you can view and analyze the data. This is perhaps the most common and important way that Excel is used with XML data. By opening an XML file you get the XML data in a workbook. You can then add other elements, such as Excel formulas and charts, to analyze the data, create summaries, and so on. Once the workbook is complete, you can use the Refresh command (covered below) to update the workbook with the latest XML data. For example, your company's back-end server might be programmed to output all of the recent sales data at the end of each month, in XML format. You could create a workbook containing all the summary formulas and charts and then generate each month's report simply by refreshing the XML data.

When you select File→Open in Excel, the Open dialog box by default lists XML files along with other types of Excel files (when All Microsoft Excel Files is selected in the Files of Type list). You can also select XML files from this list if you want the Open dialog box to list only XML files. Once you have selected an XML file to open, Excel displays the dialog box shown in Figure 8-5.

You must select one of the three ways to open an XML data file:

- As an XML list
- As a read-only workbook
- Use the XML Source task pane

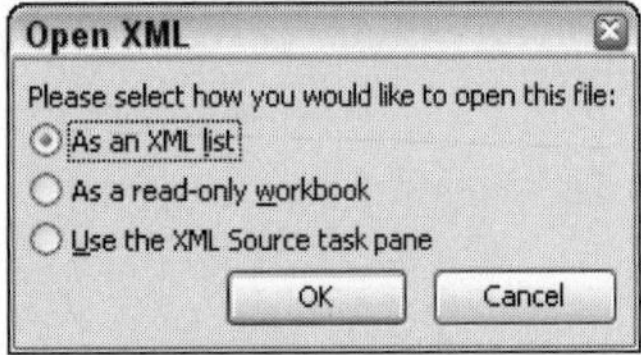


Figure 8-5: Selecting how an XML file is to be opened.

These options are discussed in the following sections. Excel also has a command to import XML data that is covered later in the chapter. Opening and importing XML data are very similar; the major difference is that opening an XML file creates a new workbook that contains the XML structure and data, while importing XML data inserts the data into an existing workbook.

# Open as an XML List

When you open an XML data file as an XML list, Excel creates a table in the worksheet with one column for each element or attribute in the XML file's schema. If the schema is not specified or not available, Excel infers the schema from the structure of the XML data. Data from the file is displayed in the table in the appropriate columns. The file's map is displayed in the XML Source task pane, as shown in Figure 8-6 for the Employees data file that was presented earlier in the chapter in Listing 8-1.

| | A | B | C | D | E | F |
|---|---|---|---|---|---|---|
| 1 | gender | name | ID | dateOfHire | department | salary |
| 2 | female | Wendy Smith | 78234 | 5/1/1998 | Sales | 34500 |
| 3 | male | Arthur Jackson | 61439 | 6/1/1995 | Marketing | 54900 |
| 4 | female | Carlotta Gomez | 73219 | 9/15/1996 | Sales | 48000 |
| 5 | male | Wilson Anderson | 51432 | 10/1/2000 | IT | 31200 |
| 6 | female | Elizabeth Poe | 77812 | 12/1/1997 | Marketing | 43600 |
| 7 | * | | | | | |
| 8 | | | | | | |
| 9 | | | | | | |

Figure 8-6: After opening the Employees XML file as an XML list.

Please note the following in the figure:

- Each column has the field or attribute name in the first row as a column label.
- Each column label has a down arrow next to it. Click this arrow to access Excel's regular data commands for sorting and filtering the list.
- The asterisk in row 7 marks the location where you will enter any new data that you want to add to the table.

Once you have opened an XML data file this way, you can treat the data like any other data in Excel. You can edit the data, add or delete records, use the database functions and charts to perform analysis – the fact that the data came from an XML file does not place any restrictions on you. Note that Excel doesn't perform data validation against the schema when you open an XML file in this manner.

At this point the data is divorced from the original XML file, and changes you make in Excel do not affect the original XML data file. You can, however, refresh the data by selecting Data → XML → Refresh XML Data, or by clicking the Refresh button on the List and XML toolbar. This command reads the XML data file again and refreshes the worksheet with any changes. The XML file must be available, of course. Other actions you can take with an XML list are covered in the "Working with XML Lists" section later in the chapter.

When you save the data, it's saved as a regular Excel workbook (or any of the other save options that Excel offers). You can also export the XML data, which also is explained later in the chapter.

# Open as a Read-Only Workbook

When you open an XML data file using the Open as Read-Only Workbook option, you have access not only to the file's data but to other details as well. Figure 8-7 shows the Employees data file from Listing 8-1 after being opened using this option.

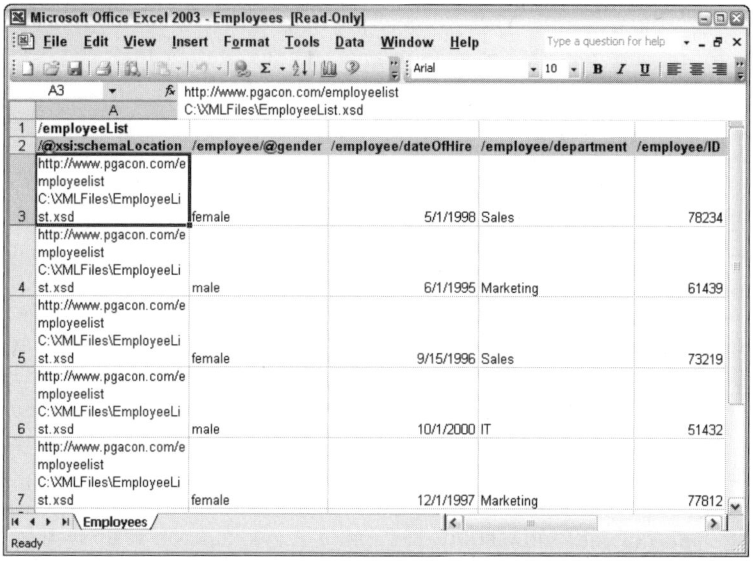

| | A | | | | |
|---|---|---|---|---|---|
| 1 | /employeeList | | | | |
| 2 | /@xsi:schemaLocation | /employee/@gender | /employee/dateOfHire | /employee/department | /employee/ID |
| 3 | http://www.pgacon.com/employeelist C:\XMLFiles\EmployeeList.xsd | female | 5/1/1998 | Sales | 78234 |
| 4 | http://www.pgacon.com/employeelist C:\XMLFiles\EmployeeList.xsd | male | 6/1/1995 | Marketing | 61439 |
| 5 | http://www.pgacon.com/employeelist C:\XMLFiles\EmployeeList.xsd | female | 9/15/1996 | Sales | 73219 |
| 6 | http://www.pgacon.com/employeelist C:\XMLFiles\EmployeeList.xsd | male | 10/1/2000 | IT | 51432 |
| 7 | http://www.pgacon.com/employeelist C:\XMLFiles\EmployeeList.xsd | female | 12/1/1997 | Marketing | 77812 |

Figure 8-7: An XML file opened using the Open as Read-Only Workbook option.

The following information is available:

- Cell A1 displays the name of the root XML element.

- Row 2 displays element and attribute names with information about the file structure. Attribute names are preceded by the ampersand character (@). For example, cell B2 contains /employee/@gender which means "the gender attribute of the employee element which is a child of the root element." Cell B3 contains /employee/dateOfHire, which means "the dateOfHire element which is a child of the employee element which is a child of the root element."
- Column A contains information about each repeating element – <employee> in this case. It shows the namespace the element belongs to, http://www.pgacon/com/employeelist in this example. If there is an associated XSD schema, the name of the schema file is shown as well (c:\XMLFiles\EmployeeList.xsd in this example).
- The remaining cells contain the data from the XML file.

When you open an XML file in this manner you cannot use the File→Save command to save it because it is opened as a read-only file. You must use File→Save As to assign a new name to the file in order to save it. This restriction is a safety feature that prevents you from inadvertently overwriting the original XML file.

# Open Using the XML Source Task Pane

Opening an XML data file using the XML Source task pane provides you with maximum flexibility for placing the XML data in your workbook. Rather than creating a single table for all of the XML data, as the Open as an XML List option does, using the XML Source task pane lets you select which XML elements to insert in the worksheet and where to place them.

When you open an XML file using this option, Excel does not read any data into the worksheet. Instead, it creates a map of the XML file's structure in the XML Source task pane. The map is based on the XML file's schema or, if a schema is not specified or available, is inferred from the structure of the XML data. Once you have this map, you place elements in your worksheet by dragging them from the XML Source task pane and dropping them at the desired location. This process was described in detail earlier in the "Using Maps" section of this chapter. You can map only those elements whose data you need in the worksheet, omitting those you do not need. Once you have completed the mapping, use the Refresh command to read the data from the file into the mapped worksheet locations.

This process may be clearer with an example. These steps assume that you have the XML data file and schema from Listings 8-1 and 8-2 available on your system.

1. Create a new, blank workbook.
2. Choose File→Open, and select the Employees.xml file to open.
3. When prompted, select the Open Using the XML Source Task Pane option. Excel displays the structure of this XML file in the XML Source task pane, as shown in Figure 8-8.

Figure 8-8: The structure of the Employee.xml file is displayed in the XML Source task pane.

4. Drag the `<name>` element from the XML Source task pane and drop it in cell A2.
5. Drag the `<department>` element to cell B2.
6. Complete the mapping by dragging the `<salary>` element to cell D2.
7. Click the Refresh button on the List and XML toolbar. Excel reads the data from the XML file and places it in the worksheet, which now should look like Figure 8-9.

| | A | B | C | D | E | F |
|---|---|---|---|---|---|---|
| 1 | | | | | | |
| 2 | **name** | **department** | | **salary** | | |
| 3 | Wendy Smith | Sales | | 34500 | | |
| 4 | Arthur Jackson | Marketing | | 54900 | | |
| 5 | Carlotta Gomez | Sales | | 48000 | | |
| 6 | Wilson Anderson | IT | | 31200 | | |
| 7 | Elizabeth Poe | Marketing | | 43600 | | |
| 8 | | | | * | | |
| 9 | | | | | | |
| 10 | | | | | | |

Figure 8-9: The worksheet after refreshing the XML data.

When looking at Figure 8-9, note that Excel has created a single XML table. Even though the table is in two parts – cells A2:B7 and cells D2:D7 – it is considered a single table because both parts were mapped from the same XML file. The different parts of the table do not even have to be on the same rows. For example, the `<salary>` element could have been mapped to cell C12 and it still would be part of the table, with corresponding rows.

**Copying and Moving Lists**

If you move an entire list (using the Edit→Cut command followed by Edit→Paste, the list definition moves with it so that subsequent refresh operations will refresh the data in the new location. If you copy a list, however, you copy the data only – the list remains in its original location. A refresh will affect the original list and not the copy. You can, of course, use a formula to copy list data to other worksheet locations so it too can be refreshed. If you move part of a list, you move the data only – the cells from which you cut the data will be empty until the next refresh.

Actions you can take with an XML list are covered later in the chapter in the section "Working with XML Lists."

# Importing XML Data

Importing XML data is similar in many respects to opening an XML file, as was discussed earlier in this chapter. The main differences are:

- You can import XML data into an existing workbook, whereas opening an XML file creates a new workbook.
- You can validate XML data against its schema when you import the data but not when you open an XML file.

When you import data, the result is a list in the worksheet that is linked to the XML data file (and its schema, if any).

## Importing into a New List

To import XML data and create a new list, the procedure is as follows:

1. (Optional.) Place the cell pointer at the location where you want the top-left corner of the list located.
2. Choose Data→XML→Import or click the Import button on the List and XML toolbar. Excel displays the Import XML dialog box. Select the XML file to import, and click Import.
3. Excel displays the Import Data dialog box, shown in Figure 8-10. Select the location for the list:

- As a list in the current worksheet with the top-left corner of the list located at the indicated cell. The default cell is the location of the cell pointer. You can edit the cell address directly or click the adjacent button to indicate the list position by pointing in the workbook.
- As a list in a new worksheet. The list will be placed with the top-left corner in cell A1.

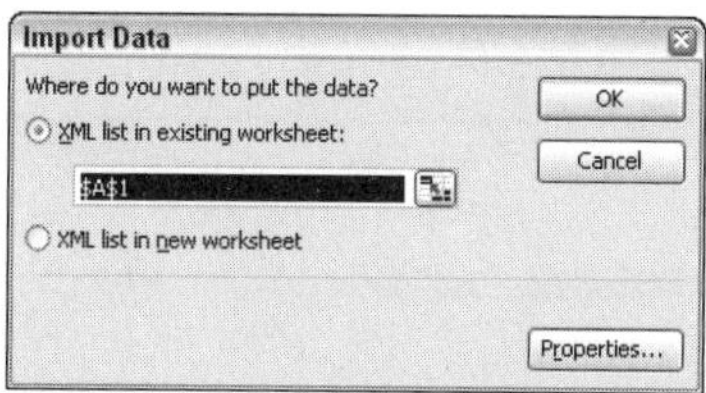


**Figure 8-10: The Import Data dialog box.**

4. Click the Properties button if you want to change the list's properties. (These are explained in detail later in the chapter. Most importantly, you must change a property if you want the XML data validated against its schema when it is imported.)
5. Click OK to close the Import Data dialog box and perform the import operation.

If you have chosen to validate the data during importing, Excel displays a message describing any validation violations that are found. Violations do not prevent the data from being imported.

## Importing into an Existing List

You can import XML data into an existing list. Before doing so, you must decide whether the newly imported data will replace existing data in the list or will be appended at the end of the list. The structure of the data to be imported must match the structure of the XML mapping. With the List and XML toolbar displayed, here's what to do:

1. Put the cell pointer in the XML list that you want to import into.
2. Click the XML Map Properties button on the List and XML toolbar to display the XML Map Properties dialog box.
3. In the When Refreshing/Importing Data section of the dialog box, choose whether you want new data to overwrite existing data or to be appended at the end of the list.
4. Click OK to close the dialog box.

### Refreshing versus Importing

It might seem that importing data to an existing XML list and refreshing the list do the same thing. Almost, but not quite. Refreshing a list always reads data from the same XML file, whereas importing data lets you read data from a different XML file (as long as it follows the same mapping). You would use refreshing to ensure that your list always contains the latest data from a specific XML file, while you would use importing to obtain data from different XML files.

5. Click the Import button on the List and XML toolbar to display the Import XML dialog box.
6. Select the XML file to import, and click Import.

Once you have imported the XML data, you can work with the list as described in the following section.

# Working with XML Lists

Once you have an XML list in a workbook, what can you do with it? As mentioned earlier, XML data can be used just like any other worksheet data for formulas and charts. In addition, there are some special techniques for working with XML lists. They are explained in this section.

## XML List Properties

Each XML list in a workbook has a set of properties that control certain aspects of how the list works. You can access these properties in several ways:

- By clicking the Properties button in the Import XML dialog box when importing XML.
- By clicking the XML Map Properties button on the List and XML toolbar when the cell pointer is in the list.
- By choosing Data → XML → XML Map Properties when the cell pointer is in the list.

The XML Map properties dialog box is shown in Figure 8-11. Each list, or map, has its own set of independent properties. The name of the map is displayed in the Name field at the top of the dialog box. Other property settings are described in Table 8-1.

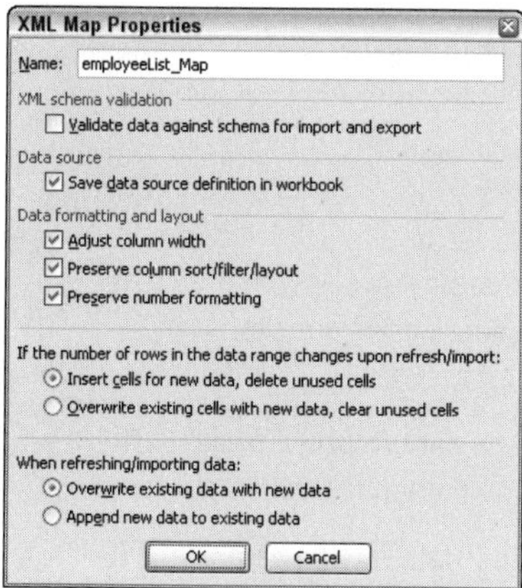


Figure 8-11. The XML Map Properties dialog box.

**TABLE 8-1 PROPERTY SETTINGS FOR AN XML MAP**

| Property | Description | Default Setting |
|---|---|---|
| Validate data against... | If selected, the XML data is validated against the associated schema during importing and exporting. See the section "XML Data Validation" for more details. | Off |
| Save data source definition... | If selected, the XML list remains linked to the XML data file and can be refreshed with new/changed data. If not selected, the link between the XML list and the XML data file is removed, meaning that the data becomes static and cannot be refreshed. | On |
| Adjust column width | When selected, column width is automatically adjusted to suit the table data. | On |
| Preserve column sort/filter/layout | When selected, the layout, filtering, and sort order of columns in the list are preserved. | On |
| Preserve number formatting | When selected, the formatting of numbers in the list is preserved. | On |
| Insert cells for new data... | When selected, new cells are inserted into the worksheet to accommodate new data during a refresh or import operation; existing worksheet data is not overwritten. | On |

*Continued*

**TABLE 8-1 PROPERTY SETTINGS FOR AN XML MAP** *(Continued)*

| Property | Description | Default Setting |
|---|---|---|
| Overwrite existing cells... | When selected, existing worksheet data is overwritten if there is not enough space for new data during a refresh/ import operation. | Off |
| Overwrite existing data with new data | If selected, then during a refresh new data returned from the XML data file overwrites existing data in the list. | On |
| Append new data to existing data | If selected, then during a refresh new data returned from the XML data file is appended at the end of existing data in the list. | Off |

Excel is inconsistent with terminology, and you'll find XML List and XML Map used to refer to the same thing.

# Formulas in Lists

Placing formulas in lists is a powerful technique supported by Excel. By putting a formula in a list, as opposed to somewhere else in the workbook, the result of the calculation can be exported with the other list data. This enables you to import XML data, use Excel formulas to perform calculations on the data, and then export the results of the calculations as XML for use by other programs.

In order to include a formula in an XML list, the list must contain an XML element with a data type that Excel interprets as a number, a date, or a time. You place the formula in that column of the list in the worksheet. As with any list, formulas are automatically filled in when new data rows are added. When you export the list, the result of the formula is included as the element's content.

To illustrate, I'll use a modification of the EmployeeList schema that was presented earlier in the chapter. The modification consists of adding an optional element named `<monthlySalary>`, which is data type float. The resulting map is shown in the XML Source task pane in Figure 8-12.

The schema was mapped to the worksheet by dragging the `<employee>` element from the XML Source task pane to cell A2. Then, the `Employees.xml` data file was imported into the map. At this point, the list looks like Figure 8-13. The `<monthlySalary>` column is empty because it is an optional element in the map and the `Employees.xml` file does not contain data for this element.

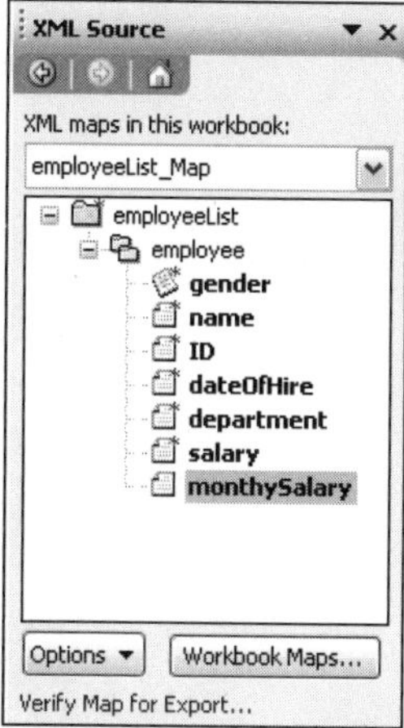


Figure 8-12: The modified EmployeeList map with the optional <monthlySalary> element.

| | A | B | C | D | E | F | G |
|---|---|---|---|---|---|---|---|
| 1 | | | | | | | |
| 2 | gender | name | ID | dateOfHire | department | salary | monthySalary |
| 3 | female | Wendy Smith | 78234 | 5/1/1998 | Sales | 34500 | |
| 4 | male | Arthur Jackson | 61439 | 6/1/1995 | Marketing | 54900 | |
| 5 | female | Carlotta Gomez | 73219 | 9/15/1996 | Sales | 48000 | |
| 6 | male | Wilson Anderson | 51432 | 10/1/2000 | IT | 31200 | |
| 7 | female | Elizabeth Poe Smith | 77812 | 12/1/1997 | Marketing | 43600 | |
| 8 | * | | | | | | |
| 9 | | | | | | | |
| 10 | | | | | | | |

Figure 8-13: After importing Employees.xml into the modified EmployeeList map.

The next step is to enter the formula `=F3/12` into cell G3 and then copy the formula to cells G4:G7. After formatting columns F and G as Currency, the worksheet looks like Figure 8-14.

| | A | B | C | D | E | F | G |
|---|---|---|---|---|---|---|---|
| 1 | | | | | | | |
| 2 | gender | name | ID | dateOfHire | department | salary | monthySalary |
| 3 | female | Wendy Smith | 78234 | 5/1/1998 | Sales | $34,500.00 | $ 2,875.00 |
| 4 | male | Arthur Jackson | 61439 | 6/1/1995 | Marketing | $54,900.00 | $ 4,575.00 |
| 5 | female | Carlotta Gomez | 73219 | 9/15/1996 | Sales | $48,000.00 | $ 4,000.00 |
| 6 | male | Wilson Anderson | 51432 | 10/1/2000 | IT | $31,200.00 | $ 2,600.00 |
| 7 | female | Elizabeth Poe Smith | 77812 | 12/1/1997 | Marketing | $43,600.00 | $ 3,633.33 |
| 8 | * | | | | | | |
| 9 | | | | | | | |
| 10 | | | | | | | |

Figure 8-14: The <monthlySalary> column contains a formula.

To verify that the formula results can be exported, you can export this list to an XML file (the details on how to export an XML list are covered in the next section). If you open the resulting XML file in a text editor, you can see that the data in the `<monthlySalary>` column has been included. Here's a snippet of XML data that shows one `<employee>` element from the exported XML file:

```
<ns1:employee gender="male">
  <ns1:name>Wilson Anderson</ns1:name>
  <ns1:ID>51432</ns1:ID>
  <ns1:dateOfHire>2000-10-01</ns1:dateOfHire>
  <ns1:department>IT</ns1:department>
  <ns1:salary>31200</ns1:salary>
  <ns1:monthySalary>2600</ns1:monthySalary>
</ns1:employee>
```

You are not limited to including formulas in the same list that contains the data that the formula will use. A formula in one list can make use of data in one or more other lists, as well as data from nonlist parts of the worksheet.

# Exporting an XML List

Excel lets you export a list to an XML file with some restrictions. The most important restriction has to do with how many levels are present in the XML map. The map shown in Figure 8-15, for example, is from the Booklist schema that you saw in Chapter 7. You can think of this map as having two levels because the `<firstname>` and `<lastname>` elements are children of the `<book>` element, which is in turn a child of the root element `<books>`. Put another way, if you start at the root element you have to go down two levels to get to the `<firstname>` and `<lastname>` elements. Excel refers to this kind of map – with two or more levels – as containing lists of lists, and they cannot be exported.

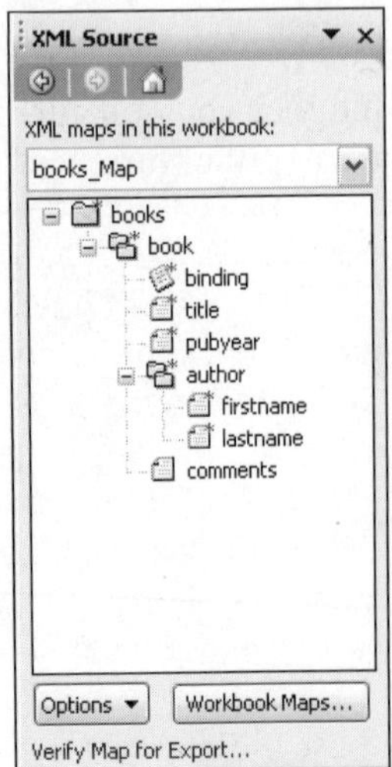


Figure 8-15: An XML map that contains two levels.

Compare this with the map shown in Figure 8-16. This second map contains the same elements as the first map but they are all on one level. This kind of map can be exported.

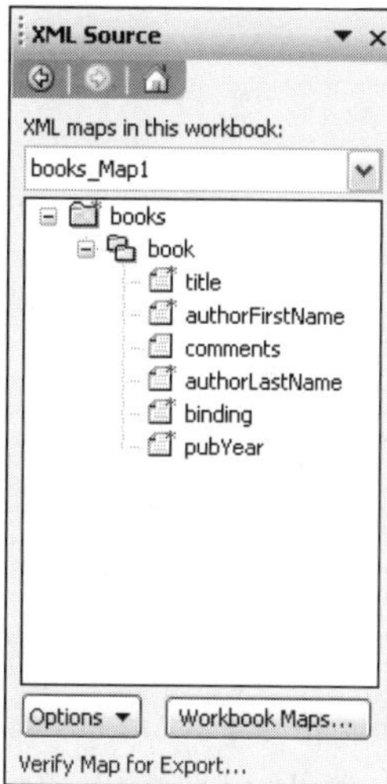


**Figure 8-16: An XML map that contains the same elements as the map in Figure 8-15 but on only one level.**

Why does Excel distinguish between single-level maps and multilevel maps when it comes to exporting the data? After all, Excel can import data from both kinds of maps. Here's what happens. When you import data using a multilevel map such as the one in Figure 8-15, Excel *flattens* the data. Each element in the map gets a column in the worksheet, but the information about the relative position of each element in the map is lost. For example, the fact that `<firstname>` is a child of `<author>` which is itself a child of `<book>` is lost. If the data were exported, its structure would not agree with the original map (schema), and this is why Excel does not permit it.

In contrast, when you open a single-level map such as the one shown in Figure 8-16 the data is already flat and no information about structure is lost when it is exported.

If you try to export an invalid map, Excel displays a dialog box with an explanation. You can also check a map in the XML Structure task pane. With the map displayed, click the Verify Map for Export command at the bottom of the task pane, and Excel tells you if it is valid for export or not and, if not, the reasons why the map is invalid.

There are two ways to export an XML map. The first requires that the cell pointer be in the map that you want to export. Then, select Data → XML → Export. If the map is valid for export, Excel displays the Export XML dialog box in which you select a destination and specify a name for the XML file.

The second method lets you export any XML map in the workbook without regard to the location of the cell pointer:

1. Choose File → Save As. Excel displays the Save As dialog box.
2. Select XML Data in the Save As Type list.
3. Enter a filename for the exported file and click Save.
4. XML displays a warning that saving the file as XML data will result in the loss of certain worksheet features. Click Continue to proceed to export the file.

These two methods are equivalent as to the XML file that is created. They differ as follows:

- After using the Export command, you continue working in the active workbook. Subsequent File → Save commands save the workbook with formatting and all changes.
- After using the Save As XML Data command, you are working in the XML data file and not the workbook. Subsequent File → Save commands save the data but not any formatting or other such elements you have added.

When you export XML data, Excel follows these rules:

- UTF-8 encoding is always used for the output file.
- Any use of the "http://www.w3.org/2001/XMLSchema-instance" namespace is deleted, including references to a schema file.
- All namespaces are defined in the root element.
- Existing namespace prefixes are overwritten with prefixes of ns0 for the default namespace and ns1, ns2, and so on for additional namespaces.
- Empty elements are created for blank cells that correspond to required elements but not for cells that correspond to optional elements.
- Comments are not preserved.

For example, Listing 8-3 shows an original XML data file before being imported into Excel, and Listing 8-4 shows the result of exporting this data from Excel.

**Listing 8-3: The Original XML Data File**

```
<?xml version="1.0" encoding="UTF-8"?>
<books xmlns="http://www.pgacon.com/flatbooklist"
  xmlns:xsi="http://www.w3.org/2001/XMLSchema-instance"
  xsi:schemaLocation="http://www.pgacon.com/flatbooklist
C:\XMLFiles\FlatBookList.xsd">
  <book>
    <title>Hamlet</title>
    <authorFirstName>William</authorFirstName>
    <authorLastName>Shakespeare</authorLastName>
    <binding>hardcover</binding>
    <pubYear>1995</pubYear>
    <comments>With commentary</comments>
  </book>
</books>
```

**Listing 8-4: The Exported XML Data File**

```
<?xml version="1.0" encoding="UTF-8" standalone="yes"?>
<ns1:books xmlns:ns1="http://www.pgacon.com/flatbooklist">
  <ns1:book>
    <ns1:title>Hamlet</ns1:title>
    <ns1:authorFirstName>William</ns1:authorFirstName>
    <ns1:authorLastName>Shakespeare</ns1:authorLastName>
    <ns1:binding>hardcover</ns1:binding>
    <ns1:pubYear>1995</ns1:pubYear>
    <ns1:comments>With commentary</ns1:comments>
  </ns1:book>
</ns1:books>
```

# Other List Commands

Excel has some additional commands for working with lists. They are accessed on the Data→List menu, and those commands that are relevant to XML lists are described in Table 8-2.

**TABLE 8-2 XML LIST COMMANDS**

| Command | Action |
|---|---|
| Resize List | Lets you specify a new size for the list. Excel automatically resizes a list as needed so you rarely need this command. |

*Continued*

**TABLE 8-2 XML LIST COMMANDS** *(Continued)*

| Command | Action |
|---|---|
| Convert to Range | Unlinks the list from its data source (XML file). |
| Total Row | Inserts a row at the bottom of the list with formulas that sum each column that contains numerical data. |
| Hide Border of Inactive Lists | Hides the border of inactive lists (lists that do not contain the cell pointer). Affects all lists in the workbook. |

# XML Data Validation

Excel can validate XML data against its schema when the data is imported and when the data is exported. Excel does not validate data as you work in the worksheet. For example, if you enter an invalid value in a cell of an XML list, it will not be caught and marked as invalid until you export the XML data.

Validation is controlled by the Validate Data Against Schema option in the XML Map Properties dialog box, as was covered earlier in this chapter. Each individual map in the workbook has its own set of properties, so you can enable validation for some maps and not for others. To validate data during import, you must set this option during the import process as was described earlier in the "Importing XML Data" section.

When Excel validates data during export, a validation error does not prevent the exporting from occurring. Rather, the invalid data is exported and Excel displays a message notifying you of the violation and explaining the nature of the problem. Figure 8-17 shows an example.

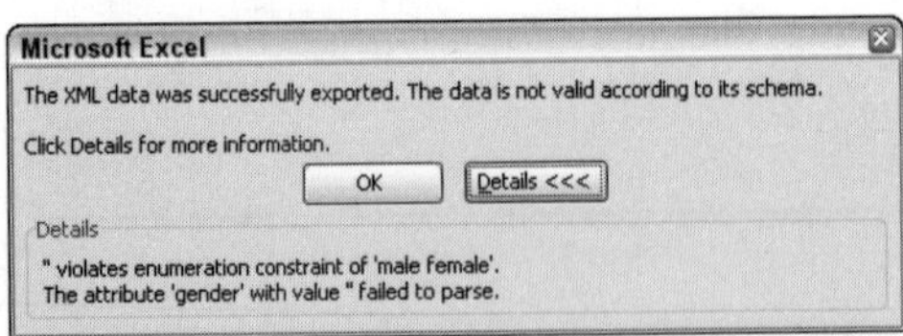


**Figure 8-17: Excel displays a message when data fails validation during export.**

You can use Excel's own data validation tools with XML data. These are completely separate from XML schema validation. Use the Data→Validation command to access these tools.

# Saving Workbooks as XML

Saving an Excel workbook as XML is entirely different from exporting data from an XML list or saving a mapping as XML data, procedures that were covered earlier in the chapter. When you save a workbook as XML, Excel uses a special XML vocabulary called XML Spreadsheet (XMLSS). XMLSS is designed to encompass essentially all the contents of a workbook, not just selected data. Its purpose is to enable you to save an entire workbook in XML format, permitting other programs to access the information in the workbook without having to be able to read Microsoft's proprietary WKS file format.

The XMLSS format saves most but not all aspects of a workbook contents. Content that is not retained includes

- Auditing trace arrows
- Charts and other graphics objects
- Macro sheets
- Dialog sheets
- Custom views
- Drawing object layers
- Outlining
- Scenarios
- Shared workbook information
- User-defined functions
- VBA projects

To save a workbook in XML Spreadsheet format:

1. Select File → Save As.
2. Select XML Spreadsheet in the Save as Type list.
3. Enter a name for the file.
4. Click Save.

After saving a workbook in XMLSS format, you can continue working in the program as usual. Subsequent File → Save commands continue to save the workbook in XMLSS format. To save again in standard Excel WKS format, you must issue the File → Save As command and select Microsoft Excel Workbook in the Save as Type list.

Chapter 9

# Access and XML

IN THIS CHAPTER

- Importing XML data
- Understanding Access and XML data types
- Exporting Access objects
- Understanding the ReportML vocabulary
- Examining export options

THERE ARE MANY PARALLELS between Access (or any database management program) and XML. After all, both are technologies for structuring and storing data. Fields in a database table have an obvious connection to elements and attributes in XML because both are used for storing data. Records in a database table are equivalent to repeating elements in an XML file. As this chapter explains, Access provides tools for both importing and exporting XML.

# Importing XML Data and Schemas

Access enables you to import both XML data and XML schemas to a database. You can import data into a new table or an existing table. When you import a schema, Access creates a new, empty table with the structure of the imported schema.

Access's XML import is limited to XML elements. Data in attributes is simply ignored. Attributes are also ignored when importing the structure of an XML file.

## XML Data and Tables

Access keeps all of its data in tables, and when importing XML data, Access looks for "tables" in the XML file. An XML file does not of course contain actual tables – what Access is looking for is data that is structured like a table and can be imported into one. In essence, this is a repeating element that is only one level deep. By "one level deep," I mean a repeating element and its child elements that contain data only. The following examples illustrate this.

The first example uses the `Employees.xml` data file that you were introduced to in Chapter 8. The structure of this file is shown in Figure 9-1; the file's one attribute is not shown because Access doesn't support attributes.

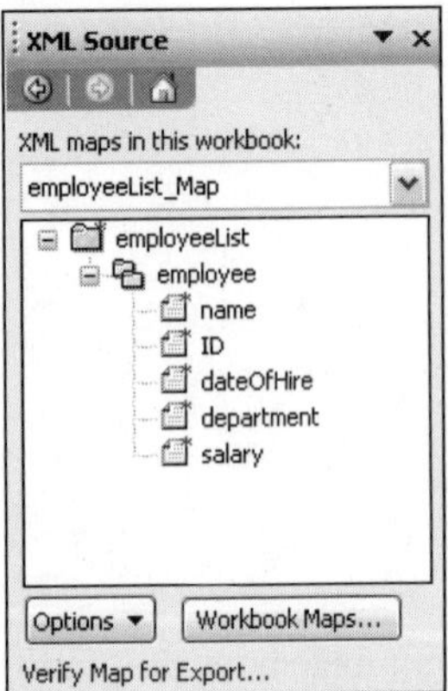


**Figure 9-1: The structure of the Employees.xml data file.**

You can see that this file has a root element named `<employeeList>`, which contains one repeating element named `<employee>`, which in turn has five child elements (`<name>`, `<ID>`, and so on). Each of the child elements holds data and none of them contains its own child elements. This structure is one level deep and Access would import it as a single table with five fields.

In contrast, Figure 9-2 shows the structure of the `MyBooks.xml` data file that you first saw in Chapter 7, "Word and XML."

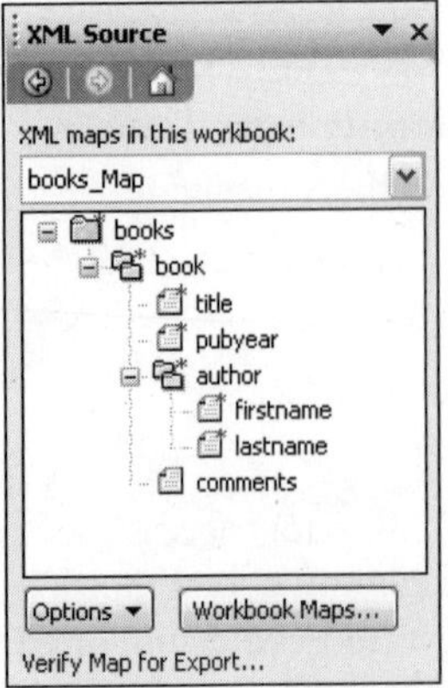


**Figure 9-2: The structure of the MyBooks.xml data file.**

This structure is not one level deep because the `<book>` element contains the child element `<author>`, which has its own child elements. There are two levels in this structure and therefore Access cannot import it as a single table. Rather, Access sees this file as containing two tables:

- A "book" table with the fields title, pubyear, and comments.
- An "author" table with the fields firstname and lastname.

When you import data from a file that contains multiple tables such as `MyBooks.xml`, Access always imports all the tables in the file. You can later delete unneeded tables from Access if desired.

# Importing Data

To import data from an XML file, follow these steps:

1. Choose File → Get External Data → Import. Access displays the Import dialog box.
2. Select XML in the Files of Type list.
3. Select the desired XML file and click Import. Access displays the Import XML dialog box with the file's tables listed, as shown in Figure 9-3. You can examine the structure of the file by expanding nodes in the Tables tree, but you cannot choose what to import because Access always imports the entire file.
4. Click the Options button to display the import options (shown in Figure 9-3). Make a selection as follows:
   - Select the Structure Only option to create a new, empty table based on the structure of the XML file.
   - Select the Structure and Data option to import the XML data into a new table (or tables, depending on the file structure).
   - Select the Append Data to Existing Table(s) option to append imported data to existing tables.
5. If you want to apply a transform to the data when it is imported, click the Transform button and select the transform in the dialog box that appears.
6. Click OK. Access imports the data and displays a message when the process is completed.

## Imported but Not Linked

It's important to realize that when you import XML data into Access it is not linked to the original XML file. This is different from Excel in which an imported XML list remains linked to the XML file and can be refreshed with new data with a single command. The only way to "refresh" a table that contains imported XML data is to repeat the import process. Access can link a table to various external data sources, but links to XML files are not supported.

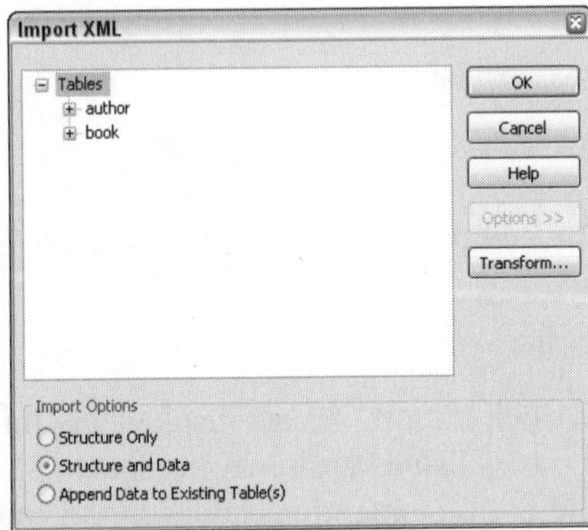


Figure 9-3: Importing XML data into Access.

When you select the Append Data to Existing Table(s) option, Access compares the structure of the table(s) being imported with tables that already exist in the database. If a match is found, the data is appended to that table. If no match is found, the data is placed in a new table. Tables are named according to the name of the XML element being imported. If the name is already in use, a number is appended to the name.

# Importing Structure

When you import an XML structure into Access you are not importing any data. Access reads the structure of the XML file and creates one or more new, empty tables in the database based on the XML structure. You can import structure from an XML data file or from an XML schema. To import XML structure:

1. Choose File → Get External Data → Import. Access displays the Import dialog box.
2. Select XML in the Files of Type list.
3. Select the desired XML file or XSD schema file and click Import. Access displays the Import XML dialog box with the file's tables listed.

4. If you selected an XML file in Step 3, click the Options button and select the Structure Only option. If you selected an XSD schema this is not necessary.
5. Click OK. Access imports the structure and displays a message when the process is completed.

## Access and XML Data Types

Access has different data types that can be assigned to fields in a table. Access's data types are similar to but not identical to the data types available in XML. When importing data or structure from XML, data types are handled as follows:

- When you import data from an XML file into a new table, all fields in the table are assigned the Text data type.
- When you import structure from an XML data file, all fields in the new table are assigned the Text data type.
- When you import structure from an XSD schema file, each field in the new table is assigned the Access data type that most closely matches the data type specified in the schema.

After importing data or a table structure, you can always use Access's table design mode to change the data type of fields. Of course, if the table contains data, the data type changes you make must be consistent with that data.

# Exporting Access Objects to XML

When discussing Access's capabilities for exporting XML data, it's important to have an understanding of Microsoft's primary motivation for including these in the program. Otherwise, you may find it strange that Access's XML export capabilities are designed the way they are.

Exporting XML from Access is a lot more than simply making data from an Access database available to other programs that can read XML. You can do this, of course, but that's only a small part of the story. More important is the fact that the data in a database is not of much use unless it can be viewed and perhaps edited. Much of Access itself is devoted to these tasks. Access forms, reports, queries, PivotTables, and PivotCharts (all considered Access objects) are designed specifically to present a database's raw data into a usable form. These Access front-end components are powerful and flexible but have the significant shortcoming that the users must have Access installed on their system. Although Microsoft Office is widespread, most Office installations are the Standard edition, which doesn't include Access. As of this writing, it isn't known whether Microsoft will follow this same pattern for distributing Office 2003, but in any case it, remains true that many users whom you might want to be able to view the data won't have Access installed.

> ### Statelessness and the Web
>
> The Web is by its very nature stateless, with each request for an HTML page being totally independent of anything that happened before or will happen after. Certain Web-based applications, such as online catalog purchases, require that some state information be maintained throughout the duration of a user's interaction with the Web site. At the server side of things, programmers have devised methods, such as a Session.State object maintained by Web server software, to keep track of individuals as they move from page to page on the Web site. On the client side, cookies are used by many Web sites to store user information. When a Web site "remembers" who you are a month after your last visit, for example, the state information is being stored in a cookie.

The solution that Microsoft decided on was to use a Web browser for the front end. Essentially every computer has a Web browser installed, and it is Internet Explorer on an increasingly large number of systems. Since IE is a free download, software availability ceases to be an issue. By making it possible to view and edit Jet or SQL Server data in Internet Explorer, Microsoft has greatly simplified the task of the Access developer.

An added advantage of this approach is that a browser-based application is, if properly designed, *stateless*. This means that each operation does not depend on the outcome of the previous operation, and the server does not have to "remember" the status, or state, of each user. As a result, the front-end application does not have to maintain a connection to the server throughout a session, reducing the load on the server hardware and software.

In broad outline, here's how browser-based database front-end applications work: the user opens the application in his or her browser, the Web server establishes a connection to the back-end database and retrieves the requested data, and the server encodes the data as HTML and returns it to the user for viewing in the browser. If the application permits editing of the data, the new or modified data is returned from the browser to the Web server, which in turn posts the changes to the database. XML is an essential part of Access's support for browser-based front ends, including Data Access Pages.

## Sample Data

When exploring a new technology it is always useful to have sample data to work with. For Access, Microsoft provides the Northwind database that includes a selection of tables, queries, forms, and reports that you can use. This database comes in two versions: `Northwind.mdb` is an Access application that uses the Jet database engine. `NorthwindCS.adp` is an Access data project that uses Microsoft SQL Server (which must be installed or available on a remote server). The examples in this section use Northwind data and objects.

## Data Access Pages and XML

A Data Access Page (DAP) is a browser-based front end that lets users view and work with data in an Access or SQL Server database. Access provides tools for designing Data Access Pages and also permits reports, queries, and tables to be saved directly as Data Access Pages (with some limitations). XML is involved in the creation of Data Access Pages, but in a behind-the-scenes manner that is invisible to the user. For this reason, Data Access Pages are not covered in this book. Exporting objects as XML provides more flexibility than a Data Access Page, as you'll see in the following sections.

To avoid changing the original sample database, I recommend that you copy the MDB or ADP file from its original folder (Samples under the Office installation folder) to another location and use the copy.

# The ReportML Vocabulary

ReportML is an XML vocabulary designed for representing Access objects (tables, reports, queries, and so forth) as XML data. ReportML represents these objects in complete detail, storing every property and value in the object regardless of whether that property or value is needed by whatever task the ReportML is being generated for. When you export XML objects from Access, the first thing that Access does is generate a ReportML file for the Access object being exported. The ReportML file is then used in the next step, which is generating the final output files that are used to provide the browser-based front-end to the Access data (as will be covered in detail soon). When this step is complete, the ReportML file is no longer needed and is deleted by default. If you're interested, it can be instructive to examine a ReportML file to see the way in which an Access object is represented in XML. For example, Listing 9-1 shows the first couple of dozen lines of the ReportML file that is created when exporting the Catalog report from the Northwind database. The entire file is almost 2,000 lines long, which is not too surprising when you consider the amount of information that needs to be represented for an Access report.

**Listing 9-1: Portion of an Access-Generated ReportXM File**

```
<?xml version="1.0" encoding="UTF-8"?>
<RPTML version="1.0">
<SYSTEM-SETTINGS>
<LOCALE>1033</LOCALE>
</SYSTEM-SETTINGS>
<REPORT reportid="Catalog">
<TITLE>Catalog</TITLE>
<DESCRIPTION></DESCRIPTION>
<LAYOUT>absolute</LAYOUT>
<OBJECT-TYPE>report</OBJECT-TYPE>
```

```
<VLINK>#800080</VLINK>
<LINK>#0000ff</LINK>
<PRINTER-ROW-SPACING>0</PRINTER-ROW-SPACING>
<PRINTER-PRINT-QUALITY>300</PRINTER-PRINT-QUALITY>
<PRINTER-ORIENTATION>portrait</PRINTER-ORIENTATION>
<PRINTER-PORT>Microsoft Document Imaging Writer Port:</PRINTER-PORT>
<PRINTER-PAPER-SIZE>letter</PRINTER-PAPER-SIZE>
<PRINTER-PAPER-BIN>form source</PRINTER-PAPER-BIN>

<PRINTER-ITEM-SIZE-WIDTH>9363</PRINTER-ITEM-SIZE-WIDTH>

<PRINTER-DEFAULT-SIZE>true</PRINTER-DEFAULT-SIZE>
<PRINTER-ITEM-SIZE-HEIGHT>0</PRINTER-ITEM-SIZE-HEIGHT>
<PRINTER-ITEMS-ACROSS>1</PRINTER-ITEMS-ACROSS>
<PRINTER-ITEM-LAYOUT>horizontal column layout</PRINTER-ITEM-LAYOUT>
<PRINTER-DUPLEX>simplex</PRINTER-DUPLEX>
<PRINTER-DRIVER-NAME>Microsoft Office Document Image Writer Driver
  </PRINTER-DRIVER-NAME>
<PRINTER-DEVICE-NAME>Microsoft Office Document Image Writer
  </PRINTER-DEVICE-NAME>
<PRINTER-DATA-ONLY>false</PRINTER-DATA-ONLY>
<PRINTER-COPIES>1</PRINTER-COPIES>
<PRINTER-COLUMN-SPACING>360</PRINTER-COLUMN-SPACING>
<PRINTER-COLOR-MODE>monochrome</PRINTER-COLOR-MODE>
<USE-DEFAULT-PRINTER>true</USE-DEFAULT-PRINTER>
<FETCH-DEFAULTS>true</FETCH-DEFAULTS>
<MOVEABLE>true</MOVEABLE>
<ALLOW-DESIGN-CHANGES>false</ALLOW-DESIGN-CHANGES>
<DIR>left-to-right</DIR>
<HAS-MODULE>false</HAS-MODULE>
<TIMER-INTERVAL>0</TIMER-INTERVAL>
<KEY-PREVIEW>false</KEY-PREVIEW>
<PALETTE-SOURCE>(Default)</PALETTE-SOURCE>
```

If you want to examine the ReportML files, you must tell Access not to delete them. This is accomplished by adding the following entry to the Windows registry:

```
HKEY_CURRENT_USER\Software\Microsoft\Office\11.0\Access\ReportML
```

If you aren't familiar with using RegEdit to edit the registry, you can insert this key into the registry as follows:

1. Use a text editor to create a file with the contents shown in Listing 9-2.
2. Save the file under any name you like and with the .reg extension.

3. Close the text editor.
4. Locate the file in Windows Explorer and double-click it.
5. When prompted as to whether you want to add the information to the registry, click Yes.

With this registry entry in place, the ReportML files that Access creates will not be deleted. After you perform an export operation (as will be described soon), you can find and open the ReportML file to examine its contents. These files are given the name `object_report.xml` where *object* is the name of the Access object you exported.

**Listing 9-2: The Registration Entry File**

```
Windows Registry Editor Version 5.00

[HKEY_CURRENT_USER\Software\Microsoft\Office\11.0\Access\ReportML]
```

You can view an XML file in any text editor, but if you have Internet Explorer version 5 or later, you may prefer to use it. IE has a default style sheet for displaying XML that uses color-coding and indentation to make the XML easier to read. Of course, you can't edit the XML in IE.

How does Access use the ReportML file to create the final exported XML objects? The answer lies in two XSL transforms:

- `RPT2DAP.XSL` generates the final HTML page from the ReportML page when you are creating a Data Access Page.
- `RPT2HTM4.XSL` generates the requested output files from the ReportML file when you are exporting XML objects.

Both of these XSL files are located in the `Office11\AccessWeb` folder. As you might expect, they are quite complex. You can open them and examine their workings if you desire, but I do not recommend changing them unless you know XSLT well and are sure of what you are doing (and always keep a backup copy!). It is possible to tweak these transforms to modify the output that is created when creating Data Access Pages or exporting XML objects, but only advanced XSLT users should attempt that.

As of this writing, Microsoft warns Access users that the `RPT2HTM4.XSL` transform is "a sample" and that applications created with it — that is, browser-based front ends created by exporting XML objects — should be thoroughly tested. In my opinion, any application should be thoroughly tested, but this warning may be a good reason to take extra care.

# Export Basics

This section explains the basics of exporting XML objects from Access. The following sections deal with the various export options that are available and explain how to make use of the exported files. You can export tables, queries, forms, and reports as follows:

1. In the Access project window, right-click the object you want to export and select Export from the pop-up menu. Access displays the Export dialog box.
2. Select XML in the Save as Type list.
3. Select a destination folder for the exported files; the default is the folder where the database file (MDB or ADP) is located.
4. Enter a name for the exported files, or accept the default suggested by Access, which is the name of the Access object being exported. Do not include an extension because Access adds it automatically.
5. Click Export. Access displays the Export XML dialog box, shown in Figure 9-4. Select the information to be exported from the following:
   - **Data (XML).** Exports an XML file containing the object's data.
   - **Schema of the data (XSD).** Exports the data schema as a separate XSD file.
   - **Presentation of your data (XSL).** Exports HTML and XSL files for data presentation.

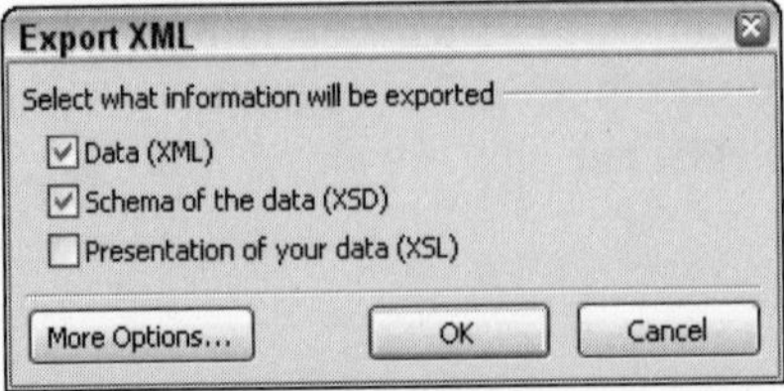


**Figure 9-4: You select what to export in the Export XML dialog box.**

6. Click the More Options button to set advanced export options (explained in the next section).
7. Click OK. Access performs the export operation.

You can also display the Export dialog box by opening the object you want to export and then selecting Export from the File menu. You must use this technique if you want to apply a sort or filter to the object that will be reflected in the exported data.

To see how this process works and what the results look like, you can use a report in the Northwind database. Open the database and display the Reports section of the project dialog box, as shown in Figure 9-5.

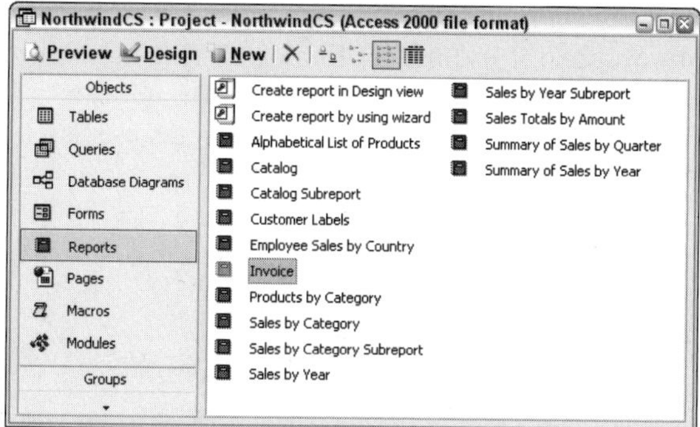


**Figure 9-5: Selecting a report in the Project dialog box.**

Double-click Invoice to see what the Invoice report looks like in Access. Figure 9-6 shows part of the report.

When you have finished viewing the report, close it. Then, follow the steps outlined above to export this report as XML. In Step 5, select all three options. When the process is complete, the following files will be in the folder where the Northwind database file is located:

- `Invoice.htm`
- `Invoice.xml`
- `Invoice.xsd`
- `Invoice.xsl`

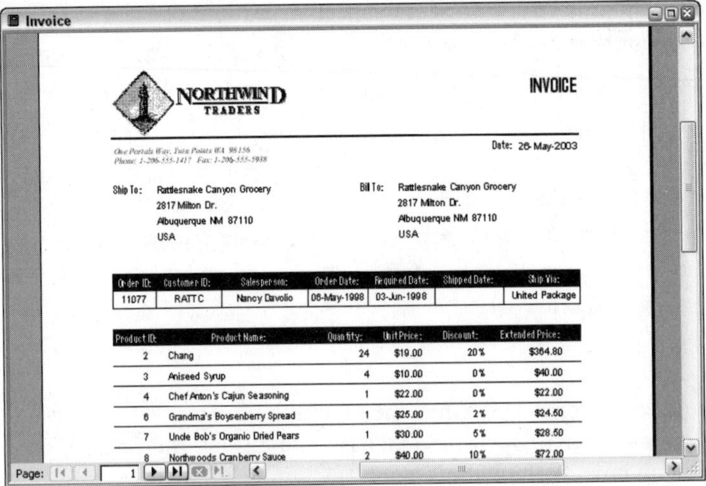


Figure 9-6: Viewing the Invoice report in Access.

Double-click the file Invoice.htm to open it in Internet Explorer. (This may take a moment or two, for reasons that will be explained later.) The file appears as shown in Figure 9-7. Compare this to the same report displayed in Access as shown in Figure 9-6. They are essentially identical.

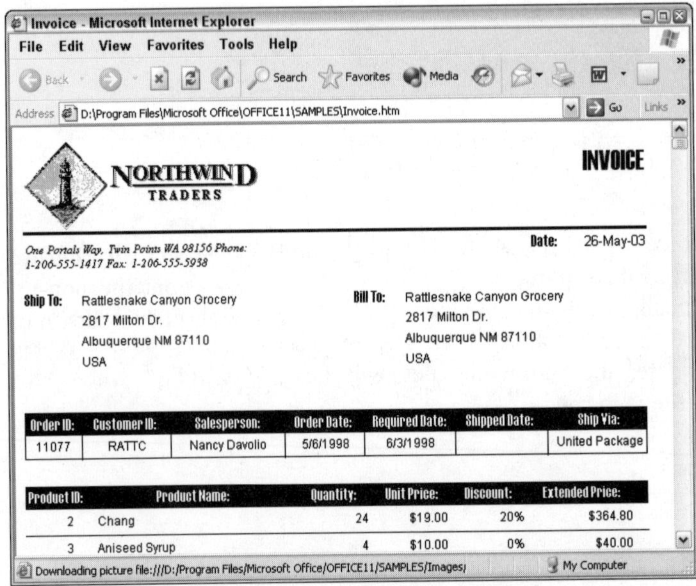


Figure 9-7: Viewing the exported Invoice report in Internet Explorer.

The next section explains how this works.

## AN ANALYSIS

To make the most effective use of Access's XML export capabilities, you should understand how the exported files enable the user to view the report in the browser. It will help if you have some understanding of HTML, VBScript, and the inner workings of Internet Explorer, but that's not really necessary.

Start with the `Invoice.html` file displayed in Internet Explorer, then select Source from IE's View menu. IE will start the Notepad application and display the raw HTML that is behind the report presented in the browser. Figure 9-8 shows the first few lines of this HTML (it is a very long file). If you browse through this file and have some knowledge of HTML, you can see that it is a standard if rather complicated HTML file.

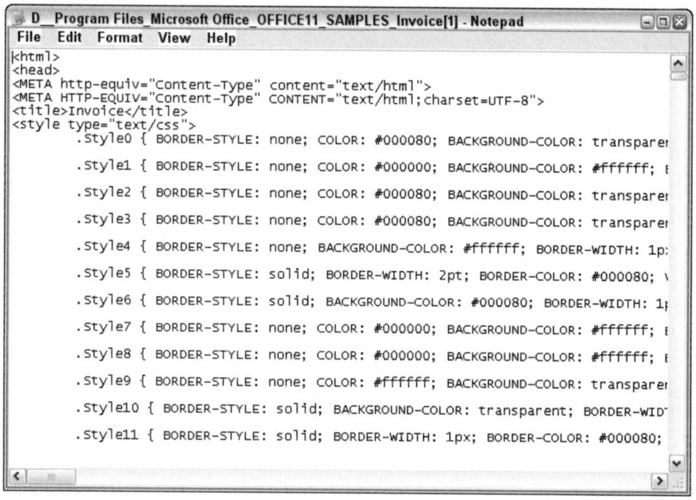

```
D_Program Files_Microsoft Office_OFFICE11_SAMPLES_Invoice[1] - Notepad
File  Edit  Format  View  Help
<html>
<head>
<META http-equiv="Content-Type" content="text/html">
<META HTTP-EQUIV="Content-Type" CONTENT="text/html;charset=UTF-8">
<title>Invoice</title>
<style type="text/css">
        .Style0 { BORDER-STYLE: none; COLOR: #000080; BACKGROUND-COLOR: transpare
        .Style1 { BORDER-STYLE: none; COLOR: #000000; BACKGROUND-COLOR: #ffffff;
        .Style2 { BORDER-STYLE: none; COLOR: #000080; BACKGROUND-COLOR: transpare
        .Style3 { BORDER-STYLE: none; COLOR: #000080; BACKGROUND-COLOR: transpare
        .Style4 { BORDER-STYLE: none; BACKGROUND-COLOR: #ffffff; BORDER-WIDTH: 1p
        .Style5 { BORDER-STYLE: solid; BORDER-WIDTH: 2pt; BORDER-COLOR: #000080;
        .Style6 { BORDER-STYLE: solid; BACKGROUND-COLOR: #000080; BORDER-WIDTH: 1
        .Style7 { BORDER-STYLE: none; COLOR: #000000; BACKGROUND-COLOR: #ffffff;
        .Style8 { BORDER-STYLE: none; COLOR: #000000; BACKGROUND-COLOR: #ffffff;
        .Style9 { BORDER-STYLE: none; COLOR: #ffffff; BACKGROUND-COLOR: transpare
        .Style10 { BORDER-STYLE: solid; BACKGROUND-COLOR: transparent; BORDER-WID
        .Style11 { BORDER-STYLE: solid; BORDER-WIDTH: 1px; BORDER-COLOR: #000080;
```

**Figure 9-8: Viewing the HTML behind the browser display of the Invoices report.**

Next, use Windows Explorer to locate the Invoice.htm file that was created during the export process. Right-click the filename, select Open With from the pop-up menu, and then select Notepad from the next menu. The text of this file is shown in Listing 9-3.

**Listing 9-3: Contents of the Invoice.htm File**

```
<HTML xmlns:signature="urn:schemas-microsoft-com:office:access">
<HEAD>
<META HTTP-EQUIV="Content-Type" CONTENT="text/html;charset=UTF-8"/>
</HEAD>
<BODY ONLOAD="ApplyTransform()">
</BODY>
<SCRIPT LANGUAGE="VBScript">
  Option Explicit
```

```
Function ApplyTransform()
  Dim objData, objStyle

  Set objData = CreateDOM
  LoadDOM objData, "Invoice.xml"

  Set objStyle = CreateDOM
  LoadDOM objStyle, "Invoice.xsl"

  Document.Open "text/html","replace"
  Document.Write objData.TransformNode(objStyle)
End Function

Function CreateDOM()
  On Error Resume Next
  Dim tmpDOM

  Set tmpDOM = Nothing
  Set tmpDOM = CreateObject("MSXML2.DOMDocument.5.0")
  If tmpDOM Is Nothing Then
    Set tmpDOM = CreateObject("MSXML2.DOMDocument.4.0")
  End If
  If tmpDOM Is Nothing Then
    Set tmpDOM = CreateObject("MSXML.DOMDocument")
  End If

  Set CreateDOM = tmpDOM
End Function

Function LoadDOM(objDOM, strXMLFile)
  objDOM.Async = False
  objDOM.Load strXMLFile
  If (objDOM.ParseError.ErrorCode <> 0) Then
    MsgBox objDOM.ParseError.Reason
  End If
End Function

</SCRIPT>
</HTML>
```

You'll notice immediately that this text is completely different from the HTML source that you viewed in IE (see Figure 9-8). Shouldn't they be the same? Not necessarily – here's how it works.

When a user opens Invoice.htm in Internet Explorer, the text shown in Listing 9-3 is loaded. This file consists mostly of VBScript, which IE executes when it loads the file. The script makes use of a software component called the Document Object Model, or DOM, that is part of the Internet Explorer installation. The DOM provides tools for working with XML – in this case, specifically the ability to apply a transform to XML data and output the data. Here's what happens when Internet Explorer loads `Invoice.htm`. You can follow this in the script code if you are familiar with VBScript.

1. IE loads the XML data from Invoice.XML into the DOM software component.
2. IE loads the transform instructions from Invoice.xsl into the same DOM software component.
3. The transform is applied to the XML data and the result of the transform, which is the HTML code that was shown in Figure 9-8, is displayed in the browser.

It's the third step that is mostly responsible for the apparently slow loading of `Invoice.htm` into the browser. A lot more is going on than just loading HTML into the browser – the entire process of performing the transform must be done as well, and for large data sets with complex transforms, this can take a while.

What about the XSD file that is generated, `Invoice.xsd` in this example? It is referenced in the `Invoice.xml` file as the schema for the data and is used during the transform process to provide information about how the data should be interpreted.

This method of exporting XML objects for browser-based data presentation offers significant flexibility. Once the files are in place and accessible to the users (via the Internet, an intranet, or a shared server), you need only regenerate the XML data file to update the data. Also, if you are conversant with XSL, you can modify the transformation to create a different output, perhaps altering some aspects of the report's appearance or layout.

## SPEEDING THINGS UP

One advantage of this method of providing browser-based data viewing is that it is easy to update the data by regenerating the XML data file. The data that the user actually sees is generated on the fly from this XML data by the transform. This can be a liability as well, however. As you have seen, the transform process can take some time, and if the XML data has not changed, the output of the transform, and therefore what the user sees, will be the same each time. Why make each user wait for the slow transform process to complete each time the data is viewed? If the data changes infrequently, as would be the case for a weekly or monthly report, you can run the transform only when the data changes and make the transform output directly available to the users. There are various non-Office tools available for running transforms, but even without these tools you can do this. Here are the steps required. I'm using the filenames from the Invoice example, but the steps would be the same in any case.

1. Generate the XML, XSD, XSL, and HTM export files as described earlier.
2. Change the name of Invoice.htm to something else such as InvoiceOriginal.htm (do not change the extension).
3. Open the renamed file from Step 2 in Internet Explorer. The transform will be executed.
4. In IE, use the View → Source command to view the transform output in Notepad.
5. In Notepad, use the File → Save As command to save the HTML code under the original name `Invoice.htm`.

After you perform these steps, users opening `Invoice.htm` in their browser will get the already transformed text – there's no need to run the time-consuming transform and the page loads a lot faster. Whenever the data behind the report changes, repeat these steps to generate the changed `Invoice.htm` file.

With some databases Access lets you publish live data to the Web in which data updates are performed automatically and do not require manual updating (re-exporting) of the XML data file. This is covered later in this chapter.

# XML Export Options

When you are exporting XML data, the Export XML dialog box (shown earlier in Figure 9-4) has a More Options button that you click to set advanced export options. The options are related to the three types of XML objects you can export: data, schema, and presentation. Each group of options is on its own tab in the dialog box that is displayed when you click the More Options button. When you have finished setting options, click the OK button to perform the exporting.

## DATA EXPORT OPTIONS

Data export options control the data that is exported, that is, the data that's exported to the *object*`.xml` file. These options are set on the Data tab, which is shown in Figure 9-9. They're explained in Table 9-1.

**TABLE 9-1 XML DATA EXPORT OPTIONS**

| Option | Description |
|---|---|
| Export data | Select this option to export the object's data as an XML file. This is the same as the Data (XML) option in the previous dialog box. |

| Option | Description |
|---|---|
| Data to export | If the object being exported has subsections, you can choose to export the entire object or just part of its data. |
| All records | Select this option to export all the object's records to XML. |
| Apply existing filter | If the object is open and a filter is applied, select this option to export only those records selected by the filter. |
| Current record | If the object is open and a record is current, select this option to export only that record. |
| Apply existing sort | If the object is open and a sort is applied, select this option to export the data in the specified order. |
| Transforms | Click this button to select an XSL transform to apply to the data during export. |
| Encoding | Select UTF-8 or UTF-16 encoding for the exported XML. You should use the default UTF-8 unless you have a specific reason to use UTF-16. |
| Live data | Select this option to export live data. This option is not available for all types of Access databases. See the "Exporting Live Data" section later in this chapter for more information. |
| Export location | Specify the name and location for the exported XML file. |

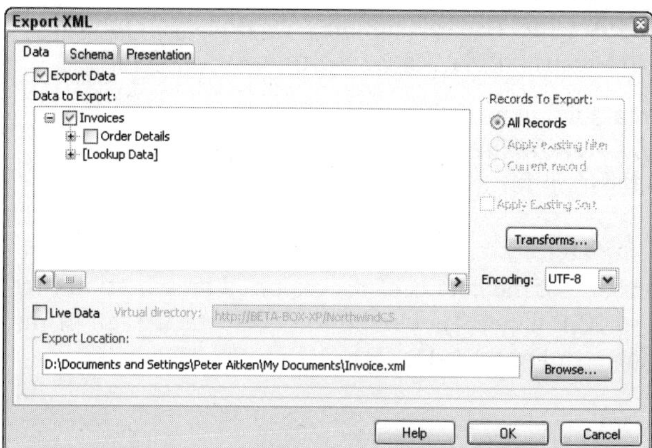


Figure 9-9: Setting data export options.

### SCHEMA EXPORT OPTIONS

The schema export options control the way that the Access object's schema is exported. They are set on the Schema tab of the dialog box, as shown in Figure 9-10.

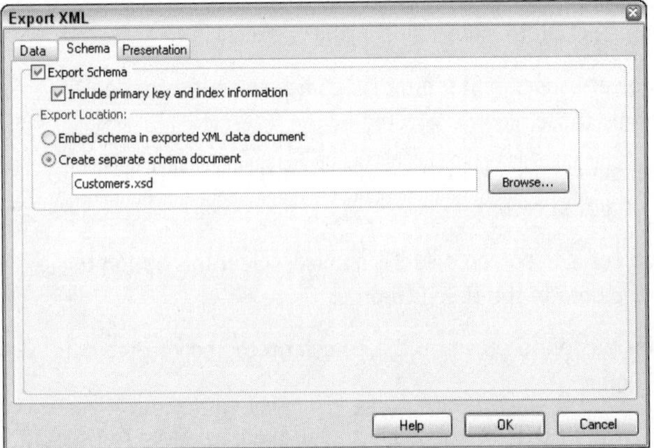


Figure 9-10: Setting schema export options.

The options in the Export XML dialog box are as follows:

- **Export schema.** Select this option to export the object's schema as an XSD file. This is the same as the Schema of the Data (XSD) option in the previous dialog box.
- **Include primary key and index information.** Select this option to include the object's key and index information in the schema.
- **Embed schema in exported XML document.** Select this option to embed the schema in the XML data file. Use this option only when you have a specific reason to do so because it may cause the transform to fail.
- **Create separate schema document.** Select this option to save the schema in a separate XSD file. Enter the filename and use the Browse button to specify the name and location for this file.

### PRESENTATION EXPORT OPTIONS

The presentation export options determine details of the exported presentation files (the XSL transform and HTM or ASP page). They're on the Presentation tab of the Export XML dialog box, as shown in Figure 9-11.

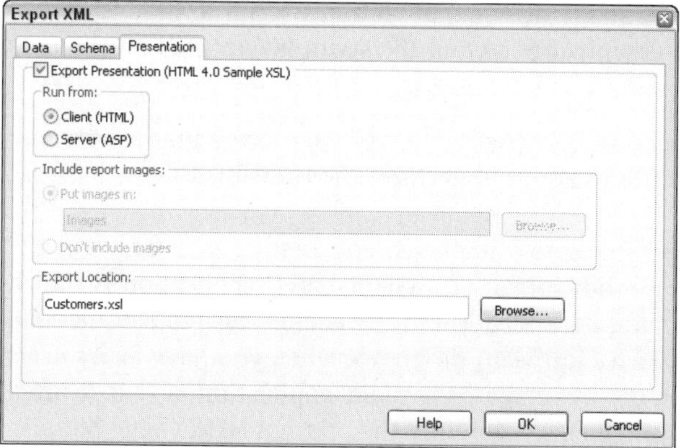


Figure 9-11: Setting presentation export options.

Here's an explanation of the available options:

- **Export Presentation.** Select this option to export the object's presentation as XSL and HTM/ASP files file. This is the same as the Presentation of Your Data (XSL) option in the previous dialog box.
- **Run From.** Choose whether you want the presentation to run on the client or the server. There's more information about this in the next section, "Client versus Server."
- **Include Report Images.** These options are available only if the object being exported contains images. If you choose to include images, they are exported as separate image files, which are then linked to from the HTML file. By default, these files are placed in the `Images` folder off the main export folder. If you want them placed elsewhere you can specify the location.
- **Export Location.** Specify the name and location of the export files.

## Client versus Server

When you are creating a browser-based front end using XML export, you have the option of creating an application that runs on the client or one that runs on the server. You select the type of application to create on the Presentation tab when setting XML Export options (see Figure 9-11). The example presented earlier in the chapter was client-based. Here are the primary differences:

- **Client.** Access produces an HTML file that contains script to perform the transform; this file is downloaded to and the script is executed on the client machine.
- **Server.** Access produces an ASP (Active Server Page) page that resides on the server. This file contains script to perform the transform.

There are trade-offs between these two methods, and neither is better than the other in all situations. The major advantage of a client-based application is that it offloads the process of performing the transform to the client. This reduces the load on the server, and that can make a significant difference when you have many users accessing the application. The disadvantage of a client application is that it often increases the downloading requirements – not only the original HTML page but also the XML data file, the XSL transform file, and, in some cases, the XSD schema file must be downloaded to the client. In contrast, a server-based application requires only that the final generated HTML be downloaded to the client. You make the choice based on the details of your situation and your server configuration.

## XML Exporting versus HTML Exporting

Access offers an HTML export feature that directly creates a Web page containing an Access object such as a report. This is simpler and less resource-intensive than exporting a static XML application as has been described, mainly because the XML does not have to be transformed into HTML each time a user accesses the application. In the real world, for instance, the export example that I presented earlier in this chapter would probably be better done using HTML exporting instead of XML exporting.

When would you prefer XML exporting over HTML exporting for static objects? Perhaps the most common situation is when you have an automated process that updates the XML data file. There's no reason why this file has to originate in the Access export process. Once the original export file set has been created, you can create the XML data file any way you want as long as it has the correct structure. For example, you could create a script that gets data from the database and writes out an updated XML data file, and then schedule the script to run once per week.

To export an object as HTML, follow the same procedure as is used for exporting an object as XML but, in the Export dialog box, select HTML Documents in the Save as Type list.

## Exporting Live Data

The export techniques that you have seen so far are for exporting static data. In other words, the exported object is not automatically updated when the data in the database changes – you must re-export the XML data file to make new or changed data available to the application. Access also has the ability to export browser-based front-end applications that are live and automatically reflect changes to the underlying data in the database.

Exporting live data is supported only by Access data projects that connect to an SQL Server database.

Exporting live data works by establishing a connection to the database each time a user logs on to the application. In other words, rather then getting its data from a static XML file that was exported from the database at some time in the past, a live application establishes a connection to the back-end database – that is, SQL Server – and gets the most recent data. You'll see this if you compare the HTML file generated for a static application with one generated for a live application. Here are the two lines of VBScript code from the static application that load the `Invoices.xml` file into the DOM for subsequent processing by the transform:

```
Set objData = CreateDOM
LoadDOM objData, "Invoice.xml"
```

Now, look at the equivalent code from a live application (the last three lines are actually a single line split to fit on the page):

```
Set objData = CreateDOM
LoadDOM objData, "http://localhost/NorthwindCS?
  sql=SELECT+*+FROM+%22dbo%22%2E%22Invoices
  %22+for+xml+auto,elements&root=dataroot"
```

The code does the same thing, loading the XML data so that it can be transformed, but the second example gets the latest data directly from the database server. You needn't worry about the details of this statement because Access creates it for you. It contains details about the computer that the database server is on, the name of the database, and the details of what data to retrieve.

To create a live front end, check the Live Data option on the Data tab when setting XML Export options. The Live Data option is displayed in this dialog box only if the Access database that you are exporting from supports live data XML export. In the adjacent Virtual Directory field, you must enter the URL of the folder on the server that the export process is to use.

If you select the Live Data option, you must export the entire Access object and cannot select part of it for export in the Data to Export box. Also, Live Data does not permit you to apply a transform during export.

## Deploying Your Application

When you export a static Access object, the application is self-contained because it does not depend on anything outside of the exported files. To deploy the project on the Internet or an intranet, all you need to do is copy these files to a folder on your Web server. This could be the root Web folder, but more often it's a virtual folder created specially for the application. Please see the documentation for your Web server software for details on folder locations and the steps required to create a virtual folder.

A live-export object is self-contained except that it must be able to contact the database server. You publish a live application in the same way as a static application, placing it in a folder on your Web server. The server, of course, must support ASP pages.

A static application does not need to be published to a Web server. It can be made available over a LAN by placing the file set in a publicly available folder and directing users to open the HTML file from that folder.

Remember that users need Internet Explorer version 5 or later to view these applications.

Chapter 10

# FrontPage and XML

IN THIS CHAPTER

- Editing XML in FrontPage
- Using Web Parts
- Using Data Views
- Filtering, sorting, and formatting in Data Views

THE NEW FRONTPAGE provides a variety of powerful tools for connecting your Web pages to data. XML is one of the kinds of data that FrontPage can use. This chapter shows you how to use XL data on your FrontPage Web pages.

## XML-Based Data for the Web

XML is a means for structuring data and, in today's ever-more-connected world, data often needs to be presented on the Web. FrontPage is the Web site authoring component of Office, so it is not surprising that Microsoft has built tools into it that let you present XML-based data on a Web page. For FrontPage, XML is just one of several different data sources that a Web page can be connected to. Many of the things you can do with data in FrontPage are the same regardless of whether the source is an XML file, a database, or a Web service. This chapter focuses on using XML in FrontPage Web sites.

Many of FrontPage's data-related features, including those new ones that are related to XML, are available only when a Web site is being hosted on a server that supports SharePoint services. If you do not have an account on a SharePoint server, you will not be able to use most of the tools described in this chapter. Please note that I assume that you already know how to use FrontPage to author Web sites. This chapter deals only with the XML-related features of FrontPage.

## The Sample Data

The examples in this chapter make use of the `StockItems.xml` data file. This file, shown in Listing 10-1, maintains information about items in a hardware store's inventory, containing data for the item name, the supplier, and the wholesale and retail prices.

**Listing 10-1: The StockItems.xml Data File**

```
<?xml version="1.0" encoding="UTF-8"?>
<stockitems xmlns="http://www.pgacon.com/stockitems"
  xmlns:xsi="http://www.w3.org/2001/XMLSchema-instance"
  xsi:schemaLocation="http://www.pgacon.com/stockitems
  C:\XMLFiles\StockItems.xsd">
  <item>
    <name>Claw hammer</name>
    <supplier>Ajax Manufacturing</supplier>
    <wholesaleCost>12.50</wholesaleCost>
    <retailPrice>19.95</retailPrice>
  </item>
  <item>
    <name>Needle-nosed pliers</name>
    <supplier>Miller Manufacturing</supplier>
    <wholesaleCost>8.45</wholesaleCost>
    <retailPrice>15.89</retailPrice>
  </item>
  <item>
    <name>Wire stripper</name>
    <supplier>Ajax Manufacturing</supplier>
    <wholesaleCost>11.25</wholesaleCost>
    <retailPrice>21.00</retailPrice>
  </item>
  <item>
    <name>Paint scraper</name>
    <supplier>Clyde Co.</supplier>
    <wholesaleCost>4.10</wholesaleCost>
    <retailPrice>8.00</retailPrice>
  </item>
  <item>
    <name>Crescent wrench</name>
    <supplier>Baxter Foundry Inc.</supplier>
    <wholesaleCost>12.60</wholesaleCost>
    <retailPrice>23.95</retailPrice>
  </item>
</stockitems>
```

# Viewing and Editing XML

FrontPage lets you open and view or edit any XML file that is part of the Web site. To do so, right-click the name of the file in the Folder pane and choose Open from the pop-up menu. Figure 10-1 shows the `StockItems.xml` file opened in FrontPage. You can see that the lines are numbered. Not visible in the figure is the color-coding that FrontPage uses to distinguish attribute names and values from other text.

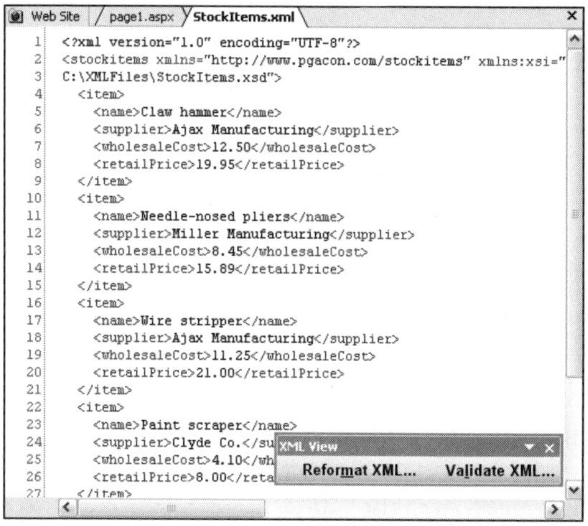

Web Site / page1.aspx / StockItems.xml

```
<?xml version="1.0" encoding="UTF-8"?>
<stockitems xmlns="http://www.pgacon.com/stockitems" xmlns:xsi="
C:\XMLFiles\StockItems.xsd">
  <item>
    <name>Claw hammer</name>
    <supplier>Ajax Manufacturing</supplier>
    <wholesaleCost>12.50</wholesaleCost>
    <retailPrice>19.95</retailPrice>
  </item>
  <item>
    <name>Needle-nosed pliers</name>
    <supplier>Miller Manufacturing</supplier>
    <wholesaleCost>8.45</wholesaleCost>
    <retailPrice>15.89</retailPrice>
  </item>
  <item>
    <name>Wire stripper</name>
    <supplier>Ajax Manufacturing</supplier>
    <wholesaleCost>11.25</wholesaleCost>
    <retailPrice>21.00</retailPrice>
  </item>
  <item>
    <name>Paint scraper</name>
    <supplier>Clyde Co.</su
    <wholesaleCost>4.10</wh
    <retailPrice>8.00</reta
  </item>
```

XML View

Reformat XML... Validate XML...

Figure 10-1: Displaying an XML file in FrontPage.

This figure also shows the XML View toolbar, which is automatically displayed when you open an XML file (you can display or hide this and other toolbars in the usual manner, with the View→Toolbars command). This toolbar has two commands on it:

- **Reformat XML.** Formats the XML so there is one element per line and child elements are indented with respect to their parent. The XML in the figure is formatted this way.
- **Validate XML.** Checks the XML for well-formedness.

The Validate command is somewhat misleading. You might think that this would validate the XML against its schema (assuming the schema is available and linked from the XML file), but this is not the case. All it does is check the XML for proper XML syntax, such as each opening tag having a closing tag and elements being nested legally. In XML parlance, this is called being *well formed.*

# Using XML Web Parts

An XML Web Part is one of the tools that FrontPage provides for displaying XML data on a Web page, specifically a Web Part Web Page in FrontPage lingo. Specifically, an XML Web Part lets you apply an XSLT transform to XML data and display the result. You cannot use an XML Web Part to display raw (that is, untransformed) XML data.

## Creating an XML Web Part

To add an XML Web Part to the page you are designing:

1. Place the cursor at the desired location on the page.
2. Choose Data → Insert Web Part. FrontPage displays the Web Part Gallery task pane.
3. On the task pane, select XML Web Part in the Web Part List.
4. Click the Insert Selected Web Part button. FrontPage inserts the XML Web Part.

When an XML Web Part is first inserted onto a page, it is not yet connected to any XML data. You must set its properties by double-clicking the Web Part to open the Web Part Properties dialog box, as shown in Figure 10-2.

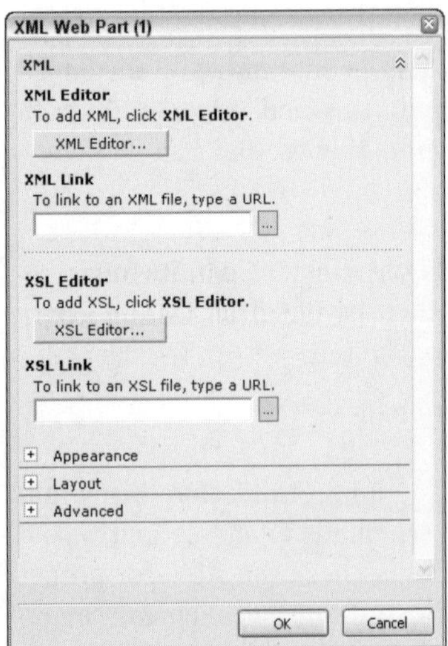


Figure 10-2: Setting properties of an XML Web Part.

You set properties as follows:

- **XML Editor.** Click this button to open the editor if you want to enter the XML directly (or copy and paste it from another application).
- **XML Link.** To link the Web Part to an existing XML file, enter the file's URL in this field. You can also click the adjacent... button to browse for the file.
- **XSL Editor.** Click this button to open the editor if you want to enter the XSL transform directly (or copy and paste it from another application).
- **XSL Link.** To link to an existing XSL file, enter the URL or click the button to browse for the file.
- **Appearance.** Click the + symbol to display the Web Part's appearance properties, with which you can affect the Web Part's appearance, including its title and size.
- **Layout.** Click the + symbol to display the Web Part's layout properties, including whether the Web Part is visible on the page and the text direction (left to right or right to left).
- **Advanced.** Click the + symbol to display the Web Part's advanced properties, including whether it can be minimized and its description.

What's the point of creating an XML Web Part that is not visible on the page? The answer lies in FrontPage's capability to create dynamic pages whose appearance changes in response to user input. Thus, an XML Web Part could be displayed or hidden when the user clicks a button on the page.

# A Web Part Example

I think it would be helpful for you to see an example of using an XML Web Part to display XML. The source data is the `StockItems.xml` data file from Listing 10-1. The goal of the Web page designer is to display a list of all the items in the data file, with the list containing only the item name and the retail price for each item. Additionally, the item name should be in boldface, and the price should be displayed with a leading dollar sign. The XSL transform to accomplish this is shown in Listing 10-2. I used the name `StockItemsDisplay.xslt` for this file.

**Listing 10-2: Stylesheet for Displaying StockItems.xml Data**

```
<?xml version="1.0" encoding="UTF-8"?>
<xsl:stylesheet version="1.0"
  xmlns:sl="http://www.pgacon.com/stockitems"
```

*Continued*

Listing 10-2 *(Continued)*

```
  xmlns:xsl="http://www.w3.org/1999/XSL/Transform">
<xsl:output method="html" version="1.0" encoding="UTF-8"
  indent="yes"/>

<xsl:template match="/">
  <xsl:apply-templates select="//sl:item"/>
</xsl:template>

<xsl:template match="sl:item">
  <p><b><xsl:value-of select="sl:name"/></b> $<xsl:value-of
    select="sl:retailPrice"/></p>
</xsl:template>
</xsl:stylesheet>
```

This is a fairly simple stylesheet, containing only two templates. It's the second template that does the work. For each `<item>` element it outputs in this order:

1. The HTML tag to start a paragraph.
2. The HTML tag to turn boldface on.
3. The value of the current `<name>` element.
4. The HTML tag to turn boldface off.
5. A space followed by a dollar sign.
6. The value of the `<retailPrice>` element.
7. The HTML tag to end a paragraph.

To create this XML Web Part, you must have FrontPage open and be editing a Web page that is on a SharePoint server. The page on which you are going to place the Web Part should be in design mode (click the Design tab at the bottom of the FrontPage window). The XML data file and the XSLT transform file should have been imported to your Web site using FrontPage's File→Import command. Then:

1. Place the cursor at location on the page where you want the Web Part placed.
2. Choose Data→Insert Web Part to display the Web Part Gallery task pane.
3. Select the XML Web Part entry in the Web Part list.
4. Click the Insert Selected Web Part button.
5. On the page, double-click the new Web Part to open its properties dialog box.

6. Click the button next to the XML Link field and locate the `StockItems.xml` file.
7. Click the button next to the XSL Link and locate the `StockItemsDisplay.xslt` file.
8. Click OK to close the properties dialog box.

At this point the XML Web Part is finished. The data will appear on the design screen, and you can verify that the stylesheet is doing what it is designed for. Click the Preview tab at the bottom of the screen to see what the Web Part will look like in actual use. This is shown in Figure 10-3. The other page elements shown in this figure are default items that FrontPage puts on the page, and you need not be concerned with them.

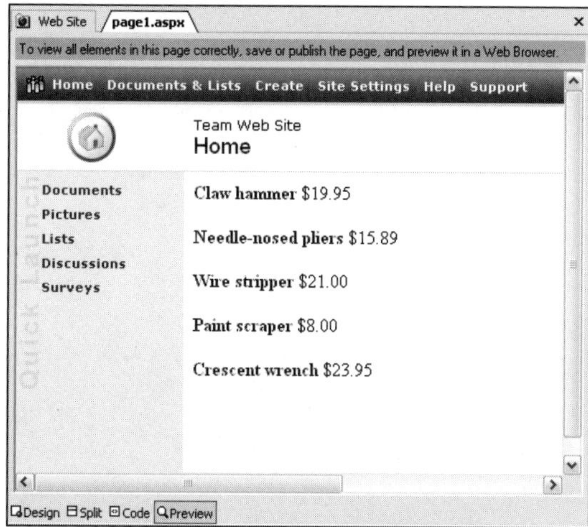


**Figure 10-3: The XML Web Part displaying the stock items data as filtered by the stylesheet.**

If you examine the stylesheet in Listing 10-2, you'll notice that it is different from other stylesheets that are designed to convert XML to HTML. The reason is that this stylesheet is outputting only the HTML to display the XML data as part of an HTML page – it is not outputting the entire page. Thus, there is no need to create certain HTML tags, such as `<HTML></HTML>` and `<BODY></BODY>`, that would be required for an entire Web page.

# Using Data Views

FrontPage also can use and display XML data with a Data View. Compared to an XML Web Part, a Data View is a more traditional way of displaying data. A Data

View uses a tabular row-and-column format and does not provide for applying a stylesheet to the data. It does, however, provide various options for filtering and sorting the data and modifying the formatting. A Data View can be bound to various data sources including SharePoint lists, databases, and Web services. This section explains how to create a Data View that is bound to an XML data file.

## Creating a Data View

To create a Data View bound to XML data, the XML data file must be available either on the Web site you are editing or in another location. Then:

1. Place the cursor at the location on the page where you want the Data View located.
2. Choose Data → Insert Data View to display the Data Source Catalog task pane (see Figure 10-4).

Figure 10-4: Selecting an XML file to bind to a Data View.

3. Click the + symbol to open the XML Files node. This node lists the XML files that are part of the Web site that you are authoring. There are three such files listed in Figure 10-4.
4. If the desired XML file is listed, proceed to Step 6.

5. If the desired XML file is not listed, click the Add to Catalog command on the task pane and follow the prompts to locate the desired XML file (on a local disk, for example) and add it to the project. The selected file is then listed on the task pane.

6. Click the name of the desired XML file on the task pane and select Insert Data View from the pop-up menu. FrontPage retrieves the XML data and inserts the Data View in the page.

When you insert a Data View bound to an XML file, FrontPage creates the Data View using the default settings. For example, Figure 10-5 shows the default Data View based on the `StockItems.xml` data file from earlier in the chapter. You can see that this is a straightforward table with the XML filename as the title, the repeating field names as column headings, and the data in rows. These same elements will be displayed when the page is published. Unless this default appearance is what you want, your next steps will be to customize the Data View.

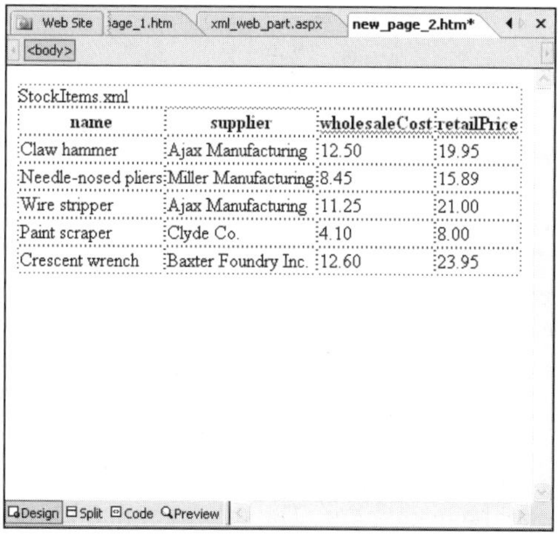

StockItems.xml

| name | supplier | wholesaleCost | retailPrice |
|---|---|---|---|
| Claw hammer | Ajax Manufacturing | 12.50 | 19.95 |
| Needle-nosed pliers | Miller Manufacturing | 8.45 | 15.89 |
| Wire stripper | Ajax Manufacturing | 11.25 | 21.00 |
| Paint scraper | Clyde Co. | 4.10 | 8.00 |
| Crescent wrench | Baxter Foundry Inc. | 12.60 | 23.95 |

**Figure 10-5: The StockItems.xml file as a Data View.**

You can see that a Data View uses the XML element names for the column headings. You can edit these and apply formatting, if desired, directly on the page using FrontPage's usual text editing techniques. These names are for display only, and the original element names are still used to refer to the elements when defining filter criteria and other tasks (covered later in the chapter).

## The Data View Details Task Pane

When you create a Data View, FrontPage displays the Data View Details task pane, shown in Figure 10-6, which gives you access to the Data View's properties. If this task pane is not displayed, you can display it by right-clicking the Data View and selecting Data View Properties from the pop-up menu.

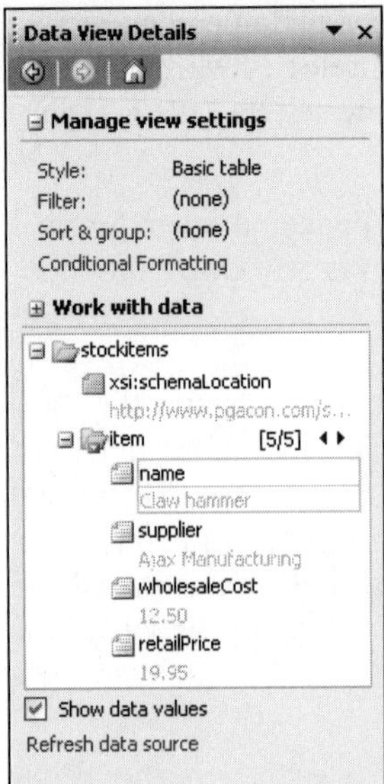


Figure 10-6: The Data View Details task pane.

The list in the middle of the task pane displays the structure of the data. If an element is repeating, a single instance of the element and its children is shown (the `<item>` element in Figure 10-6, for example). To the right of the element name is an indication of which of the repeating elements is shown. In Figure 10-6, it shows that the fifth of five `<item>` elements is displayed. Click the adjacent arrows to move forward and backward in the list. You can display the element names and their data or just the element names based on the setting of the Show Data Values option at the bottom of the task pane.

The Refresh Data Source command refreshes the Data View from the XML file and should be used if you think the file may have changed. The other commands at the top of the task pane, under Manage View Settings, are described in the following sections.

### DATA VIEW STYLES

When you construct a Data View as described earlier in this chapter, it is created using the basic table style. There are several other styles available. To change the style of a Data View:

1. Select the Data View.
2. Click the Style command on the Data View Details task pane.
   FrontPage displays the General tab in the View Styles dialog box, shown in Figure 10-7.

3. Scroll the HTML View Style list to see the available views, and click the desired one. FrontPage displays a description of the selected view in the Description section of the dialog box.
4. Click OK to apply the selected view to the Data View.

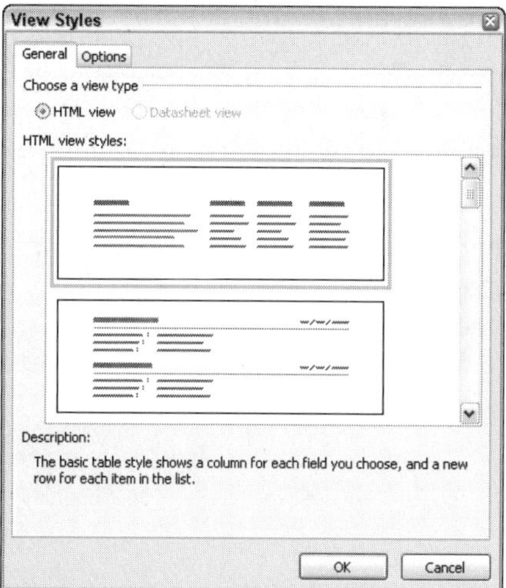


Figure 10-7: Selecting a view style for a Data View.

Not all of the available views are appropriate for a specific situation. You can easily switch a Data View to different styles to see which is best for your application. For example, Figure 10-8 shows the same data as Figure 10-6 displayed using the repeating form style – the items are listed sequentially rather than in a table.

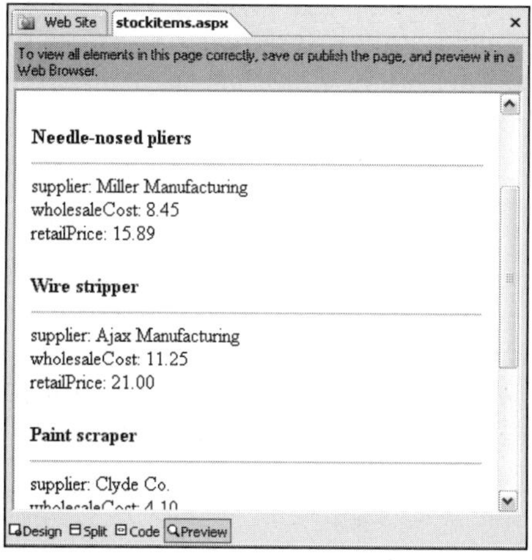


Figure 10-8: A Data View using the repeating form style.

The View Styles dialog box also has an Options tab, shown in Figure 10-9. These options control certain aspects of the Data View display on the finished Web page, as follows:

- The Toolbar section enables you to display a toolbar at the top of the Data View to let the user filter, sort, and/or group the data. The individual options determine which capabilities are available on the toolbar.
- The Header and Footer section controls whether a header and/or footer is displayed in a Data View. If the Enable Sorting on Column Headers option is selected, a user can sort the data on a column by clicking the column heading.
- The Record Sets section has options that determine how many items (that is, rows) are displayed at one time. If you choose to display fewer items than the data contains, FrontPage includes, at the bottom of the Data View, an indication of which items are displayed, such as `Items 7 to 12`. FrontPage also displays Next and Previous links that let the user move forward and backward in the data.

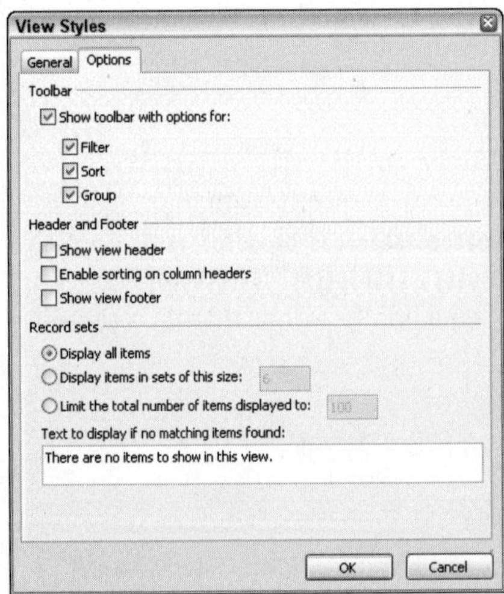


**Figure 10-9: The Options tab in the View Styles dialog box.**

## DATA VIEW FILTERS

A filter lets you define criteria to determine which records of the XML data are displayed. By default all data is displayed. To define a filter, click the Filter command on the Data View Details task pane. FrontPage displays the Filter Criteria dialog box as shown in Figure 10-10.

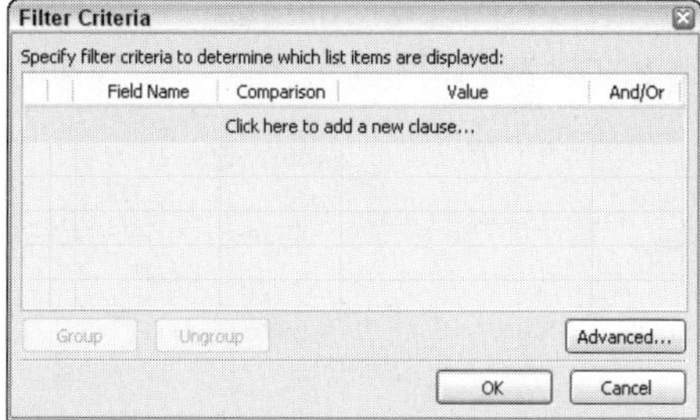


**Figure 10-10: The Filter Criteria dialog box.**

To define a filter, click where it says Click here to add a new clause@@@Initial cap this, "Click Here to Add a New Clause"?@@@. FrontPage inserts a blank clause in the dialog box. Select or enter values in the first three columns as follows:

- **Field Name.** Select the name of the field (XML element) that the filter will be based on.
- **Comparison.** Select the type of comparison to be performed, such as Equals or Greater Than.
- **Value.** Enter the value that the comparison is to be performed against.

To enter additional criteria, select And or Or in the fourth column to determine how the current criterion and the new one are to be combined:

- **And.** Both criteria must be met for the item to be displayed.
- **Or.** Either criterion, or both, must be met for the item to be displayed.

Define the new criteria the same way you defined the first filter criterion. When you close the Filter Criteria dialog box, the Data View will display the result of the filter. If the filter excludes all data, a message to that effect is displayed.

If you click the Advanced button in the Filter Criteria dialog box, FrontPage displays the XPath expression that will be used to implement the filter. If you are familiar with XPath syntax, you can enter the filter criteria here as an XPath predicate rather than using the Filter Criteria dialog box. You can also edit the XPath expression created by FrontPage.

To remove a criterion, select it by clicking the arrow in the left margin and pressing Del.

Figure 10-11 shows an example of filter criteria for the `StockItems.xml` data. These criteria will display data only for items whose `retailPrce`is less than 10 and whose supplier is Ajax Manufacturing.

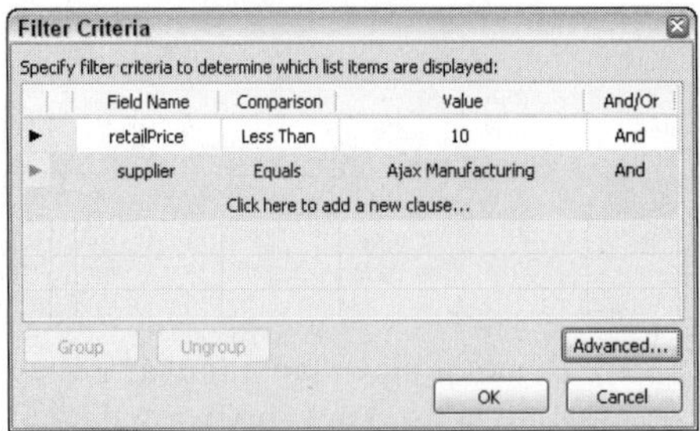


**Figure 10-11: A two-part criteria defined for the StockItems data.**

## DATA VIEW SORTING AND GROUPING

Sorting refers to the order in which the data is presented in the Data View. Grouping lets you display that data so that items are grouped together when they have the same data in a specified field. For example, Figure 10-12 shows the StockItems Data View grouped by the supplier field. The two items from Ajax Manufacturing are grouped together under a heading identifying the supplier; this is the only group with more than one entry because no other supplier has more than one item.

Web Site | stockitems.aspx*

<body> <form> <WebPartPages:DataViewWebPart>

StockItems.xml

| name | supplier | wholesaleCost | retailPrice |
|---|---|---|---|
| - **supplier**: Ajax Manufacturing | | | |
| Claw hammer | Ajax Manufacturing | 12.50 | 19.95 |
| Wire stripper | Ajax Manufacturing | 11.25 | 21.00 |
| - **supplier**: Baxter Foundry Inc. | | | |
| Crescent wrench | Baxter Foundry Inc. | 12.60 | 23.95 |
| - **supplier**: Clyde Co. | | | |
| Paint scraper | Clyde Co. | 4.10 | 8.00 |
| - **supplier**: Miller Manufacturing | | | |
| Needle-nosed pliers | Miller Manufacturing | 8.45 | 15.89 |

Design Split Code Preview

**Figure 10-12: A Data View with grouping applied.**

To specify sort order and define groups:

1. Select the Data View.
2. Click the Sort & Group command on the Data View Details task pane. FrontPage displays the Sort and Group dialog box (see Figure 10-13).

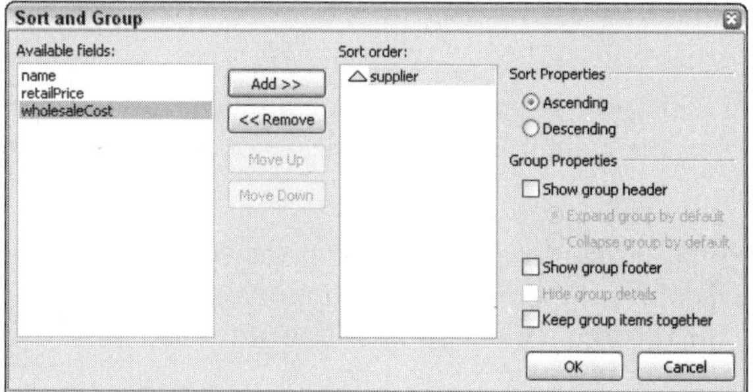


Figure 10-13: Defining sort order and group display options for a Data View.

3. Select a field in the Available Fields list and click Add to move it to the Sort Order list.
4. Select either Ascending or Descending in the Sort Properties section. A small yellow arrow next to the field name indicates the sort direction for that field.
5. Select group display options as follows:
   - **Show Group Header.** A header is displayed at the top of each group (as in Figure 10-12). The group can be expanded or collapsed by default; the user can expand or collapse groups as needed when the page is displayed.
   - **Show Group Footer.** A footer is displayed at the bottom of each group.
   - **Hide Group Details.** Available only when a header is displayed. This displays only the header, with no other details.

When you are sorting on more than one field, the sort is applied to the fields in the order they are listed in the Sort Order list. To change the priority of a field, select it in this list and use the Move Up and Move Down buttons to change its position.

## CONDITIONAL FORMATTING

Conditional formatting means that the format of specified text on the page depends on one or more data values in the XML file. For example, you could use conditional formatting to display negative numbers in red. Conditional formatting also lets you hide or show text depending on data conditions. You can apply conditional formatting to any text in a Data View, not just to the data values. In the StockItems example, for instance, you could specify that the name of an item be displayed in blue text when the item's retail price is less than 10. To apply conditional formatting:

1. Select the text to which the formatting will be applied. If you select a repeating data item, the formatting automatically is applied to all repeats of that item.
2. Click the Conditional Formatting command on the Data View Details task pane. FrontPage displays the Conditional Formatting task pane. Any conditional formats for this Data View are listed on this task pane.
3. Click the Create button and select one of the commands from the pop-up menu:
   - **Show Content.** Displays the selected text only when certain conditions are met.
   - **Hide Content.** Hides the selected text only when certain conditions are met.
   - **Apply Formatting.** Applies text formatting when certain conditions are met.
4. FrontPage displays the Condition Criteria dialog box, shown in Figure 10-14. Use this dialog box to specify the conditions for the formatting to be applied. It works the same way as the Filter Criteria dialog box that was covered earlier in this chapter. When the criteria are complete, click OK to close the dialog box.
5. If you selected Show Content or Hide Content in Step 3, you're finished. If you selected Apply Formatting, FrontPage displays the Modify Style dialog box.
6. Click the Format button and follow the prompts to specify the formatting that you want applied when the conditions are met.
7. When you've finished, click OK to close the dialog box.

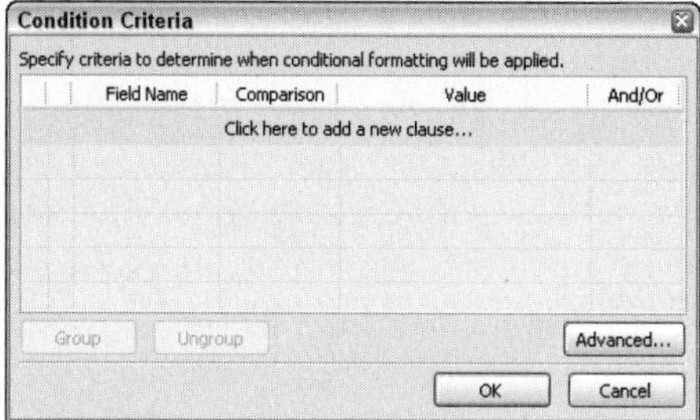


Figure 10-14: Specifying criteria for conditional formatting.

When a Data View has conditional formatting defined, the individual conditions are listed on the Conditional Formatting task pane. To work with an existing conditional format, select the item on this task pane, click the adjacent arrow, and select options from the pop-up menu as follows:

- **Edit Condition.** Modify the conditions under which the formatting is applied.
- **Modify Style.** Change the formatting that is applied (not available for Show Content or Hide Content conditions).
- **Delete.** Delete the entire conditional formatting rule.

You'll see a real-world example of conditional formatting in Chapter 14, "Connecting FrontPage and InfoPath."

# Part IV

## Case Studies

## IN THIS PART:

Part IV takes the material that you learned in the first three parts and applies it to real-world problems. Each case study shows how to use XML to integrate two Office applications to create a solution for a specific need. Each of the case studies provides a foundation on which you can build in using Office and XML for your own specific needs.

Chapter 11

# Connecting Word and InfoPath

IN THIS CHAPTER

- Creating a schema
- Designing the form
- Creating and applying a stylesheet
- Creating a stylesheet with formatting

YOU'VE ALREADY LEARNED about the powerful XML-related capabilities of the Office applications. Now, it's time to see some of these tools in action. This is the first of six chapters that takes you though the design and creation of an application that uses Office and XML to implement a complete solution. This chapter presents an example in which Word is used to format and print data that is entered using an InfoPath form.

## Overview

Word has the ability to open and display any XML data. In and of itself, this is not particularly exciting. However, things get a lot more interesting when you consider Word's ability to apply stylesheets to the data. A stylesheet, called a *solution* in Word, can transform the XML data in just about any way you can imagine. Because Word can support multiple stylesheets for a single XML document, you can have two or more views of the same XML data instantly available. Coupled with Word's powerful formatting tools and the WordML markup language, a lot of possibilities are available to the developer.

## The Scenario

Your company needs a system to handle interoffice memos. The goal is to have memos created on-screen by using a standard form, and also to have the memo information available online in XML format to provide access to the data. For various reasons, memos are still delivered as hard copies, so a method is also needed to format and print the memos. You decide to create an InfoPath form for memo creation, and to use Word and a stylesheet to provide the formatting.

The solution presented here is, from a real-world perspective, only partial. You would not expect the user to manually open memos in Word for printing – this is more likely to be handled automatically by means of scripts or back-office automation. These tasks, as well as printing, are not related to XML, however, so they are omitted. The goal of this example is to show you how InfoPath and Word can be used to input and format XML data.

# Create the Schema

The first step in this project is to create the schema for the InfoPath form. The data layout is quite simple, consisting of the root element `<memo>` with five nonrepeating child elements: `<date>`, `<to>`, `<from>`, `<subject>`, and `<body>`. All of these child elements are type text except for `<date>`, which is type date. The schema is associated with the target namespace http://www.pgacon.com/memo, which you can replace with your own namespace. If you decide to use your own namespace, be sure to make that change in the other listings as well. Listing 11-1 shows the schema file.

**Listing 11-1: Sample Schema File**

```
<?xml version="1.0" encoding="UTF-8"?>
<xs:schema targetNamespace="http://www.pgacon.com/memo"
  xmlns:xs="http://www.w3.org/2001/XMLSchema"
  xmlns="http://www.pgacon.com/memo" elementFormDefault="qualified"
  attributeFormDefault="unqualified">
  <xs:element name="memo">
    <xs:complexType>
      <xs:sequence>
        <xs:element name="date" type="xs:date"/>
        <xs:element name="to" type="xs:string"/>
        <xs:element name="subject" type="xs:string"/>
        <xs:element name="body" type="xs:string"/>
        <xs:element name="from" type="xs:string"/>
      </xs:sequence>
    </xs:complexType>
  </xs:element>
</xs:schema>
```

# Design the InfoPath Form

With the schema ready, you can start designing the form. First create a new form based on the schema. Here are the steps to follow:

1. Choose File→Design a Form to display the Design a Form task pane.
2. Click the New From Data Source command on the task pane to display the Data Source Setup Wizard.
3. Select the XML Schema or XML Data File option, and then click Next.
4. Click the Browse button and locate the schema file that you created in the previous section.
5. Click Finish. InfoPath creates a new form with the schema displayed in the Data Source task pane.

Now you can start designing the form's visual interface. You can create your own interface if you like, or follow these steps to duplicate what I did:

1. On the Data Source task pane, click the Layout command to display the Layout task pane.
2. In the Insert Layout Tables list, click the Table with Title entry. InfoPath inserts a layout table onto the form.
3. Click the table where it says "Click to Add Title" and enter Create a Memo.
4. Display the Data Source task pane.
5. Drag the `<memo>` group from the Data Source task pane and drop it on the form where it says "Click to Add Form Content." InfoPath displays a pop-up menu.
6. Select Controls from the pop-up menu. InfoPath inserts labels and controls for the five child elements of `<memo>`.
7. Modify the sizes and positions of the labels and controls as needed, being sure to make the body text box extra large.

The finished form looks more or less like the one in Figure 11-1. Don't forget to save the form with a descriptive name. Once the template is complete, fill out a form based on this template, entering a practice memo and saving the form. You'll need this XML data file later for testing the stylesheet.

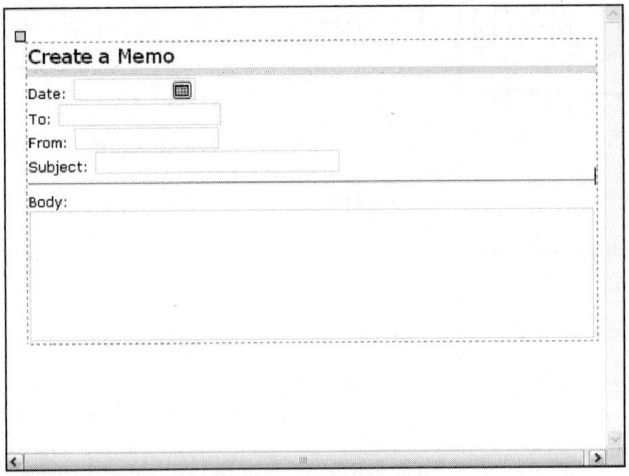

Figure 11-1: The completed memo form.

# Create the Stylesheet

The next phase in this project is to create the stylesheet, or transform, that will determine how the memo is displayed when it's opened in Word. To start with, we will create a relatively simple stylesheet that displays text and data in the Word document but does not apply any formatting. The document that results when the stylesheet is applied to the XML data from the form should have the following:

- A heading that says Interoffice Memo
- The label Date:, followed by the `<date>` value from the InfoPath form
- The label To:, followed by the `<to>` value from the InfoPath form
- The label From:, followed by the `<from>` value from the InfoPath form
- The label Subject:, followed by the `<subject>` value from the InfoPath form
- The data from the `<body>` value from the InfoPath form

An XSL stylesheet that does this is shown in Listing 11-2. Note that the ns0 namespace must match the namespace that was used in the schema. Some portions of the stylesheet code are explained in more detail following the listing. You can see that the stylesheet uses several WordML tags, those with the `w` namespace prefix. Later in the chapter I'll show you how to determine the tags that WordML uses for various things.

**Listing 11-2: The Memo Stylesheet**

```
<?xml version="1.0" encoding="UTF-8"?>
<xsl:stylesheet version="1.0"
  xmlns:w="http://schemas.microsoft.com/office/word/2003/2/wordml"
  xmlns:ns0="http://www.pgacon.com/memo"
  xmlns:xsl="http://www.w3.org/1999/XSL/Transform">

<xsl:template match="/">
 <w:wordDocument>
   <w:body>
     <xsl:apply-templates select="/ns0:memo"/>
   </w:body>
 </w:wordDocument>
</xsl:template>

<!-- the memo heading -->
<xsl:template match="ns0:memo">
   <w:p><w:r><w:t>Interoffice Memo</w:t></w:r></w:p>
   <ns0:memo>

<!-- the Date line -->
  <w:p>
  <w:r><w:t>Date:</w:t></w:r>
  <w:r><w:t xml:space="preserve">   </w:t></w:r>
  <ns0:date>
  <w:r><w:t><xsl:value-of select="ns0:date"/></w:t></w:r>
  </ns0:date>
  </w:p>

<!-- the To line -->
  <w:p><w:r><w:t>To:</w:t></w:r>
  <w:r><w:t xml:space="preserve">   </w:t></w:r>
  <ns0:to>
  <w:r><w:t><xsl:value-of select="ns0:to"/></w:t></w:r>
  </ns0:to>
  </w:p>

<!-- the From line -->
  <w:p><w:r><w:t>From:</w:t></w:r>
  <w:r><w:t xml:space="preserve">   </w:t></w:r>
  <ns0:from>
  <w:r><w:t><xsl:value-of select="ns0:from"/></w:t></w:r>
  </ns0:from>
  </w:p>
```

*Continued*

Listing 11-2 *(Continued)*

```
<!-- the Subject line -->
  <w:p><w:r><w:t>Subject:</w:t></w:r>
  <w:r><w:t xml:space="preserve">   </w:t></w:r>
  <ns0:subject>
  <w:r><w:t><xsl:value-of select="ns0:subject"/></w:t></w:r>
  </ns0:subject>
  </w:p>

<!-- the memo body -->
  <w:p>
  <ns0:body>
  <w:r><w:t><xsl:value-of select="ns0:body"/></w:t></w:r>
  </ns0:body>
  </w:p>

 </ns0:memo>
</xsl:template>
</xsl:stylesheet>
```

The second line of this file is the opening `<xsl:stylesheet>` tag that identifies the content as a stylesheet. Note that there are three namespace prefixes defined, one (`w`) for the WordML vocabulary, one (`xsl`) for the stylesheet vocabulary, and one (`ns0`) for the schema in use.

The next section, repeated here, defines a template that will be applied to the XML file's root element:

```
<xsl:template match="/">
 <w:wordDocument>
   <w:body>
     <xsl:apply-templates select="/ns0:memo"/>
   </w:body>
 </w:wordDocument>
</xsl:template>
```

This template does the following:

1. Writes a `<w:wordDocument>` tag to the output.
2. Writes a `<w:wbody>` tag to the output.
3. Applies other templates, or in this case, a single template (described next), to elements that match `/ns0:memo`.
4. Writes a `</w:wbody>` tag to the output.
5. Writes a `</w:wordDocument>` tag to the output.

The remainder of the stylesheet consists of the other template that is applied by the <xsl:apply-templates> element described earlier. Here's the first part of the template, from Listing 11-2:

```
<xsl:template match="ns0:memo">
<w:p><w:r><w:t>Interoffice Memo</w:t></w:r></w:p>
<ns0:memo>
```

The first line of this section opens the template and specifies that it applies to <ns0:memo> elements (there will be exactly one of these elements in the XML file).

The second line writes the text "Interoffice memo" to the output. The XML tags in this line, such as <w:p>, are WordML tags that identify a paragraph and text.

The third line writes the <ns0:memo> tag to the output.

The next section, repeated here, has the job of writing the Date part of the document:

```
<w:p><w:r><w:t>Date:</w:t></w:r>
<w:r><w:t xml:space="preserve">→</w:t></w:r>
<ns0:date>
<w:r><w:t><xsl:value-of select="ns0:date"/></w:t></w:r>
</ns0:date>
</w:p>
```

The first line writes the text Date: to the document along with the required WordML tags. The second line writes a tab character. Note the use of the xml:space="preserve" attribute to instruct Word to preserve the tab. (The tab is designated by an arrow symbol in the listing here; you use an actual Tab instead when you create the code.)

The third line writes the opening tag <ns0:date> to the output. The fourth line writes the data that is in the <date> element of the XML data file (the date that the user entered on the form). The fifth line writes the closing tag </ns0:date> to the output, and the final line writes a WordML tag marking the end of a paragraph.

The remaining parts of the stylesheet follow the same pattern as what's already been described, writing labels and data for the other elements of the memo. When the file is complete, save it using either the XSL or the XML extension.

# Apply the Stylesheet

In order to try out the stylesheet, you will need all three files that you created earlier in this chapter: the XSD schema (see Listing 11-1), the saved InfoPath form, and the stylesheet (see Listing 11-2). Then:

1. Start Word.
2. Choose Tools→Templates and Add-ins to display the Templates and Add-ins Dialog box.
3. Click the Schema Library button to display the Schema Library dialog box.
4. Click the Add Schema button to open the Add Schema dialog box.
5. Locate and select the schema file that you created, and then click Open.
6. Enter an alias such as Memo for the schema and click OK. You return to the Schema Library dialog box. The alias of the schema you just added is included in the Select a Schema list.
7. Click the name of the schema you just added.
8. Click the Add Solution button to display the Add Solution dialog box.
9. Locate and select the stylesheet file that you created, and click Open.
10. Enter an alias for this stylesheet such as MemoPlain.
11. At this point the Schema Library dialog box looks like Figure 11-2. Click OK to close this dialog box and return to the Templates and Add-ins dialog box.
12. Click OK to close the dialog box.

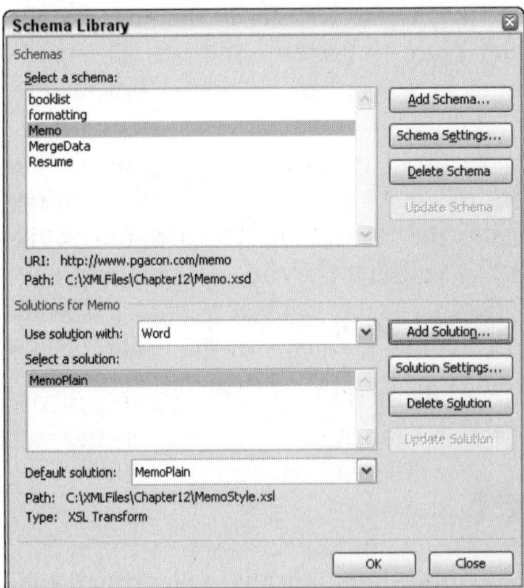


**Figure 11-2: Adding the schema to Word's Schema Library.**

Now both the schema and the stylesheet (which Word calls a *solution*) are loaded into the Schema Library. Open the XML data file by choosing File→Open and locating the XML file that you saved when you filled out the InfoPath Form. When you open this file, Word associates it with the schema and solution that you loaded because they all use the same namespace. The stylesheet is applied to the document and the output is displayed as shown in Figure 11-3.

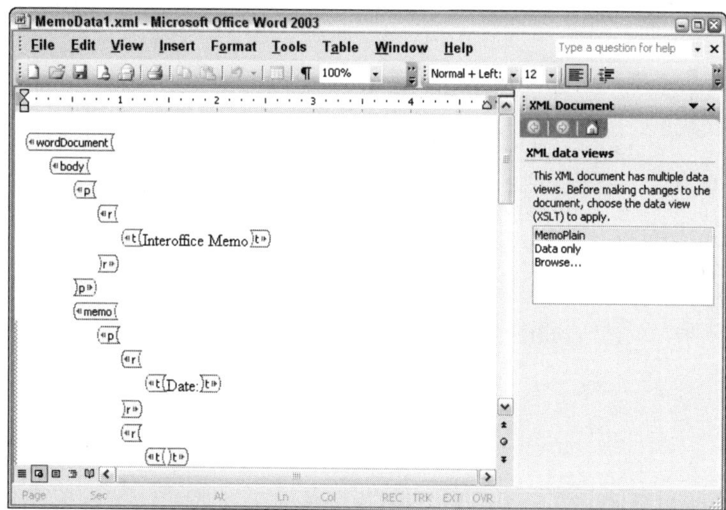


Figure 11-3: The InfoPath document with the stylesheet applied and XML tags displayed.

Please note that the document's XML tags are displayed. To hide them, turn off the Show XML Tags in the Document option on the XML Structure task pane (see Figure 11-4). Note also that the XML Document task pane displays a list of three options:

- **MemoPlain.** Display the document using the MemoPlain solution.
- **Data only.** Display the document without applying a stylesheet; only the XML data and tags will be displayed.
- **Browse.** Locate another stylesheet to apply to the document.

You need to address the question of how (or whether) the WordML document will be validated. The document won't pass validation against the memo schema because of all the WordML tags that are added. You have two choices. One is to simply turn off validation. InfoPath already will have validated the data, so you may feel that it is unnecessary for Word to validate it also. However, the user can change the data in Word, so you may want to leave validation in place. It is a call that you must make based on the details of your specific application. To turn validation off:

1. Choose Tools → Templates and Add-Ins to display the Templates and Add-ins dialog box.

2. On the XML Schema tab, deselect the Validate Document Against Attached Schema option and select the Allow Saving as XML Even If Not Valid option.

3. Click OK to close the dialog box.

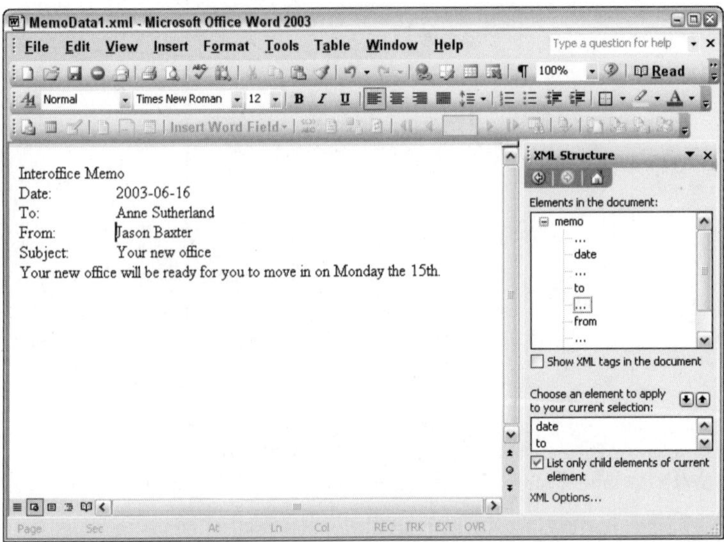


Figure 11-4: The memo document with the XML tags hidden.

Your second option is to instruct Word to ignore mixed content in the document when performing validation. This means that the validation process will check to see that the memo elements contain the data as specified in the schema, but will ignore other elements (namely, the WordML elements). To use this technique:

1. Choose Tools → Templates and Add-Ins to display the Templates and Add-ins dialog box.

2. On the XML Schema tab, click the XML Options button to display the XML Options dialog box.

3. Select the Ignore Mixed Content option.

4. Click OK twice to close all dialog boxes.

With the validation options set, you can save the document as WordML using the File → Save As command (if you use File → Save, it will overwrite the InfoPath form file). You can open the WordML file in Notepad or another text editor to see what it looks like. You'll see that there are a lot of elements at the start of the file that perform tasks such as defining styles and listing document properties. The actual content is located toward the end of the file. It should be clear to you that

WordML is a very complicated vocabulary. The idea of writing WordML from scratch may appear daunting, yet it would be very useful to do so. For the current example, writing some WordML – or more specifically, creating a stylesheet that outputs WordML – would permit you to automatically apply formatting to the memo in Word. To my knowledge, Microsoft has not released the full WordML specification, but there are techniques you can use to get the WordML you need. These are explained in the following sections.

# Creating a Stylesheet with Formatting

If you knew that WordML is required to create the desired formatting, the rest of the process would be straightforward. All you'd need to do is modify the stylesheet so that it generates the WordML required to define the style(s) you are using and apply them to the memo elements. Fortunately, you can get Word to do most of the work for you. Here are the basic steps:

1. Define the desired style in the document.
2. Apply the style to part of the text.
3. Save the document as WordML.
4. Open the document in a text editor and locate the WordML elements.
5. Copy these elements to the stylesheet, making sure to copy any needed namespace definitions as well.

The following sections walk you though the process of doing this for the memo example. The object is to define a style and apply it to the memo heading.

## Define and Apply the Style

These steps require that you have the memo document open in Word and have used Save As to save it as an XML file under another name.

1. Choose Format → Styles and Formatting to display the Styles and Formatting task pane.
2. Click the New Style button to display the New Style dialog box.
3. Enter MemoHead as the name for the new style.
4. Use the dialog box commands to define the style as you like. I used a larger font in boldface, gray shading, and a black border at the bottom.
5. When the style definition is complete, click OK to close the dialog box.

6. Select the first line of the memo and apply the MemoHead style to it. The document now looks like Figure 11-5.
7. Save the file.

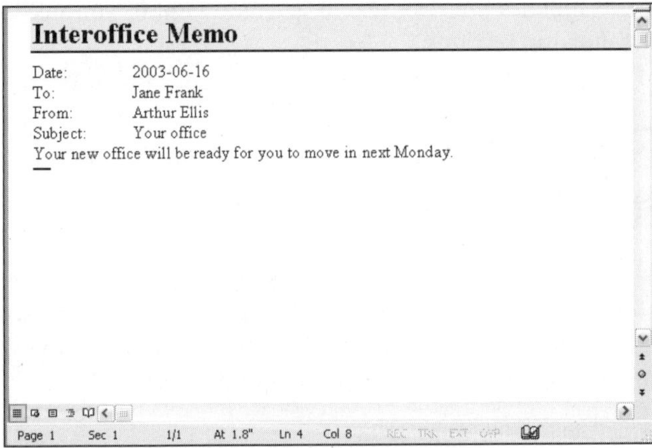


Figure 11-5: A memo in Word with formatting applied.

The next step is to extract the WordML elements from the file you just saved and insert them into the stylesheet.

## The Style Definition

To find the WordML elements, open the file that you saved in the previous section in a text editor such as Notepad. It is preferable, however, to use a specialized XML editing program such as XML Spy, because Word does not format WordML files nicely and you are likely to find lots of elements run together on each line, making them difficult to read.

First, locate the style definition. A WordML file contains a <styles> element that contains individual <style> elements for each style. You'll find more than one style defined in the WordML file – the one you want is the one named MemoHead, as indicated by its `w:styleId` attribute and <w:name> tag. Here's the relevant <style> tag:

```
<w:style w:type="paragraph" w:styleId="MemoHead">
  <w:name w:val="MemoHead"/>
  <w:basedOn w:val="Normal"/>
  <w:rsid w:val="2D5055"/>
  <w:pPr>
    <w:pStyle w:val="MemoHead"/>
    <w:pBdr>
      <w:bottom w:val="single" w:sz="12" wx:bdrwidth="30"
         w:space="1" w:color="auto"/>
```

```
    </w:pBdr>
    <w:shd w:val="clear" w:color="auto" w:fill="E6E6E6"/>
    <w:spacing w:after="120"/>
  </w:pPr>
  <w:rPr>
    <wx:font wx:val="Times New Roman"/>
    <w:b/>
    <w:sz w:val="40"/>
    <w:sz-cs w:val="40"/>
  </w:rPr>
</w:style>
```

Now that you have located the required element, you need to copy it to the stylesheet:

1. In your text editor, open the stylesheet file that you created earlier in the chapter.
2. Save the file under a new name, retaining the XSL or XSLT extension.
3. Place the cursor immediately after the first `<w:wordDocument>` element, which is right after the `<xsl:template match="/">` element.
4. Type in a `<w:styles>` element and a `</w:styles>` element.
5. Copy the `<style>` element from the WordML document and paste it between the `<w:styles>` element and the `</w:styles>` element.

With the MemoHead style definition in place, you're ready to apply the style to the document.

# Apply the Style

This step locates the WordML that applies the MemoHead style to the memo heading. By including this WordML in the stylesheet output, you are, in effect, applying the style to text in the memo.

Switch to the editor in which the WordML file is open. Then, search for the text Interoffice Memo (this is the text to which you applied the style). The relevant Word ML is as follows:

```
<w:p>
  <w:pPr>
    <w:pStyle w:val="MemoHead"/>
  </w:pPr>
  <w:r>
    <w:t>Interoffice Memo</w:t>
  </w:r>
</w:p>
```

Compare this to the corresponding WordML in the original stylesheet; the only difference is lines 2↵n4. All you need to do is copy these three lines from the WordML file and paste them at the corresponding location in the stylesheet file.

# Checking Namespaces

WordML uses a variety of namespaces, and your new stylesheet must define any that are used in the new elements that you just added. If you miss a namespace, you'll get an error later when you try to use the stylesheet, so it's better to catch them now. An examination of the new code shows only one new prefix, wx, that is used in the style definition. Locate the definition of this namespace prefix near the start of the WordML file and copy it to the stylesheet where the other namespace prefixes are defined. After you have done so, the <xsl:stylesheet> element will look like this:

```
<xsl:stylesheet version="1.0"
 xmlns:w="http://schemas.microsoft.com/office/word/2003/2/wordml"
 xmlns:ns0="http://www.pgacon.com/memo"
 xmlns:xsl="http://www.w3.org/1999/XSL/Transform"
 xmlns:wx="http://schemas.microsoft.com/office/word/2003/2/auxHint">
```

# Other Details

Because WordML stores complete information about a Word document, you can expect that document properties are included. This is, in fact, the case, which means that you can include WordML tags in the stylesheet to set certain properties in the document that the stylesheet is creating. Specifically, you can set the validation-related properties that were discussed earlier in the chapter. You can also specify that displaying of XML tags is off by default. Properties are specified within a <w:docPr> element. The specific WordML code for the present example is as follows:

```
<w:docPr>
    <!-- Do not allow saving of invalid document -->
     <w:saveInvalidXML w:val="off"/>

    <!-- Do not display XML tags. -->
    <w:showXMLTags w:val="off"/>

    <!-- Ignore mixed content in validation -->
     <w:ignoreMixedContent/>
</w:docPr>
```

These elements should be placed in the stylesheet immediately after the closing </w:styles> element that you inserted earlier, and just before the <w:body> element. The completed stylesheet is shown in Listing 11-3. The new elements that have been added since the original stylesheet are in bold.

**Listing 11-3: Completed Stylesheet with Formatting Elements**

```
<?xml version="1.0" encoding="UTF-8"?>
<xsl:stylesheet version="1.0"
 xmlns:w="http://schemas.microsoft.com/office/word/2003/2/wordml"
 xmlns:ns0="http://www.pgacon.com/memo"
 xmlns:xsl="http://www.w3.org/1999/XSL/Transform"
 xmlns:wx="http://schemas.microsoft.com/office/word/2003/2/auxHint">

<xsl:template match="/">
<w:wordDocument>
  <w:styles>
    <w:style w:type="paragraph" w:styleId="MemoHead">
      <w:name w:val="MemoHead"/>
      <w:basedOn w:val="Normal"/>
      <w:rsid w:val="2D5055"/>
      <w:pPr>
        <w:pStyle w:val="MemoHead"/>
        <w:pBdr>
          <w:bottom w:val="single" w:sz="12" wx:bdrwidth="30"
             w:space="1" w:color="auto"/>
        </w:pBdr>
        <w:shd w:val="clear" w:color="auto" w:fill="E6E6E6"/>
        <w:spacing w:after="120"/>
      </w:pPr>
      <w:rPr>
        <wx:font wx:val="Times New Roman"/>
        <w:b/>
        <w:sz w:val="40"/>
        <w:sz-cs w:val="40"/>
      </w:rPr>
    </w:style>
   </w:styles>

<w:docPr>
    <!-- Do not allow saving of invalid document -->
     <w:saveInvalidXML w:val="off"/>
```

*Continued*

**Listing 11-3** *(Continued)*

```
    <!-- Do not display XML tags -->
    <w:showXMLTags w:val="off"/>

    <!-- Ignore mixed content in validation -->
     <w:ignoreMixedContent/>
</w:docPr>

 <w:body>
     <xsl:apply-templates select="/ns0:memo"/>
   </w:body>
 </w:wordDocument>
</xsl:template>

<!-- the memo heading -->
<xsl:template match="ns0:memo">
        <w:p>
          <w:pPr>
            <w:pStyle w:val="MemoHead"/>
          </w:pPr>
          <w:r>
            <w:t>Interoffice Memo</w:t>
          </w:r>
        </w:p>
   <ns0:memo>

<!-- the Date line -->
  <w:p>
  <w:r><w:t>Date:</w:t></w:r>
  <w:r><w:t xml:space="preserve">   </w:t></w:r>
  <ns0:date>
  <w:r><w:t><xsl:value-of select="ns0:date"/></w:t></w:r>
  </ns0:date>
  </w:p>

 <!-- the To line -->
  <w:p><w:r><w:t>To:</w:t></w:r>
  <w:r><w:t xml:space="preserve">   </w:t></w:r>
  <ns0:to>
  <w:r><w:t><xsl:value-of select="ns0:to"/></w:t></w:r>
  </ns0:to>
  </w:p>

 <!-- the From line -->
```

```
  <w:p><w:r><w:t>From:</w:t></w:r>
  <w:r><w:t xml:space="preserve">   </w:t></w:r>
  <ns0:from>
  <w:r><w:t><xsl:value-of select="ns0:from"/></w:t></w:r>
  </ns0:from>
  </w:p>

<!-- the Subject line -->
  <w:p><w:r><w:t>Subject:</w:t></w:r>
  <w:r><w:t xml:space="preserve">   </w:t></w:r>
  <ns0:subject>
  <w:r><w:t><xsl:value-of select="ns0:subject"/></w:t></w:r>
  </ns0:subject>
  </w:p>

<!-- the memo body -->
  <w:p>
  <ns0:body>
  <w:r><w:t><xsl:value-of select="ns0:body"/></w:t></w:r>
  </ns0:body>
  </w:p>

 </ns0:memo>
</xsl:template>
</xsl:stylesheet>
</xsl:stylesheet>
```

## Load and Apply the New Stylesheet

To see the new stylesheet in action, you must first load it into Word's schema library. Here's what to do:

1. Choose Tools → Templates and Add-ins to display the Templates and Add-ins dialog box.
2. On the XML Schema tab, click the Schema Library button to display the Schema Library dialog box.
3. In the Select a Schema List, click the Memo schema.
4. Click the Add Solution button and locate the new stylesheet that you just created.
5. When prompted, enter an alias such as MemoFormatted for the solution.
6. Click OK twice to close all dialog boxes.

At this point you have to solutions – the two stylesheets you created – associated with the Memo schema and its namespace, http://www.pgacon.com/memo (or whatever namespace you used). When you open the InfoPath form file, Word uses its namespace to associate it with the schema and the two solutions. This is shown in Figure 11-6, just after opening an InfoPath file created from the Memo form template. You can see that the XML Document task pane offers both solutions (stylesheets), and the document is displayed using the new `MemoFormatted` solution. You can switch to the old, unformatted view by clicking MemoPlain in the task pane.

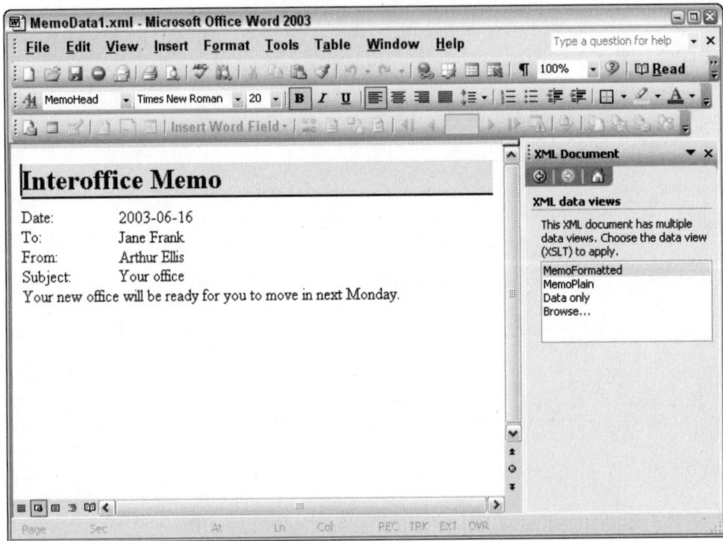


Figure 11-6: A memo document displayed using the new stylesheet.

The memo shown in Figure 11-6 appears identical to the one shown earlier in Figure 11-5, and that's the point. In the first memo, the formatting was applied manually by using Word's formatting commands. In the second, the formatting was created automatically by the stylesheet and applied to the data from the InfoPath XML file.

You may want to use additional formatting for the memo. You can use the techniques outlined in this chapter to apply formatting to the other memo elements such as the To and From lines, and then incorporate the WordML elements in a new stylesheet.

Chapter 12

# Connecting Excel and InfoPath

IN THIS CHAPTER

- Creating a schema
- Designing the InfoPath form
- Creating the workbook
- Importing data
- Analyzing results

THIS IS THE SECOND of six chapters that works through the creation of a complete solution using Office and XML. The example presented here pairs InfoPath and Excel to create a data entry and analysis application.

## Scenario

The scenario for this case study is as follows: Your company is involved in running telephone surveys, and the old methods of gathering, tabulating, and analyzing the data have become a problem, reducing efficiency and productivity. You want a new solution that will provide the following:

- An on-screen form that the telephone operator can use to record information while talking to a respondent
- A method of getting the data from the data collection program to the data analysis program without the need for re-keying or the chance for errors
- A way to quickly generate both statistical and graphical summaries of the data

InfoPath is the obvious choice for an easy-to-use on-screen form. For analysis, Excel is the best option because it offers both charts and statistical calculations. The survey data will be saved from InfoPath as an XML file, which will be imported into Excel for analysis.

# Planning

Once you have decided which Office applications will be involved in this project, there's still a lot of planning to be done, including deciding the order in which the parts of the application will be designed. Will you create the InfoPath form first and then the analysis workbook, or the other way around? It is actually a good idea in most cases to decide on the structure of the data first and then create the schema that defines it, because both InfoPath and Excel can make use of the schema to simplify the task of creating the form and workbook.

Once the schema is complete, the next logical step is to design the InfoPath form. Having the form enables you to create sample XML data files to use when designing and testing the Excel workbook. Of course, the process of creating an application, even a relatively simple one such as this, is rarely a linear start-to-finish process. You almost always have to go back and change things that you hoped were finished. That's okay, and it does not mean that your planning was a failure. In most situations, good planning minimizes but doesn't eliminate these changes, and that's all you can expect.

# Create the Schema

The first step in creating the schema is to decide on the data that the survey will collect. Table 12-1 shows the data for our sample program.

TABLE 12-1 DATA TO BE COLLECTED BY THE SURVEY

| Field | Data | Validation |
|---|---|---|
| date | The date of the survey | Any valid date; today's date will be entered by the user |
| age | The age of the respondent as a positive integer | In the range 18–65 because the survey is limited to people in that age range |
| education | The level of education achieved by the respondent with four possible choices: did not finish high school, high school diploma, college degree, graduate degree | Not needed because it is an enumeration |
| voted | A true/false value indicating whether the respondent voted in the last election | Not needed because it is a Boolean value |

| Field | Data | Validation |
|---|---|---|
| income | The respondent's annual income as a positive integer | Zero or greater |
| flavor | The respondent's favorite flavor of ice cream with six choices: vanilla, chocolate, strawberry, coffee, cherry, and other | Not needed because it is an enumeration |

Now that you know the data that the schema has to specify, you can create the schema. If you know the XSD schema language, you could use any text editor to write the schema manually, but that's a lot of work even for simple schemas – and is prone to errors. It's much better to use one of the many specialized XML and schema editors that are available, some as freeware, others as shareware or commercial programs. (My favorite is XML Spy.) Unfortunately, Office provides no direct way to create a schema. While InfoPath lets you define what is essentially a schema when you create a data source, this information is saved as part of the form template and is not available as a separate XSD file.

Regardless of how you create the schema, it ends up looking something like the one shown in Listing 12-1 (because the XSD language is so flexible, the same schema definition can be written in different ways so your schema file may be different). When you create your schema, be sure to use an appropriate namespace in place of the one in the listing. When the schema is complete, save it with an appropriate name and the .xsd extension (I named mine `survey.xsd`).

**Listing 12-1: Schema for the Survey Data**

```
<?xml version="1.0" encoding="UTF-8"?>
<xs:schema targetNamespace="http://www.pgacon.com/survey"
   xmlns:xs="http://www.w3.org/2001/XMLSchema"
   xmlns="http://www.pgacon.com/survey"
   elementFormDefault="qualified"
   attributeFormDefault="unqualified">
  <xs:element name="surveyResults">
    <xs:complexType>
      <xs:sequence>
        <xs:element name="respondent" minOccurs="0"
             maxOccurs="unbounded">
          <xs:complexType>
            <xs:sequence>
              <xs:element name="date" type="xs:date"/>
```

*Continued*

**Listing 12-1** *(Continued)*

```
              <xs:element name="age">
                <xs:simpleType>
                  <xs:restriction base="xs:positiveInteger">
                    <xs:minExclusive value="18"/>
                    <xs:maxExclusive value="65"/>
                  </xs:restriction>
                </xs:simpleType>
              </xs:element>
              <xs:element name="education">
                <xs:simpleType>
                  <xs:restriction base="xs:string">
                    <xs:enumeration value="No high school"/>
                    <xs:enumeration value="High school"/>
                    <xs:enumeration value="College degree"/>
                    <xs:enumeration value="Graduate degree"/>
                  </xs:restriction>
                </xs:simpleType>
              </xs:element>
              <xs:element name="voted" type="xs:boolean"/>
              <xs:element name="income" type="xs:positiveInteger"/>
              <xs:element name="flavor">
                <xs:simpleType>
                  <xs:restriction base="xs:string">
                    <xs:enumeration value="Vanilla"/>
                    <xs:enumeration value="Chocolate"/>
                    <xs:enumeration value="Strawberry"/>
                    <xs:enumeration value="Coffee"/>
                    <xs:enumeration value="Cherry"/>
                    <xs:enumeration value="Other"/>
                  </xs:restriction>
                </xs:simpleType>
              </xs:element>
            </xs:sequence>
          </xs:complexType>
        </xs:element>
      </xs:sequence>
    </xs:complexType>
  </xs:element>
</xs:schema>
```

With the schema complete, you can proceed to the InfoPath form.

# Design the InfoPath Form

When you start designing the InfoPath form, you'll see why creating the schema first was a good idea – it really simplifies your task.

## Create a New Form Template

To begin, you need to construct a template for the survey. Start by generating a new form template based on the schema. Here are the steps to follow:

1. Start InfoPath.
2. Choose File→Design a Form.
3. On the Design a Form task pane, click New from Data Source. InfoPath opens the Data Source Setup Wizard.
4. On the first screen, select the XML Schema or XML Data File option, and then click Next.
5. Click the Browse button, and then locate and open the schema file for the survey data (the schema you just created).
6. Click Finish.

At this point, InfoPath displays a blank form ready for design and, in the Data Source task pane, the structure of the schema that you selected, as shown in Figure 12-1.

Go ahead and save the template now. I used the name `SurveyFormTemplate`, but you can use any name you like. Remember to save the template regularly as you work on it, to prevent the chance of data loss.

# Selecting a Layout

Recall from Chapter 4, "Designing InfoPath Forms, Part 1" that in designing a form's visual interface, you first select a layout. This form is based on a simple schema and doesn't require a complex layout, nor does it require multiple views or optional sections. A good choice for the layout is a one-column table with a title as described in the following steps.

1. Click the Layout command on the task pane to display the Layout task pane.
2. In the Insert Layout Tables list, click the Table with Title item. InfoPath inserts the table, with placeholder text, into your form.
3. On the form, click where it says "Click to add a Title" and type the title for the form.

At this point, you can add any desired formatting for the title text, such as changing the font or alignment. Figure 12-2 shows the form with the title centered.

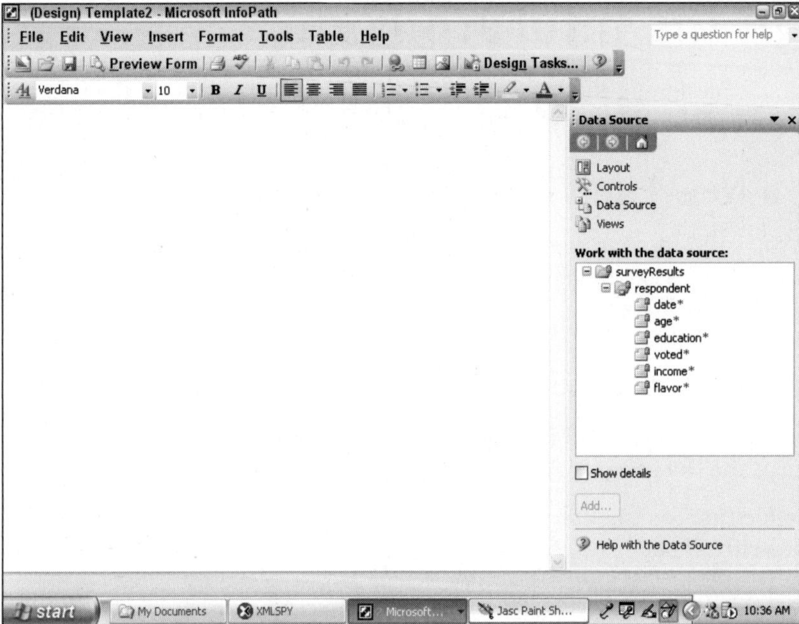


Figure 12-1: A new form template based on the schema.

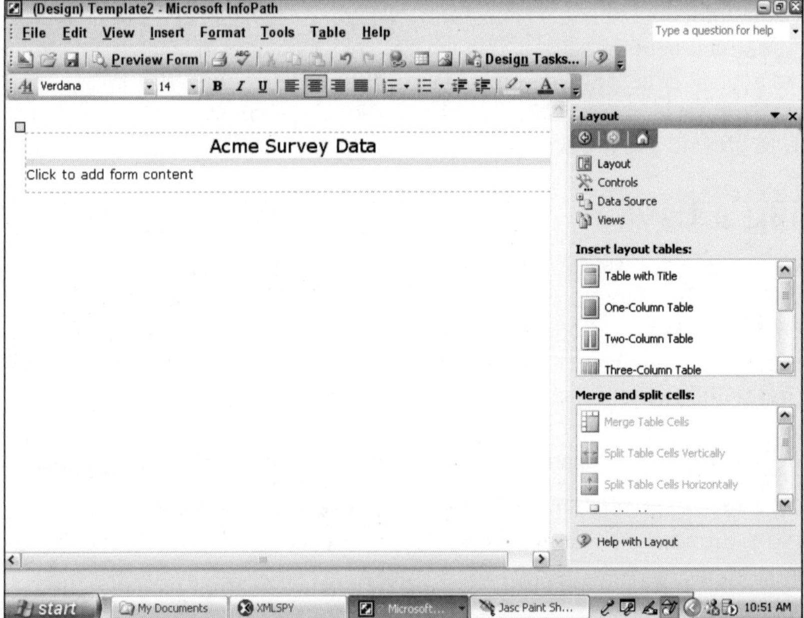


Figure 12-2: The form after adding a layout table and title.

## Adding Controls

The survey data is structured as a repeating element, `<respondent>`, that holds the responses from one survey participant. The repeating element contains six child elements that hold the individual pieces of data. This data structure is a perfect match with InfoPath's repeating design elements – either a repeating table or a repeating section. Either would be suitable for this project; I decided to use a repeating section and let InfoPath decide on the controls to use. Here are the required steps:

1. Click on the form where it says "Click to add form content."
2. On the task bar, click the Data Source command to display the Data Source taskbar.
3. Right-click the respondent element in the data source, then select Repeating Section with Controls from the pop-up menu.

The result of these actions is that InfoPath inserts a repeating section into the form. This section contains controls with the type of control determined by the type of data of the corresponding element. Thus:

- The Date field is a Date Picker control because it is type Date.
- The Education and Flavor fields are Drop-Down List Box controls because they are enumerations.
- The Voted field is a Check Box control because it contains Boolean data.
- The Age and Income fields are Text Box controls for entry of data from the keyboard.

Note that each control in the repeating section has been given a label based on the name of the bound element in the data source. At this stage in design the form template looks like the one shown in Figure 12-3.

The form could be used as it is now, but with a little effort you can make it easier to use and more attractive.

## Fine-Tuning the Form

The fundamentals of the data entry form are now complete, but there are some additional design steps that will improve the appearance and usability of the form.

### FORMATTING THE SECTION

For a more attractive screen display, and to make each copy of the section clearly distinct from others, you can change the background color and add a border.

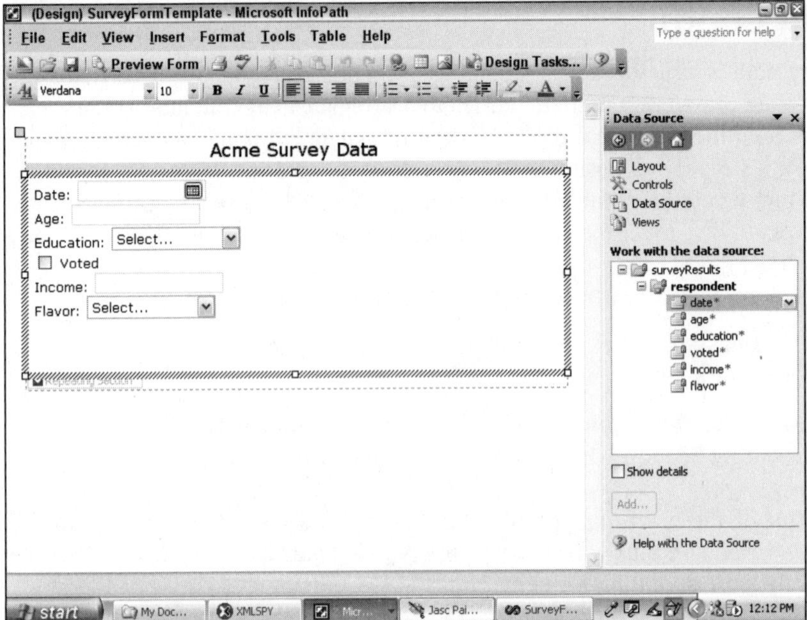


**Figure 12-3: The form template after adding the repeating section with controls.**

1. Right-click the section (between controls) and select Borders and Shading from the pop-up menu. InfoPath displays the Borders and Shading dialog box.
2. On the Borders tab, select the solid style and a width of 3 points. You can select a color other than black if you like – I used a dark blue.
3. In the Border diagram on the right side of the dialog box, click at the bottom of the sample to place a border there.
4. Click the Shading tab in the dialog box.
5. Select the Color option and select a light gray from the list.
6. Click OK to close the dialog box.

Your form now displays with a gray background and a blue border at the bottom. Remember, you can preview the appearance of the form at any time by clicking the Preview Form button on the toolbar. The preview shows how the form will appear when it is being filled out. Figure 12-4 shows the form preview at this stage of its design.

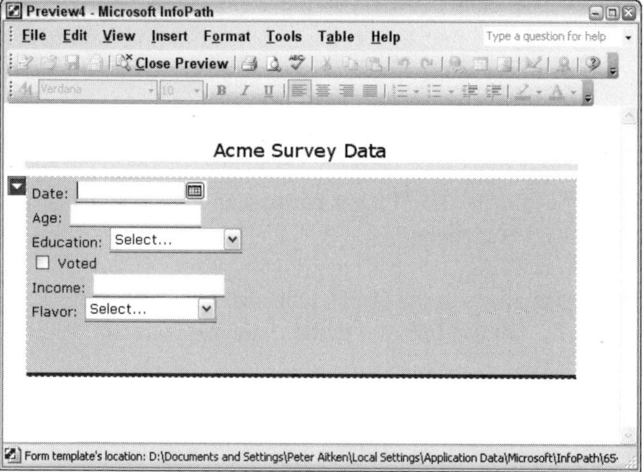


Figure 12-4: Previewing the form design.

## MODIFYING LABELS AND CONTROL POSITION

Next, we want to change some of the labels on the form and also make some changes to the arrangement of controls on the form. The labels were created automatically when the repeating section was inserted, and they are based on the bound data source field names. You can change a label to be more informative by simply clicking it and editing the text.

When modifying control position, remember that an InfoPath form uses a *flow* layout. Unlike some other visual form design tools, you cannot simply drag items to the desired location. The items on an InfoPath form – specifically text and controls – are treated like text in a document that flows from the top left of the form, across, and then down to a new line. A new line starts either when the designer presses Enter or when content reaches the right margin and is wrapped to a new line.

For example, look at the form in Figure 12-4. Starting at the top left, this form contains:

- The text "Date:"
- A Date Picker control
- A carriage return (Enter) to start a new line
- The text "Age:"
- A Text Box control, and so on

Taking this method of form layout into account, editing tasks must be carried out accordingly. For example, suppose that you want to move the Age control and its label up to be on the same line as the Date control. Here's how you would do it:

1. Click to the right of the Date Picker control to place the editing cursor there. If the cursor is already on that line you can press the End key for the same result.
2. Press Del to delete the carriage return at the end of the line. The Age Text Box and label move up to the top line.
3. To change the space between the Date Picker control and the Age label, add or delete spaces in between them.

Go ahead and make the desired changes to the form's labels and layout. Figure 12-5 shows the changes that I made; you can use this as a guide or devise your own design.

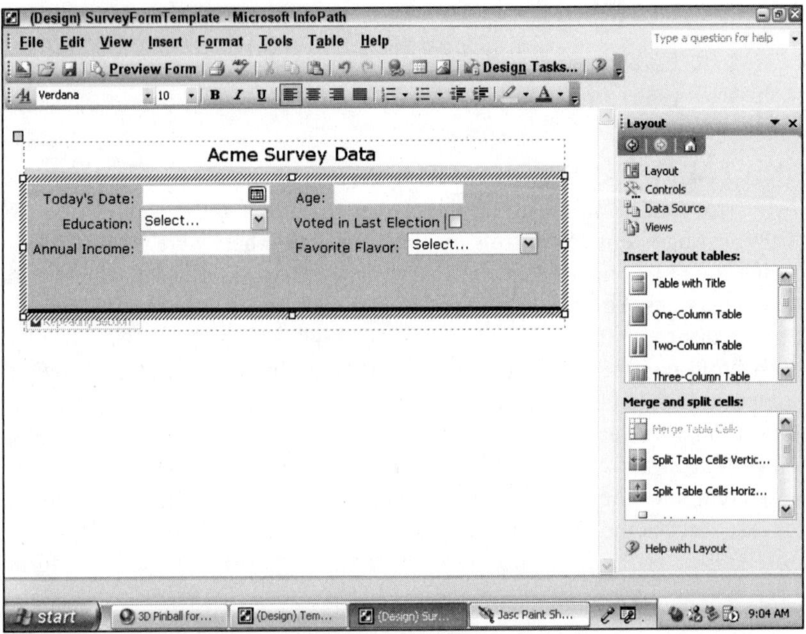


Figure 12-5: Changing the form's labels and control positions.

## FORMATTING THE INCOME FIELD

InfoPath fields, or controls, provide the form designer with some degree of flexibility over the format of data display. For our example form, the only place that such formatting is appropriate is the Income field, which can be formatted to display data as currency (with a comma separating thousands and a dollar sign). Here's how:

1. Right-click the Income Text Box control and select Text Box Properties from the pop-up menu.
2. On the Data tab, click the Format button to display the Integer Format dialog box (see Figure 12-6).

3. Select the Currency option.
4. Click OK twice to return to the form.

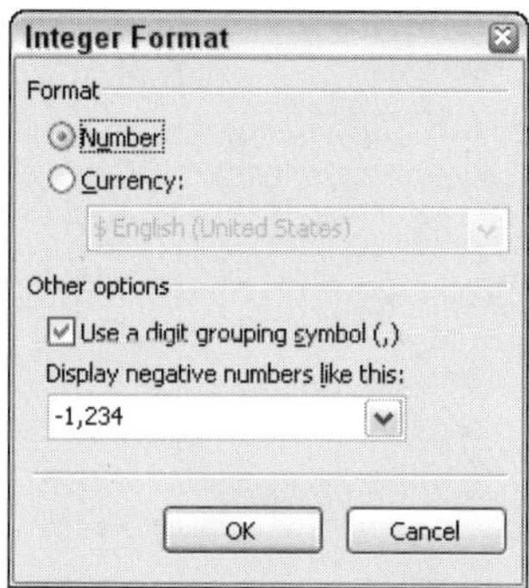


Figure 12-6: Specifying currency format for the Income control.

## TESTING THE FORM

The form is now complete and ready for testing. There are two ways to test a form. One, which you should do first, is to select Preview Form from the InfoPath toolbar. This lets you work with the form as if you were filling it out, adding data, inserting new sections, and so on. You cannot, however, save the data. The second and final testing should be done by actually filling out a form based on the template and saving the data. Here's how:

1. Make sure that you have saved the final version of the template.
2. On the InfoPath menu, select Fill Out a Form. InfoPath displays the Fill Out a Form task pane.
3. In the Fill Out a Form section of the task pane, click the name of the template that you just created. InfoPath opens a new, blank form.
4. Fill out the form, adding at least one additional section. Remember, to add a new section you can either right-click an existing section and select from the pop-up menu, or you can choose Insert → Section → Respondent from the menu.
5. Once you have added data for two or three respondents, save the form (File → Save).

Figure 12-7 shows the form with data for three respondents. Assuming that the form worked properly and you do not need to go back to make design changes, let's turn our attention to the Excel workbook that will analyze the survey data.

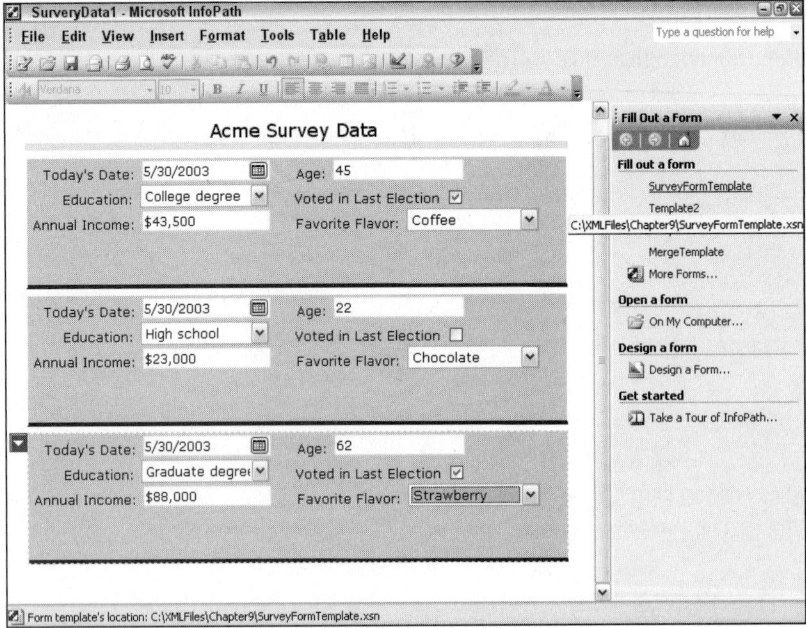

Figure 12-7: Filling out the survey form.

# Create the Workbook

With the InfoPath form design completed, it's time to design the workbook that will analyze and summarize data from the survey.

## Import the Map

First, you have to import the map for the survey data XML file. Here are the steps to follow:

1. Start Excel.
2. If necessary, choose View→Task Pane to display the task pane.
3. Open the task pane menu (Hint: click the down arrow in the task pane title bar) and select XML Source to display the XML Source task pane.
4. Click the Workbook Maps button to display the XML Maps dialog box.
5. In the XML Maps dialog box, click the Add button to display the Select XML Source dialog box.
6. Locate the XSD schema file for the survey data. You could also base the map on the sample XML data file that you created in the previous section, but it is preferable to use the schema when it is available.

7. Click Open. The selected map will not be listed in the XML Maps dialog box.
8. Click OK to close the XML Maps dialog box.

The XML Source task pane, shown in Figure 12-8, displays the structure of the map that you just opened.

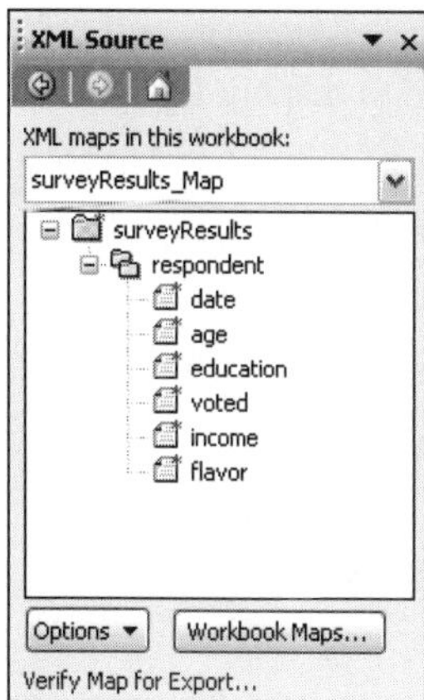


Figure 12-8: The survey data XML map displays in the XML Source task pane.

# Creating the XML List

Now that you have access to the map of the XML survey data, you need to map it to a worksheet range in order to create the XML list where the data will be imported. As you learned in Chapter 8, "Excel and XML," you can map individual fields to different worksheet locations, but that won't be necessary for this project. It is sufficient to map the entire collection of fields – in other words, the `<respondent>` element – to a cell and let the individual fields fall where they may. To do so:

1. Select Sheet3, which will be the worksheet for the XML data.
2. Double-click the sheet's tab and change its name to Raw Data.
3. From the XML Source task pane, drag the `<respondent>` element and drop it on cell A1. Excel maps the six fields to columns A through F, as shown in Figure 12-9.

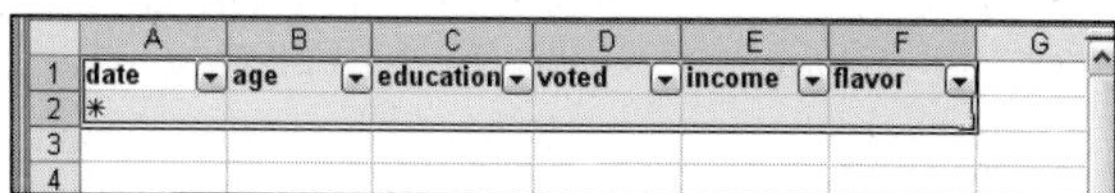


Figure 12-9: The XML list is created in the worksheet.

# Importing the Sample Data

Next, you can import the sample XML data file that you created when you were testing the InfoPath form. You'll need this data in the workbook when designing and testing the analysis functions. These are the steps to follow:

1. Place the cell pointer on a cell in the XML list that you created in the previous step.
2. If necessary, choose View → Toolbars → List and XML to display the List and XML toolbar.
3. Click the Import button on the toolbar. Excel displays the Import XML dialog box.
4. Locate and select the XML data file that you saved from InfoPath, and then click Import.

Figure 12-10 shows the XML list with my sample data in it. With this data in place, you can begin work on the analysis functions of the workbook.

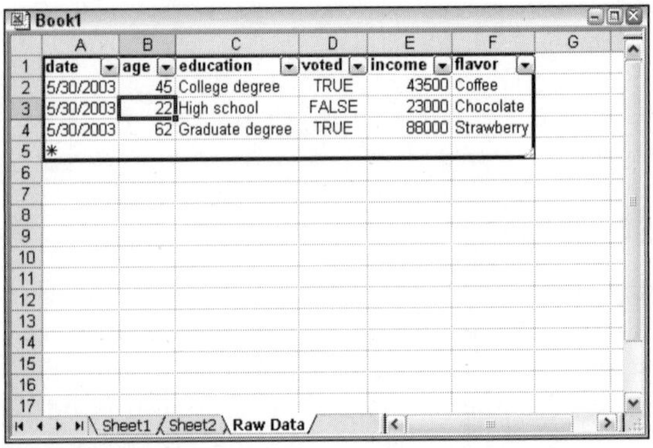

| date | age | education | voted | income | flavor |
|---|---|---|---|---|---|
| 5/30/2003 | 45 | College degree | TRUE | 43500 | Coffee |
| 5/30/2003 | 22 | High school | FALSE | 23000 | Chocolate |
| 5/30/2003 | 62 | Graduate degree | TRUE | 88000 | Strawberry |

**Figure 12-10: The XML list after importing the sample data from InfoPath.**

# The Workbook Analysis Functions

Once you have the XML data in your workbook, you can use any of Excel's powerful analysis tools to provide the summary information that you need. Let's run through a sample summary analysis that determines what percentage of respondents prefers each of the six flavor choices. The example is relatively simple because, after all, this is a book about XML and Office and not about Excel's other capabilities. The point is to show you how to use Excel to provide "instant" analysis of data with little effort on the part of the user.

## SUMMARIZING FLAVOR PREFERENCE

To begin with, the Excel tool for ascertaining the flavor preference percentages is the `DCount` data function, which takes a list and counts the number of records in it that meet a specified criteria. You need to use this function six times, once for each of the six flavor choices. The function requires a criterion range, located somewhere in the workbook, on which to filter. A criterion consists of the field name in one cell and the value in the cell below. For example, to count the records where the Flavor field is "vanilla" you would put the text "Flavor" in one cell and the text "vanilla" in the cell below.

It's usually a good idea to place criteria in an out-of-the-way part of the workbook. For this project I placed them in their own worksheet. Here are the steps to follow:

1. Make Sheet2 active.
2. Double-click its tab and change the worksheet name to "Criteria."
3. Put the label "flavor" in cell A1, and then copy it to cells B1:F1.
4. Create the first criterion by entering the text "vanilla" in cell A2.
5. Create the other five criteria (chocolate, strawberry, coffee, cherry, and other) in the cells to the right, so that your worksheet looks like the one in Figure 12-11.

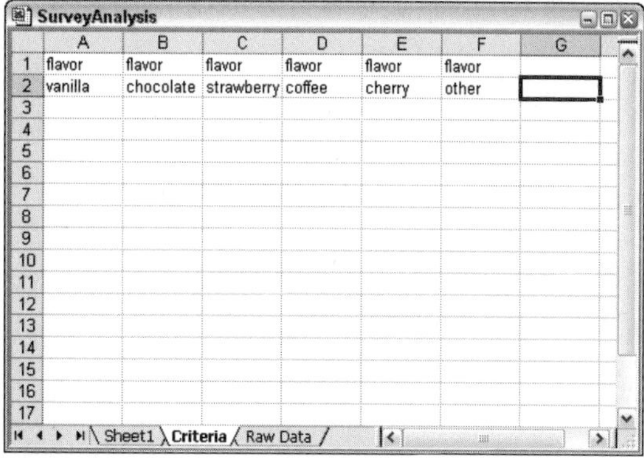


**Figure 12-11: After creating the flavor criteria.**

With the criteria in place you can now insert the `DCount` functions. The first worksheet is used to display the analysis results. Follow these steps:

1. Make Sheet1 active.
2. Change the worksheet name to Analysis.
3. Put the label "Flavor Preferences" in cell A2.

4. Put the names of the six flavor choices in cells C2:C7.
5. Put the corresponding `DCount` function next to each label, in cells D2:D7. Creating these functions is explained next.

The `DCount` function requires the following three arguments:

- **Database.** The workbook range that contains the database, or list, of data. This can be expressed as a named range or a specific range address such as A1:F200. In this application, however, you do not know ahead of time how many rows the list will contain because the data imported from InfoPath expands as the survey progresses. In this case you simply specify columns and Excel automatically locates the last record in the list. The Database argument, therefore, is `'Raw Data'!A:F`. Note the single quotes around the worksheet name – these are essential because the name contains a space.
- **Field.** The list field, or column, on which the function is to perform its calculation. This can be specified as a column name or a relative position (1 is the first column; 2, the second; and so on). The `DCount` function counts nonempty cells, and because there will be no empty cells in this list (all fields are required according to the schema), it does not matter which field is used. I used the value `1` for this argument.
- **Criteria:** The workbook range containing the criteria for the function. This is `Criteria!A1:A2` to count instances of "vanilla," `Criterial!B1:B2` to count instances of "chocolate," and so on.

When you enter these functions in cells D2:D7, make sure that each function references the correct criterion range to match the adjacent label. For example, in the cell adjacent to the "Strawberry" label, the function is

```
=DCOUNT('Raw Data'!A:F,1,Criteria!C1:C2)
```

In the cell adjacent to the "Cherry" label, the function is

```
=DCOUNT('Raw Data'!A:F,1,Criteria!E1:E2)
```

When you have finished entering the functions, the Analysis worksheet looks like Figure 12-12. Note that the functions are correctly totaling the flavor preferences for the sample data (refer to Figure 12-10).

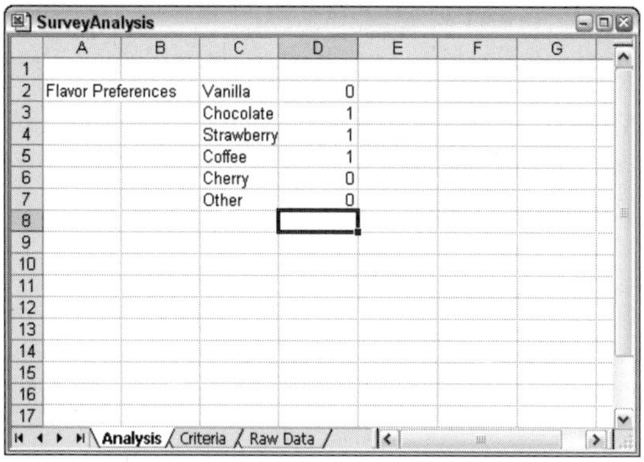

SurveyAnalysis

| | A | B | C | D |
|---|---|---|---|---|
| 1 | | | | |
| 2 | Flavor Preferences | | Vanilla | 0 |
| 3 | | | Chocolate | 1 |
| 4 | | | Strawberry | 1 |
| 5 | | | Coffee | 1 |
| 6 | | | Cherry | 0 |
| 7 | | | Other | 0 |

Analysis / Criteria / Raw Data

**Figure 12-12: After entering the DCount functions to total flavor preferences.**

## DISPLAYING PERCENTAGES RATHER THAN TOTALS

As useful as the totals for each flavor may be, displaying them as percentages is usually preferred. Remember, the total changes each time new data is added to the list. In order to calculate percentages, you need to know the total number of respondents, which is a useful piece of information in itself. To find this, you can make use of a feature of the `DCount` function: when it is given a blank criterion, it counts all records in the list. Thus, the following function returns the total number of records in the list:

```
DCOUNT('Raw Data'A:F, 1, Criteria!G1:G2)
```

Note that this is dependent on cells G1 and G2 in the Criteria worksheet remaining blank. To include the total respondent count on the Analysis worksheet, follow these steps:

1. Insert two new rows at the top of the worksheet so that the existing content now starts in row 4.
2. Enter the text "Respondents" in cell A2.
3. Enter the function `DCOUNT('Raw Data'A:F, 1, Criteria!G1:G2)` in cell C2.

Now that you have the total number of respondents, you can modify the formulas in cells D4:D9 to display percentages rather than totals. For the vanilla category, for example, the calculation is simply the number preferring vanilla divided by the total number of respondents. For example, the new formula in cell D4 will be

```
=DCOUNT('Raw Data'!A:F,1,Criteria!A1:A2)/C2
```

You can go ahead and change all six formulas, dividing each by the value in cell C2. After formatting cells D4:D9 as Percentage the worksheet will look like Figure 12-13.

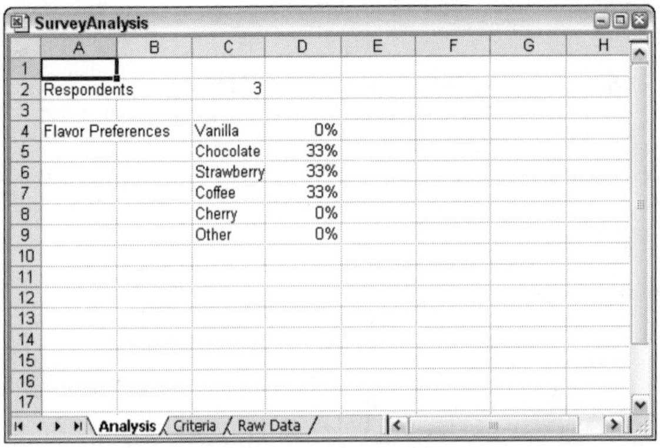

SurveyAnalysis

| | A | B | C | D |
|---|---|---|---|---|
| 1 | | | | |
| 2 | Respondents | | 3 | |
| 3 | | | | |
| 4 | Flavor Preferences | | Vanilla | 0% |
| 5 | | | Chocolate | 33% |
| 6 | | | Strawberry | 33% |
| 7 | | | Coffee | 33% |
| 8 | | | Cherry | 0% |
| 9 | | | Other | 0% |

Analysis / Criteria / Raw Data

Figure 12-13: Displaying percentages for flavor preferences.

## CREATE A CHART OF FLAVOR PREFERENCES

The final step in this analysis is to create a chart displaying the flavor preference data. This task is greatly simplified by Excel's Chart Wizard. Here are the required steps.

1. Select cells C4:D9 in the Analysis worksheet.
2. Click the Chart Wizard button on the toolbar, or choose Insert→Chart. Excel displays the Chart Wizard dialog box.
3. Select Column under Chart Type, and Clustered Column under Chart Sub-type, then click Next.
4. In the next dialog box (Step 2 of 4) there are no changes needed, so click Next to proceed.
5. In the next dialog box (Step 3 of 4), display the Legend tab and deselect the Show Legend option. Because this chart has only one data series, a legend is not needed. Then, click Next.
6. In the final wizard dialog box, select the As Object In option and make sure that Analysis is selected in the drop-down list. This creates the chart as an object embedded in the Analysis worksheet.
7. Click Finish to create the chart.
8. In the worksheet, drag the chart to the desired position and size.

When you have completed creating the chart your analysis worksheet will look like Figure 12-14.

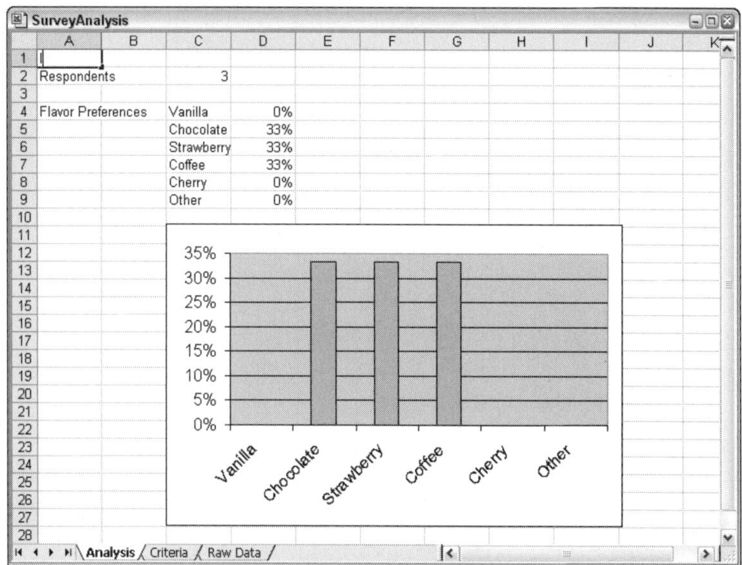


Figure 12-14. Displaying a chart of flavor preferences.

### TESTING WITH MORE DATA

It's always good idea to test an analysis worksheet with additional data. You can see that your functions and chart work when there are three records in the list—will they still work properly when the list expands? To check this:

1. Go back to the InfoPath form and add a number of additional data records to the three you entered earlier.
2. Save the file.
3. Switch to Excel and display the Raw Data worksheet.
4. Click the Refresh button on the List and XML toolbar. Excel imports the new records from the InfoPath form.
5. Display the Analysis worksheet. It should have automatically updated to reflect the added data, as shown in Figure 12-15.

# Additional Considerations

When designing a data entry and analysis solution that uses InfoPath and Excel, there are a few other concerns that you need to keep in mind.

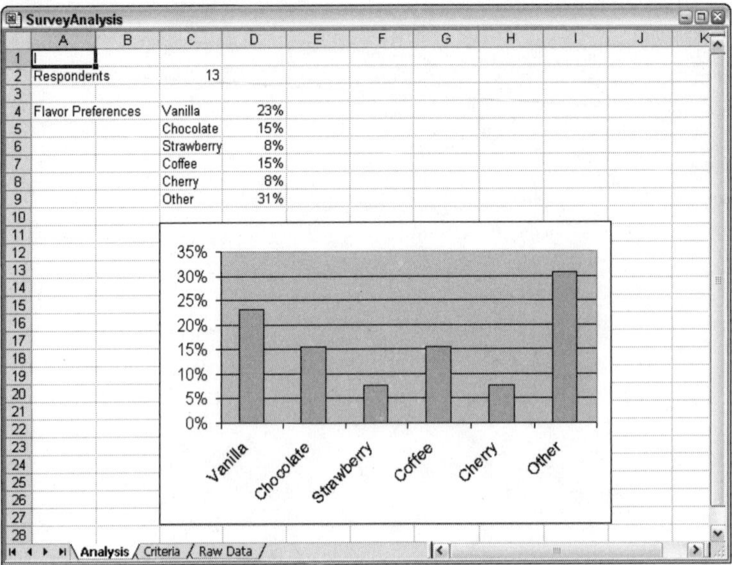


**Figure 12-15: The analysis worksheet automatically updates with new data.**

# Data Validation

One concern is data validation. InfoPath always validates a form when it is being filled out, but it does allow the user to save a form that contains validation violations. Likewise, Excel can validate XML data against its schema when it is imported, but this is an option that must be specifically enabled for an XML list (in the Properties dialog box). It is somewhat pointless to have validation required in both InfoPath and Excel. When designing the solution, you need to make a choice:

- The person filling out the InfoPath form is not permitted to save invalid data. You can then be sure that the data imported into Excel is valid. You do not need to use Excel's validation option or to design the workbook's analysis functions to take into account the possibility of invalid data.
- The person filling out the InfoPath form is permitted to save invalid data. Your Excel workbook must then take into account the possibility of invalid data being imported. You may want to use Excel's validation option, but you should design the workbook's analysis functions to take into account the possibility of invalid data.

In my experience the first option is always to be preferred. After all, one of the main benefits of using XML and InfoPath is the ability to validate data so that programs that use the data – in this case, the Excel workbook – can do their jobs without all the added complexity of having to deal with the possibility of invalid data.

## Data Flow

A second concern is the way your data flow is designed. Using this chapter's application as an example, one important question is whether there will be only a single person or multiple people collecting survey data and entering it into InfoPath.

The data flow design task is somewhat simplified in the case of a single person, but there are still decisions to be made. Will the operator start a new InfoPath form every day or every week, or how often? In our example, each time the data is imported into the Excel workbook, the import contains only new data, with data from previous imports already present in the worksheet. This requires that a property of the XML list be set so that new data is appended to existing data. The other approach is to have the operator always use the same InfoPath file so that new data is added to old. In other words, the InfoPath data file always contains all the data, old and new. When it is imported into Excel, the old data in the worksheet does not need to be kept. The XML list property must be set so that new data overwrites existing data.

To set XML list properties, click the XML Map Properties button on the List and XML toolbar. These properties were covered in detail in Chapter 8.

If survey data is to be collected by more than one person, things get a bit more complicated and there is more than one way to design the data flow. One approach is to use InfoPath's form merge capability (as was described in Chapter 3, "Introduction to InfoPath," and Chapter 5, "Designing InfoPath Forms, Part 2"). When a form is designed so that merging is supported, your data flow could have each operator fill out his or her own InfoPath form, and merging those forms into a "master" form that is then saved and imported into Excel. Another approach is to import each operator's form data separately into Excel.

Chapter 13

# Connecting Access and InfoPath

IN THIS CHAPTER

- Creating the database
- Designing the InfoPath form
- Adjusting the views
- Using the form

INFOPATH FORMS make it easy to enter, view, and edit information in an Access database. This chapter walks you though the process of creating an application that uses InfoPath forms to do just that.

## The Scenario

You work for the Save the Chipmunk charitable organization, and your boss has told you to design an efficient, computer-based method of keeping track of donors and donations. A database is the ideal solution for storing the data, and InfoPath forms are a good choice for entering and viewing data. Because InfoPath form design is simplified when you start with an existing data source, your first task is to design the Access database.

## Creating the Database

For this case study, you first need to create the Access database that will be connected to InfoPath. You may be wondering why I'm not using the Northwind sample database that is provided as part of the Access installation. The most important reason is that by creating the database yourself, you will gain an intimate understanding of its internal structure and will be better able to relate it to the InfoPath forms you'll create later. In addition, the database you will create is very simple. In contrast, the Northwind database is rather complex and would be more difficult to work with.

## Database Design

The database that we are designing here is simple but sufficient to illustrate the use of InfoPath with an Access database. There are two tables:

- A Donors table that contains information about the individual donors such as their name and phone number
- A Donations table that contains information about each individual donation: the date, the amount, and the identity of the donor

The two tables will be linked so that each entry in the Donations table is associated with a single entry in the Donors table, identifying the person who made the donation. Because each person is likely to make multiple donations as time goes by, this arrangement, called a *relational* database, simplifies many aspects of database design. This sort of relationship is called *one to many* because each item in the Donors table can be linked to multiple items in the Donations table (when one person makes two or more donations), but each item in the Donations table is linked to only one item in the Donors table (because each donation comes from a single person).

## Creating a New Database and the Donors Table

Here's how to create the new database and define the Donors table:

1. Start Access.
2. Choose File→New to display the New File task pane.
3. Click the Blank Database command on the task pane.
4. In the next dialog box, select a location and enter a name for the database (I used DonorList).
5. Click Create.

At this point, Access displays the Tables list for the new database. There are no tables yet, of course. The list contains three ways to create a new table: in Design View, by using a wizard, and by entering data. If you are familiar with these tools, you can use any method you like as long as the resulting table has the correct structure (described later). These steps use Design View:

1. Double-click the Create Table in Design View entry in the DonorList tables dialog box. Access opens Design View, as shown in Figure 13-1.
2. In the first row of the Field Name column enter DonorID.
3. Press Tab to move to the Data Type column. Access automatically specifies the Text data type. Use the drop-down list to change this to AutoNumber.

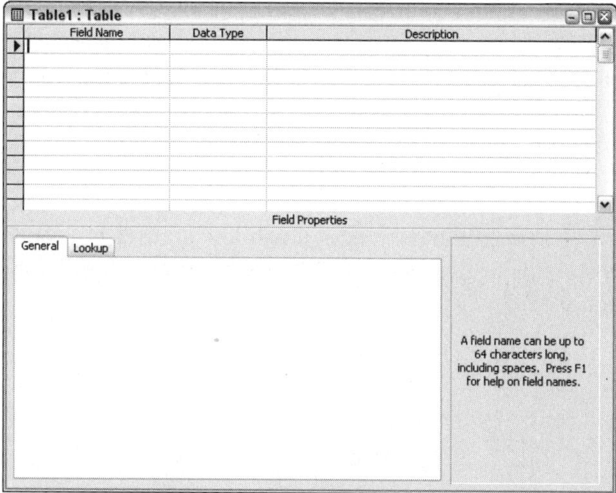


Figure 13-1: The table designer at the start of designing a new table.

4. Move to the second row and enter FirstName as the field name and accept Text as the data type.
5. With the cursor still on the row for the FirstName field, use the General tab at the bottom of the design dialog box to change the Field Size to 16 and Allow Zero Length to No. This specifies that the last name can hold up to 16 characters and that it cannot be left blank.
6. Repeat Steps 2–5 to enter the following fields specified below with the indicated field size values. For all of these fields the data type should be Text and Allow Zero Length should be No.

| Field | Size |
|---|---|
| LastName | 20 |
| Address | 25 |
| City | 15 |
| State | 2 |
| PostalCode | 5 |
| HomePhone | 12 |

7. When all the fields have been defined, right-click the DonorID field and select Primary Key from the pop-up menu. A small key symbol is displayed to the left of the DonorID row to indicate that this field is a primary key.

The final step is to specify how the table records should be sorted. We want them to be sorted by last name and then by first name. Here's how:

1. Right-click anywhere in the table design window and select Properties from the pop-up menu. Access displays the Table Properties dialog box, shown in Figure 13-2.

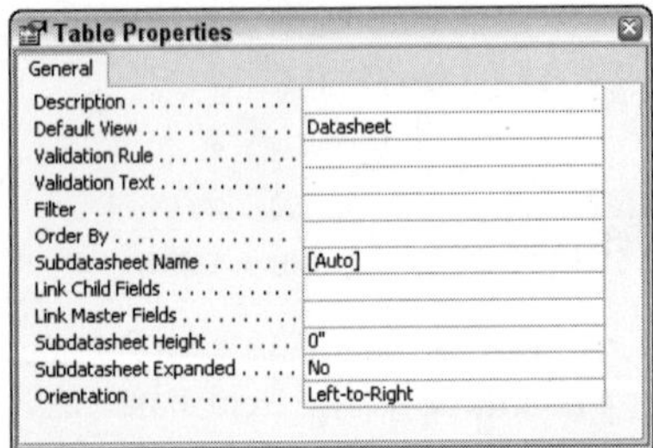


**Figure 13-2: The Table Properties dialog box.**

2. Enter LastName, FirstName in the Order By property.
3. Close the dialog box by clicking the X in the title bar.

Figure 13-3 shows what the completed table design looks like now.

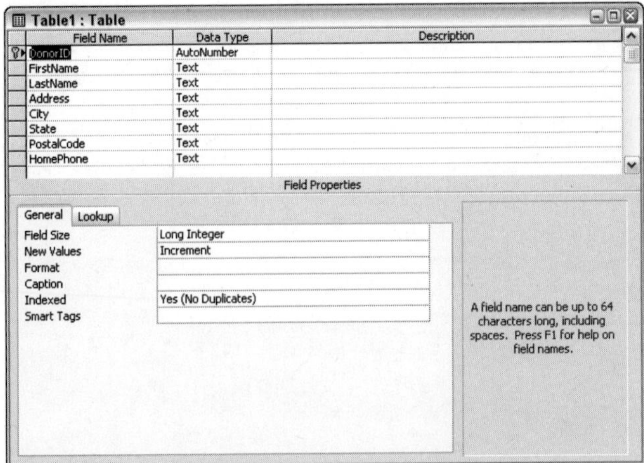


**Figure 13-3: After completing the design of the Donors table.**

Close the designer by clicking the X in the title bar. When prompted to save the table select Yes, and then enter Donors as the table name.

For readers who are not familiar with databases, some explanation is in order. Most of the fields are self-explanatory – they will be used to hold name, address, and other information about an individual donor. But what about the DonorID field? Why is it type AutoNumber and also designated as the primary key? Here's why:

- The AutoNumber designation means that Access will automatically enter sequential numbers in this field as donors are added to the table. The user need not enter this information.
- The primary key is the field that can be used to uniquely identify each record. This field cannot be left blank and must contain a unique value for each record (donor).

# Define the Donations Table

Now it's time to define the Donations table. This table is simpler that the Donors table, containing fewer fields. Follow the procedures just described for the Donors table to create this table. The four fields are as follows:

| Field | Data Type |
|---|---|
| ID | AutoNumber |
| DonorID | Number |
| Date | Date/Time |
| Amount | Currency |

Set the ID field as the primary key.

After these fields are defined, use the Table Properties dialog box to specify Date as the sort field. Save this table as Donations. Figure 13-4 shows the Design View when you've finished.

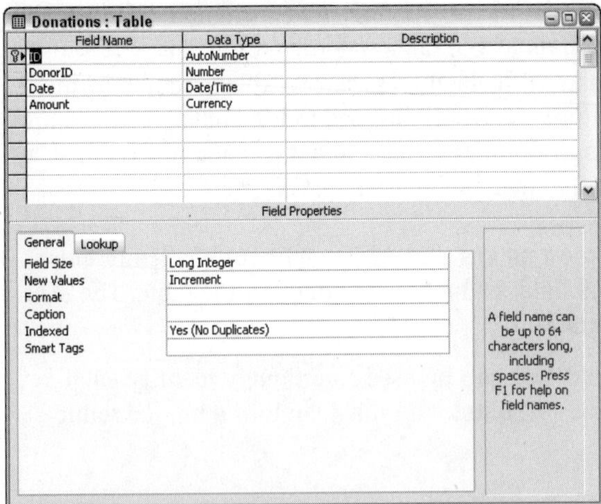


Figure 13-4: The completed design of the Donations table.

# Defining the Relationship

You've probably figured out that the Donors and Donations tables are going to be linked, or related, by the DonorID field. Even though the field name is the same in both tables, Access cannot guess that this is the relationship to create – you must do it yourself. Here's how:

1. Make sure that both tables are closed because Access cannot create a relationship with an open table.
2. Click the Relationship button on the toolbar or select Tools→Relationships. Access opens the Relationships window and the Show Table dialog box.
3. In the Show Table dialog box, the Tables tab lists both of the tables you created. Select each table in turn and click the Add button. This adds the tables to the Relationship window.
4. Click Close to close the Show Table dialog box. Figure 13-5 shows the Relationship window displaying the two tables but no relationship.

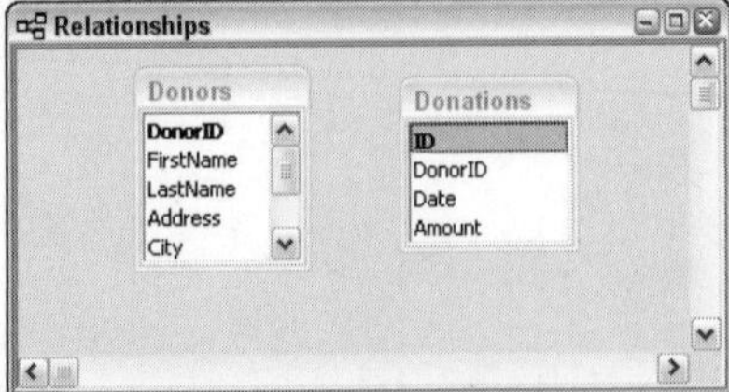


Figure 13-5: Before defining the relationship between Donors and Donations.

5. Point your cursor at the DonorID field in the Donors table (it's displayed in boldface because it is the table's primary key). Drag it to the Donations table and drop it on the DonorID field of that table. Access displays the Edit Relationships dialog box, shown in Figure 13-6.

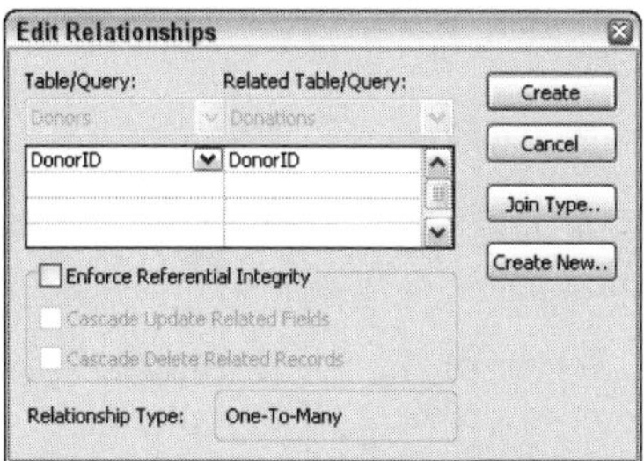


Figure 13-6: The Edit Relationships dialog box.

6. Because the default settings for this relationship are correct, you do not need to make any changes in this dialog box. Click Create to create the relationship and close the Edit Relationships dialog box.

7. The relationship is now indicated by a connecting line in the Relationships window, as shown in Figure 13-7.

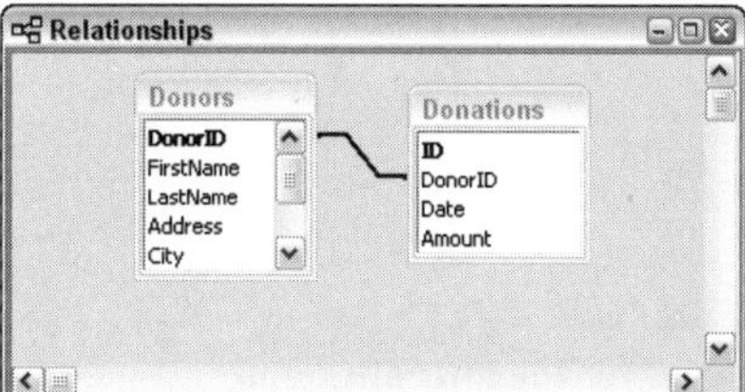


Figure 13-7: The relationship is indicated graphically in the Relationships window.

8. Close this window by clicking the X in the title bar.

The database is now complete and you can turn to the next task, designing the InfoPath form.

# Designing the InfoPath Form

The InfoPath form will be designed to let the user enter new donors, enter new donations, and search for donors by specified criteria. This may sound complicated, but I think you'll be surprised at how easy InfoPath makes it.

## Connect to the Data Source

Your new InfoPath form will be based on a data source – namely the Access database that you created earlier in this chapter. Here are the steps required to create a new form based on the data source:

1. Start InfoPath.
2. Choose File → Design a Form to display the Design a Form task pane.
3. On the task pane, click the New From Data Source command. Access displays the Data Source Setup Wizard.
4. Select the Database (Microsoft SQL Server or Microsoft Access Only) option, and click Next.
5. In the next dialog box, click the Select Database button. Access displays the Select Data Source dialog box.
6. Locate the DonorList database file that you created earlier in the chapter. Select it and click Open.
7. Access displays the Select Table dialog box, as shown in Figure 13-8.

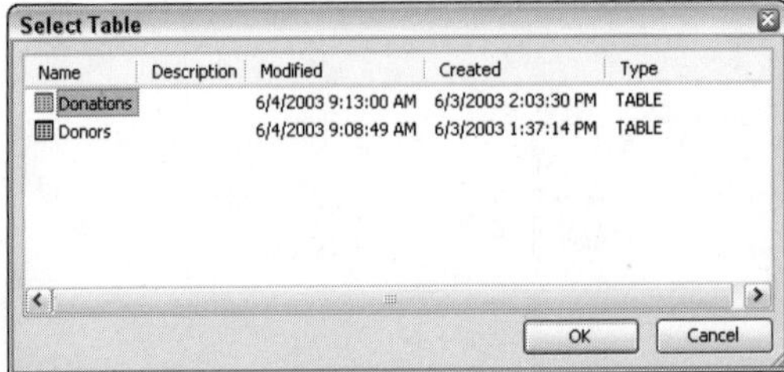


**Figure 13-8: Selecting data source tables for the InfoPath form.**

8. The database's two tables, Donations and Donors, are listed. Select the Donors table and click OK.
9. The next Data Source Setup Wizard dialog box, shown in Figure 13-9, lists the fields in the table that you selected. Fields with a check mark will be included in the form's data source. Since this form requires all fields, there are no changes needed here. Click the Add Table button to add the Donations table.

In Figure 13-9 you'll see that the DonorID field is grayed out and cannot be deselected. That's because this is the table's primary key field.

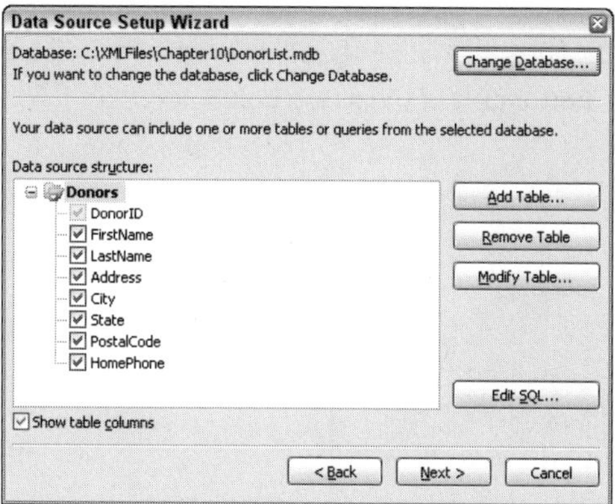


Figure 13-9: Selecting fields from the Donors table.

10. Access again displays the list of the tables in the data source. Select the Donations table and click Next.

11. The Edit Relationships dialog box is displayed, as shown in Figure 13-10. Access suggests a relationship between the DonorID fields in the two tables based on the field names being the same. You could use this dialog box to specify other relationships if necessary, but for this example the suggested relationship is correct and you can simply click Finish.

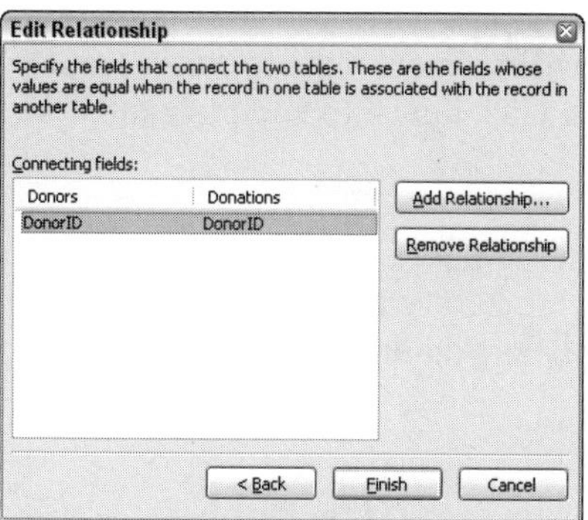


Figure 13-10: Specifying the relationship between the tables.

12. Access displays the Data Source Setup Wizard dialog box again, as shown in Figure 13-11. You can see that the Donations table and its fields are listed as a child of the Donors table. You could deselect individual fields at this time if they were not needed in the InfoPath form, but the form will use all the fields so this is not necessary. Note that the ID and DonorID fields in the Donations table are grayed out and cannot be deselected. The ID field is required because it is the table's primary key, and the DonorID field is required because it is the link to the Donors table.

If the names of the table fields are not displayed, select the Show Table Columns option at the bottom left of the dialog box.

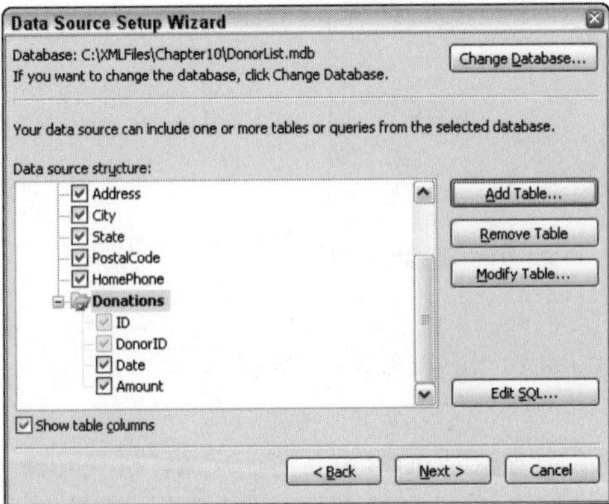


**Figure 13-11: After adding the Donations table to the data source.**

13. Click Next to display the wizard's final dialog box. It presents a summary of the data source that you defined, and gives you the option of designing the Query View or the Data View first (more on these views soon). Select the Query View option, and then click Finish to complete the design of the data source.

When you're done, Access creates the new form template. You need to understand how this form is created before you start working on its design. Be sure to save the form template now and regularly as you design it.

# The New Form

The form that Access creates has quite a few components already present on it. Perhaps most importantly, the new form has two views defined: a Query View and a Data Entry View.

InfoPath automatically creates the Query View, shown in Figure 13-12.

This view has the following components:

- A layout table at the top with a "Query Form" title and some explanatory text. If you click the explanatory text, it is deleted and you can enter your own text in this area if desired.

- Another layout table that contains the remainder of the view's components.
- A New Record button that the user will click to add a new record (that is, a new donor) to the database.
- A set of text boxes for the fields in the Donors table. The user enters query information here.
- A Run Query button that the user clicks to perform the query based on the information entered in the text boxes.

The form's second view, the Data Entry View, is initially blank – you must design it from scratch. This is the view that is used to view and enter data. For example, if the user runs a query using the Query View, the records that are retrieved by the query are displayed in the Data Entry View for the user to examine or edit. Likewise, if the user clicks the New Record button, a new, blank record is displayed in the Data Entry View for the user to fill in.

Your task now is to take the preliminary InfoPath-created form and make modifications and additions to meet the needs of your application. The one thing that is required is to design the Data Entry View. Other changes and additions – such as data validation, conditional formatting, and changes to the Query View – are optional.

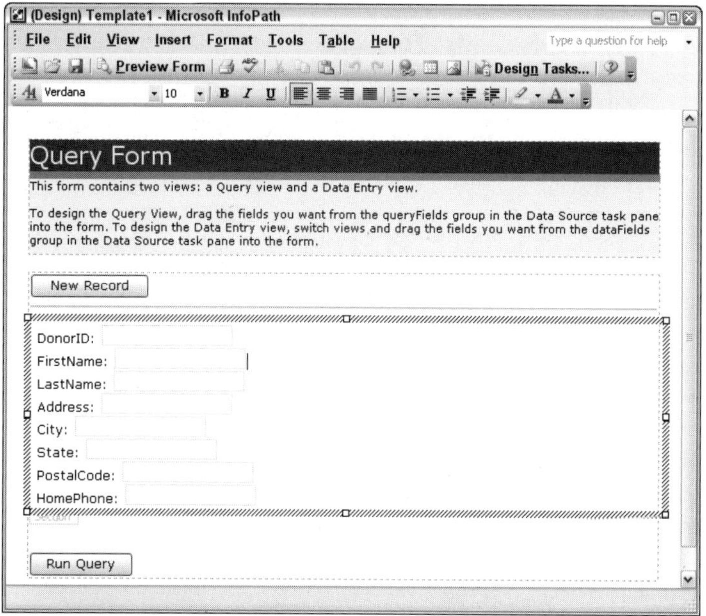


Figure 13-12: The Query View created by InfoPath.

# About the Data Source

Figure 13-13 shows the data source that InfoPath created based on the DonorList database. The structure of this data source may require some explanation.

**Figure 13-13:** The data source created from the DonorList database.

There are two main groups in the data source: queryFields and dataFields. Each of these groups contains the two tables Donors and Donations with all of their fields, so why are there two separate groups? The answer lies in the fact that form information is treated differently when it is part of a query than when it is simply data. As a result, form controls on the form's Query View are bound to fields in the queryFields part of the data source, while controls on the form's Data Entry View are bound to fields in the dataFields part. You must keep this distinction in mind when designing the form, making sure to use the correct binding when adding controls.

# Modifying the Query View

The Query View that InfoPath created is perfectly functional as it is, but you may want to make some changes. For example, the layout table at the top of the form – the one with the Query View title in it – is superfluous, and can be deleted by right-clicking it and choosing Delete → Table from the pop-up menu.

If there are fields on which you won't be running queries, you can delete the associated controls and labels. For example, it isn't likely you will need to find donors based on DonorID, because that is just an arbitrary numerical value, so you should delete it. You can also enhance the formatting of the view with fonts, colors, and so on. I leave this to your discretion. For the example application I deleted the DonorID field but otherwise left this view unchanged.

Formatting InfoPath forms is covered in Chapter 4 "Designing InfoPath Forms, Part 1."

## Starting the Data Entry View

The main remaining task is designing the form's Data Entry View. InfoPath's tools make this a lot easier than you might expect. Here's how to get started:

1. Display the Views task pane.
2. Click Data Entry (default) to display the Data Entry View, which is currently blank.
3. Display the Layout task pane.
4. In the Insert Layout Table list, click Table with Title. InfoPath inserts a table with placeholder text.
5. Click where it says Click to add a title, and type your form title – for example, Save the Chipmunks Donors.
6. Click where it says Click to add form content.
7. Display the Data Source task pane.
8. If necessary, open the `dataFields` node of the tree.
9. Right-click the `d:Donors` group under `dataFields` and select Repeating Section with Controls from the pop-up menu. InfoPath inserts the section and bound controls on the form.

Figure 13-14 shows what the form looks like now. Examine the form to see exactly how much work InfoPath has done for you.

Except for the title, the form consists of just one repeating section. You can see this by the Repeating Section tab at the bottom of the form. The section contains controls for the eight fields in the Donors table – DonorID through HomePhone. The section repeats because the Donors table will contain multiple donors. When the form is in use, there will be one copy of the section displayed on the form for each donor that was returned by a query or is being entered by the user.

The repeating section also contains a repeating table as identified by the repeating Table tab. This table has controls for the four fields in the Donations table. It is a repeating table because each donor can have one or more associated donations.

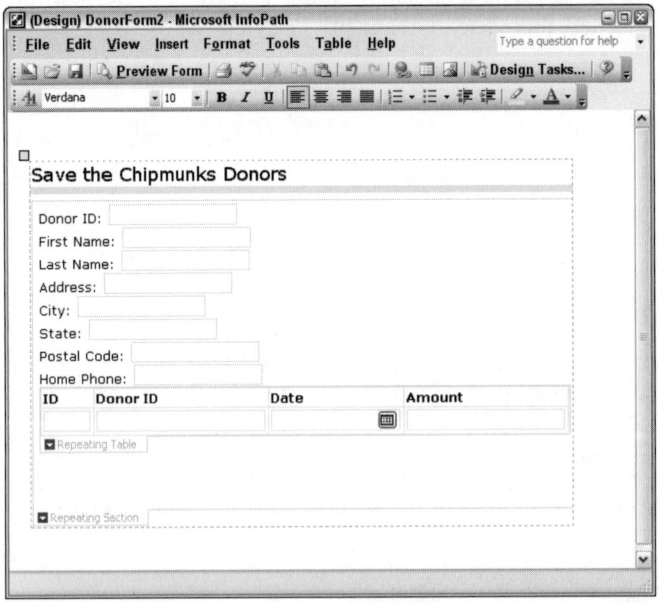

Figure 13-14: The data entry form after adding the repeating section.

How was InfoPath able to automatically create this form so easily? It has to do with the way the data source is defined. Back when you created the data source, you specified that there was a one-to-many relationship between the Donors and Donations tables. With this information, InfoPath was able to create the repeating section containing a repeating table to match the structure and relationship of the two tables.

The form's functionality is essentially complete, but you could still make a few modifications, which are discussed in the following section.

# Fine-Tuning the Data Entry Form

The first phase in fine-tuning the form is to remove controls that are not needed because they are bound to fields whose data the user will not need to see or modify. These are the DonorID fields for the Donors and the Donations tables, and the ID field for the Donations table. Remember that removing these controls from the form does not affect the data source – the corresponding fields are still present even if they are not visible.

To remove the DonorID field from the Donors table:

1. Select the text box next to the Donor ID label at the top of the form by clicking it.
2. Press Del to delete the control.
3. Press Backspace as many times as needed to delete the `Donor ID` label.
4. Press Del to delete the empty line and bring the First Name field to the top of the section.

Deleting the ID and Donor ID fields from the repeating table is a bit more complicated. You cannot just delete the controls because that would leave blank columns in the table. Instead, you must delete the entire table columns:

1. Drag over the first two columns in the table to select them. The column labels will be displayed with a gray background.
2. Select Table→Delete→Columns to delete the ID and Donor ID columns from the table.

Figure 13-15 shows how the form looks at this point.

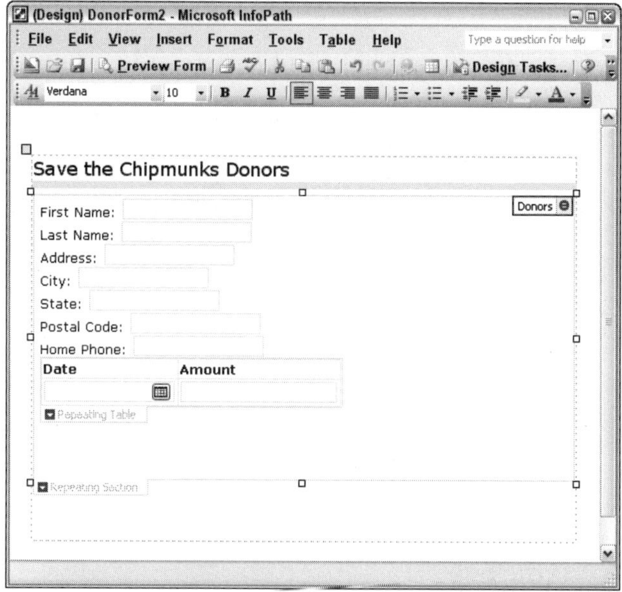


Figure 13-15: The Data Entry View after removing unneeded controls.

The Data Entry View contains only those controls that are required. Even so, the form still can be improved, primarily in terms of its appearance. Here are some suggestions; I won't describe the required steps in detail, because you already know them:

- Rearrange the controls and labels so they are not spread out one to a line.
- Change the size of some controls to better match the data they will contain.
- Insert a line (choose Insert→Horizontal Line) to visually separate the repeating table from the other controls.
- Format the Amount field as currency.
- Add a border at the bottom edge of the repeating section so that each one will be clearly delineated from the next.

You'll see how the form looks after adding a Submit button, the next step in form design.

## Adding a Submit Button

As it stands, the form can be submitted to the database by choosing File→Submit. It's a nice touch to add a Submit button to the form so the user can submit the form without using the menus. This phase of form design is completely optional but does add user-friendliness to the form. Here's how to add the button:

1. Click on the form below the Repeating Section tab but within the section border.
2. Choose Insert→More Controls to display the Controls task pane.
3. In the Insert Control list, click Button. InfoPath inserts a Button control.
4. Right-click the button control and select Button Properties from the pop-up menu. InfoPath displays the Button Properties dialog box, as shown in Figure 13-16.

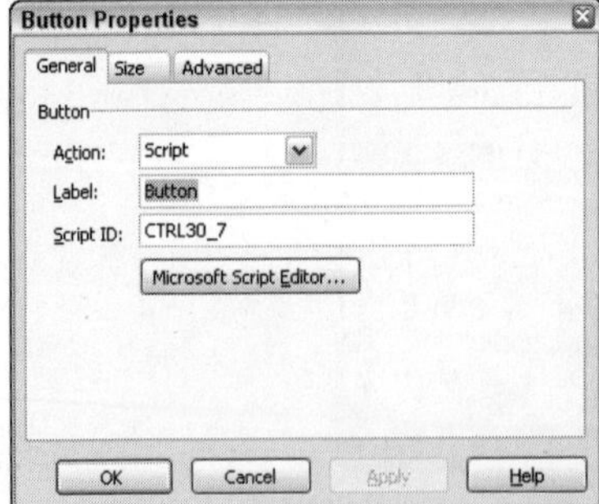


Figure 13-16: The Button Properties dialog box.

5. Select Submit in the Action drop-down list. InfoPath displays the Submit Forms dialog box.

6. Accept the default options and click OK to return to the Button Properties dialog box.
7. Enter Submit in the Label field.
8. Click OK to close the dialog box.

Figure 13-17 shows the form in Form Preview mode of the Data Entry View after formatting changes were applied and the Submit button added.

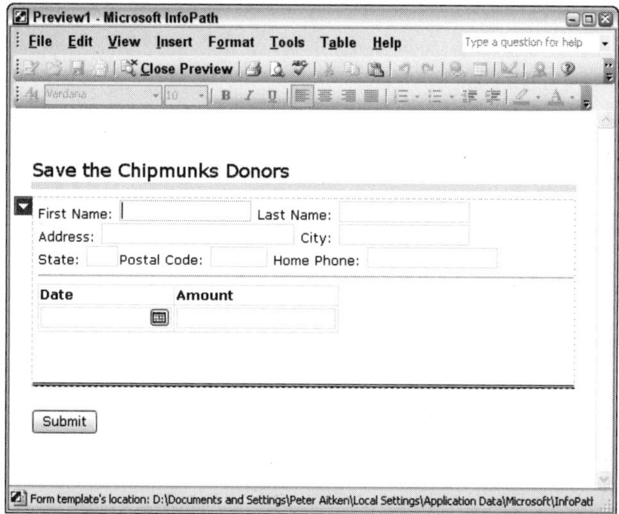


Figure 13-17: The Data Entry View in form in Preview mode showing a Submit button.

## Setting Form Submission Options

InfoPath provides several options for form submission. It is important to set these to suit the requirements of your application. Here's how:

1. Right-click the button that you just added to the form and select Button Properties from the pop-up menu. InfoPath displays the Button Properties dialog box.
2. On the General tab, click the Define Action Parameters button. InfoPath displays the Submitting Forms dialog box.
3. Click the Submit Options button. InfoPath displays the Submit Options dialog box (see Figure 13-18).

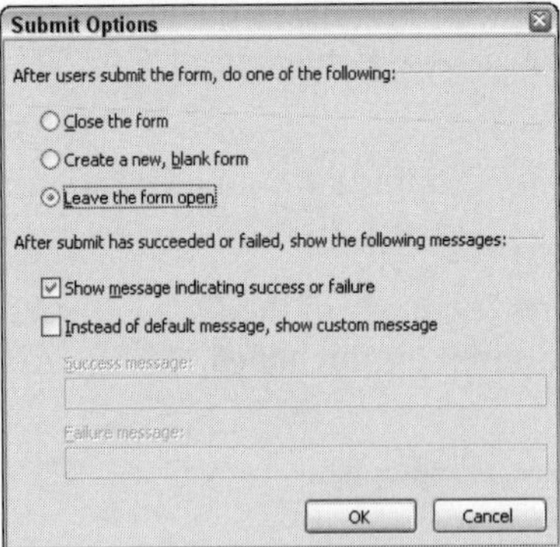


Figure 13-18: Setting form submission options.

The form submission options determine what happens to the form when it is submitted. The choices are:

- **Close the form.** Appropriate when the users submit the form when they are finished editing or viewing data.
- **Create a new, blank form.** Appropriate when the user will be submitting data in batches.
- **Leave the form open.** Appropriate when the user needs to continue viewing/editing the same data after submission.

For this application the second option, Create a New, Blank Form, is best. It lets the user enter or edit data in the database, submit the new and/or changed records to the database, and start again with a blank form.

4. Select the Create a New, Blank form option, and click OK.
5. Click OK twice more to close all dialog boxes and return to the form.

The form is complete. It's time to try it out.

# Using the Form

Using the form that you just designed to interact with the DonorList database is an excellent example of the power of InfoPath when teamed up with Access. Follow these steps to get started:

1. Start InfoPath.
2. Choose File→Fill Out a Form to display the Fill Out a Form task pane.

3. On the task pane, click the name of the form template that you designed earlier in this chapter. Because the database is currently empty, InfoPath displays the form's Query View.

4. Click the New Record button to enter data for a new donor and donation. InfoPath switches to the Data Entry View and displays a blank record, as shown in Figure 13-19.

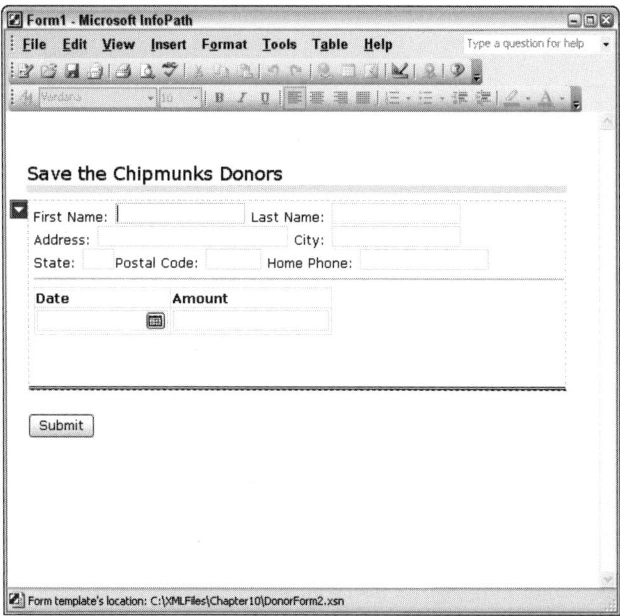


Figure 13-19: Adding a new donor to the database.

5. Enter information for a donor and a donation.

6. Choose Insert → Section → Donors to add a new, blank donor section to the form.

7. Add information for the second donor and his donation to the form. The form now looks something like Figure 13-20.

You are now ready to submit this data to the Access database. Click the Submit button and, when prompted, select Yes. InfoPath submits the form and, assuming that there are no errors, displays a message that the submission has been successful. Finally a new, blank form is displayed with the Query View active.

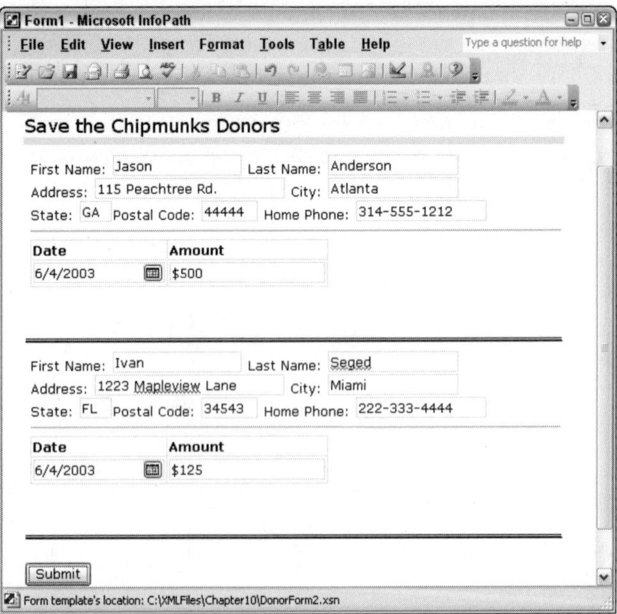


**Figure 13-20: After adding two donors and donations to the form.**

The data you entered is in the Access database but the form is blank. You can verify this by choosing View→Data Entry – you'll see a blank form that does not contain the previously entered records. You can enter and submit more data if you like, but it will be instructive to see how the Query View works. Here's how to enter a donation for someone who has made donations previously.

1. If necessary, display the Query View again by choosing View→Query.
2. In the Last Name field, enter the last name of one of the donors that you entered previously.
3. Click the Run Query button. InfoPath switches to the Data Entry View and displays the data for the donor whose last name you specified.
4. Right-click the Donations table and select Insert Donations from the pop-up menu. InfoPath adds a new, empty row to the donations table.
5. Enter the information for the new donation as shown in Figure 13-21.
6. Click the Submit button and follow the prompts to submit the new information to the database. InfoPath displays a new, blank form.

To retrieve all records in the Donors table, leave the query form blank and click Run Query.

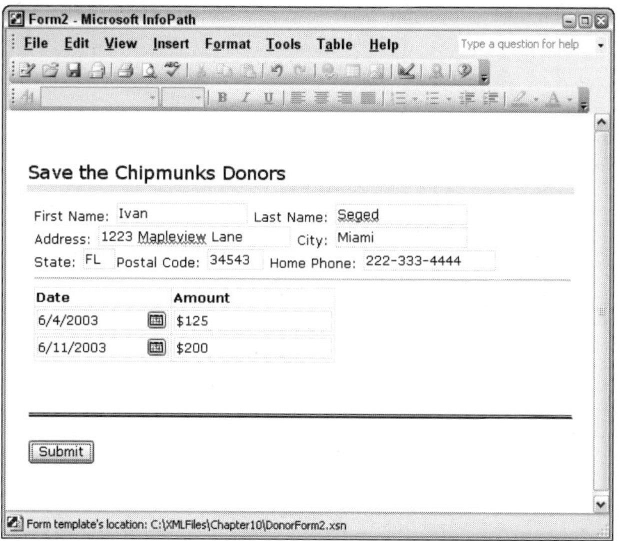


**Figure 13-21: After adding a second donation for an existing donor.**

An InfoPath form designed in this way provides you with all the tools you need for most database tasks. You've already seen how to add a new donor and donation and how to add a donation for an existing donor. Here are some other things you might want to do:

- To delete a donor from the database along with all of his or her donations, right-click the donor in Data Entry View and select Remove Donors from the pop-up menu.
- To change a donor's data, display it in the Data Entry View and make the necessary changes.
- To delete a single donation for a donor, click the row in the donations table that you want to remove. Then, click the adjacent down arrow and select Remove Donations from the pop-up menu.

These changes are recorded in the database when the form is submitted.

This chapter has shown you how InfoPath and Access can be used together for data entry and editing needs. When you create an InfoPath form template based on a data source such as an Access database, some aspects of the form-design process are automated, making your job even easier.

Chapter 14

# Connecting FrontPage and InfoPath

IN THIS CHAPTER

- Designing the InfoPath form
- Using the form
- Designing the Web page
- Using the Web page

FRONTPAGE ENABLES you to design Web pages that are connected to XML data, and InfoPath is designed for entering and editing data that will be saved as XML. If this sounds like a perfect match, you are right! This chapter walks you through the process of using InfoPath and FrontPage for publishing data on the Web.

## The Scenario

Your company sells specialty food items and wants you to design a Web page that lists the items that are available. The objective is to have two lists on the page: one of items that are in stock, and the other for items that are temporarily out of stock. A third category is for items that are in the master list but won't be listed on the Web page at all – for example, items that are on long-term back order. You have decided to approach this project by designing an InfoPath form for entering and editing the food items and creating a FrontPage SharePoint page for the display.

## Design the InfoPath Form

The first part of this project is to create the InfoPath form that will be used to enter and edit information on the gourmet items that are offered by your company. There are five required pieces of information:

- The name of the item
- The unit the item comes in, such as 8-ounce can, pound, or 1-liter bottle

- The price of the item
- A true/false value indicating whether the item is in stock
- A true/false value indicating whether the item should be listed on the Web page

For this form, you can design the data source in InfoPath rather than relying on an external schema (although you could use the latter technique if you wanted to). Here are the steps required:

1. In InfoPath, choose File→Design a Form.
2. On the Design a Form task pane, click the New Blank Form command. InfoPath opens a new, blank form and displays the Design Tasks task pane.
3. Click the Data Source command on the task pane. InfoPath displays the Data Source task pane.
4. Right-click the myFields element and choose Properties from the pop-up menu to display the Field or Group Properties dialog box.
5. Change the Name field from myFields to foodItems, and then click OK to close the dialog box.
6. Right-click the `foodItems` element in the data source and select Add from the pop-up menu to display the Add Field or Group dialog box.
7. Specify `item` as the name and Group as the type, and select the Repeating option.
8. Click OK to close the dialog box.
9. Right-click the `item` element in the data source and select Add from the pop-up menu to add each of the five child elements as described in Table 14-1.

**TABLE 14-1 CHILD ELEMENTS OF THE ITEM GROUP**

| Name | Type | Data Type | Other |
|---|---|---|---|
| name | Field (element) | text | Cannot be blank |
| unit | Field (element) | text | Cannot be blank |
| price | Field (element) | double | Cannot be blank |
| inStock | Field (element) | True/false | Default value true |
| list | Field (element) | True/False | Default Value True |

10. When the data source is complete, save the form under a descriptive name such as `FoodItemsData`.

At this point the Data Source task pane looks like the one in Figure 14-1.

Figure 14-1: The completed data source.

With the data source complete, you can turn your attention to designing the form's visual interface. The interface will be straightforward, consisting of a title and a repeating table. Here are the steps to follow:

1. Click the Layout command on the task pane to display the Layout task pane.
2. Click the Table with Title item to add a layout table to the form.
3. Click on the form where it says Click to Add Title, and enter a title for the form.
4. Click where it says Click to Add Content.
5. On the task pane, click the Data Source command to display the Data Source task pane.
6. Right-click the `item` element and select Repeating Table from the pop-up menu. InfoPath inserts a repeating table in the form.
7. Right-click the Price field to display the Text Box Properties dialog box.
8. On the Data tab, click the Format tab to display the Decimal Format dialog box.

9. Select the Currency option.
10. Click OK twice to close both dialog boxes and return to the form.
11. Edit the table, changing the column widths to fit the data they contain.

When you are finished, the new form will look more or less like Figure 14-2. Don't forget to save the completed form template.

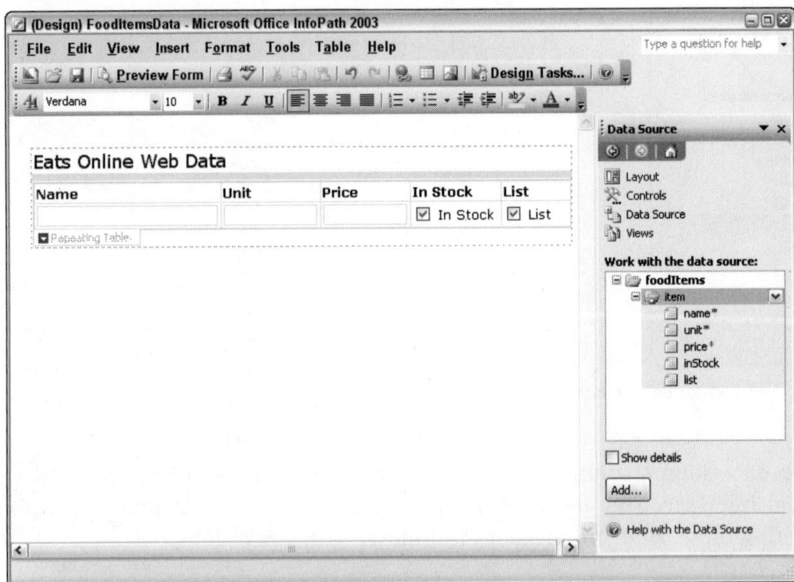


Figure 14-2: The completed form template.

# Fill Out and Save the Form

Before you start designing the Web page in FrontPage, you need some sample data to work with. In InfoPath, choose File → Fill Out a Form to create an instance of the form that you designed. Enter some data on it. When creating this data be sure that some items have In Stock set to `true` and others have this field set to `false`. The same goes for the List field. When you are finished, your form will look something like Figure 14-3.

When the data entry is complete, you must save the form. If your system is set up so that your Web site is listed under My Network Places, you may be able to save it directly to your Web site. Otherwise, save it locally and import it to the Web site later.

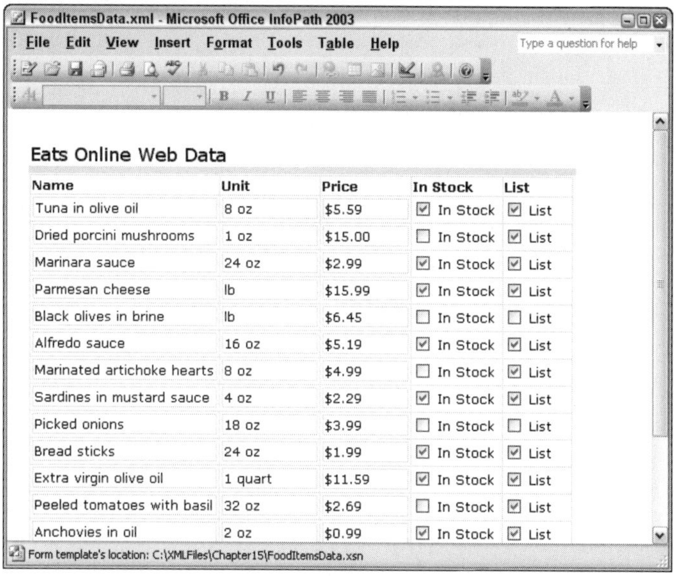
FoodItemsData.xml - Microsoft Office InfoPath 2003

File Edit View Insert Format Tools Table Help

Type a question for help

Eats Online Web Data

| Name | Unit | Price | In Stock | List |
|---|---|---|---|---|
| Tuna in olive oil | 8 oz | $5.59 | ☑ In Stock | ☑ List |
| Dried porcini mushrooms | 1 oz | $15.00 | ☐ In Stock | ☑ List |
| Marinara sauce | 24 oz | $2.99 | ☑ In Stock | ☑ List |
| Parmesan cheese | lb | $15.99 | ☑ In Stock | ☑ List |
| Black olives in brine | lb | $6.45 | ☐ In Stock | ☐ List |
| Alfredo sauce | 16 oz | $5.19 | ☑ In Stock | ☑ List |
| Marinated artichoke hearts | 8 oz | $4.99 | ☐ In Stock | ☑ List |
| Sardines in mustard sauce | 4 oz | $2.29 | ☑ In Stock | ☑ List |
| Picked onions | 18 oz | $3.99 | ☐ In Stock | ☐ List |
| Bread sticks | 24 oz | $1.99 | ☑ In Stock | ☑ List |
| Extra virgin olive oil | 1 quart | $11.59 | ☑ In Stock | ☑ List |
| Peeled tomatoes with basil | 32 oz | $2.69 | ☐ In Stock | ☑ List |
| Anchovies in oil | 2 oz | $0.99 | ☑ In Stock | ☑ List |

Form template's location: C:\XMLFiles\Chapter15\FoodItemsData.xsn

**Figure 14-3: The form after entering some sample data.**

# Design the Web Page

The Web page will contain two Data Views, both based on the same XML file. One of the Data Views will list items that are in stock as indicated by the `inStock` element in the XML file, and the other will list out-of-stock items. Items in which the list element is false won't be included in either Data View.

To begin, open your SharePoint Web site in FrontPage and select File→New to create a new, blank page. Next, add the page's descriptive text, including a title and labels to identify the two Data Views that will be added. You can design this part of the page any way you like; my design is shown in Figure 14-4. Don't forget to save the page now and then as you work on it.

## Adding the In-Stock Data View

Follow these steps to add the Data View that will list in-stock items:

1. Place the cursor at the location for the Data View that will display in stock items.
2. Select Data→Insert Data View. FrontPage displays the Data Source Catalog task pane.
3. If you saved the InfoPath XML file to the Web site, it should already be listed in the XML Files section of the task pane. If not, use the Add to Catalog command on the task pane to locate the file and import it into the Web site.

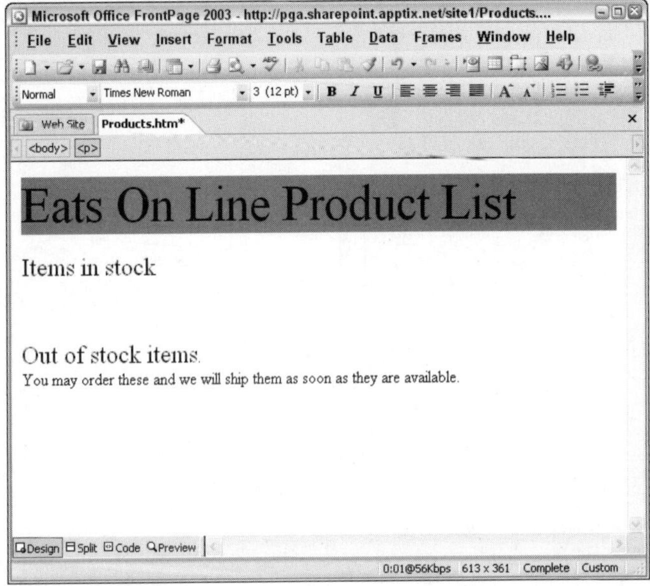


Figure 14-4: The page before adding the Data Views.

4. Click the XML filename and select Insert Data View from the pop-up menu. FrontPage inserts a Data View into the page, as shown in Figure 14-5.

When you insert the Data View in Step 4, FrontPage may display a dialog box informing you that the page's extension must be change to .aspx. This is so because plain HTML pages, which is what FrontPage creates by default when you start a new blank page, do not support Data Views. To change the extension, choose File → Save As and change the filename extension from .htm to .aspx.

The Data View's default appearance is clearly not acceptable. The following is the minimum you need to do. First, edit the names at the top of the first three columns. Then, delete the right two columns, since the user does not need to see this information. Here's how:

1. Put the cursor in the column to be deleted.
2. Choose Table → Select → Column.
3. Choose Table → Delete Columns.

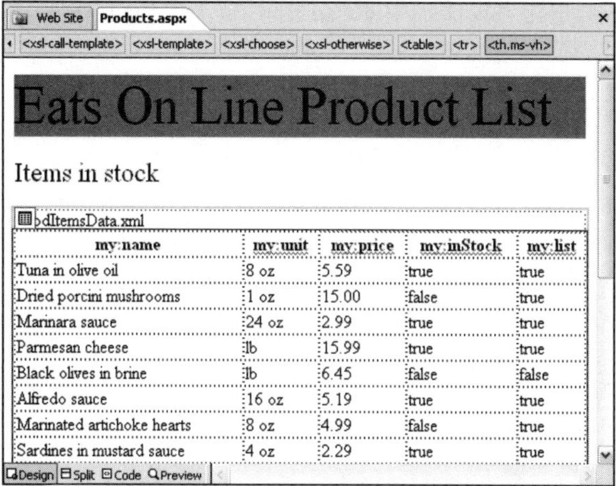


**Figure 14-5: After inserting the first Data View.**

Add a dollar sign to the Price column:

1. Click any individual cell in the Price column.
2. Use the arrow keys to move the cursor to the left edge of the cell.
3. Type in a dollar sign. The symbol is displayed in all cells in the column.

Delete the title of the Data View (`FoodItemsData.xml` in the figure).

1. Double-click the title in the Data View. FrontPage opens a dialog box whose title is the name of the XML file.
2. In the dialog box, click the + symbol next to Appearance.
3. Delete the text in the Title field.
4. Click OK to close the dialog box.

In the prerelease version of FrontPage being used in the writing of this book, you cannot delete the title of the Data View in design mode. If you erase the title as described in the preceding steps, FrontPage displays "Untitled." However, when the page is published and viewed in Internet Explorer, the title is not shown.

Finally, you need to filter the data in this Data View so that the list displays only those items for which both the `inStock` and the `List` elements are true:

1. Right-click the table and select Data View Properties from the pop-up menu. FrontPage displays the Data View Details task pane.
2. Click the Filter command o the task pane. FrontPage displays the Filter Criteria dialog box.
3. For this Data View, `inStock` must be `true` and `list` must be `true`. Enter these required criteria in the dialog box, as shown in Figure 14-6.
4. Click OK to close the dialog box.

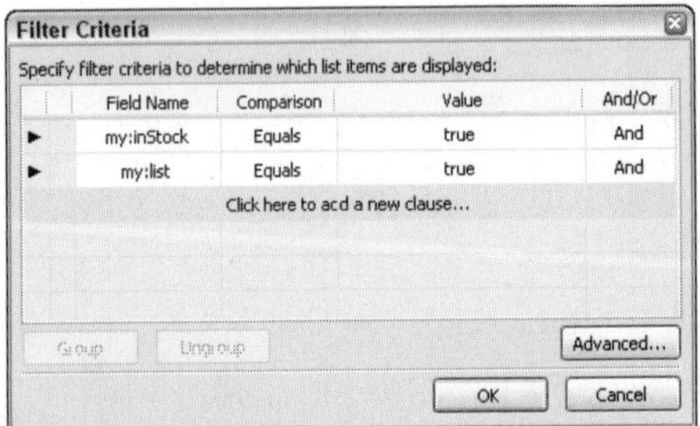


Figure 14-6: The criteria for the Data View.

When entering the criteria, be sure to match the case used. Enter `true` as shown in the figure and not `True`. This sort of comparison is case-sensitive.

At this point the in-stock Data View is complete. Your page will look more or less like Figure 14-7 (this is shown in FrontPage's Preview mode).

## Adding the Out-of-Stock Data View

The out-of-stock Data View is essentially identical to the in-stock Data View, and you can follow the procedures described in the preceding section to add it to the page. The only difference is in the filter criteria that you must define. For this Data View, `inStock` must be `false` and `list` must be `true`, as shown in Figure 14-8.

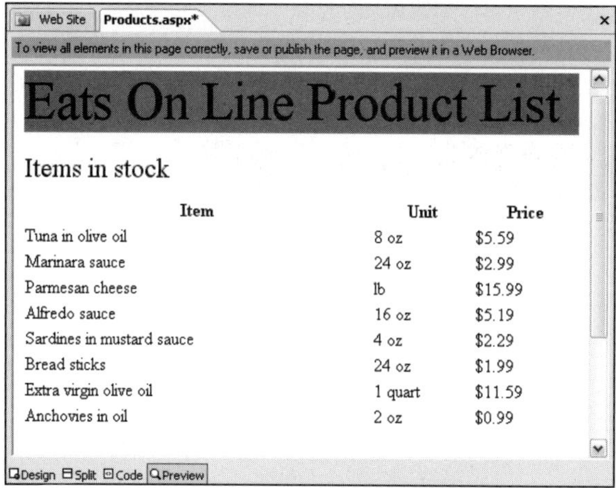


# Eats On Line Product List

Items in stock

| Item | Unit | Price |
|---|---|---|
| Tuna in olive oil | 8 oz | $5.59 |
| Marinara sauce | 24 oz | $2.99 |
| Parmesan cheese | lb | $15.99 |
| Alfredo sauce | 16 oz | $5.19 |
| Sardines in mustard sauce | 4 oz | $2.29 |
| Bread sticks | 24 oz | $1.99 |
| Extra virgin olive oil | 1 quart | $11.59 |
| Anchovies in oil | 2 oz | $0.99 |

Figure 14-7: Previewing the in-stock Data View.

Filter Criteria

Specify filter criteria to determine which list items are displayed:

| Field Name | Comparison | Value | And/Or |
|---|---|---|---|
| my:inStock | Equals | false | And |
| my:list | Equals | true | And |

Click here to add a new clause...

Group Ungroup Advanced...

OK Cancel

Figure 14-8: The filter criteria for the out-of-stock Data View.

# Using the Web Page

After your page is complete and saved to your Web site, you can give it a try by navigating to the page using Internet Explorer. Figure 14-9 shows the final Web page in a browser.

When the data changes, all that is required is to open the InfoPath form from the Web site in InfoPath, make the necessary changes, and save it back to the Web site. Users will see the new XML data when they open or refresh the Web page.

This case study has shown you how InfoPath and FrontPage can be used to enable easy entry and editing of data that is automatically reflected in a Web page.

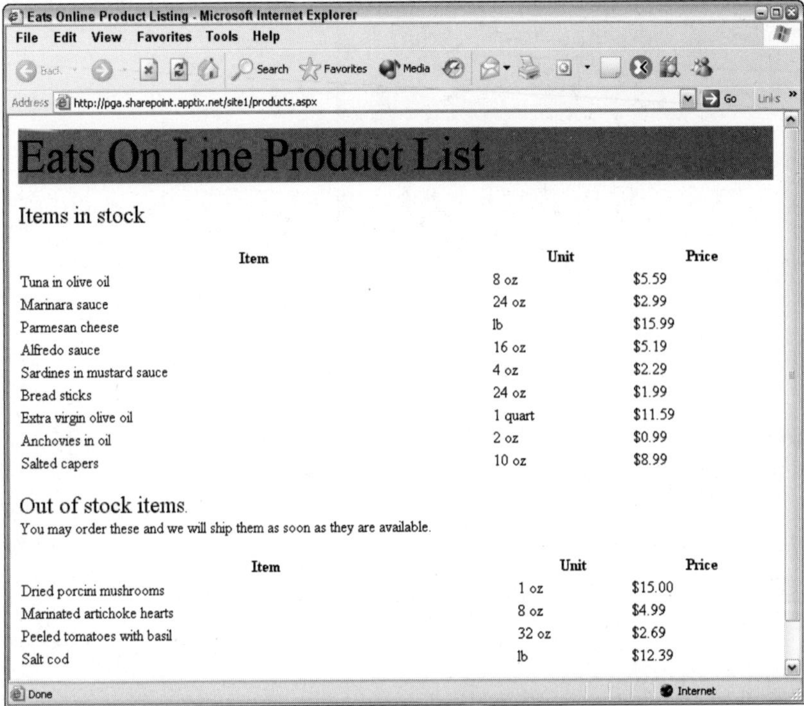


Eats On Line Product List

Items in stock

| Item | Unit | Price |
|---|---|---|
| Tuna in olive oil | 8 oz | $5.59 |
| Marinara sauce | 24 oz | $2.99 |
| Parmesan cheese | lb | $15.99 |
| Alfredo sauce | 16 oz | $5.19 |
| Sardines in mustard sauce | 4 oz | $2.29 |
| Bread sticks | 24 oz | $1.99 |
| Extra virgin olive oil | 1 quart | $11.59 |
| Anchovies in oil | 2 oz | $0.99 |
| Salted capers | 10 oz | $8.99 |

Out of stock items.

You may order these and we will ship them as soon as they are available.

| Item | Unit | Price |
|---|---|---|
| Dried porcini mushrooms | 1 oz | $15.00 |
| Marinated artichoke hearts | 8 oz | $4.99 |
| Peeled tomatoes with basil | 32 oz | $2.69 |
| Salt cod | lb | $12.39 |



**Figure 14-9: The final Web page displayed in a browser as a user would see it.**

Chapter 15

# Connecting Word and FrontPage

IN THIS CHAPTER

- Creating the schema
- Creating the template
- Creating the Web page

ALTHOUGH MOST of the case studies presented in the book involve InfoPath and another Office application, there's no reason that InfoPath has to be involved in a business solution that uses XML to enable two Office applications to work together. This chapter presents a case study that uses Word and FrontPage.

## The Scenario

Your firm keeps track of monthly sales figures by category. The sales manager, who is responsible for these figures, has two related tasks. First, the figures must be included in a report for upper management. This report will also include narrative text that provides details on the period being reported and forecasts for the future. Second, the raw sales figures must be posted to an internal company Web site so they are available to the sales force.

Word, with its sophisticated editing and formatting tools, is an obvious choice for creating an attractive report to submit to the higher-ups. By creating a Word template, you can make it possible for the sales manager to enter the sales figures and narrative and then print or e-mail the report to the recipients. By associating the template with a schema (one that you will create in the next section), the relevant data in the report – specifically the date and the sales figures – can be marked up and will be accessible to other programs.

For the Web page, FrontPage is really the only choice. Specifically, the XML Web Part that FrontPage provides is an ideal tool for the present needs. It enables you to apply an XSLT transform to the WordML file, extracting the relevant data from the WordML document and formatting it for display on a Web page.

# Create the Schema

This case study requires a Word document that is marked up with both WordML for the formatting and a custom set of XML tags to structure the data. In order to do this, a schema must be associated with the Word document, or more specifically, with the template that the document will be based on.

The data requirements are fairly simple. The schema should define a root element named `salesFigures`. This element will have five child elements, one named date that is type string, and four others, all type double, named software, computers, consulting, and repairs. The `date` element will contain the month and year that the figures are for (hence the use of type string rather than type date), while the four other elements will contain the sales figures for each category. The resulting schema is shown in Listing 15-1. Note that a target namespace has been defined for the schema. You can use this one or provide your own, but if you change it be sure to change it throughout the chapter as well.

**Listing 15-1: The Sales Figures Schema**

```
<?xml version="1.0" encoding="UTF-8"?>
<xs:schema targetNamespace="http://www.pgacon.com/salesfigures"
  xmlns:xs="http://www.w3.org/2001/XMLSchema"
  xmlns="http://www.pgacon.com/salesfigures"
  elementFormDefault="qualified" attributeFormDefault="unqualified">
  <xs:element name="salesFigures">
    <xs:complexType>
      <xs:sequence>
        <xs:element name="date" type="xs:string"/>
        <xs:element name="software" type="xs:double"/>
        <xs:element name="computers" type="xs:double"/>
        <xs:element name="consulting" type="xs:double"/>
        <xs:element name="repairs" type="xs:double"/>
      </xs:sequence>
    </xs:complexType>
  </xs:element>
</xs:schema>
```

With the schema is finished, you can turn to designing the Word template.

# Creating the Template

The process of creating the template has two stages. First, you must create a template that has the required schema attached to it and design the visual appearance of the template. Second, you must mark up the template with the tags from your schema so that the data entered by the user can be identified properly.

## Template Design: Schema and Visual Appearance

The following steps create a new Word template, associate the Sales Figures schema with it, and design the template's visual elements.

1. Start a new, blank Word document.
2. Choose Tools→Templates and Add-ins to display the Templates and Add-ins dialog box.
3. Click the XML Schema tab.
4. Click the Add Schema button and locate the schema that you created earlier in this chapter. Follow the prompts to add the schema to the Schema Library.
5. When you return to the Templates and Add-ins dialog box (see Figure 15-1) make sure that:
   - The schema you just added is checked (in Figure 15-1, Sales Figures is the alias that I assigned to the schema).
   - No other schemas are checked.
   - The Validate Document Against Attached Schemas option is checked.
   - The Allow Saving as XML Even if Not Valid option is not checked.

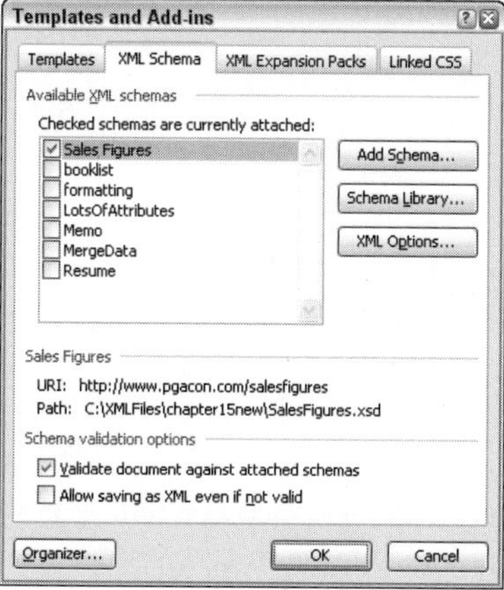

Figure 15-1: Attaching the Sales Figures template to the template.

6. Click the XML Options button to display the XML Options dialog box.
7. Select the Ignore Mixed Content option (the reason for this is explained later in the chapter).

8. Click OK twice to close both dialog boxes and return to the document.
9. Choose File→Save to display the Save As dialog box.
10. Select Document Template in the Save as Type list.
11. Enter a name for the template (I used SalesFigures).
12. Click OK to save the template and close the dialog box.

You have created the Word template (which is still blank, of course) and associated it with your schema, so now you can design the template's contents. My approach is to create a template with a table for the sales figures and placeholders for the information that the user will enter (date and each sales figure), as shown in Figure 15-2.

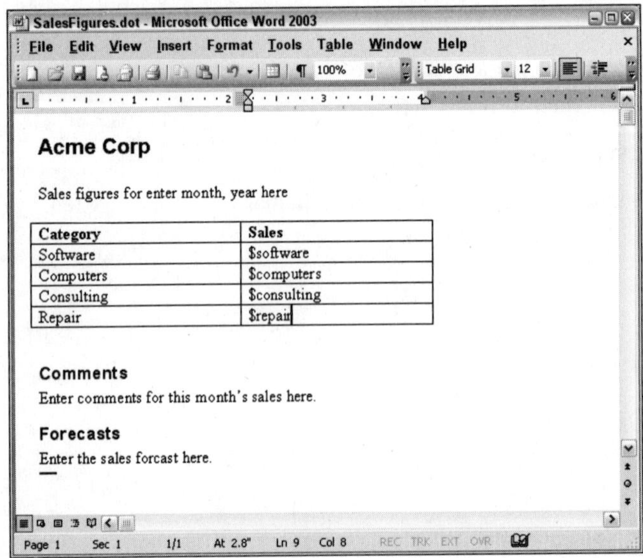


**Figure 15-2: The template includes placeholders for the data that will be entered.**

When creating a document based on the template, the user will select the text "enter month, year here" and type in the month and year. Likewise, he or she will select the text "software" in the second column of the table and enter the sales figure for that category. Note the leading dollar sign in each cell of the second column, so the sales figures that the user enters will be displayed as currency amounts.

As you may be aware, Word provides an array of tools for template design, and there are certainly other approaches that you could take in creating this template. For this project, however, I decided to keep the template as simple as possible in order to clearly demonstrate the XML techniques that are the purpose of this case study.

# Template Design: XML Mapping

The next phase is to map the XML elements to the template. Specifically, you map XML elements to the placeholders in the template. Then, when the user replaces the placeholder with the actual data, it is associated with the corresponding XML element. Here are the steps to follow:

1. If necessary, display the XML Structure task pane.
2. Position the cursor anywhere in the template.
3. In the list of elements on the task pane, click `salesFigures`. Word displays a dialog box asking where the element should be applied. Click the Apply to Entire Document button.

Word puts an opening `<salesFigures>` tag at the start of the document and a closing `<salesFigures>` tag at the end of the document. These are visible in the document (see Figure 15-3) if the Show XML Tags in the Document option is selected on the XML Structure task pane.

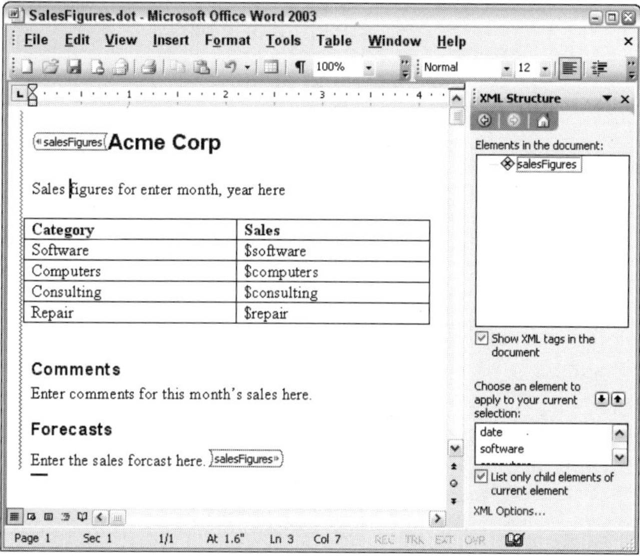


**Figure 15-3: After applying the root salesFigures element to the entire document.**

Please note the following in this figure as well:

- The entire document is marked with a wavy red line in the left margin. This is due to the fact that the `salesFigures` element fails validation because it does not contain the child elements that are defined in the schema. This is to be expected at this point.

- The XML Structure task pane lists the `salesFigures` element with an X icon next to it. This icon is also the result of the validation violations.
- The list of elements includes the child elements – `date`, `software`, and so on. This is because, now that the root `salesFigures` element is in place for the whole document, it is legal (according to the schema) to apply these child elements to the document.

When you associated the schema with the document, you selected the Ignore Mixed Content option. Now, you can see the reason for this. The way that you mapped the `salesFigures` element resulted in its containing not only the child elements (to be added soon) but also the boilerplate text and placeholders in the template. Because the schema does not define the `salesFigures` element as containing such mixed content, it will cause a validation violation unless the Ignore Mixed Content option is selected. With this option in force, the validation will check only the content of the child elements.

Your next task is to map the child XML elements to the placeholders in the template:

1. Select (highlight) the text "enter month, year here" in the document.
2. Click the date element name on the XML structure task pane.
3. Select the text "software" in the second column of the table (do not include the $ in the selection).
4. Click the software name on the XML structure task pane.
5. Repeat Steps 3 and 4 to map the other three placeholders in the table to the corresponding XML elements.

Figure 15-4 shows how the document looks when you've completed the mapping. At this point the template is complete, and you can save and then close it.

You may note that the document still fails validation, this time because the four elements that you mapped to the table placeholders do not contain valid data (type double) as required by the schema. Why, then, are you permitted to save the template? The template restrictions are applied only when saving the document as XML. In this case, you are saving the document as a Word template, and the template restrictions don't come into play (although they are still displayed on-screen).

## Create a Sample Data File

Before starting work on the Web page part of this project, you should create a sample data file. You'll need it for testing the FrontPage elements that you will be creating.

1. In Word, choose File→New to display the New Document task pane.
2. In the Templates section, click the On My Computer command.

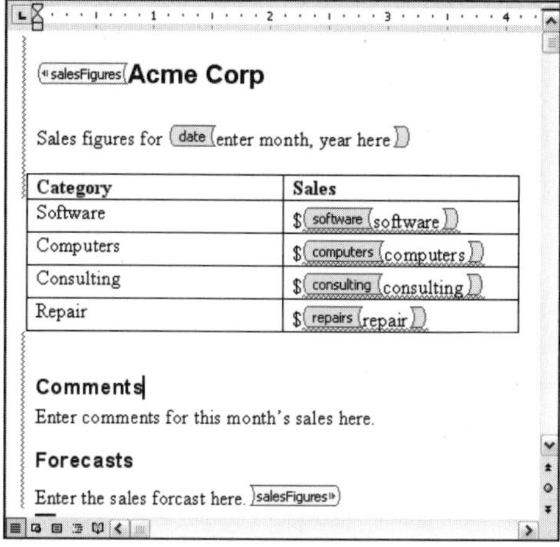


Figure 15-4: After mapping all the XML elements to placeholders in the template.

3. Locate the template that you created earlier, and click OK. Word opens a new document based on the template.
4. Edit the document, replacing the placeholder text with sample data in the following table (also see Figure 15-5).

| Placeholder Text | Data |
|---|---|
| date | May 2003 |
| software | 12550.45 |
| computers | 24199.00 |
| consulting | 18711.65 |
| repairs | 5600.00 |

5. Choose File→Save As to display the Save As dialog box.
6. Select XML Document in the Save as Type list.
7. Enter a name for the file, such as `SalesFiguresSampleData`.
8. Click Save.

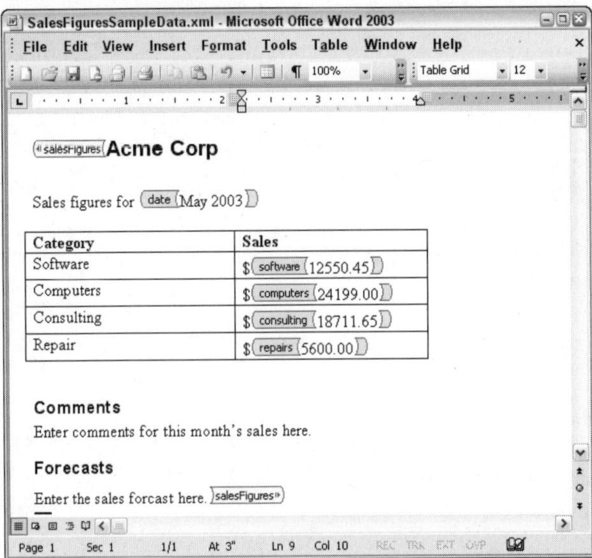


Figure 15-5: After entering sample data in the document.

Please note two things about the sample data. First, there is no need to enter data in the Comments or Forecasts sections because they are not marked up with XML and therefore are irrelevant to designing the Web page. Second, be sure to enter the sales data as plain numbers, as shown in the figure. If you use commas or any other formatting elements, validation will fail because the data type for these elements is a numeric type.

# Create the Web Page

The most demanding part of creating the Web page is the design of the XSLT transform that will extract the sales data from the WordML file and output it for display on a Web page. Once the transform has been created, the only remaining phase is to put an XML Web Part on the page and connect it to the XML data file and the transform.

## Create the Transform

The transform has two related tasks: to locate the relevant XML data in the WordML file, and to output that data along with the required HTML tags for displaying on the Web page. For this example, the display is kept very simple but you can make it more elaborate if you desire.

In order to write the transform, you need to take a look at the sample XML data that you created earlier in this chapter. The reason is that when the Word document is saved as WordML, the relevant data is marked up by both the tags defined in your schema and by WordML tags. To write the transform, or more specifically the XPath expressions that the transform will use to locate and select the relevant data, you need to know these tags. The best way to do this is to open the WordML file in a specialized XML editor such as XML Spy. Lacking this, you can use any text editor.

The first relevant bit of data is the date element. Using the search function you can locate this in the WordML file. You'll see that it is marked up as follows:

```
<ns0:date>
  <w:r>
    <w:t>May 2003</w:t>
  </w:r>
</ns0:date>
```

The `w:` prefix is associated with the WordML namespace http://schemas.microsoft.com/office/word/2003/wordml, and the `ns0:` prefix is assigned by Word to the namespace in the schema (http://www.pgacon.com/salesfigures, in this example). This information tells you two things that you need to know for the transform:

- The transform has to use both of the preceding namespaces.
- The date information will be marked up within `<ns0:date>`, `<w:r>`, and `<w:t>` tags.

Next, search the WordML file for the data for the software category. You'll find it marked up in a manner almost identical to the date data:

```
<ns0:software>
  <w:r>
    <w:t>12550.45</w:t>
  </w:r>
</ns0:software>
```

Armed with this information, you can proceed to write the transform that FrontPage will use to display the data in an XML Web Part. As usual, there is more than one way to write a transform for a desired goal; the one I wrote is shown in Listing 15-2.

**Listing 15-2: Stylesheet to Display the Sales Figures Data in an XML Web Part**

```
<?xml version="1.0" encoding="UTF-8"?>
<xsl:stylesheet version="1.0"
  xmlns:sf="http://www.pgacon.com/salesfigures"
  xmlns:w="http://schemas.microsoft.com/office/word/2003/wordml"
  xmlns:xsl="http://www.w3.org/1999/XSL/Transform">
<xsl:output method="html" version="1.0" encoding="UTF-8"
```

*Continued*

Listing 15-2 *(Continued)*

```
   indent="yes"/>
<xsl:template match="/">
  <h1>Acme Corp Latest Sales Data</h1>
  <xsl:apply-templates select="//sf:date/w:r/w:t"/>
  <xsl:apply-templates select="//sf:software/w:r/w:t"/>
  <xsl:apply-templates select="//sf:computers/w:r/w:t"/>
  <xsl:apply-templates select="//sf:consulting/w:r/w:t"/>
  <xsl:apply-templates select="//sf:repairs/w:r/w:t"/>
</xsl:template>

<xsl:template match="sf:date/w:r/w:t">
  <p><b>Sales report for <xsl:value-of select="."/></b></p>
</xsl:template>

<xsl:template match="sf:software/w:r/w:t">
  <p>Software: $ <xsl:value-of select="."/></p>
</xsl:template>

<xsl:template match="sf:computers/w:r/w:t">
  <p>Computers: $ <xsl:value-of select="."/></p>
</xsl:template>

<xsl:template match="sf:consulting/w:r/w:t">
  <p>Consulting: $ <xsl:value-of select="."/></p>
</xsl:template>

<xsl:template match="sf:repairs/w:r/w:t">
  <p>Repairs: $ <xsl:value-of select="."/></p>
</xsl:template>

</xsl:stylesheet>
```

## Create the XML Web Part

Now you're ready to create the XML Web Part. A real Web page would include more than just a Web Part, at least in most situations, but other page elements are omitted here because they aren't relevant to using the XML data, which is the purpose of this case study.

To begin, you need to have the sample data file that you saved from Word as well as the XSLT transform file available on the Web site. If you haven't already moved them to the Web site, use FrontPage's File→Import command to do so. Then, follow these steps to create the XML Web Part:

1. Start FrontPage and open the Web site that the new page will be part of.
2. Create a new page or open an existing page.
3. Place the cursor at the location where you want the XML Web Part located.
4. Choose Data → Insert Web Part to display the Web Parts task pane.
5. Select XML Web Part in the Web Part list, then click the Insert Selected Web Part button. FrontPage inserts a blank Web Part on the page.
6. Double-click the new Web Part to open its properties dialog box (see Figure 15-6).

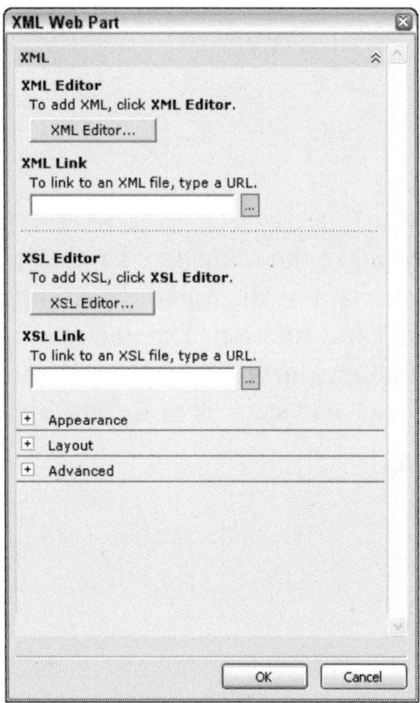


Figure 15-6: Setting the properties of the new XML Web Part.

7. Click the button next to the XML Link field and locate the XML data file.
8. Click the button next to the XSL Link field and locate the XSLT transform file.
9. Click the + symbol next to Appearance and delete the text in the Title field.
10. Click OK to close the dialog box.

Figure 15-7 shows what the XML Web Part definition looks like when viewed in FrontPage's preview mode. The XSLT transform has extracted just the relevant data from the WordML file and formatted it for displaying on the Web page.

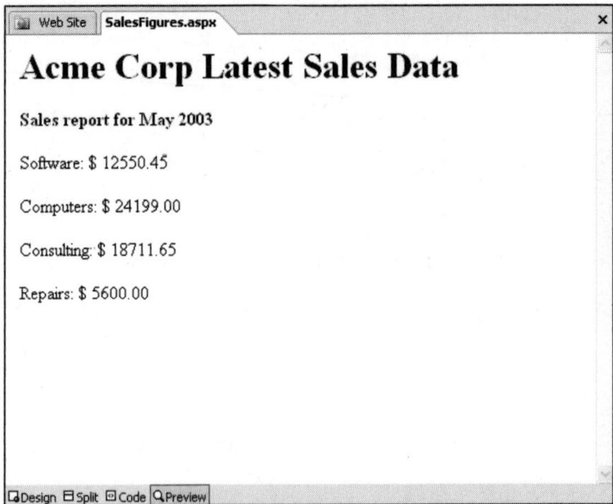


Figure 15-7: The completed XML Web Part displayed in FrontPage's Preview mode.

This case study ties Word and FrontPage together to make the same data available in two ways. Each month, the sales manager will create a new document based on the Word template and enter the sales figures and other information. The document can be printed or e-mailed to people who need the complete, formatted report. Then, by saving the document as WordML to the Web site, the raw sales data figures are automatically made available to others.

Chapter 16

# Connecting Web Publishing and InfoPath

IN THIS CHAPTER

- Designing the InfoPath form
- Saving the form as a Web page
- Using a transform to create a Web page
- Using an InfoPath script to apply a transform

XSL TRANSFORMS, or stylesheets, can be used to convert InfoPath form data into a Web page. Although Chapter 14 showed how InfoPath can be used in conjunction with FrontPage to facilitate Web publishing of data, the fact is that not everyone uses FrontPage for these tasks. Even so, the power of InfoPath can still be part of your Web publishing strategy.

## Overview

While FrontPage is considered to be part of the Office suite, some Office users may prefer not to use it for some or all of their Web publishing needs. Perhaps you prefer another Web design and publishing tool. More likely, it's just that the capabilities of FrontPage simply aren't necessary in some situations. Many Web publishing tasks require only that an HTML page be created and copied to the Web server, and the sophisticated design and publishing tools provided by FrontPage are not needed. This case study shows you two approaches to using InfoPath for entry and editing of data to be published as a Web page.

## The Scenario

It's the policy of your firm to assign the duties of being available for telephone and e-mail inquiries on a rotating basis. Each week, several members of the sales staff are selected for this task. The number of people assigned varies but is typically 2–4. At the beginning of each week, it is necessary to post a page to the company's

Web site listing these people and their contact information. Your job is to design a system whereby the supervisor can enter this information on an InfoPath form and save it as a Web page to be placed on the site. This case study presents two related approaches to this task, but the first job for both approaches is to design the InfoPath form.

# Designing the Form

The data requirements for the InfoPath form are rather simple. It has to list information for several people, including their name, phone number, e-mail address, and the name of the company branch office where they are based.

## Creating the Data Source

There is no need to provide for validation against a schema because the data is simple and won't be used by another program. This means that designing the data source in InfoPath is the best approach. Here are the steps to follow:

1. Start InfoPath.
2. Choose File → Design a Form to display the Design a Form task pane.
3. Click New, Blank Form on the task pane. InfoPath opens a new, blank form.
4. Click the Data Source command on the task pane to display the Data Source task pane.
5. Right-click the myFields group on the Data Source task pane, and then select Properties from the pop-up menu to display the Field or Group Properties dialog box.
6. Change the Name field to "dutylist." Click OK.
7. Click the Add button. InfoPath displays the Add Field or Group dialog box (see Figure 16-1).

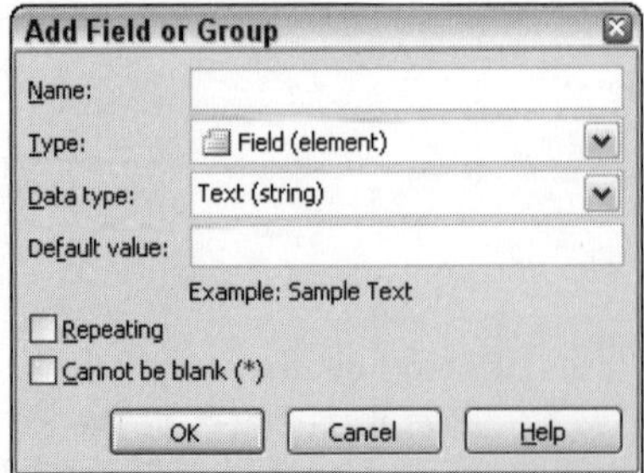


Figure 16-1: Adding a new field or group to the data source.

8. Enter "salesrep" in the Name field.
9. Select Group in the Type list.
10. Select the Repeating option.
11. Click OK.
12. Make sure that the salesrep group is selected in the list, and then click the Add button to display the Add Field or Group dialog box again. This time, you are adding a child element to `salesrep`.
13. Enter "name" in the Name field.
14. Select Field in the Type list.
15. Leave the Data Type field at the default selection of "Text (string)."
16. Click OK.
17. Repeat Steps 12–16 to add three more fields as children of the salesrep field. The names should be telephone, e-mail, and district. All should be type Text (String).

Figure 16-2 shows the completed data source. Don't forget to save the form template occasionally as you work on it.

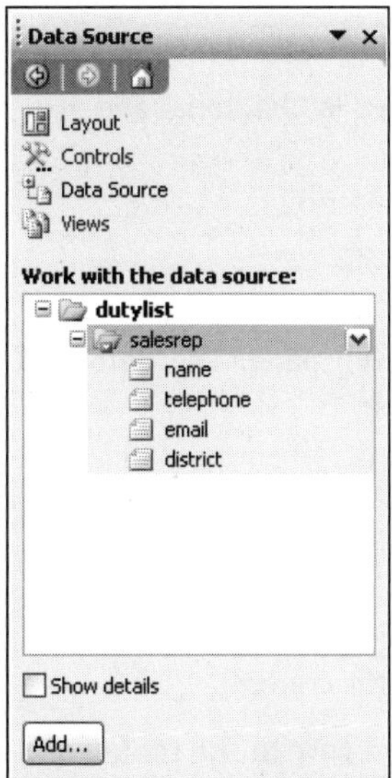


Figure 16-2: The completed data source.

## Designing the Form

To design the visual interface of the InfoPath form, follow these steps:

1. Click Layout on the task pane to display the Layout task pane.
2. In the Insert Table Layouts list, click One-Column Table to insert a table in the form.
3. Click in the newly added table and enter "Acme Widgets Information Center."
4. Format the text as desired.

I leave the details of the formatting up to you. For the example, I did the following:

- Increased the font side to 18 points
- Made the text boldface
- Centered the text both vertically and horizontally in the cell
- Decreased the table row height
- Changed the table background shading to blue
- Changed the font color to white

Formatting techniques for InfoPath forms are covered in Chapters 4 and 5.

The layout table you just added is for the title of the Web page. The data and additional items go in another table that you add as follows:

1. Make sure the cursor is on the form just below the title.
2. On the Layout task pane, click One Column Table. InfoPath inserts a second table onto the form.
3. Click in the new table where it says Click to add form content.
4. Choose Table→Insert→Rows below to add a second row to the table.
5. Click in the second row of the table and add the following explanatory text (as shown in Figure 16-3) or compose your own text.

The sales representatives listed above are available to answer your questions about our products. You can contact them either by telephone or by e-mail. In the case of e-mail it is our goal to respond by the next business day.

6. On the task pane, click Data Source to display the Data Source task pane.
7. Drag the salesrep group from the task pane and drop it in the top row of the table. A pop-up menu appears.
8. Select Repeating Table from the pop-up menu. InfoPath inserts a repeating table with four columns, one for each field in the data source.

The functional aspects of the form are complete at this point. You can apply additional formatting if desired; again I leave this to your discretion. Figure 16-3 shows the final form using InfoPath's preview mode.

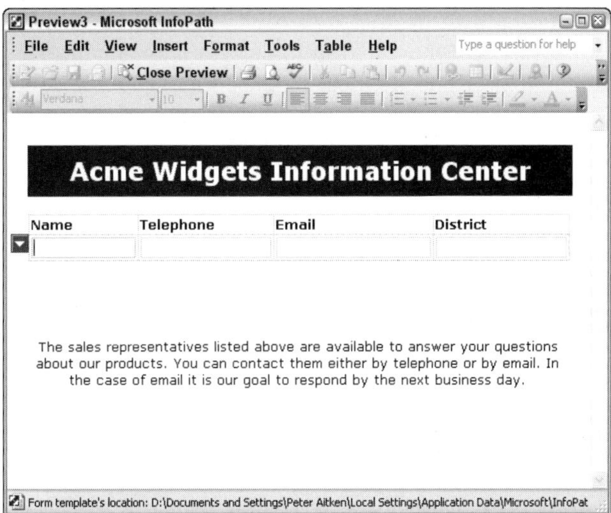


**Figure 16-3: The completed form displayed in preview mode.**

After saving the form template, it is available to be filled out with the information about each week's duty roster. Filling out InfoPath forms was covered in Chapter 3 and won't be covered further here. The next question is, of course, once the form has been filled out, how can it be saved as a Web page? There are two ways to do this: saving the InfoPath form as a Web page and using a transform to create a Web page. I discuss both of these in the following sections.

### About an Exported Web Page's Format

You should be aware that InfoPath's Export to Web command creates a special kind of HTML document called a *single file Web page*. This is also referred to as MHTML format. The file is given the MHT extension rather than HTM or HTML. The single file Web page format is designed so that the page's complete content is contained in the one file, including images and other elements that are normally external and included in the page by means of links. In other words, a Web page in MHTML format is completely self-contained and does not depend on any external items for completeness. Microsoft's Internet Explorer browser supports this format.

# Save the Form as a Web Page

The easiest way to convert an InfoPath form to a Web page is to use the Export command. InfoPath has the capability to export a form to an HTML document. The resulting Web page looks very similar if not identical to the form. Once the form has been filled out, choose File → Export To → Web and then enter the name for the HTML document. Figure 16-4 shows what the result looks like when the form is filled out and exported in this way.

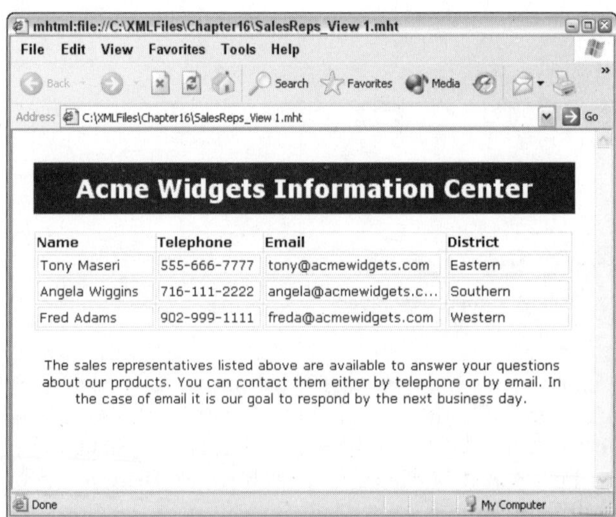


Figure 16-4: After exporting the form to the Web.

After you have exported the form as a Web page, you can post it directly to the Web page where it is available for viewing.

# Use a Transform to Create a Web Page

The second technique for publishing an InfoPath form as a Web page is a bit more complex than simply using the Export to Web command, but it provides far more flexibility. It involves saving the InfoPath form as an XML file, and then using an XSL transform to generate a Web page from the XML data file. By creating your own transform you can make the Web page come out pretty much any way you like it – you don't have to imitate the formatting on the InfoPath form.

The difficulties with this approach are probably obvious. For one thing, you need to know how to write XSL transforms (sometimes called *stylesheets*), and the underlying language is rather complex. You also need to know HTML syntax so you can determine what the output of the transform should be.

An additional problem is how to apply the transform. You might think that InfoPath would offer the option of applying a transform when a form is saved, but it doesn't. For the present, at least, you have two options:

- Go outside of Office to apply a transform to an InfoPath XML data file. There are many third-party tools available for this task, such as XML Spy. You need to refer to the documentation for whatever tool you use for instructions on how to apply a transform.
- Use a script in InfoPath to apply the transform. This is covered later in this chapter.

Despite these hurdles, this technique is so flexible that it may be worth the extra effort. The remainder of this chapter shows you how to use a transform to create a custom Web page from the InfoPath form you developed earlier in the chapter.

## Designing the Transform

To start with, look at the XML file (see Listing 16-1) that results when the SalesReps form is saved. The part of the file that contains data starts with the `<my:dutylist>` element. This root element contains one or more `<my:salesrep>` elements. Each of these elements in turn contains child elements that hold the actual data. The goal of the transform is to read this XML and output an HTML file that displays the data and other elements. The data itself will be displayed in an HTML table.

**Listing 16-1: The InfoPath SalesReps XML File**

```
<?xml version="1.0" encoding="UTF-8"?>
<?mso-infoPathSolution solutionVersion="1.0.0.5"
  productVersion="11.0.4920" PIVersion="0.9.0.0"
  href="file:///C:\XMLFiles\Chapter16\SalesReps.xsn" ?>
```

*Continued*

**Listing 16-1** *(Continued)*

```
<?mso-application progid="InfoPath.Document"?>
<my:dutylist
    xmlns:my="http://schemas.microsoft.com/office/infopath/2003/
    myXSD/2003-06-06T16:47:19" xml:lang="en-us">
<my:salesrep>
  <my:name>Tony Maseri</my:name>
  <my:telephone>555-666-7777</my:telephone>
  <my:email>tony@acmewidgets.com</my:email>
  <my:district>Eastern</my:district>
</my:salesrep>
<my:salesrep>
  <my:name>Angela Wiggins</my:name>
  <my:telephone>716-111-2222</my:telephone>
  <my:email>angela@acmewidgets.com</my:email>
  <my:district>Southern</my:district>
</my:salesrep>
  <my:salesrep>
  <my:name>Fred Adams</my:name>
  <my:telephone>902-999-1111</my:telephone>
  <my:email>freda@acmewidgets.com</my:email>
  <my:district>Western</my:district>
</my:salesrep>
</my:dutylist>
```

The task of the XSL transform is to process this XML and output an HTML file that will display the information in the browser. A detailed explanation of HTML syntax or of XSL transform rules is beyond the scope of this book. If you are considering using this technique, it's likely that you already have some familiarity with these topics. The following section describes the parts of the stylesheet so that you can understand what they are doing in terms of creating the output.

# Initial Stylesheet Elements

An XSL stylesheet is itself an XML document, so the first element in it is the standard `<xml>` tag. The second element identifies the document as a stylesheet and defines the needed namespaces. Here are those two elements for this stylesheet:

```
<?xml version="1.0" encoding="UTF-8"?>
<xsl:stylesheet version="1.0"
  xmlns:xsl="http://www.w3.org/1999/XSL/Transform"
  xmlns:my="http://schemas.microsoft.com/office/infopath/2003/
  myXSD/2003-06-06T16:47:19">
```

Note that there are two namespace prefixes defined: the `xsl` prefix is associated with the standard transform namespace, and the `my` prefix is associated with the same namespace that is used in the InfoPath XML data file.

The next element in the stylesheet is an `<xsl:template>` element. Most of the stylesheet is, in fact, contained in this element. It's shown here with the lines numbered so you can refer to them in the explanations that follow the listing. Note that the indentation in this file is purely for visual clarity and does not affect its operation at all.

```
1. <xsl:template match="/">
2.   <html>
3.     <head>
4.       <title>Sales Rep Roster</title>
5.     </head>
6.     <body>
7.     <h1>Acme Widgets Information Center</h1>
8.    <hr/>
9.     <table border="2" cellpadding="4">
10.      <thead>
11.         <tr>
12.            <td>Name</td>
13.            <td>Telephone</td>
14.           <td>E-mail</td>
15.           <td>District</td>
16.         </tr>
17.      </thead>
18.       <xsl:apply-templates select="//my:salesrep"/>
19.     </table>
20.     <hr/>
21. The sales representatives listed above are available to answer
22. your questions about our products. You can contact them either
23. by telephone or by e-mail. In the case of e-mail it is our goal
24. to respond by the next business day.
25. </body>
26. </html>
27. </xsl:template>
```

Here are the details of this code:

- Line 1: This is the opening tag for the `<xsl:template>` element. The match parameter specifies the part of the XML document to which the template applies. In this case / means the root element, so this template will be applied once for the XML document's `<my:dutylist>` element.

- Lines 2–17 are written directly to the output without changes. You can see that they are HTML tags that define the HTML document's <head> section and title (lines 3–5), the start of the <body> section (line 6), a heading (line 7), a horizontal line (line 8), and the start of a table with a row of labels at the top (lines 9–17).
- Line 18 is an <xsl:apply-templates> tag that instructs the processor to apply other templates that are defined in the stylesheet. Specifically it applies templates that are defined for the <my:salesrep> elements in the XML data file. We'll get to those soon, but the important point is that the output of these other templates will go at this location in the HTML file.
- Lines 19–26 are also written to the output file without changes. They complete the HTML table (line 19), insert another horizontal line (line 20), add the additional explanatory text (lines 21–24), and close the body section and end the HTML document (lines 26–27).

## Other Stylesheet Elements

The next part of the stylesheet is the template that processes the <my:salesrep> elements. It looks like this:

```
1.  <xsl:template match="my:salesrep">
2.    <tr>
3.      <xsl:apply-templates/>
4.    </tr>
5.  </xsl:template>
```

Here's the description:

- Line 1 opens the xsl:template element and specifies that it applies to <my:salesrep> elements in the XML data file.
- Line 2 writes an HTML tag to the output. This tag marks the start of a row in a table.
- Line 3 tells the processor to apply other templates in the stylesheet. There is no specification about which templates to process, which results in all remaining templates (there's only one more in this project) being processed, which is exactly what we want. The output of the remaining template will be inserted at this location in the HTML file.
- Line 4 writes another HTML tag, this one marking the end of a table row.
- Line 5 ends the xsl:template element.

The final template writes the actual XML data to the HTML file:

```
1.  <xsl:template match="my:name | my:telephone |
2.     my:email | my:district">
3.    <td>
4.      <xsl:value-of select="."/>
5.    </td>
6.  </xsl:template>
```

Here are the details:

- Lines 1 and 2 are a single tag that is split over two lines. This tag opens the xsl:template element. The match parameter specifies that this template will be applied to all four of the listed elements.
- Line 3 writes an HTML tag to the document. This tag marks a table cell.
- Line 4 writes the data in the current XML element to the output.
- Line 5 closes the HTML table.
- Line 6 ends the `xsl:template` element.

# Trying It Out

Listing 16-2 shows the entire stylesheet, including the code given in the preceding sections plus the required closing tab.

**Listing 16-2: Completed Stylesheet for Transforming XML File into HTML**

```
<?xml version="1.0" encoding="UTF-8"?>
<xsl:stylesheet version="1.0"
xmlns:xsl="http://www.w3.org/1999/XSL/Transform"
  xmlns:my="http://schemas.microsoft.com/office/
  infopath/2003/myXSD/2003-06-06T16:47:19">

<xsl:template match="/">
  <html>
    <head>
    <title>Sales Rep Roster</title>
    </head>
    <body>
    <h1>Acme Widgets Information Center</h1>
    <hr/>
    <table border="2" cellpadding="4">
```

*Continued*

Listing 16-2 *(Continued)*

```
    <thead>
    <tr>
  <td>Name</td><td>Telephone</td><td>E-mail</td><td>District</td>
    </tr>
    </thead>
    <xsl:apply-templates select="//my:salesrep"/>
    </table>
    <hr/>
The sales representatives listed above are available to answer
your questions about our products. You can contact them either by
telephone or by e-mail. In the case of e-mail it is our goal to
respond by the next business day.
  </body>
  </html>
</xsl:template>

<xsl:template match="my:salesrep">
  <tr>
    <xsl:apply-templates/>
  </tr>
</xsl:template>

<xsl:template match="my:name | my:telephone |
     my:email | my:district">
  <td>
    <xsl:value-of select="."/>
  </td>
</xsl:template>

</xsl:stylesheet>
```

Figure 16-5 shows the resulting Web page in a browser (I'll show you how to apply the transform to the data in a moment). You can examine the relationship between the XML data, the stylesheet commands, and the output by looking at the HTML output Listing 16-3.

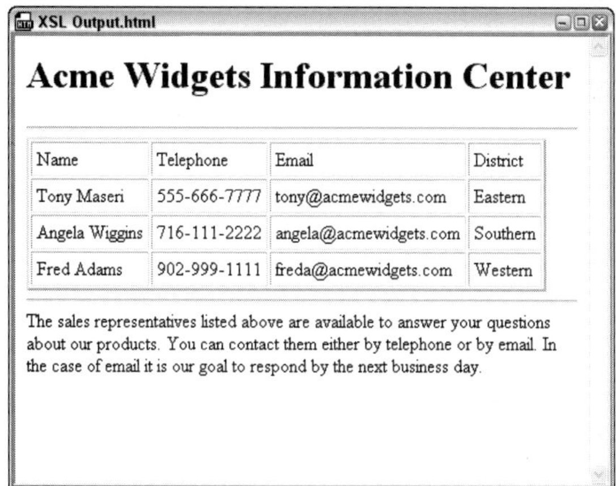


Figure 16-5: The Web page created by the transform in Listing 16-2.

**Listing 16-3: HTML Created by the Stylesheet**

```
<html>
<head>
<META http-equiv="Content-Type" content="text/html; charset=UTF-16">
<title>Sales Rep Roster</title></head><body><h1>Acme Widgets
Information Center</h1>
<hr>
<table border="2" cellpadding="4">
<thead>
<tr>
<td>Name</td><td>Telephone</td><td>E-mail</td><td>District</td>
</tr>
</thead>
<tr>
<td>Tony Maseri</td>
<td>555-666-7777</td>
<td>tony@acmewidgets.com</td>
<td>Eastern</td>
</tr>
<tr>
<td>Angela Wiggins</td>
<td>716-111-2222</td>
<td>angela@acmewidgets.com</td>
```

*Continued*

**Listing 16-3** *(Continued)*

```
<td>Southern</td>
</tr>
<tr>
<td>Fred Adams</td>
<td>902-999-1111</td>
<td>freda@acmewidgets.com</td>
<td>Western</td>
</tr>
</table>
<hr>
The sales representatives listed above are available to answer
your questions about our products. You can contact them either
by telephone or by e-mail. In the case of e-mail it is our goal
to respond by the next business day.
</body>
</html>
```

# Using an InfoPath Script to Apply the Transform

To finish this chapter, I want to show you how you can write a script to apply the transform and create the HTML file. You learned the basics of InfoPath scripting in Chapter 6. This script uses the `DOMDocument` object to perform a transform on the current InfoPath document. The result of the transform – the HTML file – is then written to disk. As a change from earlier script examples, this is written in JScript rather than in VBScript.

First, the XSL file must be added to the form as a resource. This ensures that the transform will be available to users of the form. All steps described here are carried out with the SalesReps form in design mode.

1. Choose Tools → Resource Manager from the InfoPath menu. InfoPath displays the Resource Manager dialog box as shown in Figure 16-6.
2. Click the Add button and navigate to the XSL file containing the stylesheet. Select the file, and then click OK.
3. The selected file is listed in the Resource Manager dialog box. Click OK to close the dialog box.

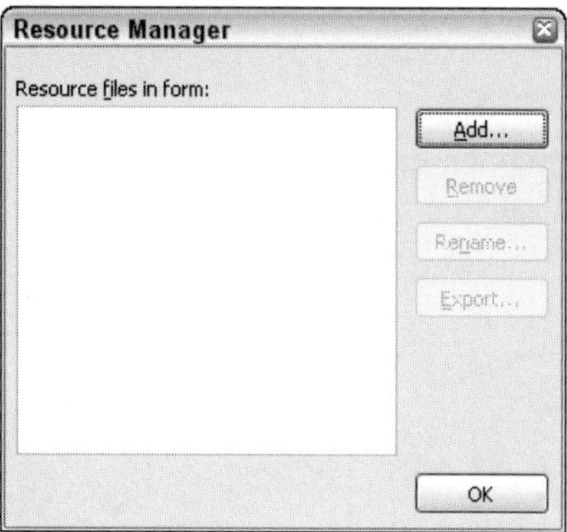


Figure 16-6: The Resource Manager dialog box.

Next, add a button to the form and write the script. These are the steps to follow:

1. Place the cursor at the end of the text at the bottom of the form.
2. Press Enter to create a new line.
3. Choose Insert→More Controls to display the Controls task pane.
4. From the Insert Controls list, select Button. InfoPath inserts a Button control on the form.
5. Right-click the control and select Button properties from the pop-up menu to display the Button Properties dialog box (see Figure 16-7).

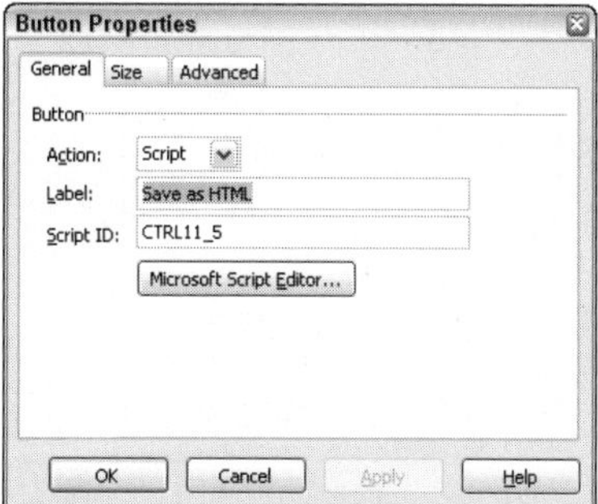


Figure 16-7: The Button Properties dialog box.

6. Select Script in the Action list.
7. Enter “Save as HTML” in the Label field.
8. Click the Microsoft Script Editor button to open the Script Editor. A blank Click event procedure for the button is displayed, as shown in Figure 16-8.

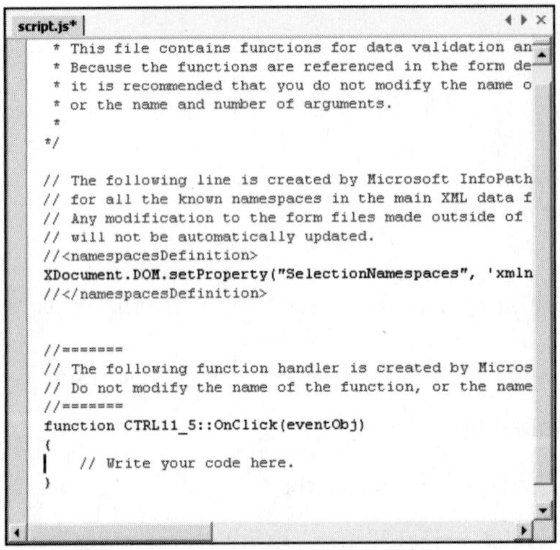

```
script.js*
 * This file contains functions for data validation an
 * Because the functions are referenced in the form de
 * it is recommended that you do not modify the name o
 * or the name and number of arguments.
 *
*/

// The following line is created by Microsoft InfoPath
// for all the known namespaces in the main XML data f
// Any modification to the form files made outside of
// will not be automatically updated.
//<namespacesDefinition>
XDocument.DOM.setProperty("SelectionNamespaces", 'xmln
//</namespacesDefinition>


//=======
// The following function handler is created by Micros
// Do not modify the name of the function, or the name
//=======
function CTRL11_5::OnClick(eventObj)
{
    // Write your code here.
}
```

Figure 16-8: Entering code for the button's Click event.

9. Enter the code shown in Listing 16-4 into the procedure, being sure not to duplicate the first line or the closing brace. Change the path and name of the output file to suit your needs.

**Listing 16-4: Code for Form Button OnClick Event**

```
function CTRL11_5::OnClick(eventObj)
{
//Create the DOMDocument object and set its properties.
var objCustomTransform = new
   ActiveXObject("MSXML2.DomDocument.5.0");
objCustomTransform.async = false;
objCustomTransform.validateOnParse = false;
//Load the transform.
objCustomTransform.load("TransformToHTML.xsl");

try{
// The file system object is used to write the result to a file.
var fso = new ActiveXObject("Scripting.FileSystemObject");
//Create the output file (blank at present).
```

```
var result = fso.CreateTextFile("c:\\xmlfiles\\output.htm", true);
//Perform the transform and write the result to the file.
result.Write(XDocument.DOM.transformNode(objCustomTransform));
//Close the output file.
result.Close();
//Display a success message.
XDocument.UI.Alert("HTML file created");}

catch(e){
//If there was an error, display an error message.
XDocument.UI.Alert(e.description);}
}
```

10. Choose File → Save to save the script.
11. Switch back to InfoPath. The form now looks like Figure 16-9.

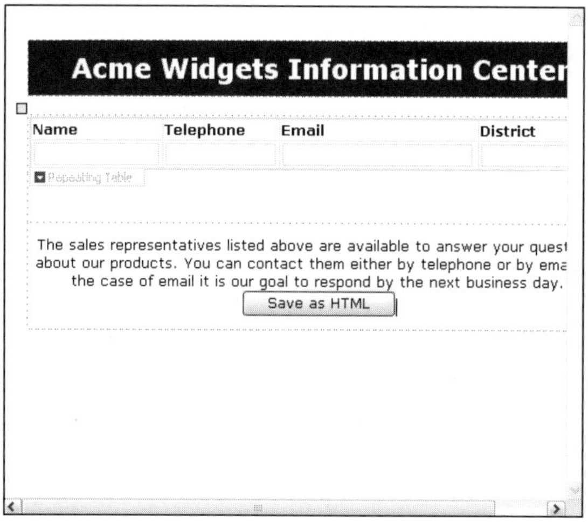

Figure 16-9: The SaleReps form after adding a button.

With the script in place, try the form again: fill out the form with the required data, and click the button. You may be asked whether an ActiveX control should be allowed to interact with the page; if so, select Yes. InfoPath will create the HTML file and display a message to that effect.

An InfoPath form is often your best choice when your users need to enter and edit information of various kinds. When that information needs to be published on the Web, you have two choices for creating the required HTML: exporting the form or using a script to apply a transform. Either way, the process is simple for both the developer and the user.

Appendix A

# What's on the Companion CD-ROM

THIS APPENDIX PROVIDES YOU with information on the contents of the CD that accompanies this book. For the latest and greatest information, please refer to the ReadMe file located at the root of the CD. Here is what you will find:

- System Requirements
- Using the CD
- What's on the CD
- Troubleshooting

## System Requirements

To use this book's CD, you need a computer equipped with a CD-ROM drive and running one of the following operating systems: Windows 95, Windows 98, Windows ME, Windows NT 4.0, Windows 2000, or Windows XP. Some of the individual applications that are provided on the CD have their own requirements, which are listed in the READ.ME file or other documentation for each application.

## Using the CD

To install the items from the CD to your hard drive, follow these steps:

1. Insert the CD into your computer's CD-ROM drive.
2. A window appears with the following options:

   **Install:** Gives you the option to install the author-created samples that are on the CD-ROM.

   **Explore:** Enables you to view the contents of the CD-ROM in its directory structure and install the shareware and trial software applications that are provided.

**eBook:** Enables you to view an electronic version of the book.

**Exit:** Closes the autorun window.

If you do not have autorun enabled, or if the autorun window does not appear, follow these steps to access the CD:

1. Click Start → Run.
2. In the dialog box that appears, type **d:\setup.exe**, where *d* is the letter of your CD-ROM drive. This brings up the autorun window described in the preceding set of steps.
3. Choose the desired option from the menu. (See Step 2 in the preceding list for a description of these options.)

# What's on the CD

The following sections provide a summary of the software and other materials you'll find on the CD.

## Author-created Materials

All author-created material from the book is on the CD in the folder named Author. This comprises all of the numbered listings in the book. Each file is named according to the listing number, for example Listing0601 for Listing 6-1. Each file's extension reflects the type of file – XML for an XML data file, XSD for a schema file, and so on.

A self-extractor that copies the files to your hard drive is also provided.

## Applications

The following applications are on the CD:

- ACDSee 5.0.1: Digital camera software for viewing, organizing, printing, enhancing, and sharing digital photos.
- Acrobat(r) Reader(r) 6.0: For viewing and printing Adobe Portable Document Format (PDF) files on major hardware and operating system platforms.
- CSE HTML Validator Professional v4.50: HTML syntax checker for validating your Web pages.
- CSE HTML Validator Lite v2.01: The "lite" version of the HTML syntax validator.

- XMLSPY Version 2004 Enterprise Edition: Powerful tool for editing and working with XML files, schemas, and XSLT transforms.
- HTML Tidy: Catches errors and other problems in HTML code and applies structured formatting.
- IBM(r) XML Schema Quality Checker v2.1.1: Checks syntax in XSD schema files.
- XML4J version 3.2.1 (XML Parser for Java): An XML parser for use in Java programs.
- expat - XML Parser Toolkit: An XML parser written in the C language.
- SP SGML parser: An SGML parser.
- XT: An XSLT implementation written in Java.
- Four Religious Works: The individual works making up the set are – *The Old Testament, The New Testament, The Quran,* and *The Book of Mormon* all in XML format.
- The Plays of Shakespeare: The complete plays of Shakespeare marked up in XML, courtesy of Jon Bosak.
- XSV 1.4 (XML Schema Validator): An open source XML schema validator.
- Instant SAXON: An XSLT processor.
- XML Specifications: Full details of the XML Recommendation from the Worldwide Web Consortium.
- XED: XED is a text editor for XML document instances.
- 4TOPS Excel Link: Links Excel worksheets to Access data.
- 4TOPS Word Link: Links Word documents to Access data.
- 4TOPS Summary Wizard: Creates statistical summaries from Access data.
- 4TOPS Filter Builder: Simplifies the process of defining data filters in Access.
- 4TOPS Document Management: Uses Access for document management tasks.
- 4TOPS Data Analysis: Statistical analysis and presentation of Access data.
- 4TOPS Excel Import Assistant: Assists in importing data into Excel.
- 4TOPS Screen Capture: Creates Access screen shots.
- Epic Editor – New product name is ArborText 5: XML-based software for multichannel publishing.
- HP EzMath v1.1: Add math formulas to Web pages.

- Hi-VisibilityT for FrontPage: Automates the search engine submission process.
- Hi-Verify for FrontPage: Provides a keyword generator, metadata policy management, and keyword density analysis.
- Hi-PositionT for FrontPage: A search engine position tracking tool.
- TagGenR for FrontPage: Wizard-driven forms for adding metatags to web pages.
- The <WebSite> Promotion SuiteT 2003:
- PATools Advanced Find and Replace v2.04: Advanced find and replace tools for Excel.
- ClipFile: Captures file names to the clipboard.
- Distributed Spreadsheet: Tools for consolidating, tracking, and controlling access to Excel worksheets.
- WebWorks Publisher 2003 for Word: Publish Word documents in various formats including HTML, HTML Help, WinHelp, and Sun JavaHelp.
- El Scripto 2: Web site components for popups, rollovers, and other effects.
- XLSTAT Pro v6.1.8: Statistical analysis tool for Excel.
- SVG Viewer 2.0: Viewer for Scalable Vector Graphics (SVG) files.
- QueryWeb v1.5: Build HTML Pages, Internet Channels, and scripts integrated with Access data.
- CD Case & Label Creator: Design and print labels and case liners for CD-ROM disks.
- Analyse-it for Microsoft Excel v1.68: Data analysis add-in for Excel.
- Gantt Chart Builder (Excel): Gantt chart builder for Excel.
- Change Management System v2.1.1: Integrates with Office to provide project management capabilities.
- BBEdit v6.1: HTML and text editor for the Macintosh.
- StyleMaker v1.4: Tool for creating stylesheets for Web sites.
- WinAce 2.2: File and data conpression in ZIP and many other formats.
- TextPad v4.5: Full-featured text editor.
- Power Utility Pak v5: Set of general purpose utilities for Excel.
- ActiveDocs v4.0: Document templates providing document automation in Office.
- HotDog Professional v7.0: Web site authoring tool.

- WinRAR: File and data conpression in ZIP and many other formats.
- XML Pro v2.01: Sophisticated XML editor.

*Shareware programs* are fully functional, trial versions of copyrighted programs. If you like particular programs, register with their authors for a nominal fee and receive licenses, enhanced versions, and technical support. *Freeware programs* are copyrighted games, applications, and utilities that are free for personal use. Unlike shareware, these programs do not require a fee or provide technical support. *GNU software* is governed by its own license, which is included inside the folder of the GNU product. See the GNU license for more details.

*Trial, demo, or evaluation versions* are usually limited either by time or functionality (such as being unable to save projects). Some trial versions are very sensitive to system date changes. If you alter your computer's date, the programs will "time out" and will no longer be functional.

## eBook version of Powering Office 2003 with XML

The complete text of this book is on the CD in Adobe's Portable Document Format (PDF). You can read and search through the file with the Adobe Acrobat Reader (also included on the CD).

## eBook version of the Office 2003 Super Bible

The Super Bible is an eBook PDF file made up of select chapters pulled from the individual Office 2003 Bible titles. This eBook also includes some original and exclusive content found only in this Super Bible. The products that make up the Microsoft Office 2003 suite have been created to work hand-in-hand. Consequently, Wiley has created this Super Bible to help you master some of the most common features of each of the component products and to learn about some of their interoperability features as well. This Super Bible consists of over 500 pages of content to showcase how Microsoft Office 2003 components work together.

# Troubleshooting

If you have difficulty installing or using any of the materials on the companion CD, try the following solutions:

- **Turn off any anti-virus software that you may have running.** Installers sometimes mimic virus activity and can make your computer incorrectly believe that it is being infected by a virus. (Be sure to turn the anti-virus software back on later.)

- **Close all running programs.** The more programs you're running, the less memory is available to other programs. Installers also typically update files and programs; if you keep other programs running, installation may not work properly.
- **Reference the ReadMe:** Please refer to the ReadMe file located at the root of the CD-ROM for the latest product information at the time of publication.

If you still have trouble with the CD-ROM, please call the Wiley Product Technical Support phone number: (800) 762-2974. Outside the United States, call 1(317) 572-3994. You can also contact Wiley Product Technical Support at www.wiley.com/techsupport. Wiley Publishing will provide technical support only for installation and other general quality control items; for technical support on the applications themselves, consult the program's vendor or author.

To place additional orders or to request information about other Wiley products, please call (800) 225-5945.

Appendix B

# XML Fundamentals and Syntax

XML IS A LANGUAGE, and as such it has a syntax – rules about what is and is not permitted. Conceptually, XML syntax is relatively simple, but there are a lot of details. Anyone who is working with XML needs to know the most important aspects of XML syntax and how XML documents are structured. These are the topics of this appendix.

## Markup and Tags

XML is a markup language that is used to give structure to data. An XML document therefore contains both the data and the XML markup that provides the structure for the data. Markup consists of *tags* that are always enclosed in angle brackets (< ... >). Here's an example that contains two tags and one piece of data:

```
<tag>Data</tag>
```

Because the `<` and `>` characters are used to delimit XML tags, you can't use them in your data. If you need to represent these symbols in your data you must use the character entities `<` (for <, the less than symbol) and `>` (for >, the greater than symbol. When working in Office, you don't need to do this because Office makes the substitution for you.

Based on this example, you might be tempted to say that anything inside brackets is a tag and anything not inside brackets is data. This is only partly true, however. Anything outside brackets is indeed data, but data can be within brackets too, as you'll learn later in the section on XML attributes.

The XML specification provides several different types of tags, and most of this appendix is devoted to explaining the details of how they work. Each type of tag has a specific purpose. The most important ones are

- Providing structure to the data
- Giving instructions for processing the XML document
- Referencing information that is stored elsewhere

# Document Structure

An XML document has both a physical structure and a logical structure. The physical structure of a document permits the components of the documents, called *entities*, to be stored separately. In other words, an XML document is not necessarily stored in a single disk file (or other storage medium). Many XML documents are, in fact, stored as a single file, but you should remember that this is not always the case. Fortunately, the end user rarely has to deal with an XML document's physical structure, which is more a concern of the person authoring the document. The processing software usually takes care of this, pulling the various physical parts of a document together as needed without your intervention.

The logical structure of a document permits the data to be organized as needed. Data is organized into named units called *elements*. As you may have guessed, XML uses tags to provide the logical structure of a document. The logical and physical structures of an XML document are completely independent of each other.

# XML Names

XML relies on names to identify tags and other elements of the document. The following rules apply to XML names:

- A name must begin with a letter, an underscore (_), or a colon (:).
- Subsequent characters in a name can be letters, digits, or the symbols period (.), underscore (_), hyphen (-), or colon (:).
- There is no length limitation.
- Names are case-sensitive. Thus, `Count` and `count` are two different names.
- Names may not start with `XML` in any combination of uppercase and lowercase. Such names are reserved for special uses.

Various non-English characters are legal in XML names. You can refer to the XML Recommendation document at `www.w3.org` for more information.

Some standard practices have developed in the XML community for creating XML names. Element and attribute names are typically created in all lowercase without a separator, for example, `lastname` rather than `LastName` or `last_name`. The colon is avoided because it is also used with namespaces (covered later in this appendix) and might cause confusion.

# Elements

An XML document's data is contained in elements. A single element is defined by its start tag, its end tag, and whatever is between these two tags. The start tag contains the element's name, and the end tag contains the element's name preceded by a slash. For example:

```
<country>
...
</country>
```

An element can contain data, other elements, or a combination of data and elements. Here's an element that contains data:

```
<firstname>Peter</firstname>
```

The following is an element `person` that contains other elements (which themselves contain data):

```
<person>
<firstname>Peter</firstname>
<lastname>Pan</lastname>
</person>
```

Finally, here's an element that contains both data and another element:

```
<person>
Peter
<lastname>Pan</lastname>
</person>
```

While legal, this kind of mixed element is best avoided.

## Nesting Elements

XML elements can be nested to any arbitrary depth. The only restriction is that each inner, or child, element must be entirely contained within the outer, or parent, element. For example, this is perfectly legal:

```
<person>
<name>Peter Pan</name>
<address>Never-Never Land</address>
</person>
```

This, however, is not because of the illegal nesting:

```
<person>
<name>Peter Pan</name>
<address>Never-Never Land
</person>
</address>
```

## The Document Element

Every XML document must contain a *Document element*, which is the parent of all other elements in the document. Its name identifies the document. You can name this element whatever you want (within the XML naming rules). What is important is the relationship of the Document element as the parent of all other elements. Sometimes the Document element is called the root element. Typically, the Document element is given a name that is descriptive of the data in the document. For example, for an XML file that contains an address list, you might call the root, or Document, element `<addressList>` as shown here:

```
<addresslist>
<person>
<firstname>Andrea</firstname>
<lastname>Morelli</lastname>
<address>123 Main Street</address>
<city>Cleveland</city>
<state>OH</state>
<zipcode>44444</zipcode>
</person>
<person>
<firstname>William</firstname>
<lastname>Jackson</lastname>
<address>32 Elm Terrace</address>
<city>Oakville</city>
<state>IL</state>
<zipcode>54321</zipcode>
</person>
...
</addresslist>
```

Note that the Document element does not contain all of the tags in an XML document, just all of the elements. Some tags, such as the DOCTYPE definition and processing instructions, are placed before the Document element.

**Document Confusion**

The term *document* is used in at least two different contexts, and it is easy to get confused. An XML document consists of all the entities, internal or external, that are declared. The only required entity in an XML document is the Document entity (or element). Thus, the Document entity is part of every XML document.

## Empty Elements

An XML element can be empty, containing no data or other elements. An element can potentially contain data and just be empty in this instance, such as a `<middlename>` element for a person who does not have a middle name. An empty element may also be designed to be empty and can never contain data. You might think that such an empty element is useless, but because empty elements can contain attributes (which will be covered soon), they do have their uses.

An empty element can be indicated by start and stop tags with nothing between them:

```
<middlename></middlename>
```

Or an empty element can be indicated by the following shorthand notation:

```
<middlename/>
```

This shorthand notation is preferred, particularly for elements that are defined as empty and cannot contain data.

# Attributes

Attributes are another method of associating information with an element. An attribute consists of a name followed by an equal sign and the attribute value enclosed in quotes (either single quotes or double quotes). Attributes are placed within an element's start tag. Here's the syntax:

```
<elementname attributename="value">
...
</elementname>
```

Attribute names follow the XML name rules presented earlier in this appendix, including case-sensitivity. An element can have multiple attributes. They are listed one after the other with a space separating them:

```
<para keyword="French history" author="P. Aitken" date='6/15/03'>
...
</para>
```

The presence of attributes has no effect on an element's contents or on its end tag. To include attributes in an empty element that uses shorthand notation, place them after the element name and before the closing /:

```
<emptyelement attribute1="value1" attribute2="value2" />
```

When there are multiple attributes in an element, each attribute name must be unique for that element.

If an attribute value is enclosed is double quotes, the value itself may contain single quotes (and vice versa).

## Special Attributes

The XML recommendation identifies two special attributes. One is the `xml:space` attribute that deals with the way white space is handled. I'll cover it in the "White Space Issues" section later in this appendix.

The other special attribute is the `xml:lang` attribute, which serves to identify the language in use. It is optional, and if omitted, the processing software will use its own default assumptions about language. When included, this attribute can be set to various values, as follows:

- A two-letter language code, such as `en` for English or `fr` for French. Please refer to `http://sunsite.berkeley.edu/amher/iso_639.html` for a complete listing.
- A two-letter language code (as the preceding) followed by a hyphen and a two-letter subcode for country. For example, `en-US` specifies American English and `en-GB` identifies British English. Please refer to `http://sunsite.berkeley.edu/amher/iso_3166.html` for the country subcodes.
- A code that follows the Internet Assigned Numbers Authority (IANA) format. IANA codes begin with `I-` or `i-` (a few other prefixes are in use as well) followed by a language identifier. For example, `i-navajo` identifies the Native American Navajo language.
- A user-defined code that begins with the prefix `x-` or `X-`.

Here's an example of XML that uses the `xml:lang` attribute. The processing software can use the proper spelling of `Theater` based on the language in use.

```
<venue xml:lang="en-US">Regency Theater</venue>
<venue xml:lang="en-GB">Regency Theatre</venue>
```

Be aware that XML processing programs are under no obligation to pay attention to `xml:lang` attributes, so their use is usually limited to situations in which you know that the processing software will utilize them.

The `xml:lang` and `xml:space` attributes apply not only to the element they are part of but also to all children of that element (unless a child has its own `xml:lang` or `xml:space` or attribute).

# Entities

In XML, the term *entity* is used in several situations when a name is defined to represent something else. All entities are declared inside the document type declaration, as follows:

```
<!DOCTYPE MyXMLDocument [
<!ENTITY ...>
<!ENTITY ...>
]>
```

XML supports several types of entities, each with its own syntax. They are covered in the following sections.

Why use entities? There are several situations in which they are important, such as

- When the data is too large to be contained efficiently in a single entity.
- When the same content is used in multiple locations. The use of an entity saves time and reduces the chance of errors.
- When content is represented differently on different platforms.
- When the content is not in an XML-compatible format, such as a binary image.

You'll see how these situations are addressed when you look at the different types of entities.

### The DOCTYPE Tag

The DOCTYPE tag is an optional item in an XML file. It is required when you are defining entities, such as this:

```
<!DOCTYPE MyXMLDocument [
<!ENTITY ...>
<!ENTITY ...>

]>
```

It's also required if you are connecting the XML document to a Document Type Definition, or DTD. DTDs are a method for defining a data model for an XML document, a function that is also performed by the newer XML Schema definitions (covered in Appendix C). Because DTDs are not supported in Office, they are not covered in this book.

Note that when an XML document contains a DOCTYPE tag, the document name in the tag must match the name of the Document element.

## The Document Element as Entity

Technically, the Document element is an entity, and in fact is the only entity that is required in an XML document. You learned about the Document element earlier in this appendix in the section "The Document Element." The Document element entity is an exception to the definition of entities in which a name stands for something else. The Document entity is the "base" of any XML document, and is where processing starts.

## Internal Text Entities

An internal text entity is defined within the XML document. It associates an entity name with some text. The syntax is:

```
<!ENTITY EntityName "Text">
```

The text can be enclosed in double quotes, in which case it can include single quotes, or it can be enclosed in single quotes and can then contain double quotes. *EntityName* must be unique within the document. Here are some examples:

```
<!DOCTYPE MyXMLDocument [
<!ENTITY myname "Peter G. Aitken">
<!ENTITY myphone "919-555-1212">
]>
```

To reference an internal text entity within the document, use the entity name preceded by an ampersand and followed by a semicolon:

```
&entityname;
```

Whenever the parser encounters an entity name like this, the name is replaced with the entity text. The effect is exactly like using a word processor's search and replace command.

## External Text Entities

An external text entity is similar to an internal text entity except that the entity text is located external to the XML document. The syntax for an entity declaration is:

```
<!ENTITY entityname SYSTEM "FileIdentifier">
```

`entityname` is the name of the entity. `FileIdentifier` identifies a file on the local system or network. It must specify the file and its location either relative to the location of the XML file that contains the entity declaration, or as a complete URI. Here are some examples:

```
<!ENTITY MyEntity SYSTEM "data.ent">
```

The entity text is contained in the file `data.ent` located in the same folder as the XML file that contains the definition.

```
<!ENTITY MyEntity SYSTEM "\entities\data.ent">
```

The entity text is contained in the file `data.ent` located in the entities folder, which is off the system's root folder.

```
<!ENTITY MyEntity SYSTEM "http://www.mywebsite.com/data.ent">
```

The entity text is located in the file `data.ent` on the specified Web site.

External text entities are referenced just like internal entities: the entity name preceded by an ampersand and followed by a semicolon:

```
&entityname;
```

Whenever the XML parser encounters an external entity name, it replaces the name with the entire contents of the referenced entity file.

There is no requirement to assign ENT or any other specific extension to external entity filenames. The ENT extension is often used, however, because it indicates that the file in intended as an entity and not as a standalone XML file.

## External Binary Entities

An external binary entity is much like an external text entity except that it references binary data rather than text data. The syntax is:

```
<!ENTITY entityname SYSTEM "FileIdentifier" NDATA datatype)
```

`FileIdentifier` specifies the source of the binary data in the same was as for external text entities. The `NDATA` keyword tells the parser that the entity data is binary and should not be parsed. *`datatype`* identifies the type of data that the entity contains. For example, the following entity references a file that contains a JPEG image:

```
<!ENTITY photo1 SYSTEM "\pictures\portrait.jpg" NDATA JPEG)
```

The XML parser uses the `datatype` value to determine how to handle the binary data. However, the parser does not “know” about any binary data types – after all, the XML standard is limited to text data – so you must tell the parser how to handle each binary format. This is done in an XML notation where you associate each `datatype` value with the application that will be used to handle it. Notations are covered later in the appendix.

External binary entities are referenced as usual: the entity name preceded by an ampersand and followed by a semicolon.

## Character Entities

A character entity refers to a character by its numerical code. Unlike text and binary entities, a character entity does not have to be defined – you can just use it anywhere it is needed. The format is as follows:

```
&#n;
```

where `n` is the decimal code for the character. You can also use hexadecimal values as follows:

```
&#xn;
```

The numeric codes can be any code from the Unicode character set. Note that the values 0–255 represent the standard ASCII character codes. For example, the registered symbol ® has the code 174 in decimal and AD in hexadecimal. To include this symbol in XML data, you could use either of the following entities:

```
&#174;
&#xAD;
```

XML defines five character entities for characters that have special meaning to the XML parser. They are < for <, > for >, & for &, " for ", and ' for '. Thus, the text data *Sam's employer* would be encoded in XML as Sam's employer.

# Character Data

By default, the entire contents of an XML document are processed by the XML parser. There are situations in which you want to include text data that will not be processed, but simply be passed along to the application as is. This is called *character data* and it is placed in a CDATA tag:

```
<![CDATA[This is the data]]>
```

The data can be as long as needed. Because it's not processed by the parser, it doesn't have the usual restrictions on special characters, so you don't have to use the character entity < to represent <, for example. All characters can be entered as themselves. The most common use for CDATA sections is when an XML document needs to quote sections of XML or programming code that contains <, >, and other characters that have special meaning in XML.

There's one exception to the rule that you do not need to use character entities in a CDATA section. If the data contains the characters ]]> then you must use > to represent the >, as shown here: ]]>. If you do not, the characters ]]> will be interpreted as marking the end of the CDATA section rather than as part of the character data.

# Notations

An XML notation is used to define how the parser is to handle external binary data in a specific format. Here's an example of an external binary entity as described earlier in this appendix:

```
<!ENTITY photo1 SYSTEM "\pictures\portrait.jpg" NDATA JPEG)
```

The JPEG part of this declaration identifies the binary data type. Because an XML parser does not know about binary data, you must tell it what to do with this data in a Notation. The syntax is:

```
<!NOTATION FormatName SYSTEM "AppIdentifier">
```

*FormatName* is the identifier that will be used for this format (JPEG in the previous example). It can be any arbitrary name but it's a good idea to use something that describes the format, such as JPEG for JPEG image files and TIFF for TIFF image files. *AppIdentifier* is the name and path of the application that the parser will call to process the binary data, or it can be a name that the operating system associates with the format. The following notation specifies that the application ShowBmp.exe will be used to process binary entity data that are associated with the BMP data type identifier:

```
<!NOTATION BMP SYSTEM "\Program Files\Graphics\showbmp.exe">
```

The following example tells the parser to use whatever application the operating system associates with TIFF (which on Windows is typically a graphics program):

```
<!NOTATION TIFF SYSTEM "TIFF">
```

# Comments

Comments are used to provide notes, reminders, and other information in an XML document. They are ignored by the XML parser and are useful only when the document is read by a person, which for the majority of XML documents does not happen. A comment is created by enclosing the text in <!-- --!> tags. For example:

```
<!-- This is the comment -->
```

A comment can span multiple lines, and contain any text with the sole restriction of a double hyphen (--). Note also that the comment text can contain single hyphens as needed as long as the last character in the comment is not a hyphen.

# Processing Instructions

A processing instruction tells the software how to process the XML. It has the following format:

```
<? target instructions ?>
```

> ### Character Encoding in XML
>
> Computers use numbers to represent characters, which means that the characters in an XML document are represented internally by numeric values. A character encoding specifies which numbers represent which characters. The XML Recommendation states that legal characters in XML documents are those that follow the Unicode standard. Unicode characters can be mapped to numbers in two ways, called Unicode Transformation Formats or UTFs. One is UTF-8, which represents standard ASCII characters. English letters, digits, and punctuation marks are represented by 1-byte values in the range 0–255, and other characters (Chinese ideographs, accented letters, special symbols, and so forth) are represented by 2- or 3-byte values. UTF-16 represents each character as a 2- or 4-byte value. XML parsers are required to support UTF-8 and UTF-16, but may support other encoding as well. Please visit `http://unicode.org/unicode/reports/tr20/` for more information on character encoding, Unicode, and XML.

*`target`* is a name identifying the application for which the instruction is intended. The target name `XML` in all upper- and lowercase variants is reserved for directing instructions to the XML parser. *`instructions`* consists of one or more parameter/value pairs in this format:

```
parameter="value"
```

The permitted parameters and values depend entirely on the target application. The only processing instruction that is used regularly is the following, and it's directed at the XML parser:

```
<? XML version="1.0" encoding="UTF-8" ?>
```

This instruction tells the parser that the document contains XML that conforms to version 1.0 (the only existing version, although there will certainly be others in the future) and that the characters in the document adhere to the UTF-8 encoding (an encoding that represents standard ASCII characters). If this processing instruction is present, as it is in essentially all XML documents, it must be the first line in the document.

# White Space Issues

The term *white space* refers to characters that are invisible themselves but have an effect on the document formatting. There are four white space characters: space, tab, line feed, and carriage return. These characters are handled differently depending on where they are located in an XML document.

The carriage return (CR, ASCII value 13) and line feed (LF, ASCII value 10) characters date from the days of teletype machines. The CR signals the print head to move to the left margin, and the LF character signals the machine to advance the paper to the next line. To start a new line of text, both characters had to be sent to the teletype. Today, Windows still uses the combInation of both (CR/LF) to start a new line. Macintosh systems Unix systems use CR alone.

Within markup (inside of tags), each white-space characters is treated as a single space. This means that you can use tabs, spaces, and new lines freely to format your XML for readability. When XML is processed, all white space within markup is converted to single spaces; this conversion is called *white-space normalization.*

Outside of markup (that is, within content), white-space issues are more complex. When it comes time to publish the data, such as by printing it, did the author insert a CR/LF because he or she wanted the output split on two lines? Or, was the CR/LF inserted as an authoring convenience that should not be reflected in the output? While you cannot read the author's mind, you can control how white space in content is handled. By including the `xml:space` attribute with the value `preserve` you instruct the parser to preserve all white space in content and pass it to the application. Setting `xml:space` to `default` results in white space being normalized. This is the default settings for parsers, you rarely see `xml:space` explicitly set to `default`.

Like the `xml:lang` attribute, the `xml:space` attribute applies to the element where the attribute is located and all of its child nodes unless the attribute is explicitly set to `default` at a child level.

## Parsers and XML Processing

The first step in processing XML is called *parsing*. A software component called a parser reads the raw XML and processes it, making the data available to an application in a form that the application can readily use. In almost all cases, the parser is an integrated part of the application rather than being separate. It's important to know that certain rules of XML apply only to the parser and not to the application itself. For example, setting the `xml:space` attribute to `"preserve"` tells the parser to preserve white space in content, meaning that the white space is included in the data passed from the parser to the application. There is no requirement, however, for the application to obey the `xml:space` directive. Different applications treat white space differently, depending on their specific needs.

# A Complete XML Document

Listing B-1 presents a complete, if simple, XML document. The lines are numbered for use in the descriptions that follow the listing.

**Listing B-1: A Complete XML Document**

```
1.  <?xml version="1.0" encoding="UTF-8" >
2.  <!DOCTYPE people [
3.  <!ENTITY otherlist SYSTEM "otherlist.ent">
4.  ]>
5.  <people>
6.  &otherlist;
7.  <person category="personal">
8.  <firstname>Mandy</firstname>
9.  <lastname>Miller</lastname>
10. <phone>919-555-1212</phone>
11. </person>
12. <person cateqgory="business">
13. <firstname>Alexander</firstname>
14. <lastname>Walczak</lastname>
15. <phone>212-333-4444</phone>
16. </person>
17. </people>
```

Line 1 is the standard processing instruction that is the first line in almost every XML document. Lines 2–4 contain the `DOCTYPE` element. It declares the Document element's name to be `people` and defines an external text entity named `otherlist` that is located in the file `"otherlist.ent"`.

Line 5 is the start tag for the `<people>` element, which in this document is the Document element. Note that its name matches the name in the `DOCTYPE` tag, as required. Line 6 has a reference to the `otherlist` entity. When the file is processed, the parser will insert the contents of the `otherlist.ent` file at this location.

Line 7 is the start tag for a `<person>` element. The tag includes an attribute that identifies this person as belonging to the category `"personal"`.

Line 8 contains an entire `<firstname>` element – start tag, data, and end tag. This is a child of the `<person>` element. Line 9 contains an entire `<lastname>` element, which is a child of the `<person>` element, and line 10 contains an entire `<phone>` element, also a child of the `<person>` element.

Line 11 is the end tag for the first `<person>` element.

Lines 12–16 contain another entire `<person>` element with its child elements.

Line 17 is the end tag for the `<people>` element. Becaused `<people>` is the root, or Document, element, this also marks the end of the document.

It is important for you to know the basics of XML syntax in order to work effectively with XML and XML applications. This appendix provides you with the most important aspects of XML syntax, and should be sufficient for the purposes of this book. You can find the complete XML Recommendation at http://w3.org/TR/REC-xml. The W3 Web site is a great source of information for other XML-related technologies as well.

Appendix C

# Data Modeling with XSD Schemas

DATA MODELING is an essential part of working with XML and Office. A data model, or schema, defines the elements, attributes, and data that an XML file can contain. To define a data model you use XSD, the XML Schema Definition language. XSD is itself written using XML, so the material you have learned about XML mostly applied to writing schemas as well. This appendix shows you the syntax and structure of XSD schemas.

## XSD Overview

A *schema*, sometimes called a *data model*, is a way to define a set of rules for an XML file. This is a very important aspect of using XML, particularly in Office. A schema can specify

- The names of the elements (tags) that are allowed in the document
- The parent-child relationships between the elements
- Which elements are required and which are optional
- The attributes that each element can have, and whether an attribute is required or optional
- The type of data each element or attribute can contain – for example, text, a date, or a number

Why is this so important? Software applications that work with XML often expect and require that the XML data be structured in a certain way. An auto-parts database, for example, expects each item to have a `<partnumber>` element, but would likely be lost if it encounters a `<flavor>` element. Likewise, in an address list, the `<firstname>` and `<lastname>` elements might be required while the `<faxnumber>` element could be optional.

When a schema is associated with an XML file, the processing software *validates* the XML against it. If there are no violations, processing continues normally. If one or more violations are found, the software takes appropriate action. An XML file that follows all the rules of its schema is said to be *valid*.

> ### What about DTDs?
>
> You may have heard about DTDs, or Document Type Definitions, as a method for defining an XML data model. In fact, DTDs were the original data model definition language and are part of the core XML specification. They are not, however, supported by Office. Why? Although DTDs are suitable for many data-modeling tasks, over the years programmers began running into limitations. The development of XSD was motivated in part by these limitations, resulting in XSD being a lot more powerful and flexible than DTDs.

A schema is defined using XML, which means that a schema file is itself an XML file. Schemas follow the rules of the XML Schema Definition Language, which is why they are called XSD schemas. By convention, schema files are saved with the XSD extension. The connection between an XML file and a schema is made in software – in other words, the schema file's name is not contained in the XML file. This provides the flexibility of associating different schemas with the same XML file at different times. It is also possible to use two or more schemas to validate different parts of the XML file through the use of namespaces, which are covered in the next section.

You'll find that you rarely have to work directly with the code in a schema file. Some software lets you define the schema using more intuitive point-and-click methods, and then generates the code for you. Other programs, such as Access, can automatically generate a schema from existing data. Finally, many published schemas are available for specific purposes. Even so, you should know the basics of defining schemas.

# Namespaces

A *namespace* provides an extra level of identification to XML elements. As an analogy, suppose that your five best friends are named Fred, Mary, Julio, Alice, and Leslie. There's no problem telling who sent you a personal message signed "Fred," unless two of your friends are named Fred. In that case, you might need the last name to identify the message sender. The last name serves a similar purpose to namespaces in XML.

In a single XML document, element names (in the absence of namespaces) must be unique. But XML offers the capability of combining the data from two or more XML documents, and the possibility of name collisions exists. By assigning different parts of a document to different namespaces, identical element names can peacefully coexist.

Namespaces also can be used to create groupings of related XML elements and attributes that can be recognized by software and processed accordingly. For example, you can use namespaces to apply different schemas to different logical parts of the document.

Some very simple XML files, including many of those used as examples in this book, do not use namespaces. In the real world, however, you'll find that namespaces are very widely used in XML files and applications.

## Default Namespace Declarations

A default namespace declaration has the following form:

```
xmlns="NameSpace"
```

`xmlns` is a reserved XML keyword used specifically for this purpose. *`NameSpace`* is the namespace identifier, specifically a unique URI (Uniform Resource Identifier) for the namespace. The namespace declaration is placed as an attribute of an element in the document, most often the Document or root element. Here's an example:

```
<rootelement xmlns="http://www.pgacon.com/xmlbook">
...
</rootelement>
```

This puts all elements and attributes in the document in the "http://www.pgacon.com/xmlbook" namespace (unless other namespaces are declared). Note that the namespace identifier looks very much like a Web URL. In fact, it is in fact a URL (my own), which is a type of URI.

Why are namespaces, most of them at least, given this form? It has nothing to do with the URI itself – the XML application does not have to retrieve information from the URI or be connected to the Web at all. It is because URIs provide unique identifiers. With this approach to assigning namespaces, the chance of duplicate namespaces is essentially eliminated because each person (or organization) will use his or her unique URI in the namespace.

### URIs, URNs, and URLs

URL stands for Uniform Resource Locator, which most people are familiar with as the addresses used to identify Web sites, such as `www.microsoft.com`. A URI, or Uniform Resource Identifier, is a broader concept that includes any string, or text, that identifies a resource. All URLs are URIs, but the reverse is not true. A URN, or Uniform Resource Name, is a URI that has an institutional commitment to remain available. All URNs are also URIs, but URNs and URLs only partially overlap. For more information please see http://w3.org/Addressing/.

Although not required, it's common practice to have a namespace URI point to a document that describes the namespace specification. This can be a help to developers who are using the namespace. They can plug the namespace URI into a browser and view the documentation. Remember, however, that a namespace URI is simply a formal identifier and does not have to point to a document on the Web.

## Explicit Namespace Declarations

In addition to or instead of using a default namespace, you can create one or more explicit namespace declarations. An explicit namespace declaration takes the form:

```
xmlns:prefix="NameSpace"
```

*prefix* is a name that can subsequently be used to apply the namespace to elements in the document. For example:

```
<rootelement xmlns:pga="http://www.pgacon.com/xmlbook">
```

With this declaration, any element or attribute in the document can be made part of the "http://www.pgacon.com/xmlbook" namespace by prefixing the element name with the namespace prefix in both the start and end tags:

```
<pga:person>
...
</pga:person>
```

A namespace prefix applies only to the specific element in which the prefix is used, and does not automatically apply to children of that element. All elements that do not use a namespace prefix belong to the current default namespace. A default namespace applies to the element in whose start tag it is declared as well as to all children that do not use a prefix, as the following example shows.

```
<rootelement xmlns="one" xmlns:zz="two">
    <element1>
        <element 2>
        <element 2>
    </element1>
    <zz:element1>
        <zz:element2>
        <zz:element2>
```

```
    </zz:element1>
    <element1 xmlns="three">
        <element2>
        <element2>
    </element1>
</rootelement>
```

Notice the following:

- The first <element1> and all of its children belong to the namespace "one".
- The second <element1> and all of its children belong to the namespace "two".
- The last <element1> and all of its children belong to the namespace "three".

The XSD namespace defined as "http://www.w3.org/2001/XMLSchema" is used for schemas This namespace is typically associated with the `xsd` prefix.

# XSD Data Types

Data types are central to XSD schemas. You use data types to specify the type of data that can be contained in XML elements and attributes. The XSD specification has two data types: simple and complex:

- A simple data type cannot contain elements or attributes – it is a unitary piece of information such as a single number or a string. Some simple data types are built into XSD; others can be defined by the programmer.
- A complex data type can contain elements and/or attributes. Complex types are made up of simple types in a specific arrangement and are always defined by the programmer.

The following sections show you how to use and define both simple and complex data types. Later, I show you how to combine these definitions to describe the data structure of an XML document.

## Simple Data Types

The simple data types apply to attributes and also to elements that contain only data (no child elements). Most of the simple types are *atomic*, which means that they cannot be broken down into parts. One simple type, the `list` type, is not atomic.

## BUILT-IN SIMPLE DATA TYPES

The XSD specification includes a wide array of defined simple data types. These types cover almost any imaginable need. The ones that are used most often are described in Table C-1. You can find a full list of data types at `http://w3.org/TR/xmlschema-2/`.

**TABLE C-1 BUILT-IN SIMPLE DATA TYPES**

| Data type | Description |
|---|---|
| anyType | Puts no restrictions on data. |
| string | A string of characters. |
| byte | An integer from –128 to 127. |
| unsignedByte | An integer from 0 to 255. |
| anyURI | A URI in relative or absolute form. |
| integer | An integer value. There is no practical limit. |
| positiveInteger | An integer with a value of 1 or greater. |
| negativeInteger | An integer with a value of –1 or less. |
| nonNegativeInteger | An integer with a value of 0 or greater. |
| nonPositiveInteger | An integer with a value of 0 or less. |
| int | An integer in the range –2,147,483,648 to 2,147,483,648. |
| unsignedInt | An integer in the range 0 to 4,294,967,295. |
| long | An integer in the range +/–9.2x$10^{18}$ (approximate). |
| unsignedLong | An integer in the range 0 to 1.8x$10^{19}$ (approximate). |
| short | An integer in the range –32,768 to 32,767. |
| unsignedShort | An integer in the range 0 to 65,535. |
| float | A floating point value in the range (approximate) +/–1.4x$10^{-45}$ to +/–2x$10^{31}$. Can take the special values INF (infinity), –INF (negative infinity), and NAN (not a number). |
| boolean | The literal values 1, 0, true, and false. |
| time | A 24-hour time in the format HH:MM:SS.sss with the fractional seconds (sss) optional. |
| date | A date in the format YYYY-MM-DD. |
| dateTime | A time and date represented as a date followed by "T" and the time. |

## USER-DEFINED SIMPLE DATA TYPES

A user-defined simple data type is a built-in type that has been customized. Specifically, you place restrictions on the data type to meet the needs of your XML document structure. For example, an XML element to hold a five-digit ZIP code could be based on the built-in type `string`, customized to permit only values that contain exactly five digits. The restrictions that are part of user-defined simple data types are called *constraining facets* or more commonly just *facets*. Here's an example:

```
<xsd:simpleType name="employeeNumber">
  <xsd:restriction base="xsd:int">
    <xsd:minInclusive value="100000"/>
    <xsd:maxInclusive value="199999"/>
  </xsd:restriction>
</xsd:simpleType>
```

This schema element defines a simple type named `"employeeNumber"`. It's based on the built-in type `int` with the added restriction that the value of the data must be in the range 100000-199999 inclusive. Note the following about this code:

- Elements in a schema all have the `xsd` prefix. This prefix will be associated with the XML Schema Definition namespace "http://www.w3.org/2001/XMLSchema".
- A user-defined simple type is defined within `<xsd:simpleType>` tags. The `name` attribute specifies the name of the type.
- The restrictions, or facets, are enclosed within `<xsd:restriction>` tags. The base attribute identifies the built-in data type on which the user-defined type is based.
- Each facet is entered as its own tag that includes information about the restriction and the associated parameter(s).

The available facets are listed in Table C-2 along with the base types they can be used with. When defining simple types, please be aware of the following:

- Do not assign a facet that conflicts with the base type's limitations. For example, the base type short has an inherent range of -32,768 to 32,767. Assigning a "maximum value" facet of 100,000 to such a type would not be permitted.
- The value assigned to a facet must agree with the base type. For example, when defining facets for a user-defined type that is based on the date type, you must assign date values to the facets. It would not make sense to assign numeric or string values to the facets in this case.

**TABLE C-2 FACETS FOR DEFINING SIMPLE DATA TYPES**

| Facet | Description | Applies to base types |
|---|---|---|
| `enumeration` | Restricts the data type to a predefined list of values. Explained later in the appendix. | All except Boolean |
| `length` | Data must contain exactly this number of characters | string, anyURI |
| `minLength` | Data must contain at least this number of characters | string, anyURI |
| `maxLength` | Data must contain this number of characters or fewer | string, anyURI |
| `minExclusive` | The data must be greater than the value | Numeric, time, and date |
| `maxExclusive` | The data must be less than the value | Numeric, time, and date |
| `minInclusive` | The data must be greater than or equal to the value | Numeric, time, and date |
| `maxInclusive` | The data must be less than or equal to the value | Numeric, time, and date |
| `pattern` | The data must match the specified pattern. Explained later in the appendix. | All types |
| `totalDigits` | The maximum number of digits in a numeric value | All integer types |

The following are some examples of user-defined simple data types. This code defines a data type called nonEmptyString for string data that contains at least one character:

```
<xsd:simpleType name="nonEmptyString">
  <xsd:restriction base="xsd:string">
    <xsd:minLength value="1"/>
  </xsd:restriction>
</xsd:simpleType>
```

This example defines a data type that is restricted to holding dates in the year 2002:

```
<xsd:simpleType name="dateIn2002">
  <xsd:restriction base="date">
    <xsd:minInclusive="2002-01-01"/>
    <xsd:maxInclusive="2002-12-31"/>
  </xsd:restriction>
</xsd:simpleType>
```

The indentation used in these examples is for appearance only. The XML parser does not care about indentation.

A user-defined simple data type can be based on another user-defined simple data type. This example builds on the nonEmptyString type previously defined to identify a new type that can hold string data from 1 to 20 characters in length. The minimum length of 1 is inherited from its base type nonEmptyString, and the maximum length is specified as a facet here.

```
<xsd:simpleType name="stringLength1To20">
  <xsd:restriction base="nonEmptyString">
    <xsd:maxLength value="20"/>
  </xsd:restriction>
</xsd:simpleType>
```

### PATTERN FACET

The pattern facet lets you define a template for a data type. For example, you could define a data type for phone numbers that must be in the form xxx-xxx-xxxx, where each x represents a digit. Here's the syntax:

```
<xsd:pattern value="template"/>
```

The template is defined as a *regular expression*, widely used syntax for defining templates that is used in other languages such as Perl. The complete regular expression language is quite complex, but fortunately you do not need to know the entire language for most purposes. The language elements that you are most likely to use are described in Table C-3.

**TABLE C-3 COMMONLY USED REGULAR EXPRESSION ELEMENTS**

| Character(s) | Description | Example |
|---|---|---|
| `(anytext)` | Matches itself. Use "`\(`" and "`\)`" to match parentheses | XML matches XML. |
| `\` | Indicates that the next character as a special character or a literal | `\n` matches the newline character. `\\` matches `\`. |
| `^` | Matches the start of text | `^Hello` matches `Hello` only at the beginning of a string. |
| `$` | Matches the end of text | `Goodbye$` matches `Goodbye` only at the end of a string. |
| `*` | Matches the preceding character zero or more times | `go*` matches `g` or `go` or `goo`, and so on. |
| `+` | Matches the preceding character one or more times | `go+` matches `go` or `goo`, and so on. |
| `?` | Matches the preceding character zero or one times | `go?t` matches `gt` and `got` but not `goot`. |
| `.` (period) | Matches any single character except a newline | `t.t` matches `tat`, `tbt`, `tct`, and so on, but not `toot`. |
| *x*\|*y* | Matches either x or y | `(b|h)ead` matches `bead` or `head`. |
| {*n*} | Matches exactly *n* times, where *n* is an integer greater than 0 | `.e{2}t` matches `feet`, `beet`, and so on. |
| {*n*,} | Matches at least *n* times, where *n* is an integer greater than 0 | `fe(2,}d` matches `feed`, `feeed`, and so on, but does not match `fed`. |
| {*n*,*m*} | Matches at least *n*-*m* times (inclusive), *n* and *m* are an integers greater than 0 with *m*>*n* | `bo{1,3}k` matches `bok`, `book`, and `boook`. |
| [*chars*] | Matches any one of the enclosed characters | `t[ac]d` matches `ted` or `tad`. |
| [^*chars*] | Matches any single character except those enclosed | `t[^ae]d` matches `tbd`, `tcd`, and so on, but not `tad` or `ted`. |
| `[a-z]` | Matches any character in the specified range | `[a-e]` matches `a`, `b`, `c`, `d`, and `e`. |

| Character(s) | Description | Example |
|---|---|---|
| `[^a-z]` | Matches any character not in the specified range | `[^a-m]` matches `n` thru `z`. |
| `\b` | Matches a word boundary | `ed\b` matches the `ed` in `fried food` but not the `ed` in "tedious job." |
| `\B` | Matches a nonword boundary | `ed\B` matches the `ed` in `tedious job` but not the `ed` in `fried food`. |
| `\d` | Matches any digit character 0–9 | Equivalent to `[0-9]`. |
| `\D` | Matches any character that is not a digit 0–9 | Equivalent to `[^0-9]`. |

Here are some examples. This pattern facet defines a data type named `"phoneNumber"` that must contain digits and dashes in the pattern ddd-ddd-dddd:

```
<xsd:simpleType name=phoneNumber">
  <xsd:restriction base="xsd:string">
    <xsd:pattern value="\d{3}-\d{3}-\d{4}"/>
  </xsd:restriction>
</xsd:simpleType>
```

This next example defines a "stockNumber" data type that has these restrictions:

- First character is always `P`.
- Second character is always another uppercase letter.
- Third character is a hyphen.
- Four remaining characters are digits.

```
<xsd:simpleType name="stockNumber">
  <xsd:restriction base="xsd:string">
    <xsd:pattern value="P[A-Z]-\d\d\d\d"/>
  </xsd:restriction>
</xsd:simpleType>
```

## ENUMERATIONS

An enumeration is a data type that is restricted to a defined set of values. A state date type, for example, might be restricted to the names of the 50 states. Each permitted value in an enumeration is specified in an <xsd:enumeration> element. The following code defines the "primaryColor" data type that can take three values: red, green, and blue:

```
<xsd:simpleType name="primaryColor">
  <xsd:restriction base="xsd:string">
    <xsd:enumeration value="red"/>
    <xsd:enumeration value="green"/>
    <xsd:enumeration value="blue"/>
  </xsd:restriction>
</xsd:simpleType>
```

The following enumeration creates a data type that is restricted to holding dates that correspond to the first day of a month in the year 2003:

```
<xsd:simpleType name="FirstOfMonthIn2003">
  <xsd:restriction base="xsd:date">
    <xsd:enumeration value="2003-01-01"/>
    <xsd:enumeration value="2003-02-01"/>
    <!-- more dates... -->
  </xsd:restriction>
</xsd:simpleType>
```

## LIST TYPES

A *list type* defines a data element that contains two or more individual data items in a single element. For example, here's an XML element that contains a list of numbers:

```
<numbers>12 14 16 18</numbers>
```

You would define a schema data type for such an element as follows:

```
<xsd:simpleType name="listOfNumbers">
  <xsd:list itemType="xsd:int"/>
</xsd:simpleType>
```

As written, this defines a type that must contain a list of numbers, but there is no specification of how many numbers. To restrict the number of items in the list, you need another schema element that uses the listOfNumbers as the base type and then puts a length restriction on it, such as this:

```
<xsd:simpleType name="listOfFourNumbers">
  <xsd:restriction base="listOfNumbers">
    <xsd:length value="4"/>
  </xsd:restriction>
</xsd:simpleType>
```

The type listOfFourNumbers is restricted to containing a list of four numbers that meet the requirements for the built-in type int.

## Complex Data Types

A complex data type can contain attributes and/or child elements. For example, here's an XML element that would be defined as a complex type:

```
<person type="sports">
<firstname>Michael</firstname>
<lastname>Jordan</lastname>
</person>
```

You use the following syntax to define a complex type:

```
<xsd:complexType name="name">
...
</xsd:complexType>
```

Between these two tags, you place other tags that define the elements and attributes that the complex type can contain. The complex type tags are summarized in Table C-4 and described in detail in the following sections.

Note that the "*name*" attribute is optional. You include it if you are defining a named data type that can be used in the schema. If it is omitted, the resulting data type is *anonymous*. Anonymous data types are covered later in this appendix.

**TABLE C-4 SCHEMA ELEMENTS USED TO DEFINE COMPLEX DATA TYPES**

| Element | Purpose |
|---|---|
| element | Defines an element within the containing element |
| sequence | Defines a sequence of elements that must be in a specified order in the containing element |
| choice | Defines two or more elements of which only one can occur in the containing element |
| group | Defines a group of elements that occurs in the containing element |
| attribute | Defines or references an attribute |
| attributeGroup | Defines or references a group of attributes |

## THE ELEMENT ELEMENT

The `element` element defines an element that the complex data type can contain. Each `element` element specifies the name of the element and its data type. This and other information about the element is specified in attributes, as detailed in Table C-5.

**TABLE C-5 ATTRIBUTES OF THE ELEMENT ELEMENT**

| Attribute | Description |
|---|---|
| `name` | The name of the element. |
| `type` | The data type of the element. |
| `default` | The element's default value. Applicable only for elements that are simple types. |
| `maxOccurs` | The maximum number of times the element can occur within its parent element. Use the value "`unbounded`" to place no limit on the number of occurrences. The default is `1`. |
| `minOccurs` | The minimum number of times the element can occur within its parent element. Must be a value between 0 and the value of `maxOccurs`. The default is `1`. |

The following code defines an element "`person`" that must contain exactly one of each of the three child elements "`firstname`", "`lastname`", and "`age`":

```
<xsd:complexType name="person">
  <xsd:element name="firstname" type="xsd:string"/>
  <xsd:element name="lastname" type="xsd:string"/>
  <xsd:element name="age" type="xsd:unsignedByte"/>
</xsd:complexType>
```

An alternate syntax has the elements defined elsewhere in the schema, and then uses the `ref` attribute to refer to them:

```
<xsd:element name="firstname" type="xsd:string"/>
<xsd:element name="lastname" type="xsd:string"/>
<xsd:element name="age" type="xsd:unsignedByte"/>

<xsd:complexType name="person">
  <xsd:element ref="firstname"/>
  <xsd:element ref="lastname"/>
```

```
  <xsd:element ref="age"/>
</xsd:complexType>
```

The advantage of this syntax is that you can define a simple element once and then use it in two or more complex types. If you need to modify the simple element – change its data type, for example – you need only make changes one location.

## THE SEQUENCE ELEMENT

The `sequence` element is used to define a group of two or more elements that must appear in a specific order. The syntax is as follows:

```
<xsd:sequence>
  <xsd:element name="firstelementname" type="type"/>
  <xsd:element name="secondelementname" type="type"/>
  ...
  <xsd:element name="lastelementname" type="type"/>
</xsd:sequence>
```

By default, a sequence must occur within its parent element exactly one time. To define a sequence that can occur within its parent element different numbers of times, use the `minOccurs` and `maxOccurs` attributes:

```
<xsd:sequence minOccurs="min" maxOccurs="max">
```

To make a sequence optional, set `minOccurs` to `0`. To place no upper limit on the number of times the sequence can occur, set `maxOccurs` to `"unbounded"`.

The following schema code defines an element named `"salesbyquarter"` that must contain the specified four child elements in the correct order, exactly once:

```
<xsd:complexType name="salesbyquarter">
  <xsd:sequence>
    <xsd:element name="qtr1sales" type="float"/>
    <xsd:element name="qtr2sales" type="float"/>
    <xsd:element name="qtr3sales" type="float"/>
    <xsd:element name="qtr4sales" type="float"/>
  </xsd:sequence>
</xsd:complexType>
```

The `sequence` element can occur within `choice`, `sequence`, `group`, `complexType`, and `restriction` elements. It can contain `choice`, `sequence`, `group`, `element`, `any`, and `annotation` elements.

## THE GROUP ELEMENT

To define a group of elements, use the `group` element. The group can then be referenced as needed for inclusion in complex types. Here's the syntax:

```
<xsd:group name="name">
  <xsd:element name="firstelementname" type="type"/>
  <xsd:element name="secondelementname" type="type"/>
  ...
  <xsd:element name="lastelementname" type="type"/>
</xsd:group>
```

The `group` element places no restriction on the order of elements; it requires only that the defined elements occur. To define a group with a specific order, use a `sequence` element within the `group` element:

```
<xsd:group name="name">
  <xsd:sequence>
    <xsd:element name="firstelementname" type="type"/>
    <xsd:element name="secondelementname" type="type"/>
    ...
    <xsd:element name="lastelementname" type="type"/>
  </xsd:sequence>
</xsd:group>
```

The following code defines a ordered group named `"quarterlysales"` then uses this group to define a complex type:

```
<xsd:group name="quarterlysales">
  <xsd:sequence>
    <xsd:element name="qtr1sales" type="float"/>
    <xsd:element name="qtr2sales" type="float"/>
    <xsd:element name="qtr3sales" type="float"/>
    <xsd:element name="qtr4sales" type="float"/>
    </xsd:sequence>
</xsd:group>

<xsd:complexType name="salesbyquarter">
  <xsd:group ref="quarterlysales"/>
</xsd:complexType>
```

The `group` element can occur within `sequence`, `choice`, `restriction`, and `complexType` elements. It can contain `sequence`, `choice`, `element`, and `annotation` elements.

## THE CHOICE ELEMENT

The `choice` element defines a set of two or more elements. One and only one of these elements can occur in the containing element. You can also specify how many times the chosen element can occur. The syntax is:

```
<xsd:choice minOccurs="min" maxOccurs="max">
  <xsd:elemement name="firstchoice" type="type"/>
  <xsd:elemement name="secondchoice" type="type"/>
  ...
  <xsd:elemement name="lastchoice" type="type"/>
</xsd:choice>
```

The default for both min and max is 1. Set min to 0 to make the element optional; set max to "unbounded" to place no restriction on the maximum number of times the element can occur.

The following code defines a complex type that can contain, exactly once, either the defined sequence, the group "SomeGroup" (assumed to be defined elsewhere in the schema), or the element "myelement".

```
<xsd:complexType name="SuperDataType">
  <xsd:choice>
    <xsd:sequence>
      <xsd:element name="element1" type="string"/>
      <xsd:element name="element2" type="string"/>
    </xsd:sequence>
    <xsd:group ref="groupdefinedelsewhere"/>
    <xsd:element name="myelement" type="string"/>
  </xsd:choice>
</xsd:complexType>
```

The choice element can occur within choice, sequence, group, complexType, and restriction elements. It can contain group, choice, sequence, any, and annotation elements.

## THE ATTRIBUTE ELEMENT

You use the attribute element to define or reference an attribute. The syntax is

```
<xsd:attribute name="name" type="type" use="use" value="value">
...
</xsd:attribute>
```

where name is the name of the attribute, and type is the data type of the attribute (either as a built-in or user-defined simple type). If type is omitted, the data type of the attribute must be defined within the body of the attribute element. use defines how the attribute is used. It is optional; possible values for use are described in Table C-6. Value is the default or fixed value of the attribute (applicable only when use is "default", "fixed", or "required".

**Table C-6 SETTINGS FOR THE ATTRIBUTE ELEMENT'S USE ATTRIBUTE**

| Setting | Description |
|---|---|
| default | The attribute has a default value as specified by the `value` attribute. If the attribute is omitted this is its value. |
| fixed | The attribute has a fixed default value as specified by the `value` attribute. The attribute cannot be assigned any other value. |
| optional | The attribute is optional. This is the default if `use` is omitted from the `attribute` element. |
| prohibited | The attribute cannot be used. |
| required | The attribute must appear once. If `value` is specified the attribute must have that value. If `value` is not specified the attribute can have any value that is legal for its data type. |

There are two ways to define an attribute. The simpler, which is less flexible, uses the `attribute` element's attributes. This example defines an optional attribute:

```
<xsd:attribute name="flavor" type="xsd:string"/>
```

The next example defines an attribute with a default value of zero.

```
<xsd:attribute name="balance" type="xsd:float" use="default"
value="0"/>
```

For additional flexibility use a `simpleType` element inside the `attribute` element. This enables you to define facets (restrictions) on the attribute's data. This works the same way as defining facets for elements as described earlier in the appendix. The following defines an attribute named `"dateIn2002"` that is restricted to dates in the year 2002. Note that this is almost identical to the code defining an element with the same restrictions as presented earlier in this appendix.

```
<xsd:attribute name="dateIn2002">
  <xsd:simpleType>
    <xsd:restriction base="date">
      <xsd:minInclusive="2002-01-01"/>
      <xsd:maxInclusive="2002-12-31"/>
    </xsd:restriction>
  </xsd:simpleType>
</xsd:attribute>
```

The second way in which you can define an attribute directly is from within a complex type as shown in the following example. The resulting complex type, named MyType, contains one element named "amount" of type float, and one required attribute named "category" of type string.

```
<xsd:complexType name="MyType">
  <xsd:attribute name="category" use="required" type="xsd:string"/>
  <xsd:element name="amount" type-"xsd:float"/>
</xsd:complexType>
```

An attribute can also be defined elsewhere and then included in a complex type by reference:

```
<xsd:attribute name="category" use="required" type="xsd:string"/>

<xsd:complexType name="MyType">
  <xsd:attribute ref="category"/>
  <xsd:element name="amount" type-"xsd:float"/>
</xsd:complexType>
```

## THE ATTRIBUTEGROUP ELEMENT

An attributeGroup element lets you define a group of two or more attributes that can then be referred to by name. This is useful when you have a group of attributes that will be used in more than one location in the schema. The syntax is

```
<xsd:attributeGroup name="name">
...
</xsd:attributeGroup>
```

The individual xsd:attribute elements that define the attributes in the group go inside the attributeGroup element. For example:

```
<xsd:attributeGroup name="carinfo">
  <xsd:attribute name="make" type="xsd:string"/>
  <xsd:attribute name="model" type="xsd:string"/>
  <xsd:attribute name="color" type="xsd:string"/>
</xsd:attributeGroup>
```

Then, apply the group to a complex type as follows:

```
<xsd:complexType name="automobile">
  <xsd:attributeGroup ref="carinfo"/>
  ...
</xsd:complexType
```

### ANONYMOUS DATA TYPES

As you have seen in most of the examples presented to far, data types are usually defined with a name (the `name` attribute), permitting the data type to be used in an element by referencing that name. Schemas also support *anonymous definitions* in which no name is assigned to a type. Instead, the type is defined directly inside the corresponding element. To illustrate, look at the following nonanonymous definition:

```
<xsd:complexType name="contactinformation">
  <xsd:element name="phonenumber" type="xsd:string"/>
  <xsd:element name="email" type="xsd:string"/>
</xsd:complexElement>

<xsd:element name="contactinfo" type="contactinformation/>
```

In this code, the structure of the `"contactinfo"` element is defined by referring to the name of the `"contactinformation"` data type that is defined elsewhere. The same result could be obtained by the following:

```
<xsd:element name="contactinfo">
  <xsd:complexType>
    <xsd:element name="phonenumber" type="xsd:string"/>
    <xsd:element name="email" type="xsd:string"/>
  </xsd:complexElement>
</xsd:element>
```

Because the data type is defined within the `<element>` tag, it does not require a name and is therefore called anonymous. Anonymous definitions are typically used when a complex type will be used only once in the schema. Because there is no separate definition of the data type, the complexity of the schema is reduced.

# The schema Element

The `schema` element must be the root element in a schema file. It must be prefixed with whatever prefix is associated with the XSD schema namespace, typically `xsd`. The `schema` element has two attributes as follows:

- **`xmlns:xsd`**. Associates the `xsd` prefix with the defined XSD namespace "http://www.w3.org/2001/XMLSchema".
- **`targetNamespace`**. Defines the namespace that will be used to associate the schema with elements in the XML files.

For example:

```
<xsd:schema xmlns:xsd="http://www.w3.org/2001/XMLSchema"
  targetNamespace="http://YourURI/YourSchema/">
```

The XSD namespace does not have to be associated with the `xsd` prefix, although it customarily is. If you want, you can use a different prefix, in which case all of the schema element names will have to use that prefix. You can also use this as the default namespace by using no prefix, as described earlier in this appendix in the section on namespaces.

All of the individual elements that make up the definition of the schema's data structure go within the `schema` element. The immediate children of the `schema` element can include `element`, `attribute`, `attributeGroup`, `group`, `simpleType`, and `complexType` elements.

# A Schema Demonstration

To give you an idea of how schemas work, let's look at a real schema and an associated data file. The goal is to create a data file to hold information about books. The desired data structure is as follows:

- The root element is `<books>`. It is in the "http://www.pgacon.com/books" namespace.
- The root element can contain any number of `<book>` child elements.
- Each `<book>` element has a required `type` attribute that can be either `"hardbound"` or `"softcover"`.
- Each `<book>` element must contain exactly one `<author>` element.
- Each `<author>` element must contain exactly one `<firstname>` element and one <lastname> element, both of type string.
- Each `<book>` element must contain exactly one `<title>` element, which must be nonblank. It is type string.
- Each `<book>` element must contain exactly one `<pubdate>` element of type date.
- Each `<book>` element can but does not have to contain one `<comments>` element or type string.
- Elements must be in the order presented here.

Listing C-1 shows a short XML data file that follows this structure.

**Listing C-1: books XML Data File**

```
<?xml version="1.0" encoding="UTF-8">
<books xmlns="http://www.pgacon.com/books">
  <book type="hardbound">
    <author>
      <firstname>Kingsley</firstname>
      <lastname>Amis</lastname>
    </author>
    <title>The King's English</title>
    <pubdate>1997-06-01</pubdate>
  </book>
  <book type="softcover">
    <author>
      <firstname>Thomas</firstname>
      <lastname>Mann</lastname>
    </author>
    <title>Death in Venice</title>
    <pubdate>1994-09-10</pubdate>
    <comments>The cover is torn</comments>
  </book>
</books>
```

Listing C-2 shows the associated schema file. Comments explain what each part of the schema does.

**Listing C-2: Schema for books XML Data File**

```
<xsd:schema xmlns:xsd="http://www.w3.org/2001/XMLSchema">

<!-- The root element is called books and is based
on the booklist data type. -->
<xsd:element name="books" type="booklist"/>

<!-- Defines the "booktype" data type, which will be used for the
"type" attribute. This is an enumeration containing "hardbound"
and "softcover" -->
<xsd:simpleType name="booktype">
  <xsd:restriction base="xsd"string">
    <xsd:enumeration value="hardbound"/>
    <xsd:enumeration value="softcover"/>
  </xsd:restriction>
</xsd:simpleType>

<!-- Defines the "authordata" type, which is used for the "author"
element. -->
```

```
<xsd:complexType name="authordata">
  <xsd:element name="firstname" type="xsd:string"/>
  <xsd:element name="lastname" type="xsd:string"/>
</xsd:complexType>

<!-- Defines the "titledata" type, which is used for the
"title" element. -->
<xsd:simpleType name="titledata"
  <xsd:restriction base="xsd:string">
    <xsd:minLength value="1"/>
  </xsd:restriction>
</xsd:simpleType>

<!-- Defines the "singlebook" data type used for "book"
elements. -->
<xsd:complexType name="singlebook>
  <xsd:attribute name="type" type="booktype" use="required"/>
  <xsd:sequence>
    <xsd:element name="author" type="authordata"/>
    <xsd:element name="title" type="titledata"/>
    <xsd:element name="pubdate" type="xsd:date"/>
    <xsd:element name="comments" type="xsd:string" minOccurs="0"/>
  </xsd:sequence>
</xsd:complexType>

<!-- Defines the "booklist" type, which is the type of the XML
document's root element. It can contain 0 to any number of
<book> elements. Each <book> element is of type "singlebook". -->
<xsd:complexType name="booklist">
  <xsd:element name="book" type="singlebook" minOccurs="0"
     maxOccurs="unbounded"/>
</xsd:complexType>

</xsd:schema>
```

This example illustrates how schemas are an essential part of XML. When an XML data file is valid, you know that its structure follows the requirements set out in the associated schema. The software that will use the XML data file can then proceed without the errors that can be caused by invalid data.

Appendix D

# XSLT and XPath

EXTENSIBLE STYLESHEET LANGUAGE, for Transformations (XSLT) is part of the Extensible Stylesheet Language (XSL), which is designed for transforming and formatting XML data. XSLT is supported by many Office applications. This appendix explains the basics of using XSLT. The appendix also provides an introduction to XPath, a technology that is used to identify parts of the document on which a transform is to operate.

## XSLT

As the *transformation* part of its name implies, XSLT is used for transforming, or changing, XML files. When you apply a transform to XML data, the output of the process is the result of applying the transform's rules and instructions to the XML data. The original XML data is not changed in any way. Depending on the specific situation, the output of the transform might be displayed on-screen, saved in a file, or submitted to a Web site.

Transforms are sometimes referred to as *stylesheets*.

What exactly can a transform do? Just about anything you can imagine. Here are some examples:

- Change the order of elements
- Select certain elements and omit others
- Output text as well as XML data
- Filter the output based on data values
- Perform simple calculations based on data in the XML

One of the tasks for which XSLT is commonly used is converting XML data to HTML for display in a browser. Other XSLT applications include creating a table of contents or index for an XML document, arranging XML data into tables, or converting XML data from one schema to another.

XSLT is actually one of two parts of the XSL specification. The other is Formatting Objects (FO), a vocabulary for applying specific formatting to data. Office does not support FO, so it isn't considered further here. XSL itself is a W3C Recommendation, and you can find complete details at `http://w3.org/Style/XSL/`.

# XSLT Structure

An XSLT transform is actually an XML vocabulary. In other words, an XSLT file is itself an XML file, and therefore the first element in the file is the standard `<xml>` tag. The content of the file is identified as a stylesheet by the `xsl:stylesheet` tag as shown here:

```
<?xml version="1.0"?>
<xsl:stylesheet
    xmlns:xsl="http://www.w3.org/1999/XSL/Transform"
    version="1.0">
<!-- stylesheet contents go here-->
</xsl:stylesheet>
```

The `xsl:stylesheet` tag includes the XSLT namespace definition, which is usually associated with the `xsl` prefix, as in this example, although sometimes the `xs` prefix is used. This tag often includes other application-specific namespace declarations as well.

The `xsl:transform` element is sometimes used as a synonym for `xsl:stylesheet`.

The contents of the stylesheet – the instructions that define what the stylesheet actually does – are placed between the tags as shown in the preceding code snippet. Stylesheet organization will become more clear when you look at the example in the next section.

# An XSLT Demonstration

Before getting to the details of XSLT syntax it will be useful to look at a simple example. The XML data to be transformed is shown in Listing D-1. This is a data file containing information for an inventory.

**Listing D-1: The XML Data File**

```
<?xml version="1.0" encoding="UTF-8"?>
<stockitems xmlns="http://www.pgacon.com/stockitems">
```

```
  <item>
    <name>Claw hammer</name>
    <supplier>Ajax Manufacturing</supplier>
    <wholesaleCost>12.50</wholesaleCost>
    <retailPrice>19.95</retailPrice>
  </item>
  <item>
    <name>Needle-nosed pliers</name>
    <supplier>Miller Manufacturing</supplier>
    <wholesaleCost>8.45</wholesaleCost>
    <retailPrice>15.89</retailPrice>
  </item>
  <item>
    <name>Wire stripper</name>
    <supplier>Ajax Manufacturing</supplier>
    <wholesaleCost>11.25</wholesaleCost>
    <retailPrice>21.00</retailPrice>
  </item>
  <item>
    <name>Paint scraper</name>
    <supplier>Clyde Co.</supplier>
    <wholesaleCost>4.10</wholesaleCost>
    <retailPrice>8.00</retailPrice>
  </item>
  <item>
    <name>Crescent wrench</name>
    <supplier>Baxter Foundry Inc.</supplier>
    <wholesaleCost>12.60</wholesaleCost>
    <retailPrice>23.95</retailPrice>
  </item>
</stockitems>
```

The stylesheet to perform the required transformation is shown in Listing D-2. The goal of the stylesheet is to transform the data to HTML for display in a browser, as follows:

- Only the name and price data will be displayed.
- Each item and its price will be on its own line.
- The name of the item will be in boldface.
- The price will be prefixed with a dollar sign.

The line numbers in the listing are not part of the stylesheet, but are used in the explanation following the listing.

**Listing D-2: The XSLT Transform File**

```
<?xml version="1.0" encoding="UTF-8"?>
1.  <xsl:stylesheet version="1.0"
    xmlns:sl="http://www.pgacon.com/stockitems"
    xmlns:xsl="http://www.w3.org/1999/XSL/Transform">
2. <xsl:output method="html" version="1.0" encoding="UTF-8"
     indent="yes"/>

3. <xsl:template match="/">
4.   <html><head>
5.   <title>Stock Parts List</title>
6.   </head><body>
7.   <xsl:apply-templates select="//sl:item"/>
8.   </body></html>
9. </xsl:template>

10. <xsl:template match="sl:item">
11.   <p><b><xsl:value-of select="sl:name"/>
12.   </b> $<xsl:value-of select="sl:retailPrice"/></p>
13. </xsl:template>

14. </xsl:stylesheet>
```

Let's examine the stylesheet line by line to get a feel for how it works.

Line 1 is the opening `xsl:stylesheet` tag. It provides the required XSLT namespace declaration as well as an application-specific namespace associated with the `sl` prefix.

Line 2 is the XSLT tag specifying that the output of the transform is HTML. Another option for this tag would be to specify XML output.

The tag in line 3 marks the start of an XSLT template element. As you'll see later in the appendix, template elements are in many ways the heart of a stylesheet. The `match` attribute uses an XPath expression to specify what part of the XML file the template applies to. In this case the / identifies the root element of the XML file. In other words, this template is applied exactly once during processing.

Lines 4–6 text that is output as is. If you are familiar with HTML, you will recognize them as HTML elements and a title. Line 7 tells the processor to apply additional templates. The select attribute uses an XPath expression to specify that the templates for `sl:item` elements are to be applied (see line 10).

Line 8 contains additional text that is output after the templates are applied (Line 7). In other words, this text, which is the closing HTML tags, will be the last thing output by the stylesheet. Line 9 is the closing tag for this template.

Line 10 is the opening tag for another template. The `match` attribute uses an XPath expression to specify that this template applies to `sl:item` elements. Thus, this template will be applied once for each `sl:item` element in the XML data.

Line 11 starts by outputting the text `<p><b>`, which are the HTML tags to start a paragraph and start boldface text. Then, it uses the `value-of` tag to output data. The `select` attribute identifies the data – in this case, the content of the `sl:name` element in the XML data.

Line 12 outputs the text `</b>`, which is the HTML tag to turn off boldface. The it outputs a space, a dollar sign, and the value of the `sl:retailPrice` element. Finally, it outputs the text `</p>` to mark the end of a paragraph and the start of a new line.

Line 13 marks the end of the template, and Line 14 marks the end of the stylesheet.

Applying this stylesheet to the XML data in Listing D-1 results in the output shown in Listing D-3. Some details of the output will depend on the specific XSLT processor that is used – for example, some will include the source namespace in the output while others won't. The important thing is that the XSLT instructions are carried out to create the HTML required to display the data as desired.

**Listing D-3: Output from Applying the Stylesheet to the XML Data File**

```
<html>
<head>
<title>Stock Parts List</title>
</head>
<body>
<p><b>Claw hammer</b> $19.95</p>
<p><b>Needle-nosed pliers</b> $15.89</p>
<p><b>Wire stripper</b> $21.00</p>
<p><b>Paint scraper</b> $8.00</p>
<p><b>Crescent wrench</b> $23.95</p>
</body>
</html>
```

Figure D-1 shows the output displayed in a browser.

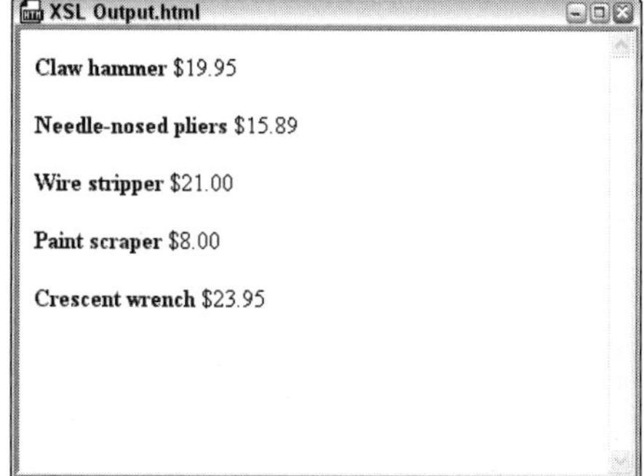


**Figure D-1:** The stylesheet output displayed in a browser.

# XSLT Templates

A template is an XSLT instruction that creates output based upon certain criteria. The criteria for a template identify a part or parts of the XML document to which the template is to be applied. The contents of the template, or *template body,* define the output that is to be created when the template is executed. A template is defined in an xsl:template element with the following syntax:

```
<xsl:template match="pattern">
...
</xsl:template>
```

*"pattern"* is an XPath expression that identifies elements in the XML document. A simple pattern is an element name or the / symbol to match the root node. You'll learn more about XPath expressions later in the appendix.

Inside the template body you place other XSLT processing instructions that are carried out when the template is processed. The processing instructions you will use most often are explained in the following sections.

# Literal Text

If you place literal text in a template body, it is output as is. Literal text is any text that is not part of an XSL tag. Here's an example:

```
<xsl:template match="item">
  <center><xsl:value-of select="."/></center>
</xsl:template>
```

This template outputs the text <center> followed by the value of the "item" element and finally the text </center>. You can also output literal text using the xsl:text instruction, described next.

# The xsl:text Element

The xsl:text element outputs literal text. Here's the syntax:

```
<xsl:text disable-output-escaping="value">
text to be output
</xsl:text>
```

The disable-output-escaping attribute can be set to "yes" or "no". If set to "yes", characters that have special meaning in XML, such as < and >, are output as themselves. If set to "no", such characters are output as the corresponding entity references (< and > for < and >, for example). The attribute is optional and if it's omitted, the default is "no".

An `xsl:text` element outputs white space unchanged. This differs from white space by itself that is not in an `xsl:text` element – that is, literal text. Such white space is normalized unless an enclosing element has the `xml:space` attribute set to `"preserve"`. If, for example, you wanted the output to consist of a part name followed by a tab and then the price, you would write the following (there's a tab between the `<xsl:text>` and `</xsl:text>` elements):

```
<xsl:value-of select="partname"/>
<xsl:text>	</xsl:text>
<xsl:value-of select="price"/>
```

# The xsl:value-of Element

The `xsl:value-of` element writes the value of an expression to the output. This is the syntax:

```
<xsl:value-of select="expression"/>
```

`"expression"` is the XPath expression to be evaluated and output. A common use of `xsl:value-of` is to output the text data from an XML element, which is accomplished by using `"."` as the select expression:

```
<xsl:value-of select="."/>
```

For example, the following XSLT fragment writes the value of the `"name"` element to the output:

```
<xsl:template match="name">
  <xsl:value-of select="."/>
</xsl:template>
```

You can also use `xsl:value-of` with a select expression that identifies a specific element. For an example, please look at lines 11 and 12 in the stylesheet example that was presented earlier in Listing D-2.

# The xsl:if Element

You use the `xsl:if` instruction to enclose a set of instructions that will be processed only if a specified condition is met. Here's the syntax:

```
<xsl:if test="criterion">
...
</xsl:if>
```

"*criterion*" is an expression that can be evaluated as true or false. The instructions contained in the xsl:if instruction are executed only if the criterion is true. For example, the following instructions output the literal text Fiction only if the "type" attribute of the element being processed is equal to "fiction". The @ symbol is used to specify an attribute:

```
<xsl:if test="@type='fiction'">
Fiction
</xsl:if>
```

## The xsl:choose Element

Use the xsl:choose element to define a choice between two or more alternatives. The syntax is:

```
<xsl:choose>
  <xsl:when test="expression1">template-body1</xsl:when>
  <xsl:when test="expression2">template-body2</xsl:when>
  ...
  <xsl:otherwise>template-body</xsl:otherwise>
</xsl:choose>
```

You can use as many <xsl:when> elements as desired, but there can be only one <xsl:otherwise> element, which is optional. <xsl:choose> works by evaluating the test expressions associated with the <xsl:when> elements in order. When an expression evaluates as true, the associated template body is instantiated. Subsequent <xsl:when> elements are ignored even if their test expression is also true. If no test expression evaluates as true, the template body in the optional <xsl:otherwise> element is instantiated. If no test expression evaluates as true, and there is no <xsl:otherwise> element, then no template body is instantiated.

The following code fragment outputs the text Large, Medium, or Small, based on the value of the "size" attribute:

```
<xsl:choose>
  <xsl:when test="@size < 100">Small</xsl:when>
  <xsl:when test="@size > 200">Large</xsl:when>
  <xsl:otherwise>Medium</xsl:otherwise>
</xsl:choose>
```

## The xsl:for-each Element

Use the xsl:for-each element to set up a loop that is executed repeatedly for each element in a set of repeating elements. The syntax is:

```
<xsl:for-each select="expression">
...
</xsl:for-each>
```

"*expression*" is an XPath expression referencing a set of repeating elements. The instructions within the `xsl:for-each` element are executed once for each element in the set. The `xsl:for-each` instruction processes the nodes in the same order they exist in the document, unless an `xsl:sort` instruction is used to change the sort order.

The following XSLT example iterates over every "book" element that is a child of a "holdings" element. The values of the "title" and "author" elements and of the "category" attribute are output. The output is sorted alphabetically by title. The output is HTML that will display the data in a table.

```
<xsl:for-each select="holdings/book">
  <xsl:sort select="title"/>
  <tr>
    <td><xsl:value-of select="title"/></td>
    <td><xsl:value-of select="author"/></td>
    <td><xsl:value-of select="@category"/></td>
  </tr>
</xsl:for-each>
```

Note that the results of an `xsl:for-each` element can also be obtained by using the `xsl:apply-templates` instruction, as described in the next section.

# The xsl:apply-templates Element

The `xsl:apply-templates` instruction processes a set of elements. This is the syntax:

```
<xsl:apply-templates select="expression"/>
```

"*expression*" is an XPath expression returning a set of elements. You can omit the select attribute in which case the instruction processes all the child elements of the current element. When the XSLT processor encounters an `apply-templates` instruction, it locates and processes all templates that are defined (in `xsl:template` instructions) for the elements identified in *expression*. Elements are processed in the same order they exist in the document unless an `xsl:sort` instruction is used to modify the order. When you use one or more `xsl:sort` instructions, the format is as follows:

```
<xsl:apply-templates select="expression">
  <!--xsl:sort instructions go here-->
</xsl:apply-templates>
```

The following example shows how to use the apply-templates and sort instructions. Its operation is explained following the code.

```
1. <xsl:template match="/">
2.    <xsl:apply-templates select="/holdings/book">
3.      <xsl:sort select="title"/>
4.    </xsl:apply-templates>
5. </xsl:template>

6   <xsl:template match="book">
7.    <xsl:apply-templates/>
8.  </xsl:template>

9.  <xsl:template match="title | author">
10.   <xsl:value-of select='.'/>
11. </xsl:template>
```

Lines 2–4 are an xsl:apply-templates instruction that will be applied to "book" elements that are children of the "holdings" element. The xsl:sort instruction on line 3 specifies that the "book" elements will be sorted by the "title" element.

Lines 6–8 define a template for "book" elements that will be executed once for each "book" element as a result of the xsl:apply-templates instruction on lines 2–4. This template contains another xsl:apply-templates instruction that has no select attribute and therefore will iterate through all the child elements of the "book" element.

Lines 9–11 define a template for the "title" and "author" elements, which are children of the "book" element. The xsl:apply-templates instruction on line 7 causes the template to be executed in the following order:

1. For the "title" element in the first "book" element
2. For the "author" element in the first "book" element
3. For the "title" element in the second "book" element
4. For the "author" element in the second "book" element

Continuing through the "title" element in the last "book" element and the "author" element in the last "book" element.

## The xsl:sort Element

The xsl:sort element is used to specify the order in which nodes are processed by an xsl:apply-templates or xsl:for-each element. The xsl:sort element can appear only within these two elements. Here's the syntax:

```
<xsl:sort select="expression"/>
```

"*expression*" defines the sort key. The select attribute is optional. If it is omitted, the sort is done based on the string value of the element data. There are three other optional attributes for the `xsl:sort` element, described in Table D-1.

**TABLE D-1 OPTIONAL ATTRIBUTES FOR THE XSL:SORT ELEMENT**

| Attribute | Description |
|---|---|
| `order` | Specifies the sort order as either `ascending` or `descending`. The default is `ascending`. |
| `case-order` | Set to `upper-first` or `lower-first` to specify whether uppercase or lowercase letters are collated first. The default is language dependent. |
| `data-type` | Set to `text` or `number` to specify whether the data is to be collated alphabetically or numerically. The default is `text`. |

You can include more than one `xsl:sort` element in an `xsl:apply-templates` or `xsl:for-each` element. In this situation, the data is sorted according to the first `xsl:sort` expression, then by the second, and so on. The following examples demonstrate the use of the `xsl:sort` element.

This code process the "`contact`" children of the current element, sorting them alphabetically by the "`type`" attribute:

```
<xsl:apply-templates select="contact">
  <xsl:sort select="@type"/>
  ...
</xsl:apply-templates>
```

The following code would do the same function as that in the preceding example, except that when two or more contacts have the same type, they will be sorted numerically by the "`age`" attribute:

```
<xsl:apply-templates select="contact">
  <xsl:sort select="@type"/>
  <xsl:sort select="@age" data-type="number"/>
</xsl:apply-templates>
```

# XPath

When creating a transform, you need some way to specify which part(s) of the XML document are to be used. XML Path Language, or XPath, was developed specifically for this task (although its use is not limited to XSLT transforms). XPath can do more than simply identify elements for processing. XPath expressions can also perform numerical calculations and string manipulation. These are covered toward the end of this appendix. XPath version 1 is a W3C Recommendation. The XPath specification is available at `http://w3.org/TR/xpath`.

The terms *node* and *node set* are commonly used in discussions of XPath. This is nothing more than another way of referring to the contents of an XML file. A node is an XML element or attribute, and a node set is a group of multiple XML elements.

# XPath Patterns

An XPath pattern identifies a node set. You use patterns in the match attribute of `xsl:template` elements to specify which nodes the template applies to (as was covered earlier in this appendix). One way to look at it is that a pattern specifies rules, or criteria, that a node must meet in order to be included in the node set. The criteria can include the name of a node (an element or attribute name), the position of the node relative to other nodes, or the data stored in an element or an attribute. Here are some basic rules of patterns:

- To match an element by name, use the name.
- To match any name, use *.
- To specify an element by its name and also by its position relative to other elements, use the / or // characters.

A *predicate* modifies the part of the pattern that comes before it, and is enclosed in square brackets. The use of predicates usually follows this syntax:

```
x[y]
```

This is interpreted as "select nodes that meet criterion *x* but only when *y* is true."

Table D-2 presents some examples of XPath expressions.

**TABLE D-2 EXAMPLES OF XPATH PATTERN MATCHING**

| Example | Matches |
|---|---|
| `item` or `//item` | Any element named `item` |
| `/item` | Elements named `item` that are children of the root node |
| `holdings/item` | Elements named `item` that are children of the element named `holdings` |

| Example | Matches |
|---|---|
| /holdings/item | Elements named item that are children of the element named holdings, which is in turn a child of the root element |
| holdings//item | Elements named item that have the holdings element as an ancestor (a parent or higher in the node tree) |
| holdings/*/item | Elements named item that have a holdings grandparent (that is, the parent of its parent) |
| holdings[item] | Elements named holdings that have a child named item |

You can also create patterns that match based on attribute names using either the attribute:: syntax or the @ character. Be aware that there is a difference between matching an element node that has a certain attribute, and matching the attribute node itself. Table D-3 shows some examples.

**TABLE D-3 XPATH PATTERNS THAT MATCH BY ATTRIBUTE NAME**

| Example | Matches |
|---|---|
| attribute::type | Attributes named type |
| @type | Attributes named type (same effect as attribute::title) |
| *[@type] | Any element node with an attribute named type |
| holdings/*[@type] | Any child element of the holdings element that has an attribute named type |

Patterns can also define node sets based on the data n the XML file rather than the element and attribute names. The syntax is similar to that described above with the addition of the data to be matched in quotes. Table D-4 shows some examples of matching by data as well as node name.

**TABLE D-4 XPATH PATTERNS THAT MATCH BY ATTRIBUTE AND ELEMENT VALUES**

| Example | Matches |
|---|---|
| `item[@type="seafood"]` | `item` elements that have the `type` attribute with the value `"seafood"`. |
| `item[name="dried cod"]` | `item` elements that have the `name` child element with the value "dried cod". |
| `id["12321"]` | A node with a type ID attribute equal to `"12321"`. An attribute is type ID if it is defined as this type in the document schema. The name of the attribute is irrelevant. |

# XPath Expressions

An XPath expression is a construct that can be evaluated as a string, a number, a node set, or a true/false value. There are two general uses for expressions in a stylesheet: to select data from the source document for processing (which was covered in the preceding section on XPath patterns) and to manipulate data and perform calculations for outputting to the result document. This section shows you how to use XPath expressions for data manipulations and calculations.

## VARIABLES

You use a variable when you need to store some data while an XSL stylesheet is executing. XPath variables are unlike other programming language variables in that they cannot be changed: once you assign an initial value to a variable, it always has that value. (The name *variable* is not really accurate but that's the term used in XPath.)

You define a variable with the `xsl:variable` element. There are two equivalent forms of syntax. One defines the variable value as an attribute:

```
<xsl:variable name="name" select="value"/>
```

The second syntactical form defines the variable value between start and end tags as shown here:

```
<xsl:variable name="name">
value
</xsl:variable>
```

In these examples, *name* is the name of the variable and `value` is the value assigned to it. The value can be text, a number, a true/false value, or a node set. Here are two examples that create variables for text and numeric data:

```
<xsl:variable name="country" value="'Norway'"/>
<xsl:variable name="interest" value="0.05"/>
```

In the first example, note the use of double and single quotes around the value. This is necessary to indicate that it is data and not a node set. If you wrote `value="Norway"` the XPath processsor would think that `"Norway"` was a node name. (You can reverse the order of the double and single quotes if desired: `'"Norway"'`.)This isn't required for numerical values, as shown in the second example. Quotes are not required when you use the start/end tag syntax:

```
<xsl:variable name="country">
Norway
</xsl:variable>
```

The next example creates a variable that refers to the specified node set. You can then use the variable name whenever you want to reference that node set.

```
<xsl:variable name="nodeset1" value="/holdings/book"/>
```

The final example assigns the Boolean value true to the variable. XSL does not have constants to represent the values true and false so you must use the functions `true()` and `false()` for this purpose. Functions are covered later in this appendix.

```
<xsl:variable name="ToPrinter" value="true()"/>
```

To reference a variable within the stylesheet, use the variable name preceded by the `$` symbol. For example, assuming that the variable `"nodeset1"` has been assigned a node set value, the following code creates a template that will be applied to that node set.

```
<xsl:template match="$nodeset1">
...
</xsl:template>
```

The next example is an `if` element that executes only if the value of the variable `"count"` is less than 500:

```
<xsl:if test="$count < 500">
...
</xsl:if>
```

Referencing a variable that has not been assigned a value causes an error.

## Variables and Namespaces

Like almost everything else in the XML world, XSL variables can be qualified by a namespace. Simple variable names — that is, names without a namespace prefix — are not part of the default namespace but rather are considered to have a null namespace. A variable name can be qualified by a namespace prefix, such as `si:total` or `qz:sales` (the prefix must be linked to a namespace, of course). The same variable name with different prefixes, such as `x:total` and `y:total`, are considered to be different variables if the prefixes refer to different namespaces, and the same if the prefixes refer to the same namespace.

Each variable that you define in a stylesheet has a *scope*, which refers to the parts of the stylesheet where the variable may be used. A variable's scope is determined by the location where it is declared. Variables declared at the top level of the stylesheet, outside of any template body, have global scope and can be referenced anywhere in the stylesheet. Variables declared within a template body are local and can be referenced only within that template body.

The most common use for variables is when there is an expression that is used in multiple locations throughout the stylesheet. By using a variable for the expression, you can make the stylesheet more readable. Using a variable also makes it simple to change the value of the expression when needed because you must make the change in only one location (the variable definition). For instance, imagine a stylesheet that will need to select node trees consisting of people in your address book who are business acquaintances as indicated by the `"type"` attribute. You could create a variable to hold the required XPath expression, as this example shows:

```
<xsl:variable name="businessAquaintances"
   select="/addresses/person[@type='business']"/>
```

With this variable defined you could use it wherever you need to refer to this node tree:

```
<xsl:template select="$ businessAquaintances ">
...
<xsl:template>
```

You can also use variables to expand the value of an attribute. Suppose the XML data includes an optional attribute named `"count"`. When the value of count is greater than zero, you want the attribute included, but when it is zero, the attribute is omitted. from the output. To accomplish this, you need the value of `"count"` for calculations but because it is an optional attribute it may be omitted and its value won't be available. Here's how you can deal with this situation using a variable:

```
<xsl:variable name="count">
  <xsl:choose>
    <xsl:when test="@count">
      <xsl:value-of select="@count"/>
    </xsl:when>
    <xsl:otherwise>
      0
    </xsl:otherwise>
  </xsl:choose>
</xsl:variable>
```

The result of this code is that the variable `"$count"` has the value of the `"count"` attribute when it is present and zero when it isn't present. You can then use the variable in your calculations as needed.

## OPERATORS

An *operator* performs an action on data in the stylesheet. There are three categories of XSL operators:

- Mathematical operators, which perform the operations of addition, subtraction, division, multiplication, and modulus.
- Comparison operators, which compare two expressions, returning true if the comparison is true and false if it isn't.
- Logical operators, which manipulate logical (true/false) expressions.

Table D-5 provides details on the XSL operators. In this table, the characters `<` and `>` are displayed as themselves for the sake of clarity. Remember that these characters have special meaning in XML and are normally represented by `<` and `>` respectively.

**TABLE D-5 THE XSL OPERATORS**

| Operator | Operation | Example |
|---|---|---|
| + | Addition | `"$count + 5"` adds 5 to the value of the variable `$count`. |
| - | Subtraction | `"$A - $B"` subtracts the value of `$B` from the value of `$A`. |
| * | Multiplication | `"$A * $B"` multiplies `$A` by `$B`. |
| div | Division | `"44 div 11"` returns 4. |

*Continued*

**TABLE D-5 THE XSL OPERATORS** *(Continued)*

| Operator | Operation | Example |
|---|---|---|
| `mod` | Modulus | Remainder after division. `"17 mod 4"` returns `1`. |
| `=` | Equal to | `"8 = 2"` returns false. |
| `!=` | Not equal to | `"8 != 2"` returns true. |
| `>` | Greater than | `"8 > 2"` returns true. |
| `>=` | Greater than or equal to | `"2 >= 8"` returns false. |
| `<` | Less than | `"2 < 8"` returns true. |
| `<=` | Less than or equal to | `"8 <= 2"` returns false. |
| and | And | `"Exp1 and Exp2"` returns true if `Exp1` and `Exp2` are both true, and false otherwise. |
| or | Or | `"Exp1 or Exp2"` returns true if either `Exp1` or `Exp2` is true or if both are true, and returns false otherwise. |
| ! | Not | `"!Exp"` returns true if `Exp` is false, false if `Exp` is true. |

Here are some examples of using the XSL operators. This expression returns true only if `$A` is less than `$B` and `$B` is greater than 20:

```
($A &lt; $B) and ($B &gt; 20)
```

This expression returns true if the variable `$count` is an even number:

```
($count mod 2) = 0
```

This code returns true if `$A` or `$B`, but not both of them, is greater than 20:

```
(($A &gt; 20) or ($B &gt; 20)) and !(($A + $B) &gt; 40)
```

# Functions

XSL includes a variety of built-in components that perform different data manipulation tasks. These components are called *functions*. Every function returns a value to the stylesheet, and some functions are passed data to operate on, called *arguments*. Functions can be used by themselves or as a part a more complex expression. For example, the function `contains()` determines if one string is contained within another. Thus, you could determine if the attribute named `"caption"` contains the string `"Albany"` as follows:

```
contains(@caption, "Albany")
```

The function returns true or false, depending on whether the text `"Albany"` is found in the attribute value.

There are quite a few XSL functions, and they fall into several categories. It is impossible to provide information on all the available functions in this appendix, but you can find complete information at `http://w3.org/TR/xpath`. The remainder of this section covers those functions that are used most often. Table D-6 lists these functions by category, with additional explanation or examples for some functions following the table.

**TABLE D-6 COMMONLY USED XPATH FUNCTIONS**

| Function category | Function | Description |
|---|---|---|
| Aggregation | `count(`*ns*`)` | Returns the number of nodes in the node set *ns*. |
| | `sum(`*ns*`)` | Sums numerical values over the node set *ns*. |
| Arithmetic | `ceiling(`*n*`)` | Returns the smallest integer that is greater than or equal to the value *n*. |
| | `floor(`*n*`)` | Returns the largest integer that is less than or equal to the value *n*. |
| | `round(`*n*`)` | Returns the integer that is closest to the value *n*, Fractional values of .5 and below are rounded down, values above .5 are rounded up. |
| Boolean | `false()` | Returns the Boolean value false. |
| | `true()` | Returns the Boolean value true. |
| | `not(`*b*`)` | Returns the logical not of the Boolean expression *b*. Returns true if *b* is false, and *vice versa.* |
| Current context | `last()` | Returns the current context size (the number of nodes it contains). |

*Continued*

**Table D-6 COMMONLY USED XPATH FUNCTIONS** *(Continued)*

| Function category | Function | Description |
|---|---|---|
| | `position()` | Returns the value of the current context position. |
| Data conversion | `boolean(a)` | Converts its argument *a* to a true or false value. |
| | `format-number(v, f)` | Converts the value *v* to a string using the formatting instructions specified by *f*. |
| | `number(a)` | Converts its argument *a* to a number. |
| | `string(a)` | Converts its argument *a* to a string. |
| String manipulation | `concat(s1, s2, ...)` | Takes two or more arguments. The return value is the arguments converted to strings and joined end to end. |
| | `contains (s1, s2)` | Returns true if string *s1* contains string *s2*. Returns false otherwise. |
| | `starts-with (s1, s2)` | Returns true if string *s1* starts with string *s2*. Returns false otherwise. |
| | `string-length(s1)` | Returns the length, in characters, of string *s1*. If the argument is omitted, returns the length of the string value of the context node. |
| | `substring (s1, start, length)` | Returns a substring from *s1* starting at position *start* and *length* characters long. |

## THE BOOLEAN() FUNCTION

The `boolean()` function takes a single argument and returns true or false. The rules by which it operates depend on the type of argument passed, and are described in Table D-7.

**Table D-7 RULES OF THE BOOLEAN() FUNCTION**

| Argument type | Returns true if... | Returns false if... |
|---|---|---|
| Number | The argument evaluates to a nonzero value. | The argument evaluates to zero. |

| Argument type | Returns true if... | Returns false if... |
|---|---|---|
| String | The argument evaluates to a string with length greater than zero. | The argument evaluates to a zero length string. |
| Boolean | The argument is true. | The argument is false. |
| Node set | The node set is not empty. | The node set is empty. |
| Result tree fragment | The fragment contains nonempty text nodes. | The fragment only contains empty text nodes. |

The `boolean()` function can be used for tasks such as determining whether a string is zero length or a node set is empty.

## THE NUMBER() FUNCTION

You use the `number()` function to convert data to a number. Table D-8 explains the conversion rules.

**TABLE D-8 CONVERSION RULES FOR THE NUMBER() FUNCTION**

| Argument type | Result |
|---|---|
| Numeric | The value is not changed. |
| Boolean | Returns 1 for true and 0 for false. |
| String | Leading and trailing white space is removed. If the remaining string is recognized as a number, the corresponding value is returned. If the string cannot be recognized as a number, the special value `NaN` is returned. |
| Node set | The node set is converted to a string using the rules for the `string()` function. The result is converted to a number following the rule for string arguments. |
| Result tree fragment | The result tree is converted to a string using the rules for the `string()` function. The result is converted to a number following the rule for string arguments. |

Here are some examples of using the `number()` function:

```
number(12.3) returns 12.3
number("12.3") returns 12.3
number("xyz") returns NaN
number(true()) returns 1
```

### THE STRING() FUNCTION

You use the `string()` function to convert data to text. The conversion rules are explained in Table D-9.

**TABLE D-9 CONVERSION RULES FOR THE STRING() FUNCTION**

| Argument | Result |
|---|---|
| Boolean | Returns either "`false`" or "`true`". |
| Numeric | Integers are returned with no decimal point. Floating point values are returned with at least one digit on each side of the decimal point. Zero is returned as "`0`". Special return values are "`NaN`", "`Infinity`", and "`-Infinity`". |
| String | The string is unchanged. |
| Node set | The string value of the node that is first in document order. If the node set is empty, an empty string is returned. |
| Result tree fragment | The values of all descendant text nodes, concatenated in order. |
| Omitted | The default argument is a node set containing the context node. |

Conversion of data to string form is usually performed automatically, so there are few occasions where the `string()` function is needed. One exception is when you want to perform a string comparison instead of a node set comparison. For example, the following code tests if any "`item`" child of the current node has the value "`Claw hammer`":

```
<xsl:if test="item='Claw hammer'">
```

If you want to test if the first "`item`" child has the value "`Claw hammer`", you would write the following:

```
<xsl:if test="string(item)-'Claw hammer'">
```

## THE FORMAT-NUMBER FUNCTION

Use the `format-number()` to format numerical values for output. The syntax is

```
format-number(value, format)
```

*value* is an expression that evaluates to a numerical value. *format* is a string that defines the format. The rules for creating format strings are quite complex, having been designed to handle every possible eventuality. I cannot describe them all here, but cover only the most frequently used ones. You can find the complete information on the W3C Web site at `http://w3.org/TR/xslt`.

A format string is comprised of characters that represent digits and symbols in the result. For example, the format string `"$#.00"` will display a number with a leading dollar sign and two decimal places. Table D-10 explains the formatting characters used in format strings.

**TABLE D-10 CHARACTERS USED IN FORMAT STRINGS**

| Character | Meaning |
|---|---|
| 0 (zero) | A digit will always be displayed at this position. |
| # | A digit will be displayed unless it is a redundant leading or trailing zero. |
| $ | Displays a leading dollar sign. |
| . (decimal point) | Specifies the position of the decimal point. |
| , (comma) | Specifies the location of digit separators. |
| - | Specifies the minus sign. |
| % | The number is multiplied by 100 and displayed as a percentage. |
| ' (apostrophe) | Displays special characters as themselves. For example '#' displays #. |

Table D-11 shows some examples.

**Table D-11 EXAMPLES OF USING THE FORMAT-NUMBER FUNCTION**

| Function | Result |
|---|---|
| `format-number(12.34, "#.#")` | 12.3 |
| `format-number(12.34, "#.00")` | 12.34 |
| `format-number(-12.34, "#.00")` | -12.34 |
| `format-number(12.34, "000.000")` | 012.340 |
| `format-number(0.25, "##%")` | 25% |
| `format-number(456000000, "$,###")` | $456,000,000 |

## THE COUNT() AND SUM() FUNCTIONS

You use the `count()` and `sum()` functions when processing a node set. The `count()` function returns the number of nodes in the set. This is the syntax:

```
count(ns)
```

The argument is an expression or variable that evaluates to a node set. The function's return value is the number of nodes in the set. This value does not include nodes that are descendants of member nodes but which are not members in their own right.

The `sum()` function calculates the sum of a set of numeric values in a node set. The node set can refer to a text element or an attribute. The syntax is:

```
sum(ns)
```

The argument is an expression or variable that evaluates to a node set. The following example returns the sum of all `"price"` elements that are children of the `"item"` element:

```
sum(item/price)
```

The next example returns the sum of all `"size"` attributes of the `"item"` element which is a child of the `"inventory"` element:

```
sum(inventory/item/@size)
```

If any value in the node set is not a number or is absent, the `sum()` function returns the special value `NaN`, representing Not a Number.

## THE LAST() AND POSITION() FUNCTIONS

The functions `last()` and `position()` enable you to obtain information abut the current context. They take no arguments and return information as follows:

- `last()` returns the number of nodes are in the current context.
- `position()` returns a number giving the position within the current context.

You would use these functions when processing a node set – using the `xsl:for-each` element, for example. There are many things that you can do with one or both of these functions. One possibility is to label the output with item numbers. For example, you could output a list like this:

```
1: Claw hammer
2: Needle-nose pliers
3. Paint scraper
4: Crescent wrench
```

This is the code required, assuming the item name is stored in the `"name"` element (this is based on the XML data from Listing D-1)

```
<xsl:template match="item">
  <xsl:value-of select="position()"/>: <xsl:value-of elect="name"/>
</xsl:template>
```

You could also use these functions to create output like this:

```
Item 1 of 4: Claw hammer
Item 2 of 4: Needle nose pliers
Item 3 of 4: Paint scraper
Item 4 of 4: Crescent wrench
```

Here's the code for this output:

```
<xsl:template match="item">
  Item <xsl:value-of select="position()"/> of <xsl:value-of
    select="last()"/>: <xsl:value-of select="name"/>
</xsl:template>
```

Another way to use these functions is to determine when processing has reached the last node in the context (where `position()` equals `last()`). In this example, a horizontal line is inserted (using the `<hr/>` HTML tag) after the item in the list one.

```
<xsl:template match="book">
  <xsl:value-of select="name"/>
  <xsl:if test="position() = last()">
    <hr/>
  </xsl:if>
</xsl:template>
```

XSLT is an important tool for almost anyone who is working with XML data. By using an XSLT stylesheet, you can transform all or part of your XML data to meet your current needs. Many of the Office applications support this technology.

# Index

## Numbers



## A

# B

# D

*continued*

## F

*continued*

*continued*

## M

# N

## Q



## R

# S



*continued*

*continued*

*continued*

## X

*continued*

## Y

# Wiley Publishing, Inc. End-User License Agreement

READ THIS. You should carefully read these terms and conditions before opening the software packet(s) included with this book "Book". This is a license agreement "Agreement" between you and Wiley Publishing, Inc. "WPI". By opening the accompanying software packet(s), you acknowledge that you have read and accept the following terms and conditions. If you do not agree and do not want to be bound by such terms and conditions, promptly return the Book and the unopened software packet(s) to the place you obtained them for a full refund.

1. License Grant. WPI grants to you (either an individual or entity) a nonexclusive license to use one copy of the enclosed software program(s) (collectively, the "Software" solely for your own personal or business purposes on a single computer (whether a standard computer or a workstation component of a multi-user network). The Software is in use on a computer when it is loaded into temporary memory (RAM) or installed into permanent memory (hard disk, CD-ROM, or other storage device). WPI reserves all rights not expressly granted herein.
2. Ownership. WPI is the owner of all right, title, and interest, including copyright, in and to the compilation of the Software recorded on the disk(s) or CD-ROM "Software Media". Copyright to the individual programs recorded on the Software Media is owned by the author or other authorized copyright owner of each program. Ownership of the Software and all proprietary rights relating thereto remain with WPI and its licensers.
3. Restrictions On Use and Transfer.
   (a) You may only (i) make one copy of the Software for backup or archival purposes, or (ii) transfer the Software to a single hard disk, provided that you keep the original for backup or archival purposes. You may not (i) rent or lease the Software, (ii) copy or reproduce the Software through a LAN or other network system or through any computer subscriber system or bulletin- board system, or (iii) modify, adapt, or create derivative works based on the Software.
   (b) You may not reverse engineer, decompile, or disassemble the Software. You may transfer the Software and user documentation on a permanent basis, provided that the transferee agrees to accept the terms and conditions of this Agreement and you retain no copies. If the Software is an update or has been updated, any transfer must include the most recent update and all prior versions.
4. Restrictions on Use of Individual Programs. You must follow the individual requirements and restrictions detailed for each individual program in the About the CD-ROM appendix of this Book. These limitations are also contained in the individual license agreements recorded on the Software Media. These limitations may include a requirement that after using the program for a specified period of time, the user must pay a registration fee or discontinue use. By opening the Software packet(s), you will be agreeing to abide by the licenses and restrictions for these individual programs that are detailed in the About the CD-ROM appendix and on the Software Media. None of the material on this Software Media or listed in this Book may ever be redistributed, in original or modified form, for commercial purposes.

5. Limited Warranty.
   (a) WPI warrants that the Software and Software Media are free from defects in materials and workmanship under normal use for a period of sixty (60) days from the date of purchase of this Book. If WPI receives notification within the warranty period of defects in materials or workmanship, WPI will replace the defective Software Media.
   (b) WPI AND THE AUTHOR OF THE BOOK DISCLAIM ALL OTHER WARRANTIES, EXPRESS OR IMPLIED, INCLUDING WITHOUT LIMITATION IMPLIED WARRANTIES OF MERCHANTABILITY AND FITNESS FOR A PARTICULAR PURPOSE, WITH RESPECT TO THE SOFTWARE, THE PROGRAMS, THE SOURCE CODE CONTAINED THEREIN, AND/OR THE TECHNIQUES DESCRIBED IN THIS BOOK. WPI DOES NOT WARRANT THAT THE FUNCTIONS CONTAINED IN THE SOFTWARE WILL MEET YOUR REQUIREMENTS OR THAT THE OPERATION OF THE SOFTWARE WILL BE ERROR FREE.
   (c) This limited warranty gives you specific legal rights, and you may have other rights that vary from jurisdiction to jurisdiction.
6. Remedies.
   (a) WPI's entire liability and your exclusive remedy for defects in materials and workmanship shall be limited to replacement of the Software Media, which may be returned to WPI with a copy of your receipt at the following address: Software Media Fulfillment Department, Attn.: Powering Office 2003 with XML, Wiley Publishing, Inc., 10475 Crosspoint Blvd., Indianapolis, IN 46256, or call 1-800-762-2974. Please allow four to six weeks for delivery. This Limited Warranty is void if failure of the Software Media has resulted from accident, abuse, or misapplication. Any replacement Software Media will be warranted for the remainder of the original warranty period or thirty (30) days, whichever is longer.
   (b) In no event shall WPI or the author be liable for any damages whatsoever (including without limitation damages for loss of business profits, business interruption, loss of business information, or any other pecuniary loss) arising from the use of or inability to use the Book or the Software, even if WPI has been advised of the possibility of such damages.
   (c) Because some jurisdictions do not allow the exclusion or limitation of liability for consequential or incidental damages, the above limitation or exclusion may not apply to you.
7. U.S. Government Restricted Rights. Use, duplication, or disclosure of the Software for or on behalf of the United States of America, its agencies and/or instrumentalities "U.S. Government" is subject to restrictions as stated in paragraph (c)(1)(ii) of the Rights in Technical Data and Computer Software clause of DFARS 252.227-7013, or subparagraphs (c) (1) and (2) of the Commercial Computer Software - Restricted Rights clause at FAR 52.227-19, and in similar clauses in the NASA FAR supplement, as applicable.
8. General. This Agreement constitutes the entire understanding of the parties and revokes and supersedes all prior agreements, oral or written, between them and may not be modified or amended except in a writing signed by both parties hereto that specifically refers to this Agreement. This Agreement shall take precedence over any other documents that may be in conflict herewith. If any one or more provisions contained in this Agreement are held by any court or tribunal to be invalid, illegal, or otherwise unenforceable, each and every other provision shall remain in full force and effect.